Masters and Servants

SCOTT P. STEPHEN

Masters

The Hudson's Bay Company and Its North American Workforce, 1668–1786

and Servants

UNIVERSITY *of* ALBERTA PRESS

Published by

University of Alberta Press
Ring House 2
Edmonton, Alberta, Canada T6G 2E1
www.uap.ualberta.ca

LIBRARY AND ARCHIVES CANADA
CATALOGUING IN PUBLICATION

Title: Masters and servants : the Hudson's Bay Company and its North American workforce, 1668-1786 / Scott P. Stephen.
Names: Stephen, Scott P., 1972- author.
Description: Includes bibliographical references and index.
Identifiers: Canadiana (print) 20190119500| Canadiana (ebook) 20190119519 | ISBN 9781772123371 (softcover) | ISBN 9781772124972 (EPUB) | ISBN 9781772124989 (Kindle) | ISBN 9781772124996 (PDF)
Subjects: LCSH: Hudson's Bay Company—Employees—History. | LCSH: Hudson's Bay Company—History. | LCSH: Household employees—Canada—History. | LCSH: Contract labor—Canada—History. | LCSH: Fur trade—Canada—History. | LCSH: Household employees—Great Britain—History.
Classification: LCC FC3207 .S84 2019 | DDC 971.2/01—dc23

First edition, first printing, 2019.
First printed and bound in Canada by Houghton Boston Printers, Saskatoon, Saskatchewan.
Copyediting by Angela Wingfield.
Proofreading by Kirsten Craven.
Maps by Wendy Johnson.
Indexing by Stephen Ullstrom.

University of Alberta Press is committed to protecting our natural environment. As part of our efforts, this book is printed on Enviro Paper: it contains 100% post-consumer recycled fibres and is acid- and chlorine-free.

University of Alberta Press gratefully acknowledges the support received for its publishing program from the Government of Canada, the Canada Council for the Arts, and the Government of Alberta through the Alberta Media Fund.

This book has been published with the help of a grant from the Canadian Federation for the Humanities and Social Sciences, through the Awards to Scholarly Publications Program, using funds provided by the Social Sciences and Humanities Research Council of Canada.

Canada
Canada Council for the Arts Conseil des Arts du Canada
Alberta Government

Contents

Editorial Note

I CONSIDER the language used by the Hudson's Bay Company Committee and its servants to be of central importance in this study. Therefore, every effort has been made to preserve the spelling and punctuation of the archival sources quoted, although some abbreviations have been expanded to avoid too many brackets. Where I have quoted from published editions of primary sources that have modernized the text, I have not tried to undo those changes.

Wages are quoted per annum; thus, a man engaged at £10 was paid £10 per annum. A man engaged at £3-4-5-6-8 was paid £3 in his first year, £4 in his second, and so on.

All dates are given in present-day style; for example, 11 February 1681/2 is written as 11 February 1682.

Acknowledgements

NEEDLESS TO SAY, I have incurred many debts during the research and writing of this book and the dissertation upon which it is based. I would like to acknowledge the moral support and financial assistance of the University of Manitoba—particularly the Department of History, St. John's College, and St. Paul's College—and the History Department of the University of Winnipeg. Chris Kotecki and the rest of the staff of the Hudson's Bay Company Archives at the Archives of Manitoba have been very helpful. I would like to thank Garin Burbank, Jack Bumsted, Russell Smandych, Patricia McCormack, Melissa Pitts, and the anonymous reviewers of this manuscript, as well as my editors, Peter Midgley and Mary Lou Roy, and all the staff at University of Alberta Press. Jennifer and Wilson Brown have been at my side from the beginning of this undertaking, offering words of wisdom and cups of tea, and saying "Ah!" encouragingly. Roland Bohr, Tolly Bradford, Gerhard Ens, and Frieda Klippenstein have epitomized both friendship and collegiality throughout my personal and professional ups and downs. I am eternally grateful for the support of my parents, my sister, her husband, and the rest of my family; in particular, M.B. and my wonderful wife, Susan, have always been there for me in ways too numerous to mention. And I hope that one day our young son, Timothy, may shrug his shoulders and say, "Yeah, I dunno. My dad wrote some kind of book or something; I guess that's kinda cool," and I shall glow with honest pride. After my having received so much support and encouragement from so many wonderful people, it would be churlish of me if I allowed them to take the slightest blame for any errors or omissions that may be found herein.

Finally, I would like to dedicate this work to my mother and father, whom I dearly wish could have lived to see its completion.

Introduction

Governor Geyer, we have considered your faithfully [sic] *Services & indefatigable paines in our Interest, as well as your cheerfull compliance wth. our request to stay an other yeare in this Extraordinary time of danger; & the Consideration on which you doe it, hopeing (as you say) the Warre may be by that time ended, that you may Leave our Concerns there in a peaceable & florishing Condition & that you would not willingly Leave your Post before you saw them soe setled, is so ingenious & honourable in you, & kind towards us, that we assure you it hath a great influence upon us that know the value of your meritts & how happily Our affaires there have prospered under your Conduct: To Shew our Just sense therefore of your Service & due regards for your Person, after having cleared wth. Mr. Kingston your acctt. upon your Sallary, We have moreover unanimously voted & paid him allso for you a Gratuity of One Hundred Pounds, Resolving soe allwaies to discharge Our selves that the Character of a meritorious Servant & Gratefull masters may be reciprocall between us.*

—HUDSON'S BAY COMPANY to George Geyer & Council (York Fort), 17 June 1692[1]

THE "GRATEFULL MASTERS" in the 17 June 1692 letter were the Governor, Deputy Governor, and Committee of the Hudson's Bay Company (HBC). The "Extraordinary time of danger" to which they referred was King William's War, during which French traders controlled James Bay, and Port Nelson (York Fort) was the only trading post in HBC hands. The "meritorious Servant" in question was George Geyer, the HBC factor (agent) in charge of Port Nelson, a man who had indeed given "faithfully Services & indefatigable paines" for more than fifteen years—and who was very strongly suspected by his employers of trading privately, contrary to their explicit instructions. How do we—how did the Committee—reconcile the apparent paradox of a servant being both devoted and deceitful?

The Governor and Company of Adventurers of England Trading into Hudson's Bay (to give its full name) came into being on 2 May 1670 as a small, undercapitalized, high-risk, overseas fur-trading venture with well-placed shareholders but no guarantee of success. It was heavily dependent on loans from friendly creditors (including Committee members and lesser shareholders) and seriously threatened by interlopers, warfare, and fluctuating European markets. Initially, the company's survival was the paramount concern, but this underlay some ambitious attempts at expanding its operations.

The early years saw the establishment of structures and practices that persisted well into the nineteenth century, and some of them into the twentieth.[2] The basic structure consisted of an active governing Committee of leading shareholders, a small London office and warehouse staff, and a series of trading posts (large and small) in North America under the management of one or two senior factors or agents (often called governors, but not to be confused with the governor and deputy governor in London). This basic structure would be elaborated upon after 1810, but significantly new elements were only introduced with the devolution of some strategic (rather than merely tactical) decision-making to the Canadian Committee in Winnipeg in 1912.

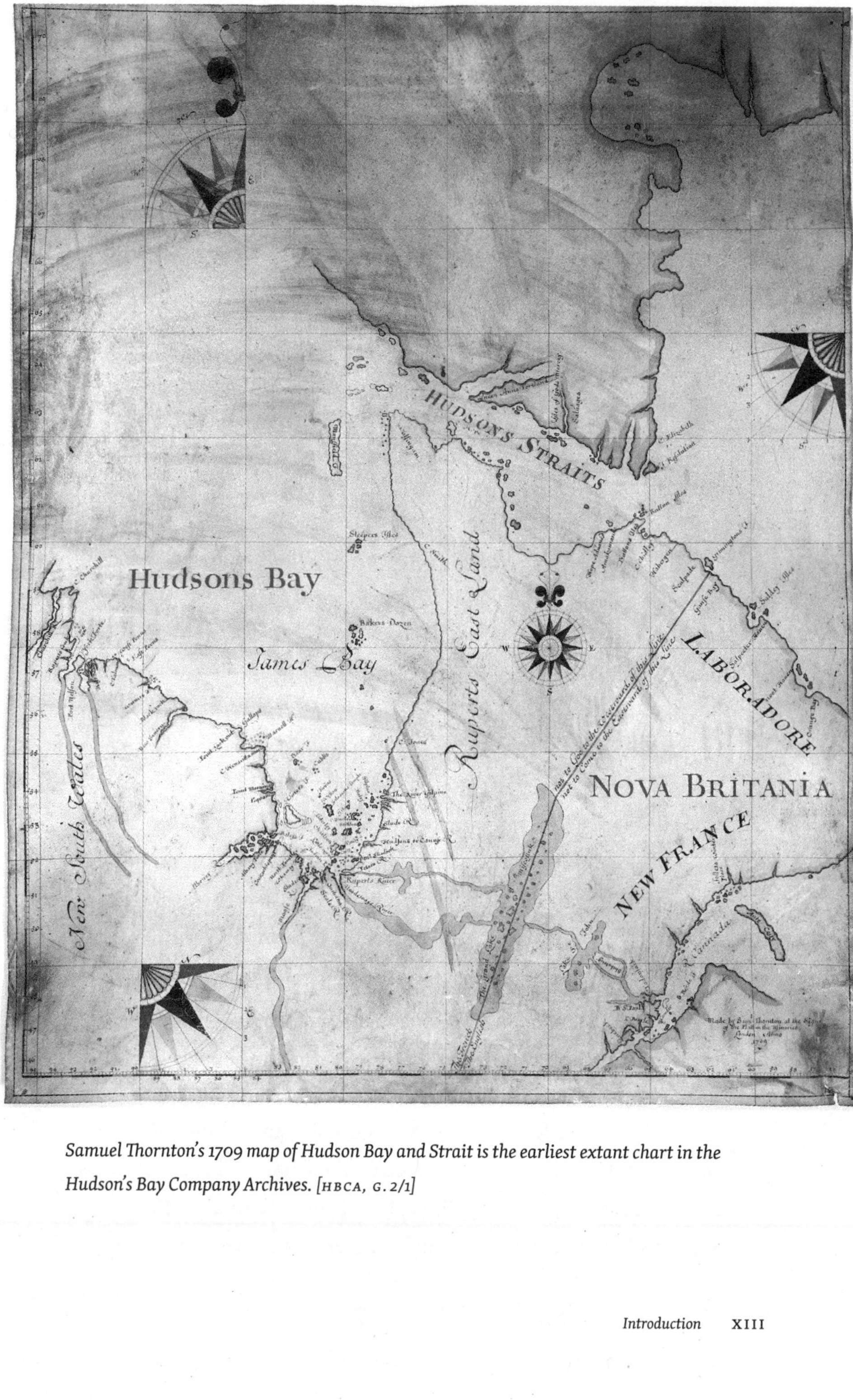

Samuel Thornton's 1709 map of Hudson Bay and Strait is the earliest extant chart in the Hudson's Bay Company Archives. [HBCA, G.2/1]

Although the shareholders were open to other avenues and resources, the trade for beaver pelts immediately emerged as the most profitable and feasible focus for the fledgling company's energies. Lacking a large workforce or any direct knowledge of the country itself (only the famous Pierre Esprit Radisson and Médard Chouart des Groseilliers had been anywhere near Hudson Bay before), the HBC created a few small outposts at the mouths of some of the major rivers emptying into Hudson and James bays. There they largely remained for the next one hundred years, a coastal model of business employed elsewhere in the empire, such as the Guinea coast of Africa.[3]

Although Albany Fort built a small outpost upriver in 1743, the HBC's move into the interior of the continent is usually dated to 1774. That year saw the establishment of Cumberland House, the first fully operational trading post inland from Hudson Bay; Albany's earlier outpost at Henley had been restricted in its trade and activities, unrealistically, as it turned out. A less obvious but more fundamental shift in the HBC's business model came in 1786, with the creation of the position of chief inland at York Fort. Whereas Cumberland House and the other early inland posts were managed from the shores of Hudson Bay—essentially (like Henley) as extensions of the coastal factories—from 1786 onward York Fort's inland operations were managed from the inland posts themselves, the senior factor leading from the front line instead of from the rear. This marked a change of more lasting significance than that of the physical move into the interior; it shifted the managerial centre of gravity, a recognition (even a self-fulfilling prophecy) that henceforth the inland experiences of both the company and its servants would become part of their basic rather than extraordinary service. It thus also marks the end date of this study.

The coastal model that persisted for more than one hundred years was made possible by the efforts of Cree, Nakoda, and Dene communities who were willing and able to act as liaisons and middlemen with First Nations that were as far inland as the foothills of the Rocky Mountains. The exchange was, on the face of it, a simple one. Indigenous traders brought in furs that they had either trapped themselves or acquired from those who had; beaver was the most sought after by the HBC for its value in the making of felt hats in Europe, but other furs (particularly marten) were exchanged as well and valued by the HBC in terms of beaver. In return, the HBC offered a variety of manufactured goods that they had imported from England and (through their suppliers) all over the world: metal edge-tools from Sheffield, woolen blankets from Oxfordshire, tobacco from Brazil, glass beads from Venice, and brandy from wherever they could get it.

Three decades of conflict with the French in Hudson Bay ended with the Treaty of Utrecht (1713). The later part of the period under review saw the fall of New France in 1760 and the (not unrelated) revolutionary reshaping of the political and economic landscape of North America in the 1770s—the latter episode, in particular, has traditionally been presented by historians as a watershed moment in imperial development. In terms of the HBC and its operations, however, the events of 1760 produced little more than a huge sigh of relief, while those of the 1770s affected the company more indirectly than might be supposed.[4] Despite increasing competition from French traders in the interior of the continent, however, with the proverbial stroke of a pen the Treaty of Utrecht ushered in a half-century of relative stability during which the company was able to rebuild and grow.

There still remained many other hazards and uncertainties that were familiar to long-distance merchants, as well as some that were confined to those whose lines of supply and communication took them north of latitude 60° north. Within the broader context of early modern international commerce, historian Patrick O'Brien felt that

> *co-ordination of markets across space, time, and cultures embodied economic and political uncertainties that even the most astute business acumen could only partially alleviate. Alien consumers with peculiar tastes, the slow diffusion of commercial intelligence, competition from fellow countrymen and enemy rivals, and the unpredictable occurrences of war, called for levels of skill, flexibility, and foresight in the*

> *management of global and Imperial trade that exceeded by a wide margin the expertise required to operate within established intra-European or domestic trades.*[5]

Though often criticized for being slothful and overly conservative during its first century of operation, the HBC profited from the innovations and rational decision-making of its London Committee and Bayside agents. In large part, the company's success depended on the development of a commercial and administrative structure that was capable of operating effectively at a great distance from the board of directors.[6]

That the HBC survived its first hundred years—indeed, that it survived its first twenty or thirty years—was due to many factors, some of them outside the company's control. One of the factors over which it could exert some control was the selection and retention of satisfactory employees. Then, as now, the ownership advantages possessed by multinational trading companies were usually different from those possessed by manufacturing firms. Instead of patent-protected technologies and recognized brand names, ownership advantages in service industries rest more in "soft" skills, embodied in people: knowledge, information, and human relationships.[7] The cultivation of such relationships within the company itself was as crucial to its success as any of its external relationships. Even the much-vaunted monopoly on the sea route through Hudson Strait (bypassing hundreds of miles of rivers and dozens of portages on the westward route from Montreal) relied more on the skills and experience embodied in the captains and crews of the company's supply ships than on any legal protection from its royal charter.

The success of long-distance ventures like the HBC was in turn crucial to the economic success of first England and then the United Kingdom. Evaluations of overseas trade and the empire's contribution to the industrializing economy, after generations of receiving little or no credit in Britain's economic growth before 1850, have recently been more generous, although most have focused on the Atlantic economy (leaving out the East India Company) and the slave trade (leaving out the HBC and others).[8]

Likewise, as Geoffrey Jones has observed, until recently, theories of the firm and of the multinational enterprise "have had little to say about trading companies" beyond "predict[ing] the demise of this type of firm in the twentieth century."[9]

Part of the scholarly shift in both focus and attitude has been an emerging desire to portray long-distance trading companies of the pre-industrial era as modern business enterprises. Ann Carlos has been at the forefront of such attempts to "rehabilitate" the HBC, while Margaret Makepeace, Emily Erikson, and others have sung the praises of the East India Company (EIC) at home and abroad.[10] New approaches to these histories are always welcome, but the recent emphasis on modernity has too often overshadowed the older elements of these corporate structures and operations, just as earlier generations of historians overlooked progressive elements.

Such approaches have pushed their way to the forefront of an older debate, in which few historians of the fur trade have participated: whether chartered trading companies were inefficient, rent-seeking monopolies; or efficient, entrepreneurial firms using their charters like a patent, allowing them to cover the costs of exploration and establish a market. Erikson's examination of private trade within the EIC illustrates the double-edged nature of this methodological sword:

> *Reframing the English [East India] Company as a networked firm, one that combines hierarchy with horizontal network structures, links the historical importance of the Company to more recent developments in organizational theory...Embedding the English Company in organizational theory also allows its example to reflect back upon our modern conception of the essential characteristics of successful firms.*[11]

Yet organizational theory, or the theory of the firm or the multinational, can provide a too-convenient framework within which to pigeonhole the experiences of historical actors. We continue to work toward the day when, as Craig Muldrew suggested in 1993, the relationship between economic theory and history becomes reversed, "so that a thickly researched historiography of the complex motivations and practices of agents acting out relationships of economic exchange—together with an understanding of how they themselves interpreted such actions—could inform future theory, rather than the other way around."[12]

To that end, I seek to understand how the HBC actually constructed a labour force that saw it through difficult times, through war and economic depression, to times of prosperity and expansion—and back again. What was the company's definition of a "good" employee? How did it go about finding and retaining such men (and they were usually men)? Were such men hard to find? Were they hard to keep? What made the relationship between employer and employee work, and what threatened that relationship?

Not under discussion here is the HBC's maritime service, the captains and crews of its supply ships criss-crossing the North Atlantic. This arm of the company's operations was sufficiently distinct, even producing its own unique series of documents, that it merits a separate study of its own—one that Michael Dove has been conducting with considerable skill at the same time as I have been conducting this one. Nor do I directly address the question of casual or seasonal Indigenous labour, which during this period was recruited in entirely different ways and for entirely different purposes than those of the HBC's permanent labour force. This study could serve as a useful starting point for an analysis of how Indigenous labour was perceived and utilized during this period, but that would be a very different book from this one.

This study seeks patterns and policies in the HBC's approach to recruiting, retaining, and dismissing Euro-Canadian (mostly British) workers for its trading stations in North America. This is not a straightforward task, for within the company's abundant surviving written records there are no policy documents or guides to "best practices." Instead, this study mines the company's correspondence, minute books, accounts, and other records for specific examples, which are used to identify and explain patterns.

One pattern that has elicited much comment from earlier scholars is found in the development of strong vertical relationships as an important element in encouraging particular kinds of behaviour. The construction of such relationships evokes the servants' willingness to identify with a dominant ideology of work, though not entirely at the expense of their own self-identified interests. Much more has been said about the HBC's active creation of "company men" than the evidence will allow, but the governing Committee certainly recognized that paternalistic personnel strategies could reap benefits, particularly the ability to retain socialized and experienced workers in the face of a competitive early modern labour "market" (an admittedly anachronistic phrase: see Appendix, "Choosing Our Words Carefully").[13]

Efforts to analyze these paternalistic strategies reflect broader debates among historians of early modern Britain. Concepts of industrial class conflict seem not to apply to this "pre-industrial" society, which has generally been characterized as exhibiting consensus based on paternalism. Instead of class consciousness, historians have emphasized vertical consciousness linking the mutual interests of masters and men—the reciprocal relationship of "a meritorious Servant & Gratefull masters" longingly referred to in this chapter's epigraph—and explained horizontal divisions within trades as arising from a failure by one party (usually masters) to live up to reciprocal obligations. Master-servant relationships in such a society may have been unequal, but imbalances of power were mitigated by the development of emotional bonds and by the tendency of servants to identify (consciously and unconsciously) with their father-figure masters.[14]

The transition from this hypothesized consensual society to one dominated by industrial class relations has proved to be a lightning rod, attracting fiery and at times thunderous debate. There is considerable disagreement over the nature of the consensus (or of the value system itself) that underpinned this pre-industrial society. For example, Richard Price (paraphrasing E.P. Thompson) differentiated "formal subordination" from "real subordination" and argued that all social relationships involving authority and obedience are characterized by a constant struggle for authority and control. Patrick Joyce placed less emphasis on workers' combativeness and called the worker-employer relationship reciprocal but ambivalent.[15] Keith Wrightson and others have suggested that the two models of social relations coexisted in England through the sixteenth and seventeenth centuries, and probably beyond.[16]

Central to most conceptions of early modern society as essentially consensual is the *moral economy*. This often vaguely defined set of customary expectations could be used to mitigate the harsher aspects of market forces, for instance by regulating the price of food after a bad harvest. This concept, and particularly E.P. Thompson's formulation of it, has been an important part of the intellectual baggage of social historians (even those who disagree with Thompson) for over forty years.[17] Explanations of moral economy often rely on the equally nebulous concept of *custom*, which Donald Woodward disparaged as "that great stand-by of the social historian and frequently invoked explanation for all that is difficult to understand."[18] These two concepts are invoked to characterize the periods preceding the development of a capitalist market economy and the rational or impersonal labour relationships that came to prevail over the moral economy and the influence of custom.[19]

To a certain extent, these debates have been given a transoceanic twist as they penetrate the field of Atlantic history. Too easily dismissed as a trendy repackaging of imperial history for a post-colonial academic world, Atlantic histories offer valuable perspectives on "the movement, across and around the Atlantic basin, of people, commodities, cultural practices, and values."[20] Even the older discipline of imperial history itself has taken a new transnational tack and perceives the Atlantic Ocean in the early modern period as "a multinational zone...[which] migrants entered more often as part of a maritime exploit, trading company, plantation complex, or social, religious or ethnocultural group than as an instrument of a European nation-state strategy."[21] Hudson Bay and its hearty band of traders have not figured very prominently in discussions of the "English" Atlantic world (its self-perception only transitioning to "British" at some much-debated point in the eighteenth century). Yet this framework does offer a more congenial approach to the low-key imperialism of the HBC, whose first two governors in London were members of the royal family; throughout this period they enjoyed at best (or worst) an arms-length relationship with state and empire.[22]

The issues raised in these ongoing discussions help contextualize the experiences of HBC workers and their employers. Although the men of Hudson Bay were working in a very different environment from that of their contemporaries in Britain, they nonetheless came from and returned to the same British labour market—or, rather, markets—which was generally characterized by a high degree of unemployment and underemployment.[23] The Atlantic labour market was a collection or conglomeration of unique working environments, including long-distance trading, whaling, and other short- or long-term migratory work. Within this early modern Atlantic world, cheap labour was usually far more in demand than quality or specialized labour.[24]

Until the HBC began actively recruiting in North America in the nineteenth century, Hudson Bay was one of many extensions of the British labour market. The movement of men to and from the Bay was just one aspect of domestic labour mobility,[25] just as Newfoundland has been described as "figuratively the western edge of the West Country; men migrated back and forth to fishery outposts, most seasonally, some staying for a few years' sojourn."[26] HBC servants numbering in the hundreds may seem inconsequential next to the more than 400,000 British people who migrated to mainland North America during this same period, but they were representative in the sense that between half and three-quarters of all the Europeans coming to the Americas did so under some form of labour contract, indentured service being the most common. However, although the HBC paid its servants' passage, board, and lodging, the various types of "freedom dues" that usually represented the juicy carrot at the end of the long stick of indentured service were conspicuously absent; all a man got at the end of his HBC contract were his wages and a free trip back to where he came from.[27]

HBC servants before the nineteenth century were not emigrants seeking a permanent home on Hudson Bay, and the company would not have allowed them to settle there. Rather, they were sojourners who came for a while and then moved on; they would have viewed the Bay as a stepping stone to better things at home or elsewhere. Hudson Bay was a life stage rather than a career.[28] Circular mobility—individuals moving away from and later returning to their point of origin—had been a common pattern in England and Scotland from the fifteenth century and probably earlier.[29] There is, in fact, no evidence from this period that any of the men under discussion here—with the possible exception of some of those who rose to the command of one of the major trading posts—saw Hudson Bay as a source of lifelong employment.

Most, if not all, men who worked for the company had other employment in their lifetimes, before and/or after their HBC service, either in Britain or in other parts of the empire. Unfortunately, it is extremely difficult to trace most of these men's previous and succeeding working lives; they are visible only while working in Hudson Bay, and their lives elsewhere are a collective mystery. It may be tempting to assume that Hudson Bay looked attractive only to men with no other options, but the evidence of men's origins that survives in the records of the HBC gives us no reason to think that its servants were significantly different from those groups seeking indentured service elsewhere in British North America. James Horn and Philip D. Morgan observed "a trend toward respectable, if modest, social origins" among indentured servants departing London and Bristol before the American Revolution. Bernard Bailyn saw no mass exodus of "destitute unskilled urban slum dwellers and uprooted peasants" but rather "certain segments of the lower middle and working classes, artisans, and craftsmen with employable skills, for whom emigration would seem to have represented not so much a desperate escape as an opportunity to be reached for."[30]

If most men entering HBC service were not seeking lifelong employment, their employers (for different reasons) were not necessarily looking for lifelong employees. Changing circumstances meant that changing expectations were placed on servants; at certain moments in the company's history each individual might be considered a vital element of survival, while at other moments a high payroll might be seen as an unnecessary or even hazardous expense. As circumstances changed, so did the relationship between the company and its men, between masters and servants.

|| Changing relationships have been at the heart of scholarly debates about pre-industrial England, which began in Britain during the 1960s and were first "imported" to the study of the North American fur trade by John E. Foster and Jennifer S.H. Brown when they were graduate students in the late 1970s. The term *pre-industrial* is often applied to the period of English history between ca. 1500 and ca. 1800, but it is seldom defined beyond these (often fuzzy) chronological goalposts. This, in turn, has raised questions about its usefulness; it has been called problematic, misleading, and "largely meaningless."[31] Patrick Joyce has warned against contrasting modern work values "with a romantic vision of 'pre-industrial' times in which the holistic virtues of self-reliance and co-operation were practised within the charmed circle of free household production." Such contrast has often been the result of assumptions about the inherent antagonism of capitalist social relations. However, more attention has been paid recently to the roles of consent, worker agency, and consensus. As our understandings of industrialization and of capitalism change, so too must our definition of *pre-industrial* (if we have one).[32]

Pre-industrial is most obviously opposed to *industrial*, but this juxtaposition is also connected with assumptions about differences between rural and urban settings, and with the dominant dichotomy of early modern British social history, *community* versus *society*. This dichotomy makes a distinction between the personal, direct, and sentimental relationships of community and the formal, abstract, and instrumental relationships of society. The transition from community to society is generally associated with the process of industrialization in the eighteenth and nineteenth centuries and is now burdened with so many connotations specific to that historical context that some scholars are seeking alternative conceptual models.[33] For these reasons, this study prefers the term *early modern*, which still implies an undefined modernity but is in most respects less problematic than the word *pre-industrial*.[34]

The hallmark of the early modern workplace is said to have been the prevalence of personal labour relationships, determined principally by social and moral obligations inherited from the Middle Ages rather than by contractual obligations negotiated in an open and individualistic market. Yet, as Wrightson and others have suggested, between these apparent polar opposites could be found a wide spectrum of actual experience. Craig Muldrew bridged the gap by arguing that early modern markets constituted a moral economy, but one formed of individualistic contractual relations:

> *[S]uch relations were much more normative than the older regulatory morality stressed by [E.P.] Thompson, and were also shared by both poor and wealthier tradesmen alike.... [I]t can be argued that in the late sixteenth and seventeenth centuries, while almost all people were involved in market relations, and in all probability had been for some time, they were not simply or even primarily concerned with self-interest in the Smithian [Adam Smith] sense, and did not interpret their behavior in such terms.*

Muldrew attributed this to the fact that, apart from wholesaling, most buying and selling was done on trust or credit, without specific legally binding instruments. Not only did this place tremendous importance on each individual's creditworthiness in his community, but "this network of credit was so extensive and intertwined that it introduced moral factors which provided strong reasons for stressing co-operation within the marketing structures of the period."[35]

A similarly amphibious situation can be identified in the Hudson's Bay Company. Although elements of the HBC's approach to its labour force can be described as modern, and all who served the company did so according to written contracts, labour relations within the company were underwritten by deep-rooted understandings of master-servant relationships within household settings until at least the nineteenth century. Of course, the social and economic structures of the HBC's establishments were influenced both by the unique circumstances of life and trade in Hudson Bay and by the military and economic threats from Canada (Quebec) and France. These factors notwithstanding, the Committee's fundamental assumptions about the social structures of its posts were similar to those made by its employees, resulting in the natural (though not inevitable) development of their forts and factories (i.e., places in which a factor or agent resided) as "household factories."

Within those households, officers and servants could potentially serve both the company and themselves. Common assumptions aside, the workplace relationships were negotiated from the company's beginnings. Early modern labour relationships were economic, social, and moral, but they were not straightforward. The appearance of deferential behaviours and the existence of strong vertical ties should not obscure the presence of tension and negotiation. The Committee and its servants all understood the nature of ideal master-servant relationships, but they also had experience of the realities of life in various kinds of households. Men at all levels of the company's hierarchy could try to shape the reality of their HBC experiences, and they did so in terms of commonly accepted ideals.

Most conflicts between masters and servants in Hudson Bay (and many in Britain, too) may thus be thought of as "family" quarrels, arising because one group or another failed to live up to reciprocal expectations.[36] Men could recognize the concept of the patriarchal family household, and even use it as a social and cultural construct, without necessarily approving of it or of their place within it. Subordinate members of the family could adopt a number of different postures, from opposition to conformity, in their relations with the master of the household.[37]

|| The HBC's decision (whether conscious or not) to use a household arrangement for its posts had a profound impact on the kind of imperial

world it shaped in North America.[38] Reproducing authority in a colonial setting was no simple task, not least of all because "traditional guarantees to liberty and law were often ambiguously located in the new political spaces of the colonies." European immigrants tried to reshape the existing physical and cultural landscapes of their new homes in a variety of ways, but the political dimension of that process was not always as straightforward as might be assumed. The "practical but theoretically vexing question of how to locate and rank divergent sources of authority in these newly defined spaces [e.g., company commissions versus royal commissions]...posed a difficult political and constitutional problem for Europeans" who found themselves far from the familiar "sets of actors, institutions, and spaces in their native metropolis."[39] In the circumstances that prevailed on the edges of the realm, legal and political authority resided most visibly in the Crown (and its representatives), rather than in English law and custom. Thus, allegiance and subjection featured as "primary modes of political affiliation": colonists could define themselves by their dependence on the Crown, just as members of any household were defined by living or working under the authority of the householder, which in turn allowed them "to represent and create authority outside of specific institutional settings and in a variety of legal and political spaces."[40] In other words, the household was an institution more transportable than English common law, or political organizations like parish and parliament.

The household factories of Hudson Bay were just one manifestation of what Alison Games has called "the astonishing range of [English] colonial and commercial experiments." For the most part, English companies "were free to create their own worlds overseas," limited only by local circumstances and the restrictions imposed by their charters (which, in the HBC's case, was an extremely flexible document).[41] The HBC's pattern of running its trading posts as large households continued throughout this period and (with modifications) beyond. Even under the early pressure of the French military threat, when the HBC needed its servants to double as soldiers (albeit reluctant ones), it never fully adopted a military model of household. The company certainly could have done so because under its charter it was granted power to make peace or war with non-Christian nations. From the mid-1600s onward, English authorities began to rein in the military discretion of colonies and companies toward other Europeans, but the right of self-defence was generally accepted.[42]

In the civilian model, diligence and defence at HBC factories resembled domestic security on a large estate or townhouse rather than a military fort, and posting a watch was little different than having one's servant sleep across the front door.[43] Compare this to the East India Company, which reacted to French aggression in the 1740s and 1750s by increasing the size of its military garrisons and proactively countering the French in India, with the result that by the 1760s the EIC had acquired a territorial empire that its directors had neither wanted nor requested.

In Hudson Bay the nature of the fur trade, the absence of colonial settlement, and the civilian nature of the household factories meant that there was no pressing need for the HBC to transform the Indigenous space around its factories into "an ordered and commodifiable colonial space attached to the national and dynastic space" of England—at least, not in the same way or to the same extent as in more southern colonies of settlement.[44] Rather than sharply identifying First Nations as "the Other," or as an enemy, the household model cast them in the light of neighbours: good or bad neighbours, as the case might be, but fellow members of a local community.

Such an approach built on lessons that Englishmen had learned in the Mediterranean and Levant trades in the sixteenth and seventeenth centuries: "a commercial demeanour defined by its style of accommodation and dissimulation... [T]he culture of trade [had] a style dictated by an acquisitive spirit inclined toward accommodation in order to extract the most advantageous terms of exchange."[45]

But the domestic roots were deeper. Like the commercial society emerging in England during this period, market relations between neighbouring English and Cree households rested upon a certain degree of mutual trust, expressed most visibly in the extension of credit. Both groups, in their own ways, understood that "[t]he very extension of credit required trust, and such trust was both acquired and maintained through neighbourly relations." Neither group made any meaningful distinction between economic and social credit in this period, so the moral language of people's credit and honesty could be applied to each other as much as it could be applied by the Committee to its servants.[46]

Keith Wrightson calls *neighbourliness* a "keyword" of early modern social relations, and the HBC's colonial world during this period appears less an empire than a neighbourhood.

> *The relationship which it [neighbourliness] defined was based upon residential propinquity, interaction of a regular kind, and a degree of consensus regarding proper conduct among neighbours within local communities.... [W]hatever the institutional framework, neighbourhood was also expressed informally, in the perennial personal contact of the inhabitants of small-scale, face-to-face communities. In this sense the neighbourhood was itself a "primary group." Its component households were interlocked in all manner of ways: rendering practical assistance and support; proffering advice or reproof; borrowing and lending; engaging in small-scale buying and selling; arbitrating quarrels; visiting the sick; celebrating the rites of birth, marriage, and death.*[47]

This is one of the contexts within which the English traders understood the Homeguard Cree, who reoriented their seasonal movement patterns in order to provide support services to the factories on a casual or seasonal basis. And HBC factors viewed each other as both neighbours and friends, with all the meanings and obligations that those relationships could entail.[48]

Each individual post, though, existed as a separate household under the overall direction of the Committee, like individual estate stewards all serving the same large landowner. Whereas many other civilian communities in British North America were conglomerations of multiple individual households, in HBC posts the factor or master (as head of the household) could speak with one voice for the community, at least symbolically. Factors were also able to prevent labour from splintering off into independent households, as it did in most other parts of British North America. Physical or spatial arrangements within the factories are significant here too; prior to the nineteenth century only the factor could expect a private room or suite (let alone a detached house of his own), and most of the men shared a single large building that was subdivided into rooms or apartments.

Similarly, land in and around the posts was kept out of individual hands until well after the end of our period (the establishment of colonial settlements in Red River and British Columbia and finally annexation by Canada in the nineteenth century). Hudson Bay was thus one of the few exceptions to the general pattern in the Americas in which the English created private property, rather than common or communal property; unlike the land corporations of New England, the HBC did not sell any of its chartered land to anyone other than Lord Selkirk until 1869.[49] This in turn mitigated the impact of capitalism on Indigenous societies during this period, for individually owned goods and chattels are perceived differently in a world where real estate is owned on a communal, familial, or corporate basis than in one where land is owned privately.

The absence of private land helped justify the absence of a court system, since much of English common law was devoted to property issues.[50] The lack of a court system was also facilitated by physical isolation; for the most part, the only vessels sailing in and out of the Bay were HBC ships, which significantly reduced the need for a local court to hear cases involving non-HBC settlers, merchants, and seamen. This, in turn, kept Hudson Bay at a legal and psychological distance from the rest of the Atlantic world.[51] These developments (or, rather, the lack thereof) help explain why court systems and other formal processes for resolving disputes quickly emerged in the fisheries, the slave trade, the East India Company's trade, and settler societies around the empire. Yet the first formal extension of English law into the fur trade country sprang from the banks of the St. Lawrence instead of the Thames: the Quebec Act of

1774[52] and the Canada Jurisdiction Act of 1803.[53] Although the 1670 charter granted the right to try civil and criminal cases in the company's territories, the HBC did not establish its own court system until it assumed the governance of the Selkirk Settlement in the 1830s.[54] Law was an important instrument of cultural transplantation elsewhere in British North America, but in Hudson Bay the role of "making physical spaces productive and social and cultural spaces agreeable" was played by the household.[55]

Therefore, an understanding of the household structure that the HBC developed and maintained through the nineteenth century, and even into the twentieth, promises to significantly enhance our understanding of how the HBC functioned as an agent of British imperialism. It had played such an imperial role from its youth; as early as 1708, John Oldmixon included a discussion of Hudson Bay (albeit not a very flattering one) in his *British Empire in America*. In addition, an understanding of HBC posts as household factories contributes to our understanding of experiences elsewhere. Thanks to the abundant documentation surviving in the company's archives, HBC posts are among the more thoroughly documented households in this period. Extrapolating from HBC contexts to other colonial contexts, and even back to Britain, will enhance our understanding of the function of households in the early modern British world.

|| Chapter 1 establishes some important contexts within which this study operates. A brief comparison of the HBC to other long-distance trading companies of the period serves (among other purposes) to demonstrate that these commercial contemporaries were often dealing with similar issues in very different circumstances and arriving at unique solutions. Fundamentally, this chapter introduces the social concepts—particularly the concept of households—that helped shape men's experiences in Hudson Bay, and ties those with their experiences in Britain.

Chapter 2 offers a brief overview of the historical development of the Hudson's Bay Company during this period. The mid-nineteenth century would see the HBC emerge as a substantial transcontinental trading concern, playing an almost vice-regal role as (usually) the sole representative of British sovereignty in a huge swath of territory from the Great Lakes to the Pacific coast and north into the Arctic, until transferring that territory to the young Dominion of Canada in one of the great real estate deals of that century (in 1870). During our period, however, those days of pseudo-imperial grandeur were far in the future, and far from certain: most of our story takes place on the shores of Hudson and James bays, with a different business model, administrative structure, and corporate outlook.

Chapters 3 and 4 examine the none-too-transparent processes by which the HBC engaged staff for its overseas stations. The 1713 Treaty of Utrecht marks a turning point here, but there was continuity as well—both in terms of how unsystematic the recruitment was and in the areas of the recruitment that remain opaque or invisible to us. Chapter 5 outlines the more visible processes by which the hired men were evaluated and the bases on which decisions were made with regard to re-engaging those whose contracts were expiring.

Chapter 6 follows the company's servants inland, exploring the experiences first of those who wintered with First Nations peoples and then of those who manned the interior posts after 1774. What began as extraordinary service performed by a handful of men would by 1786 become the new baseline for what the Committee expected from its workers. This transition challenged well-established customs and patterns and, in so doing, highlights them for our scrutiny.

Chapter 7 surveys the rhetorical tropes and practical realities that can be found in HBC correspondence. Some qualities (such as diligence, gratitude, and virtue) were clearly encouraged, while others (such as drunkenness) were seen as harmful to the well-being of the household factories. The ways in which the company's officers and servants responded to the Committee's social cues shed considerable light on how the public transcript of a cohesive master-servant relationship actually operated across the expanse of the Atlantic Ocean.

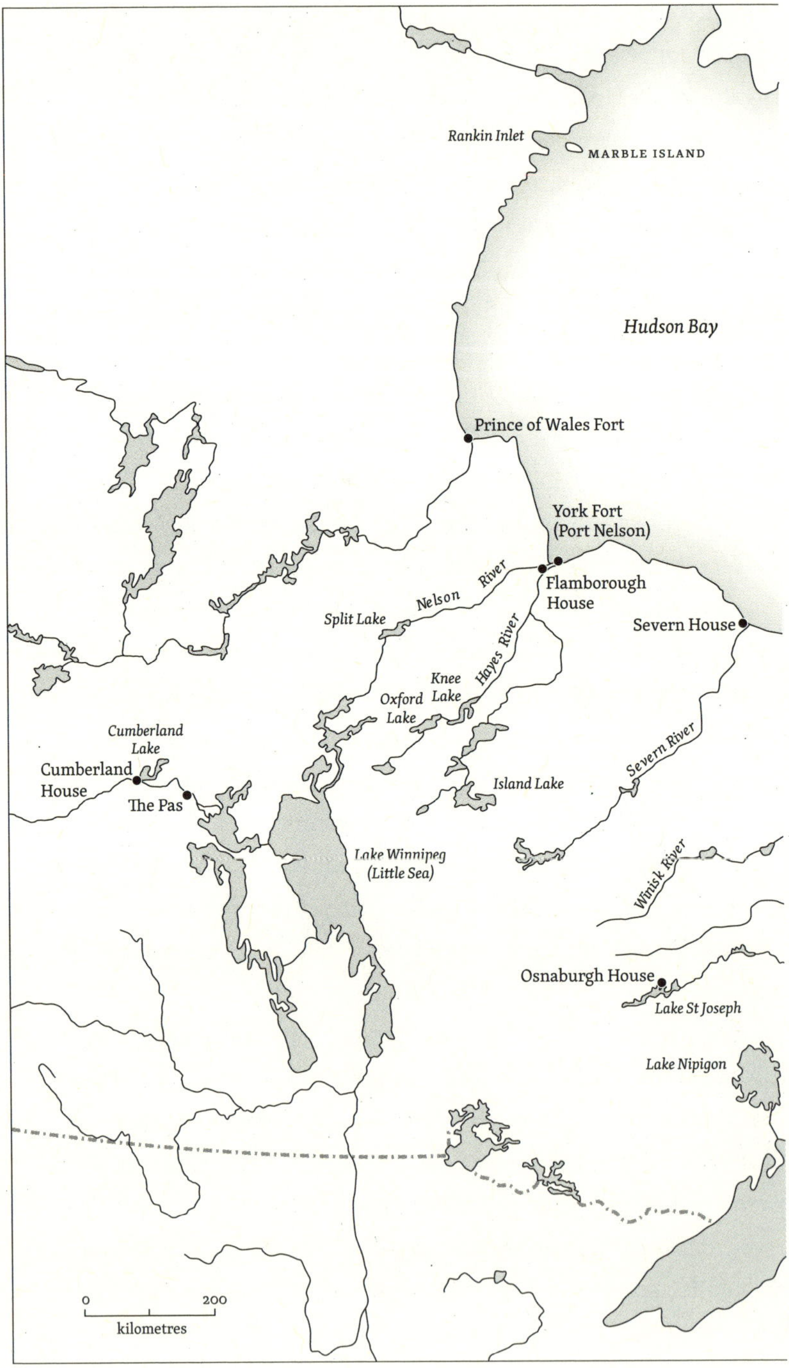

Hudson and James Bay region.

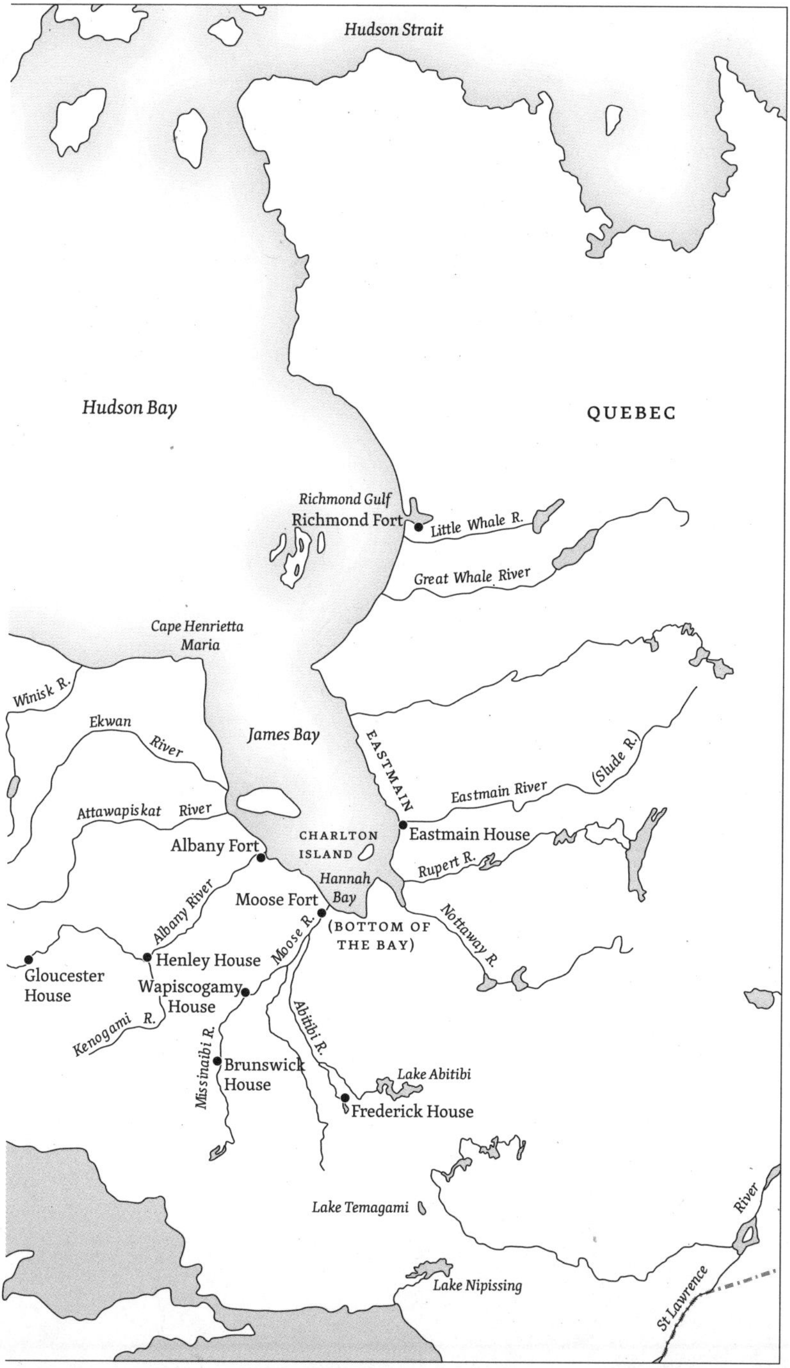
Hudson Strait
Hudson Bay
QUEBEC
Richmond Gulf
Richmond Fort
Little Whale R.
Great Whale River
Cape Henrietta Maria
Winisk R.
Ekwan River
James Bay
EASTMAIN
Eastmain River
(Slude R.)
Attawapiskat River
Eastmain House
CHARLTON ISLAND
Albany Fort
Rupert R.
Hannah Bay
Moose Fort
(BOTTOM OF THE BAY)
Nottaway R.
Albany River
Moose R.
Gloucester House
Henley House
Wapiscogamy House
Kenogami R.
Abitibi R.
Missinaibi R.
Brunswick House
Lake Abitibi
Frederick House
Lake Temagami
River
Lake Nipissing
St Lawrence

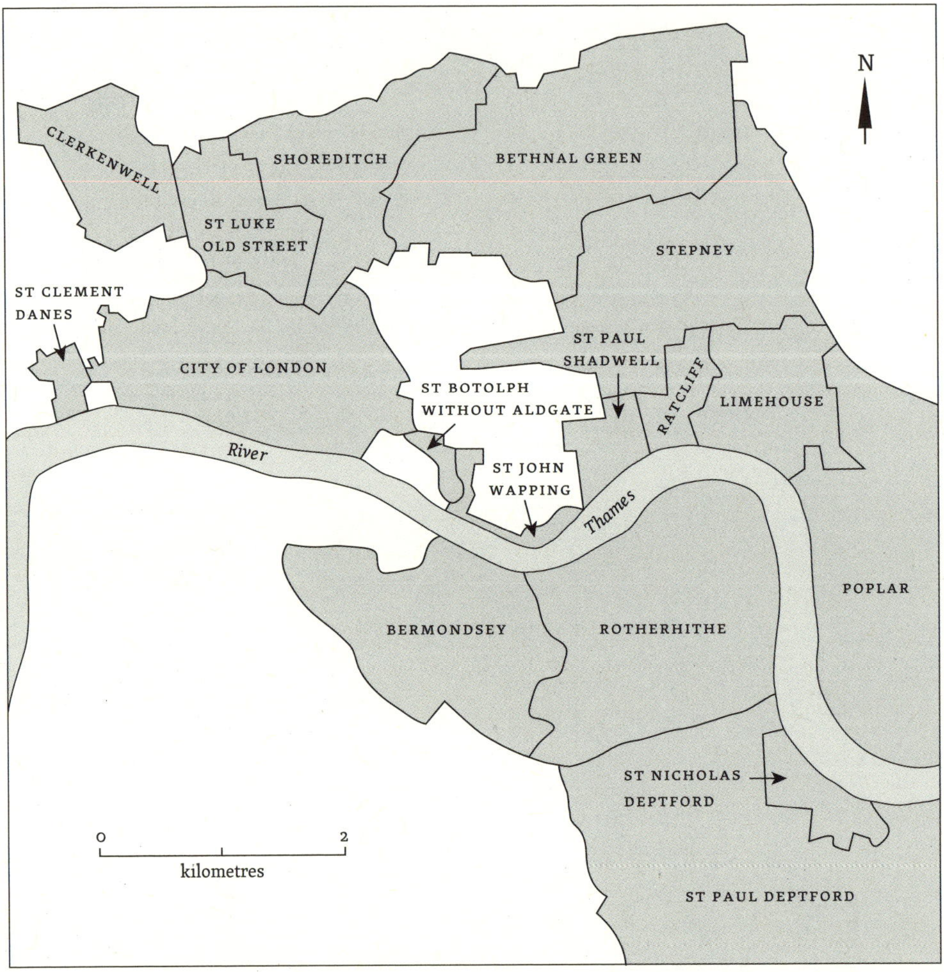

Selected London parishes in the eighteenth century.

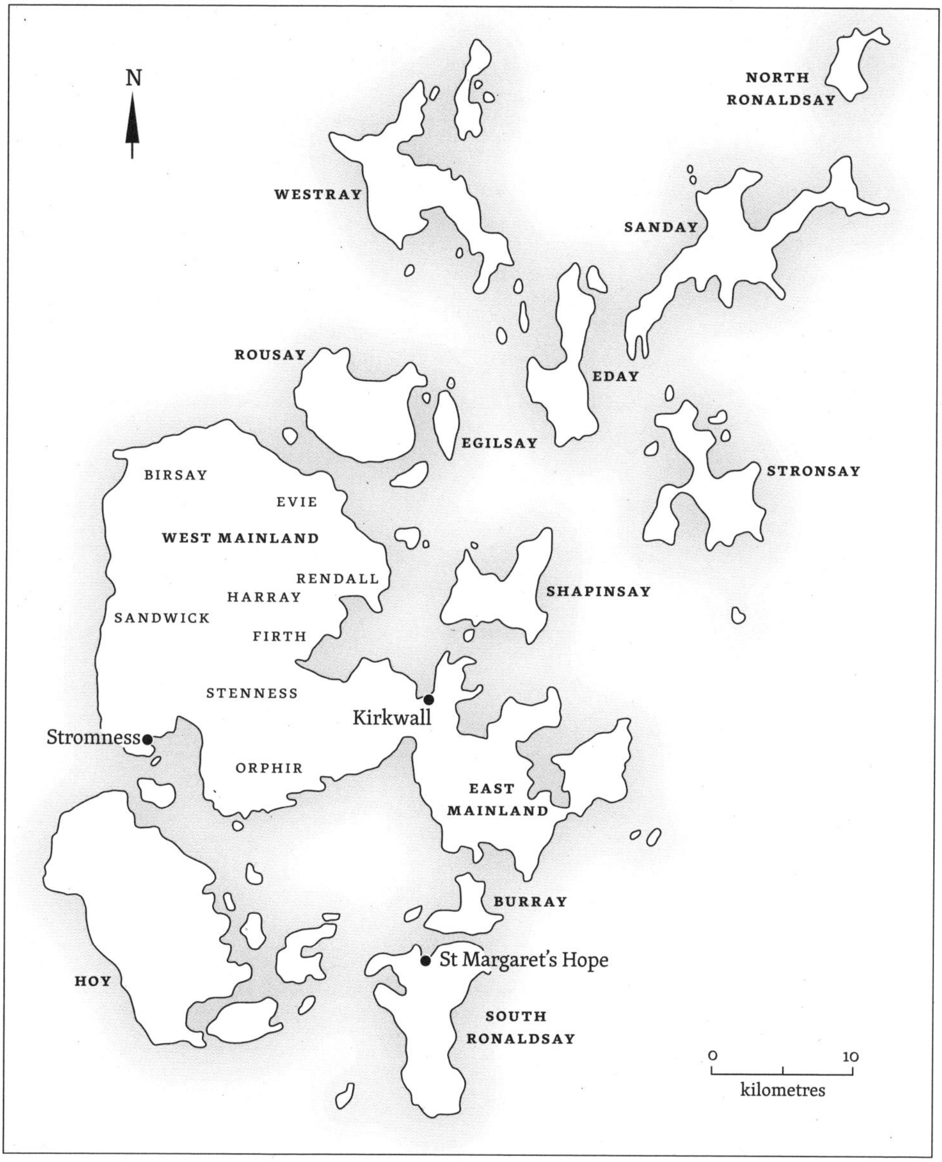

Orkney Islands.

No ideal form is ever ideal in reality, and Chapter 8 examines the two greatest threats to the stability of the household factories and thus to the model of authority and governance that the company had established in North America. Both private trade and relationships with Indigenous women were examples of men trying to operate outside the bounds of acceptable behaviour within the household model. The Committee never succeeded in eradicating these behaviours, but its ability to suppress at least their most disruptive aspects suggests both the strength of the model of household governance and the extent to which most men were willing and able to accommodate that model within their own pursuit of private goals.

Abbreviations

AF: Albany Fort

CF: Charles Fort (also known as Rupert River)

CH: Cumberland House

CHJ First Series: Rich, E.E., and A.M. Johnson, eds. *Cumberland House Journals and Inland Journal, 1775–82: First Series, 1775–79*. With an introduction by Richard Glover. London: Hudson's Bay Record Society, 1951.

CHJ Second Series: Rich, E.E., and A.M. Johnson, eds. *Cumberland House Journals and Inland Journal, 1775–82: Second Series, 1779–82*. With an introduction by Richard Glover. London: Hudson's Bay Record Society, 1952.

CI: Charlton Island

DCB: Hayne, David M., and Francess G. Halpenny, gen. eds. *Dictionary of Canadian Biography*, vols. 1–5. Toronto: University of Toronto Press, 1966–83.

EH: Eastmain House

EIC: East India Company

FH: Flamborough House

HBC: Hudson's Bay Company

HBCA: Hudson's Bay Company Archives at the Archives of Manitoba

LAC: Library and Archives Canada

Letters: Davies, K.G., and A.M. Johnson, eds. *Letters from Hudson Bay, 1703–40*. With an introduction by Richard Glover. London: Hudson's Bay Record Society, 1965.

L.O. 1680–1687: Rich, E.E., and A.M. Johnson, eds. *Copy-Book of Letters Outward &c, Begins 29th May, 1680; Ends 5 July, 1687*. With an introduction by E.G.R. Taylor. Toronto: Champlain Society for the Hudson's Bay Record Society, 1948.

L.O. 1688–1696: Rich, E.E., and A.M. Johnson, eds. *Hudson's Bay Copy Booke of Letters Commissions Instructions Outward, 1688–1696*. With an introduction by K.G. Davies. London: Hudson's Bay Record Society, 1957.

MF: Moose Fort

Minutes: Rich, E.E., ed. *Minutes of the Hudson's Bay Company, 1671–1674*. With an introduction by Sir John Clapham. Toronto: Champlain Society for the Hudson's Bay Record Society, 1942.

Minutes, First Part: Rich, E.E., ed. *Minutes of the Hudson's Bay Company, 1679–1684: First Part, 1679–1682*. With an introduction by G.N. Clark. Toronto: Champlain Society for the Hudson's Bay Record Society, 1945.

Minutes, Second Part: Rich, E.E., ed. *Minutes of the Hudson's Bay Company, 1679–1684: Second Part, 1682–1684*. With an introduction by G.N. Clark. Toronto: Champlain Society for the Hudson's Bay Record Society, 1946.

Nixon: "Report to the Governor and Committee by John Nixon, 1682." Royal Society, the Boyle Papers (Misc.), XL. Printed as appendix A in *Minutes, First Part*, 239–304.

PWF: Prince of Wales Fort (also known as Churchill River)

RAC: Royal African Company

RF: Richmond Fort

SR: Severn River

YF: York Fort (also known as Port Nelson or Fort Hayes)

1 Early Modern Contexts

Twenty eight Years have I eat your bread; Duty, and gratitude engage me Strongly in your Interest.

—HUMPHREY MARTEN (York Fort) to HBC (London), 28 August 1778[1]

THROUGHOUT THE FIRST HUNDRED YEARS and more of the Hudson's Bay Company, the relationship between its London Committee and its overseas employees was primarily that of a master and his servants. The early modern master-servant relationship was a complex one, and in this case it was heavily influenced by the circumstances of trading on Hudson Bay. Though often expanding and occasionally clinging to survival, the HBC was essentially a coastal concern before the 1770s. Labour relations within the company were framed by the physical and social constraints and possibilities of permanent coastal trading stations in a land of hunter-gatherers, as well as by the threats (real and perceived) from English interlopers and French competitors.

Labour relations within those trading stations were framed by the dominant social construct of early modern Britain, the patriarchal household family, made up of a master (the patriarch) and a family of kin, apprentices, and servants. Thus, the Bayside posts could operate as both social and economic entities; labour relations within them often appear to resemble family relations, and the clearly visible vertical ties binding the workplace community together may seem pre-eminent. Although personnel at all levels of the company's hierarchy appeared to actively cultivate such ties, these men were diverse individuals whose own interests interacted with those of their masters in complex ways.

In these and other respects, Rupert's Land (as the company's chartered territory was called) was a direct extension of early modern Britain. The company's workforce in North America remained integrated into the labour markets at home. Yet entering HBC service for five years was obviously very different from taking a year's contract a few parishes away or even signing on to a merchant ship for a voyage or a season. The physical and environmental conditions of Bayside service were more directly comparable to service with one of the other long-distance trading companies of the period—and yet, as we shall see, there really was no comparison.

Comparisons to Contemporary Long-Distance Trading Companies

The Hudson's Bay Company was relatively small and insignificant compared to some of its long-distance trading contemporaries, although it has enjoyed greater longevity than any of them. Historians have usually discussed the expansion of English trade and settlement within the context of separate ocean basins, distinguishing particularly between those companies and individuals operating in the Indian Ocean basin and those operating in the Atlantic.[2] Some recent scholarship has been more attuned to the common threads joining these disparate companies; for instance, the East India Company acquired its leadership and much of its capital from the Levant Company (active in the eastern Mediterranean), and many early modern English investors diversified their portfolios across several trading companies and other ventures in order to reduce risks and maximize returns.[3] We too must bear in mind the broader imperial and commercial contexts within which the HBC strategized (or muddled through).

This included considerable overlap among the directors of these companies. Lord George Berkeley of Berkeley was elected to three terms on the Royal African Company's (RAC's) court of assistants (board of directors) in 1674–77, 1679–82, and 1684–87, as well as being a director of the East India Company for thirty-seven years and active in the HBC throughout that period.[4] Anthony Ashley Cooper, the first Earl of Shaftesbury, was a major force in the HBC through the 1670s; he was also a founding member of the Carolina Company in 1663 and served as sub-governor of the RAC in 1672–74. Indeed, four of the eight original lords proprietor of the Carolina Company were involved in the formation of the HBC—Sir George Carteret; Christopher Monk, second Duke of Albemarle; William, Lord Craven; and Shaftesbury. Two other early HBC shareholders, Sir Peter Colleton and George Monk, first Duke of Albemarle, were respectively the son and the father of two other lords proprietor. Carteret was also prominent in the RAC and in the colony of New Jersey at this time, epitomizing what E.E. Rich called "that many-sided interest in naval, commercial and colonial projects which marked so many of the shrewd and purposeful courtiers of the Restoration period."[5] Neither was this interest confined to the late seventeenth century. For instance, Sir William Baker's time as deputy governor (1750–60) and governor (1760–67) of the HBC coincided with terms on the EIC's board of directors (1741–53, including two years as chairman), and he also had considerable business interests in New York and the Carolinas.[6]

At least some overlap may be expected in the labour forces of these different companies. Direct evidence of it in HBC records is extremely scarce, but England's vigorous expansion relied as much on the people who circulated the globe in multiple ventures as on those who stayed at home and ventured only their capital. Alison Games has spoken eloquently of "a web of empire," woven by thousands of people making thousands of journeys across thousands of miles.

> *With their trips home and new voyages out, they fabricated connections... linking ties of knowledge and custom and practice....This empire was not*

> *driven and shaped solely by events and actions from a single center, but rather continuously redefined by men who circulated around the globe.... This was an empire built on the ground, in the peripheries, in colonies and trading posts, on islands and in port towns, on board ship and within fortifications. Models devised in different colonial and commercial settings were subsequently adapted and transported around the globe by men... whose travels tangibly linked one enterprise to another. New undertakings were conceptualized in light of prior experiences.*[7]

Within this overall "web of empire," however, the HBC's ability to draw upon precedents in handling personnel issues was hampered by the many differences between them. Furs and slaves were the only trades in British North America carried out by chartered companies; other colonial trades were (more or less) open to all, which imposed distinct organizational and management challenges. Among chartered companies, the English East India Company, the Royal African Company, and others were too different in both size and structure, and the environments of their operations too divergent from Hudson Bay, to offer precedents that could be easily borrowed.[8]

One of the major differences between the HBC and its corporate contemporaries was the number of men employed. The Royal African Company claimed to have established (or re-established) eighteen factories and sent more than forty ships to Africa during its first year of operation (1660–61),[9] and at its height in 1688–89 it employed over 300 European men in its African factories, as well as an unknown number of black slaves. As the company declined in the early eighteenth century, it was not able to find recruits to keep up those numbers, nor could it afford their upkeep; however, it still had over 200 men in Africa in 1709. The East India Company, twenty years after its foundation in 1600, controlled more than a dozen trading stations, employed upwards of 200 factors, had constructed two shipyards on the Thames (which had produced seventy-six ships during those twenty years), and had become one of the largest employers in the London area.[10] In contrast, twenty years after its foundation, the

HBC controlled only one factory and employed no more than 70 men in the Bay. The East India Company maintained close to 1,000 men in India before 1756 and increased its presence after its military victory at Plassey the following year; it shipped 6,500 officers and men to India during the single decade 1762–72; and by the 1780s even its "small" establishments in Bombay had 120 military and 300 civil servants. By 1785 its London operations had grown to include 159 permanent clerical staff and 1,393 warehouse staff, besides the dockyard workers. The Hudson's Bay Company's overseas workforce did not exceed 100 until the 1730s and numbered only 180 in 1772. Inland expansion from 1774 onward required a major increase, but the HBC's 530 servants at the end of the century were still just a minor extension of the British labour supply.[11]

The factories and establishments of most early modern trading companies were much more cosmopolitan than the HBC, in whose service it was rare to find non-British subjects. The RAC recruited Irish, Dutch, French, and Portuguese men to fill gaps left by Englishmen who had died, retired, or deserted; in 1692 perhaps as few as one-quarter of the RAC's complement at Cape Coast Castle (the headquarters on the Gold Coast) were British subjects. Much of this "foreign" recruitment was done by the company's officers in the field, filling vacancies from "the human driftwood of many nationalities that found its way to western Africa." The EIC's various theatres of operation also attracted Europeans of different nationalities, who served the English company as traders, servants, and mercenaries.[12]

The European labour forces of other companies were more top-heavy than the workforce of the HBC. Europeans were concentrated in the higher ranks, while labourers tended to be drawn from the local populations, and local craftsmen were contracted as needed.[13] The RAC's Cape Coast Castle was garrisoned by 80 Europeans and 200 blacks in 1679, and by 100 Europeans and 150 blacks in the early 1690s.[14]

Europeans in lower ranks were primarily soldiers, who were not found in the HBC. The EIC's factories in the Persian Gulf were staffed by small numbers of Europeans (usually fewer than ten) including merchants, factors, writers, and a surgeon, as well as one or two linguists or interpreters (who were usually Armenians or Jews). There were also small garrisons of mercenaries, the crew of a guardship, and servants drawn from the local population to attend to the private and work requirements of the Europeans. For instance, in the 1750s the staff of the Bandar Abbass factory numbered eleven (including a Persian scribe), and the garrison was made up of one sergeant, one corporal, twenty-four Portuguese mercenaries, twenty-two sepoys, and the guardship.[15] By 1751 the EIC's growing military strength had prompted political economist Malachy Postlethwayt to suggest that it "had commenced a kind of military company instead of a trading one."[16]

HBC factories were relatively isolated outposts that needed to import their own labourers and tradesmen but did not employ military garrisons. Even at the height of the military threat from the French in the late seventeenth and early eighteenth centuries, no HBC man stepped forward to suggest—as Gerald Aungier, the EIC's president at Surat and governor in Bombay, had recommended to his employers in 1677—a "severe and vigorous" policy to ensure the stability of its trade. "Justice and necessity to your estate now require that in violent distempers, violent cures are only successful; that the times now require you to manage your general commerce with your sword in your hands."[17] Having consciously chosen to leave its sword at home, the HBC thus had very different workplaces from those found in contemporary stations established by the English in pre-existing trading centres on the coasts of Asia and Africa, where groups of white merchants supported by local servants and protected by European mercenaries were part of large and diverse trading communities. As well, the HBC and its long-distance trading contemporaries in Asia or Africa were not creating colonial settlements, which set them apart from New France and from British traders in New England and New York.

Another difference was the relative lack of possibilities for private wealth in Hudson Bay. Men entering the service of long-distance trading companies generally hoped to make their fortunes, even if only in a small way. When James Phipps sailed for Africa in the RAC's service in 1703, his father, Thomas, reminded him that he was not going "merely to see the country and take the air, but to raise yourself in the world that you may come home and enjoy your friends in much better air in your own country....[I]t is probable that your stay may not be above three years."[18] Phipps stayed in Africa for nineteen years, passing up opportunities to return home because he still hoped to make his fortune. He had heard stories of Edmund Searle and Gerrard Gore, who had become very wealthy serving the RAC on the Gold Coast at the end of the seventeenth century; however, Phipps was rising in the RAC at a time when the company itself was in significant decline. The wealth he sought eluded him, even though he left "no stone unturned to get money honestly and as I could answer it to my own conscience."[19]

India in the eighteenth century still offered many opportunities for wealth and advancement, and it was primarily such opportunities that attracted young men to those distant lands.[20] Prior to the second half of the eighteenth century their attempts to serve both the company's interests and their own were not always successful but apparently did not cause serious disruption in commerce. After the 1750s, however, unsuccessful men tried to hide their private debts by cheating the company and supplementing their private trade with smuggling or even piracy; these activities contributed to a serious decline in Indo-European trade relations. Nevertheless, in Britain the image of the East Indies as a source of great wealth was perpetuated by the "nabobs" (a corruption of the Mogul term *nawab*, meaning "governor"), EIC servants who returned home with significant fortunes and became notorious for their financial excesses.[21] No such reputation was acquired by former HBC servants, except in a very modest way in the Orkney Islands, where some ministers in the 1790s complained about men returning from the Bay with enough money to buy or rent land for themselves.[22] In this, as in most things, the HBC was not in the same league as its contemporaries.

Household Families and Household Factories

Although the HBC's major trading posts in this period had *fort* in their names, the substance of everyday life in them was decidedly civilian. They were generally referred to as factories, that is, places where factors or agents resided, and physically resembled wooden houses with tall fences around them. This resemblance had cultural significance, for Patricia Seed has argued that in the sixteenth and early seventeenth centuries Englishmen constructed their right to occupy the New World by building houses and fences and planting gardens. Houses signified stability and permanence, "a model of fixed settlement that had lasted centuries."[23]

Early modern elites often sought to supplement political and economic authority with cultural authority and to invest social relationships with meanings that encouraged hierarchy and subordination.[24] As the central social institution in British domestic and economic life, the household was an obvious template for the organization of the HBC's permanent overseas posts.[25] Although most people in Britain were rooted in their locality and its concerns, a high degree of labour mobility was possible partly because people who moved to new localities could expect to find similar customs, economic structures, and parish institutions. This extended overseas as well. Immigrants to the Chesapeake, for instance, found courts and vestries organized according to broadly familiar principles imported from England. James Horn has demonstrated how such important local institutions "instilled a sense of order and stability in societies where population turnover and mortality rates were high. Individuals might come and go but institutions remained and lent a degree of permanence to society."[26]

Hudson Bay presented no such familiar points of reference: the absence of courts in the HBC's territories before the 1830s has already been remarked upon, and Rupert's Land was not organized into parishes until around the same time. (In contrast, Virginia was organized into parishes beginning in 1610, just three years after the settlement had been established, and most of Britain's American colonies had formed some kind of parish system by the end of the seventeenth century.)[27] However,

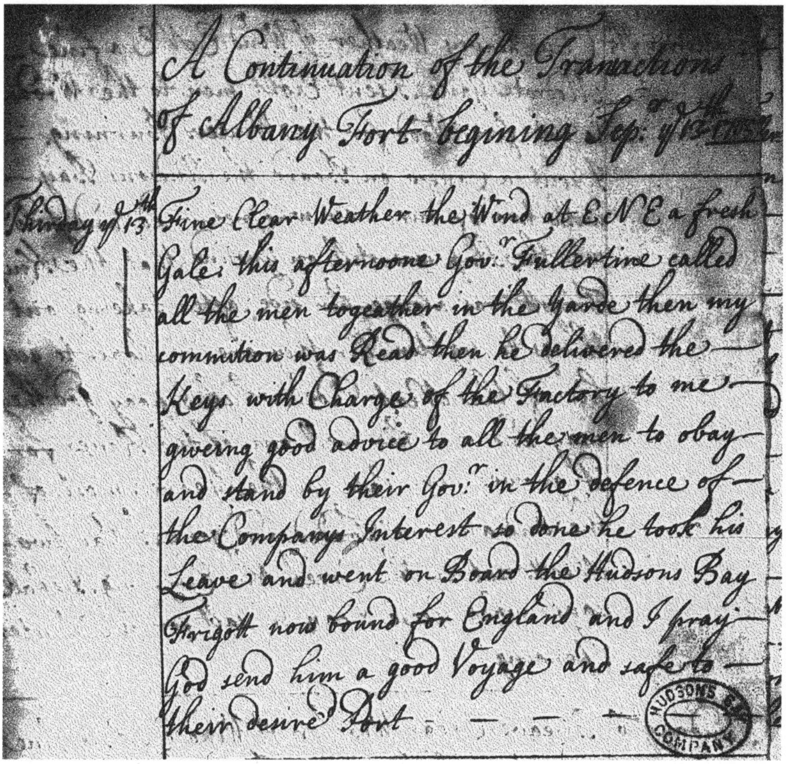

A Continuation of the Transactions
of Albany Fort begining Sepr: ye 13th 1705

Thursday ye 13th Fine Clear Weather the Wind at ENE a fresh Gale; this afternoone Govr: Fullertine called all the men togeather in the Yarde then my commition was Read then he delivered the Keys with Charge of the Factory to me giveing good advice to all the men to obay and stand by their Govr: in the defence of the Company Interest so done he took his Leave and went on Board the Hudsons Bay Frigott now bound for England and I pray God send him a good Voyage and safe to their desire Port

"A Continuation of the Transactions of Albany Fort beginning Sepr: ye 13th 1705," the earliest extant post journal from Hudson Bay. [HBCA, B.3/a/1, fol. 1]

the civilian nature of the new trading posts did offer the opportunity to transplant one of the most important points of reference in early modern England. The social regulation of the company's factories closely resembled the social structure of the household family without any party involved having to consciously construct the factories along such lines.[28]

The unit of the "household" was basic to seventeenth- and eighteenth-century English society and formed the primary organizational model for most early modern domestic and economic life. Workers were integrated into small households that were both units of family and units of production; "family" included apprentices and servants as well as kin, and the head of the household was a father figure as well as their employer.[29] The portability of the concept was illustrated in 1631 when Governor Philip Bell was instructed by the Providence Company to organize all the people of Providence into "families," each with its own "Chiefe."[30] Indeed, James Horn found family and household to be "the bedrock of civil society" in seventeenth-century Virginia and Maryland.[31] The concept of HBC trading posts as households was never articulated by the Committee; its approach to the occupation of its chartered territory was based on implicit assumptions about the organizational norms of the times and modified by trial and error.[32] As historian Keith Wrightson has observed of commercial society in early modern England, "in an environment fraught with risk the most immediate strategy of security was the maintenance of a well-ordered household."[33]

The early modern term *household* referred to the co-residential domestic group and often overlapped with meanings of *family*.[34] The *household family* included parents, children, and any resident kin, journeymen, servants, and apprentices. The precise membership was flexible, changing over time as children grew up and moved out, as apprentices completed their indentures and moved on (perhaps being replaced by new apprentices), as journeymen took other masters or became masters in their own right, and as old servants sought new situations—hence Barry Reay's characterization of the "family as process."[35] Patterns of authority and dependence are key to understanding the household family: the boundaries of membership were defined by who lived and/or worked under the authority of the (usually male) householder.[36] Kinship ties were common but not necessary; in single men's families, for instance, there might not be any kinship relations between the head of the family and the members of his household.[37] Of course, as with Indigenous societies, English kin relationships could be extended to include people not biologically related.[38]

The role of father, or of the male head of the family or the household, had different connotations within Subarctic Algonquian societies, but the rhetoric of male kinship would still have resonated with them. The patriarchal elements in the English household structure resonated with

Frenchmen too. Pierre Esprit Radisson's speech to Cree traders at Port Nelson in 1684 was probably intended to straddle these cultural perceptions: "for thirty years I had been their brother, and...I would be their father in the future if they continued to love me."[39] The original speech was meant to impress the Cree who heard it, while the recording of the speech was meant to impress the Europeans who read it.

Entry into an English household family was usually contractual, that is, on the basis of some kind of agreement setting the terms for inclusion and participation (e.g., marriage or a service contract). Many of these contracts involved the exchange of work and material benefits, and many relationships within the household family were both domestic and occupational; that is, various members had specific tasks. Concepts of family can therefore be understood in terms of instrumentality rather than sentimentality, provided that these are considered as complementary rather than as polar opposites. An increase in affection could lead to an increase in instrumentality, while greater usefulness bred greater trust, which in turn fostered greater affection.[40] HBC factor Humphrey Marten highlighted this reciprocity in a 1766 postscript, sending "My Respects to all that behaves well" at Henley House, and by implication withholding his kind regards from those who did not.[41] A well-ordered household relied on all of its members to perform their roles in order to sustain it as an economic unit.

The importance of contractual, instrumental, and occupational relationships did not eclipse relationships of blood, marriage, and friendship. Such ties were often useful in gaining access to a household, and patronage was strongly linked to both kinship and non-kinship connections.[42] Like many English masters, landowner Lord Fitzwilliam of Milton placed them on par with each other in 1705 when he asked the rhetorical question, "Who ought we to trust to but our children and our stewards?"[43]

The role of the householder, or patriarch, was social, economic, and religious.[44] In HBC journals and account books, the weekly recording of the provisions expended documented factors' roles as administrators and providers, while the regular mention of divine service on Sundays suggests a consciousness of religious duty to their men (explicitly encouraged by the Committee). Two clergymen were briefly employed in the early years of the company, but from 1686 until the early nineteenth century the Committee seems to have made no concerted effort to supply its factories with spiritual guidance; the factor, as head of the household, was responsible for domestic matters of the soul.

When supplies ran low at Albany in 1695–96, John Cartwright suggested that the men sail the factory ship home if London disappointed them again the coming year; Governor James Knight charged him with "stirring up Mutiny and Rebellion in the Factory Endeavouring the utter destruction of the Government and Countrey."[45] One of his factory mates had a more immediate suggestion, and Knight's response reveals something of the strain that this household factory was under:

> *You William Filpot, (by the malicious instigation of the Devil and the wicked inclinations of your own heart, not haveing regard either to the fear of God or man) Stand here charg'd for endeavouring to overthrow, utterly ruin and subvert from the crown of England one of his majesties plantations here in the Norwest part of America by your attempting purposing and enforcing your self to to [sic] stirr up a party to act and joyn with you in committing outrage and burglary, in forcing and breaking open the Compy Store-houses to steal, purloin, embezle and wast those provisions the Company had therein for the preservation and Safeguard of our lives and Countrey, you knowing that Wee Have had no ships these two years last past, and not unsensible that there can be no more relief then there is, Lykewise that there has been more then ordinary care taken or else wee should have fallen short of those provisions we have, so that wee must have been of necessity drove to very great extremities if such care and oversight had not been taken, Notwithstanding of all this, you have (as before mentioned) been By the Subtilty of the Devil and Malicious inclinations of your own heart, Seduced to draw over a party to Joyn with you in forceing and breaking open the Companys wairhouses to embezle and wast what wee have here to the utter destruction and losse of our lives and factory.*[46]

Both men were whipped and clapped in irons, to be sent home as prisoners at the first opportunity. The written records of their ad hoc "trials" drew the Committee's attention to their evil deeds, as well as to the "more then ordinary care" with which Knight was providing for his household factory.

These roles were not merely symbolic; one of the reasons Richard Norton was removed from the command of Prince of Wales Fort in 1727 was "that your expence of Provisions hath been very large notwithstanding which our Servants complain that they have not always had their full allowance." Henry Kelsey wrote to an earlier commander of that house, Richard Staunton:

> *[Y]ou are not for pinching unless occasion requires and it behoves all men that has charge of others to manage what provisions they have....I do not desire men Should go home to upbraid the Comp[an]y they wanted victuals in their Service neither will I be so extravigent of their [the company's] provisions or any thing else to their detriment whereby I may gain their displeasure or Merritt the name of an Ill husband.*[47]

These attitudes were clearly expected by London, but they were not merely documented to satisfy the Committee, for such responsibilities were part of the factors' perception of their roles. As Michael Lacombe observed of the early years of Jamestown and the Virginia colony at the beginning of the century when they were chronically short of food,

> *supplies were not only a tremendous logistical problem but also a dense symbol of the social status and political authority of those who controlled them....[T]he men sent by the Virginia Company to govern the settlement naturally sought to present themselves in their actions and written accounts as strong leaders whose authority was beyond question. Finding themselves in an unfamiliar context, Jamestown's leaders did this by surrounding themselves with familiar symbols and acting out familiar roles, but in doing so they appealed to markedly different visions of a*

leader. George Percy and Edward Maria Wingfield based their claims to office on patriarchal assumptions, seeing political authority as rooted in social status and legitimated through demonstrations of a leader's regard for the welfare of the ordinary sort. Captain John Smith had a very different basis for his own claim....Smith's willingness to share the rations, conditions, and labor of ordinary settlers derived from the humanist image of a leader, whose claim to authority rested above all on his willingness to subordinate his own needs to the common good.... Across the early Atlantic world, food and authority were intertwined because the labor required to procure food, the decisions about how it should be distributed, and the circumstances under which it was consumed each manifested a vision of society. Unlike other forms of symbolic communication, the pageantry of authority had to be accompanied in the case of food with something edible.[48]

By acting in a particular role, factors could define and shape relationships with their superiors and with the men under their command. All the parties involved were influenced by strong contemporary social, cultural, and religious norms regarding household governance.

Bayside servants of all ranks would have needed no prompting to think about their work environments in such a way; around 80 per cent of Englishmen who survived to adulthood married,[49] and even single men (and, less commonly, single women) could become the head of a household. Explicit references to such a mental connection in HBC documents are rare but compelling. In 1737 Richard Norton complained of being forced to reduce his complement at Prince of Wales Fort for want of provisions, "a consequence so great in our situation with so great a family." Norton himself had been apprenticed to the company, and both the concept and the practice of apprenticeship in early modern England were deeply embedded in the patriarchal household.[50]

The position of householder was achieved only after service in subordinate positions in other people's households. In this way, service and apprenticeship were integral parts of the household model. Almost half of all English households and perhaps as many as two-thirds of Orkney households contained servants; in many English parishes, servants made up between 15 and 20 per cent of the local population and may have comprised around 13 or 14 per cent of the national population. As many as two-thirds of young English men and women had left home and entered service by their late teens, and the proportion in Scotland was probably comparable.[51] Service in households was a fundamental source of social training in early modern Britain—although the high drop-out rate of apprentices in most English towns demonstrates the human fallibility of the early modern household as an icon of order and stability.[52] Nevertheless, Samuel Richardson summed up his 1734 advice manual to apprentices as "some of the necessary Rules that ought to be observed by every young Man who is put out to learn a Trade, if he intends to make a good *Servant*, or hopes to make a good *Man*."[53]

Although the term *servant* had a broad range of meanings in early modern England, it basically referred to men and women who worked for and were maintained by a single master. Their status as wage earners was secondary to their status as dependents within a household. In this sense, servants did not conceive of themselves—nor were they conceived of by others—as part of a larger labouring or proletarian class. Their freedom and independence were limited not because they had been reduced to selling their labour but because they were unmarried dependents, children in someone else's family.[54]

Significantly for the assumptions of HBC recruits, household service was associated with a particular phase of life—adolescence and young adulthood—and was rarely a lifelong employment. The great majority of servants in England were unmarried and less than twenty-seven or twenty-eight years old; it was expected that service and/or apprenticeship would be followed by marriage and the creation of one's own household.[55] In the rural estates of many of the English gentry there were a few long-serving retainers and (more commonly) stewards, but the turnover among the bulk of the domestic and agricultural servants was steady.[56] The household family being considered not only as a social institution but as an agent of socialization, craft apprentices, journeymen, domestic servants, and servants in husbandry all had a reasonable expectation of becoming their own masters one day.[57]

The association between businesses and household families was obvious to early modern Englishmen and Scotsmen. Most businesses were not identifiably separate from the households with which they were connected, and those firms that were separate were generally small; for example, few building firms permanently employed more than one or two men. Large-scale productive enterprises—the Tyneside coal pits, the naval shipyards, Sir Ambrose Crowley's ironworks—were rare.[58] Thus, HBC factories, and even the smaller outposts, were anomalous as large-scale workplaces. Men from Southampton to Stromness would have been familiar with households containing two, three, or four servants.[59] HBC factors managed households comparable in size (up to forty or fifty servants) to those of the English aristocracy. The roles of factors were thus comparable to those of estate stewards, whose employers expected them to "Study all ways to advance our Trade & promote our Interest." They were at the top of the servants' hierarchy but were still expected to show their masters proper deference and respect.[60]

Patronage, Brokerage, and Friendship

In such an intermediary role, stewards and factors illustrated one of the most recognizable manifestations of the dominant social system, the exercise of patronage. The patron-client relationship was found in all facets of English society in the seventeenth and eighteenth centuries, particularly in business and politics. In the HBC the Committee consistently portrayed itself as the sole reliable source of patronage. However, patronage was also exercised by the factors and by the captains of the supply ships, and probably also by tradesmen and "old hands" in ways largely invisible in the written record.

A patron influences the behaviour of his clients through the bestowal or withdrawal of benefits, both material and non-material. "Patronage is the art of obligation, of manipulation through rewards and punishment,"[61] past, present, and future. The patron-client relationship is a personal one, unequal but reciprocal; in exchange for the client's loyalty and service, a patron is expected to share what advantages he has at his disposal. Importantly for this study, the patron is distinguished from his client as the one who has the values of his own choosing affirmed by others.[62]

The Bayside factors played dual roles, acting as patrons to the men under their command, while also relying on the patronage of the London Committee. Being both masters and servants in this sense, factors had an "amphibious" relationship to authority, "at once its conduits and receptacles."[63] D.R. Hainsworth found the same situation among estate stewards in seventeenth-century England, who "were expected to address the great with suitable deference, to negotiate and discuss with men of middling rank, and to rebuke or encourage with bluff condescension those of lesser rank."[64] Alison Games spoke of overseas merchants of that period functioning "in two overlapping worlds, the first the local one of the trading post and the second an international world of maritime commerce, in which reputations traveled with the letters that accompanied each vessel from port to port, linking a remote outpost to an employer in London through the umbilical cord of correspondence."[65]

This chain of relationships was complicated by several variables. For instance, servants could and did correspond privately with the Committee, and sometimes appeared before the Committee in person upon their return to Britain, as they could even in the much larger EIC.[66] Factors were not mere links in a chain but rather brokers in a complex network of communication.

Whereas the patron is perceived as the source of the values that his client affirms, the broker is seen as purveying values that are not his own—although he may change their emphasis or even their content. As a middleman the broker does not dispense favours himself but attracts followers by convincing them that he can influence the patron who does dispense favours.[67] Hainsworth's colourful depiction of English estate stewards applies in an HBC context: "The prolonged absence of the lord enhanced the status of the steward in the eyes of his neighbours, even though, *au fond*, that status was governed by the status of his employer. Like the moon he shone by reflected light, and the moon is most imposing when the sun is absent."[68]

The fact that captains of the company's ships could usually travel to Hudson Bay and back in a single year allowed them to act as purveyors of information while remaining outside the central servant-factor-Committee relationship. Indigenous peoples had a variety of active roles to play. Factors acted as brokers between upland traders and both the Committee and the factory servants; factory servants connected with the Homeguard Cree acted as brokers between them and the factors; and Cree and Nakoda trading "captains" acted as brokers between the First Nations of the interior (and, to a lesser extent, the French inland traders) and the English in general.

Factors probably had the most power, as purveyors of both information and corporate values, but their power was limited by the fact that they were not the exclusive conduits of transmission. In the early 1740s James Duffield tried to make the local Homeguard Cree "sencible of ye wrong measures they had taken in Conjunction with our disafected Englishmen" at Moose, especially the recently dismissed Augustine Frost. Duffield's friend and supporter Joseph Isbister, replied from Albany, "I...ame glad to hear that ye Indians are brought to know their proper benefactor, which is ye thing that I have ever aimd at"—leaving the modern reader uncertain if the Cree's "proper benefactor" was the factor or the company.[69] Such ambiguity potentially offered men a choice of "benefactors." When Albany factor Humphrey Marten tried to stem the rising animosity between himself and William Richards at Henley House, he reminded Richards that "tho You may be an Enemy to me, and want to be master of this place [Albany]...Your own heart will tell You Sir that I have behaved to You Exceedingly well." Richards responded with outrage at "the many false charges" against him and pointedly ignored Marten's alleged past kindnesses: "my thoughts as [*sic*] been intirely bent on Establishing this place [Henley], according to my Duty to my masters."[70]

The Committee consistently portrayed itself as the principal patron within the company's organization. Allowing factors to act as patrons could both weaken central authority and tempt the factors to place their own interests ahead of the company's. The Committee, however, valued and relied upon the factor's role as a broker in transmitting expectations, praise, and censure from London. In some respects, factors may have acted as a kind of buffer between the Committee and the bulk of the servants, much as stewards and bailiffs in Britain acted as mediators between absentee landowners and the labouring poor. Hainsworth observed that the steward's fundamental objective was "the prosperity of the estate and thereby of his master."

> *The surest way to achieve this was by promoting harmony between landlord and tenant, playing a mediating role.... In any conflict between landlord and tenant, therefore, the steward would appear to be in a hopelessly compromised position since he was the salaried servant of one of the contending parties, a senior member of the lord's household.... How then could the tenants possibly trust him and if they did not trust him how was he to resolve disputes? On the other hand, since he was a member of his lord's family, his lord had a right to expect that he would always promote his interest rather than the interests of the tenants.*[71]

One is reminded of Daniel Defoe's fictional cloth worker, called before the Justice of the Peace on a complaint from his employer:

> JUSTICE. *Come in Edmund, I have talk'd with your Master.*
> EDMUND. *Not my Master, and't please your Worship, I hope I am my own Master.*[72]

As E.P. Thompson observed of this exchange, "[t]he deference which he refuses to his employer overflows in the calculated obsequiousness to 'your Worship.'" Edmund lashes out at "the immediate, daily, humiliations of dependency" without challenging the broader outlines of power and political authority.[73] As the day-to-day face of HBC authority—an image cultivated from both sides of the Atlantic—factors similarly served as lightning rods for the frustrations of the servants, as well as for their ambitions.

It is difficult to measure factors' success in acting as patrons.[74] During his time in charge of Albany, former apprentice Joseph Adams actively supported his accountant, Richard White. Adams may have given White some share of his command immediately after Joseph Myatt's death on 9 June 1730: Thomas McCliesh Jr (at York) seemed to believe that Adams and White were jointly in charge at Albany. Adams certainly recommended White to be his second, but White and the Committee could not agree on wages. In autumn 1731 Adams left White in charge of Albany while he went to Moose, and made sure to report that "at my return I found that he had Acted with a Great Deal of prudence & Delligence both in Treating the Natives well and Carr[y]ing a Good Decorum." White was a member of the Albany council in 1733 but was passed over for the position of second and was recalled to England that year over another wage dispute; Adams responded to the Committee, "I am Sorry Mr White has any ways disoblidg'd you." White re-engaged in 1735 and served as second at Prince of Wales Fort, but he came home in 1740 without ever achieving a position of command.[75]

Adams also patronized Moose accountant Samuel Maidman. William Bevan added a postscript to his 1732 letter from Moose, saying "I humbly take the liberty being desired by Mr Adames to acquaint your honours that one Samuel Maidman is a very useful man at anything." Although Maidman never achieved a position of command, in 1735 his salary was increased from fourteen pounds to twenty pounds "considering Your Usefullness at the Factory and the readiness You express to Serve Us on all Occasions"—a substantial increase, but still short of the thirty pounds he had requested. He was summoned home as part of the purge of Moose Fort in 1737: as a member of the factor's council, he felt the Committee's wrath over rampant private trade and other "mismanagement."[76]

The Committee was unable to completely control the patronage or brokerage roles adopted by its officers and servants, partly due to the complexity of relationships at play in its factories, and also to the physical distance between London and the Bay. More than one factor tartly reminded "your honours" that they had never set foot in Hudson Bay, but that situation was far from unusual in long-distance trading companies; few EIC factors, commanders, or servants became directors in the eighteenth century, and directors in office never visited India.[77] The London Committee compensated for its lack of direct knowledge of Bayside conditions by relying on the accounts of servants and others who had acquired such knowledge, especially the captains of the supply ships. To borrow a phrase from estate owner Sir John Lowther of Whitehaven, "I see with others' eyes."[78]

Returning employees could provide useful insights and advice, but they could also criticize their colleagues remaining "in the Country"—sometimes unfairly. In 1682 Governor John Nixon bemoaned the "advantage all my adversaries have above me, that they come first home, who by fraud and flatterie, can have their tale first tould, and they can be heard by you." Referring particularly to Captain Nehemiah Walker, he complained, "If I doe all things well he will rob me of the credit of it, and if badly I am sure to have all the disgrace heaped upon my back."[79] He claimed to put his faith in the Committee members' ability to detect treachery and falsehood:

> *I am confidant at last that your honours will finde, that those who goe about to put jealousies into your heads, it is for no other end but to cover their oune knaveries, or to bring their purposes to pass, or at leest to be revanged, for they hate to be looked into, I say those that are enemies to me, yow will find them to be yours first, and I pray God grant that it be not too late befor yow have found them out.*[80]

The captains were not the only intermediaries of information that Nixon had to worry about; the Committee received several complaints about him from returning servants.[81]

The company's posts represented webs of social relationships based primarily on the common experience of living and working in Hudson Bay. A man's direct social contacts were the same men with whom he had a defined work relationship.[82] Albany surgeon Eusebius Bacchus Kitchen and clerk George Humble sent their love to William Richards, master of Henley House in 1766, and he returned, "My Sincere Respects to my dear messmates."[83] Upland traders and Homeguard Cree individuals could also be defined in terms of work relationships, usually as customers or as service providers; for instance, Humphrey Marten described his Cree partner, Pawpitch, as "Daughter to the Captain of the [Albany River] Goose Hunters."[84] The social meanings with which Subarctic First Nations imbued economic relationships is well established, but it is worth adding that such relationships—especially the extension of credit and the forgiveness of debts—might have implied a fictive kinship to Englishmen of that period as well.[85] However, the more informal and routine of workers' relationships (among themselves, with their superiors, and with their Indigenous neighbours) have left little evidence in the surviving documentary record, except when serious conflict or crisis arose.

Given the small complements of HBC trading posts, where even labourers seldom formed a clear majority, it was likely that any individual's relationships would cross some boundaries of occupation and rank. Boundaries of ethnicity and culture (and sometimes gender) were also crossed when men formed relationships with Homeguard Cree. Even within an occupational group, relationships crossed boundaries of age and seniority. Thus, newly arrived young men and boys could benefit greatly from the tutelage and advice of senior men. When surgeon George Spence took charge at Albany in 1747, he wrote to James Isham at York as soon as he could, signing himself "Your Very humble Servant tho' unknown." The senior officer congratulated him on his promotion and assured him that "I

Shall be Very Glad to hear from you at all opportunity's & do assure you itt [advice] never shall be wanting on my side."[86]

Senior men might even act as surrogate fathers. Explicit evidence is rare but not unexpected, given the paternal nature of the master-servant (or master-apprentice) relationship. Writing in England in 1747, R. Campbell advised the prospective apprentice to "look upon his Master as his Parent," significant advice considering that some boys (perhaps as many as one in four in London) were fatherless by the time they entered service or apprenticeship.[87] In 1761 Humphrey Marten (whose own father had died three years earlier) lamented the "Shocking news of the Death of my beloved Friend and I may truly say Father," James Isham.[88] The power of such affective ties was again illustrated by Marten many years later, after he had succeeded to his mentor's old charge at York. He had been badly scalded in the autumn of 1778 while helping two of his men carry a tub of boiling wort in York's brewery, and he suffered from this (as well as an earlier injury to his left kidney) for several months afterwards. The care and concern of his men prompted Marten to wax affectionate in a letter to his friend Thomas Hutchins, chief factor at Albany: "to see the poor Fellows when I am in great pain, with deep sorrow in their faces, and to be inform[ed] of the heart felt prayers offer'd up for my recovery melts me in the tenderest manner, and makes me desire not to be parted from them."[89] In one case, the paternal relationship was biological as well as emotional: Henry Pollexfen Jr was named his father's accountant and second at Moose in 1758.[90]

Quasi-parental relationships could strengthen the vertical ties that bound trading post communities together, but they could also give rise to quasi-parental conflicts and may have been part of some men's reasons for leaving the service.[91] This may have been an important element of the tension between James Isham and Samuel Skrimshire at York Fort. Skrimshire, apprenticed to the company in 1733, was probably a cousin or nephew of Isham, whose mother's maiden name was Skrimshire and who acted as the young man's patron in the 1740s. Skrimshire rose to second at York but was recalled in 1750 on the basis of unfavourable reports from his superior, John Newton (a rare eighteenth-century example of the HBC "parachuting" a man into the command of a post without prior company service). Although Skrimshire returned to Hudson Bay the following year and soon regained his position as second, his relationship with Isham had soured noticeably; their correspondence between 1751 and Skrimshire's death in 1755 was frequently bitter, sarcastic, and confrontational.[92]

The sentimental and practical value of such relationships, when positive, was enhanced by the possibility of vertical mobility, but they also extended horizontally. Just as a master could become a surrogate father, so could workmates become brothers.[93] This may have been Nathaniel Bishop's feeling when he informed the Committee in 1719 that he would serve under no man but Thomas McCliesh Jr, who was probably younger than him—a declaration of loyalty and affection to which the Committee did not take kindly.[94] Joseph Isbister frequently referred to his "brother officers"; James Isham and John Potts (who was surgeon and master at Richmond) called each other "most Affect[ionate] & Lov[in]g Brother"; and Isham signed one letter to Ferdinand Jacobs at Prince of Wales Fort "Dear Friend Your Loving Bro."[95] Humphrey Marten and Andrew Graham were both deeply attached to Isham, but they were also attached to each other; they usually began and concluded their letters to each other with "Dear Friend," but Marten occasionally called Graham "My Brother" or "my dear brother" (a term probably encouraged by Marten's Quaker upbringing).[96] Contemporaries and scholars have described a "fraternity" of men in James Bay (especially at Moose Fort) in the 1730s, bound by their common origin in County Durham (especially in and around Stockton-on-Tees), although the extent of this "fraternity" is difficult to measure.[97]

Occasionally the Committee unintentionally fostered emotional relationships when providing for the training of their factors. Richard Norton, the former apprentice whose performance in charge of Prince of Wales Fort was causing concern, was transferred to York in 1727 to act as Thomas McCliesh Jr's second and learn the company's trading and accounting methods better. That working relationship became a personal one: not only did the two men become friends but Norton married one of McCliesh's daughters while on furlough in Britain in 1730–31.[98]

The Committee benefited from increased ties among their factors, which could result in better working relations between posts.[99] Ties between officers also facilitated friendship and camaraderie and perhaps resulted in a greater willingness to stay in the country. In 1692 the Committee informed Stephen Sinclair of his appointment as James Knight's deputy at Albany (at Knight's request) and expressed pleasure "that the old freindshipp bettwixt Governr. Knight & your selfe Continueth soe harty & that you are soe Ready to accompany him" on the expedition to reoccupy Albany.[100] In 1706 Anthony Beale declared to "ever had and have still a great respect" for his former superior John Fullartine: "I had the happiness of his conversation every day and I be very well satisfied we parted good freinds."[101] Samuel Richardson's 1734 advice manual for apprentices called friendship "a glorious Thing...Its noble Influences... sweeten the Ills of Life, double our Comforts, divide our Cares, and ennoble human Nature."[102]

In the eighteenth century the term *friend* could encompass kinship ties, sentimental relationships, economic ties, occupational connections, social networks, and other attachments.[103] Friendship was a multi-faceted moral relationship, requiring "friends" to support and serve each other in many different ways. Acts or tokens of friendship both illustrated and reinforced the relationship and obliged the friend in further reciprocal exchanges. Felicity Heal, discussing food gifts in early modern England, described them as expressing "local patronage and power relationships—the desire, for example, to reinforce economic and social bonds that secured further business alliance," and as creating "a predictable deferred obligation to reciprocate." More generally, Craig Muldrew has described an early modern "economy of obligation," based on credit and tied closely with exchanges among kin and friends—people who could also be called upon to underpin trust and maintain social reputation when the "economy of obligation" failed.[104] Again, these concepts would have resonated with the company's Cree trading partners; although expressed in different terms, they could nevertheless provide a basis for a mutual understanding—or at least a constructive mutual misunderstanding.[105]

Friendship was not necessarily a relationship of equality or of equity; patronage and dependence were also understood in terms of friendship, and the London Committee's letters to its Bayside posts were consistently signed, "Your Loving Friends."[106] The language of friendship (which overlapped with the language of kinship) thus represented a sentimental element in the unequal and utilitarian relationship between the Committee and its servants and emphasized the reciprocal nature of that relationship.[107] It also helped highlight the relationships, both vertical and horizontal, that tied the factories to each other as well as to London.

The Bayside correspondence is replete with examples of such rhetoric. When John Potts succeeded to the command of Moose Fort in 1747, James Isham wrote, "I most heartily congratulate you...& trust...by your Conduct & frugality you will gain the applause of yr Sincere freinds, & increase the Company's trade to their Interest & satisfaction." That same year Joseph Isbister called Thomas White (former chief at York) "ye Gentlemn yt I alway's had a Great Veneration for, having had Some Knowledge of him formerly." During a heated exchange of correspondence with Isham a few years later Isbister wrote, "You may think from the Perticular regard I Expres'd for Mr Newton...that I cannot have any respect for Mr Isham, Yes Sr and Mr Isbister would as gladly cultivate a freindly Correspondance with Mr Isham as any Man He knows although the Communication with each other had only been by writing." He declared that "it is My Exprest desire to live in Amity with You & all the rest of the Companys Cheifs," and signed himself "Your Affectionate freind & most Humb Servant." Isbister's words may seem formulaic, but Isham responded to them.

> *I cannot See how any good Harmony mutual freindship & Correspondance can be carried on while such sort of Discourse Passes, therefore in hopes of such a Hapiniss with You & any of our Neighbours, I shall here confine My Self to wt is most Conducive to ye Companys Interest & hope to Our own Satisfaction.*[108]

This network of relationships was focused primarily on Hudson Bay; most men's visibly operative social ties originated in the social universe of the factories. The appearance thus created is that company servants became "company men," defining themselves in terms of these relationships, centring themselves on their common experience of living and working for the company in Rupert's Land, and isolating themselves from their original homes in Britain. However, the frequent turnover of personnel and the consistently large proportion of "green" hands suggest that only a minority of men adapted so permanently to their Bayside environment. Most servants maintained their ties with Britain, and, throughout the period studied, more than three-quarters returned there after less than ten years in the country. Like households in Britain, the factories were permanent institutions characterized by a largely temporary membership.

Public and Private Transcripts

How do we account for the discrepancy between the consistent rhetoric of subordination and the small proportion of men who spent more than ten years in company service? Early modern power relations were more multi-faceted than they may at first appear, and thus our understanding of them may be problematic. It is tempting to assume a dichotomy between deference and confrontation, but this may lead us either to misconstrue popular politics as spasmodic and reactive, in which periods of subordination are punctuated by moments of agency, or to assume that disobedience and dissent were the norm.[109]

The relatively weak were able to manipulate for their own purposes "the texts, languages, and performances which were intended to explain, demonstrate, and justify the power of their superiors."[110] For instance, the system of poor relief in England during this period was undoubtedly an instrument of regulation reflecting elite agendas, yet those whom it sought to regulate developed a sense of entitlement: no one wanted to go on the dole, but having that option if circumstances demanded it "was becoming a new element in customary expectations."[111] In seeking to understand such manipulation, James C. Scott's fieldwork among the peasantry of Southeast Asia provides a useful distinction between the "public transcript"—"the repertoire of acceptable public behaviour between superior and subordinate in face-to-face contexts"—and the "hidden transcript"—"what each side may say or think when they are off-stage." The concept of a public transcript is similar to the "implicit contracts between employer and employed" that Patrick Joyce and others argue "provide the basis for authority in work and outside it."[112]

The deference expressed in the public transcript gives the impression—to both participants and observers—that the existing social order is a consensual one.[113] The content and boundaries of the public transcript are not simply constructed by dominant elites; they are to some extent the result of ongoing negotiations or struggles between dominant and subordinate groups, the "theatre of resistance" that Carolyn Podruchny saw played out in the Montreal-based fur trade.[114] Nor were such processes alien to their Subarctic Algonquian-speaking neighbours, whose "psychology" anthropologist Richard Preston summarized in terms of (among other things) "an adaptable collective wisdom," "readiness for pragmatic accommodation to external factors," and "an expectation of negotiability in personal relations, characterized by planning strategies in terms of past performance and future preferences."[115] Whether we characterize these negotiations as a "terrain of compromise" or as a common argument in which members of a community are engaged, the different processes that took place at different times and in different places help account for the overall flexibility of relationships between superiors and subordinates.[116]

The use of dominant discourses—such as the rhetoric of master-servant relationships or the socio-economic model of the patriarchal household family—by subordinates does not necessarily indicate a complete commitment to the social relations expressed in those discourses, nor does it preclude conflict between the two groups. Deference in master-servant relationships, and indeed in most power relations, depends on the inclusion in the public transcript of implicit promises of benefits for subordinate groups. At least some of these promised benefits must be realized, for they are what give subordinate groups their own stake in the prevailing order. This, in turn, allows them opportunity to legitimately criticize the public transcript in its own terms.[117] Thus, the patently imbalanced power relations of a position in service were made relatively palatable by the realistic promise of one moving out of service someday to become a householder and quite possibly a master with servants of one's own. As Peter Laslett observed, "the head of the poorest family was at least the head of something;" or, as *The Batchelor's Directory* put it more bluntly in 1694, "[o]ne finds nothing so sweet as the power of commanding others."[118] In the HBC that promise could take two forms, either rising through the company's ranks to become the master of a small post (or the factor of a major one), or using the savings and skills (and perhaps the connections) acquired in Hudson Bay to launch a more independent life upon return to Britain.

These conceptual models, emphasizing negotiation and confrontation between horizontally defined (and sometimes vague) groups such as "superiors" and "subordinates," may appear incompatible with the existence of vertical ties between those groups. It is not necessary, however, to think of social relations simply as a dichotomy between the sentimental (represented by vertical ties) and the instrumental (represented by horizontal ties). Both models were at work throughout early modern England. Social relations in a particular time and place represented the particular accommodation "between the forces of social identification—as kinsmen, friends, neighbours, patron and client, co-religionists, fellow countrymen—and the forces of social differentiation—as landlord and tenant, master and man, governor and governed, rich and poor."[119] Public transcripts in the early modern period emphasized vertical ties, partly to guard against horizontal divisions becoming social fissures, while hidden transcripts emphasized horizontal ties as a counterbalance to the hegemony of the dominant elite.

|| The HBC's factories and houses grew and developed within these complex contexts. However, much of the preceding discussion benefits from hindsight that was unavailable to the handful of investors who first ventured to build such outposts on the distant shores of Hudson Bay. In the late 1660s, as the idea of a maritime approach to the furs of northern North America circulated and took hold in the English capital, the scope and nature of their future establishments were perceived only dimly; even the charter granted in 1670 laid down the most general of frameworks. The household factories described here evolved over time, through opportunities and expedients, decisions and assumptions, peace and war. They began with a vague but apparently unbounded optimism and were shaped both by the collective personality of the London directors and by the personalities of the posts' residents—many of them now lost to our view.

2 The Hudson's Bay Company as Enterprise and Employer

1668–1786

The reason that I have enlarged so much upon evry subject is, to convince your judgments, that if yow will reap the profits of this country yow must use the meens, and follow the advice of your Governor, and if yow think him not capable of giveing yow advice I desire that yow would remove him, and place one in his roome upon whose judgment your Honors may better confide....I am to steer between two rocks, and am in danger of falling on the one, or on the other I strive to keep good orders, and behave my selfe in my place as I am bound, by oath, and as my duty requires to promote your bussiness, and restraine licentiousness to my power, then it is that I fall on that rack Slander, and envy, and if I buy their good worde at your coast, or neglect my deuty to satisfy their lisentiousness, then I am lyke to fall aworse, the breach of my faith, the breach of my bounds, the loss of my reputation.

—JOHN NIXON, "Report to the Governor and Committee by John Nixon, 1682," 249, 271

ON 5 JUNE 1668 two small ships sailed from Gravesend, bound for Hudson Bay. Only two of the men aboard could claim any direct knowledge of their destination, and the men who financed the expedition based their hopes for success on optimism rather than on concrete information. The ships were both ketches, well suited to long-distance travel in uncertain weather, but the *Eaglet* was forced back by storms. Her companion, the *Nonsuch*, persevered, and her backers waited patiently for her return the following October; until that happy occasion they could not be certain if she were carrying on a successful trade in the Bay or lying at the bottom of the Atlantic.

For one hundred years and more the Governor and Committee of the Hudson's Bay Company required deep reserves of patience and optimism. The daunting North Atlantic allowed only one trip in and out of Hudson Strait every year—including twelve weeks of travel to the shores of Hudson Bay and six weeks back to England—and even that one trip relied on good luck and better timing. While this was short compared to the six-month voyage to India, other American destinations such as Boston, Barbados, and the Chesapeake could be reached from London in between five and nine weeks (and there were fewer icebergs). The timing of the annual voyage to Hudson Bay was dictated entirely by the ice conditions of the North Atlantic, whereas voyages to and from warmer destinations were timed to coincide with local patterns of production and/or trade.[1] The HBC's decision makers in London had to wait from autumn until spring to respond to changing circumstances in the Bay, by which time circumstances could have changed again; similarly, their agents in the field often found their information from London incomplete and out of date. Thus, the Committee relied heavily on the discretion and ability of those agents in the field, hoping that it had not chosen frail reeds upon which to lean.[2]

Uncertain Beginnings

The 1670s were a decade of experimentation. The Committee in London and its factors and servants in Hudson Bay were each in their own ways sorting the possible from the impractical. A rapid transition from seasonal trading posts manned by the crews of the company's ships to permanent factories with their own modest garrisons demanded some kind of framework for recruitment and salaries.[3] Constructing that framework required the Committee to evaluate how they were going to structure the trade and how much overhead they considered reasonable (or sustainable); at the same time, the company's servants had to decide under what terms they were willing to stay in Hudson Bay. These overlapping questions sometimes produced tension but together laid important groundwork for the HBC's long first century.

The beginnings of the Hudson's Bay Company were thus marked by trial and error.[4] Like most metropolitan merchants, the London Committee had little experience in administering on a large scale or over such long distances. Some early HBC directors were also active in other commercial and/or colonial companies, but Hudson Bay was a novel trading environment. No clearly articulated policy inspired the company's strategies for operating in that environment. Instead, the Committee created a patchwork of experiments and expedients, similar to that of other British colonial endeavours, where experimentation and "eclectic borrowing" from other nations' experiences produced very diverse settlements.[5]

The first trading establishments in Hudson Bay were humble concerns, some little more than seasonal camps for ships' crews to live in while they traded with local Lowland Cree. The first was built by the crew of the *Nonsuch* on their initial voyage to test the trading waters of Hudson Bay; to shelter themselves through the winter of 1668–69 they built a simple wooden house near the mouth of Rupert River and named it Charles Fort after the monarch they were trying to impress.[6] Few details are known about that first expedition, although it included some men who served the company later: sailors John Hawkins and James Tottenham (Tatnum), surgeon Pierre Romieux (dit Romulus), and trader Médard Chouart, Sieur des Groseilliers. Clerk Thomas Gorst and trader Pierre Esprit Radisson were aboard the *Eaglet* and did not reach Hudson Bay that year. Although it is impossible to calculate whether the *Nonsuch* turned a profit that winter, it showed that the venture was feasible. That was enough for the initial investors to win first a royal grant of exclusive trade and then a royal charter.[7]

The charter, granted on 2 May 1670, established "The Governor and Company of Adventurers of England Tradeing into Hudson's Bay" as a legal corporate entity. It was a remarkably flexible document, which would have served equally well as the charter of a colony or as the charter of a trading monopoly. The company was to be "true and absolute Lordes and Proprietors" of the yet-to-be-mapped Hudson Bay watershed, henceforth known as Rupert's Land. They were granted the "sole Trade and Commerce" of this territory without being constrained by definitions of how exactly that trade would be carried out: corporate structure was outlined generally, strategy and tactics not at all. Regarding human resources, the charter stated simply that either the Committee or the general court of shareholders could "admit...such Servants or Factors" as they considered necessary, including a military force. Overall, the charter spoke more to undefined opportunities than to specific strategies and goals.[8]

With the new company's legal identity established in London, it was time to build upon the tentative physical presence that had been established at Charles Fort. Bayside governor Charles Bayly and his secretary, Thomas Gorst, wintered there with between ten and twenty men in 1670–71, when they built a new and more substantial house: two storeys with a brick chimney.[9] Unfortunately, the men became fed up: "so long had these poor Men liv'd in this Desart, holding a precarious Being by their Guns and Fishing Tackle. Their Patience was at last spent." Bayly was unable to get enough volunteers to stay in the country, and he led the entire expedition home in July 1671.[10]

Bayly returned to Charles Fort the following year and used it as a base for exploring the inland sea over which the king had so generously granted them dominion. The first priority was finding trading partners, without whom the company's monopoly would be of little value. Expeditions to Nelson River on the west coast of Hudson Bay in the summers of 1670 and

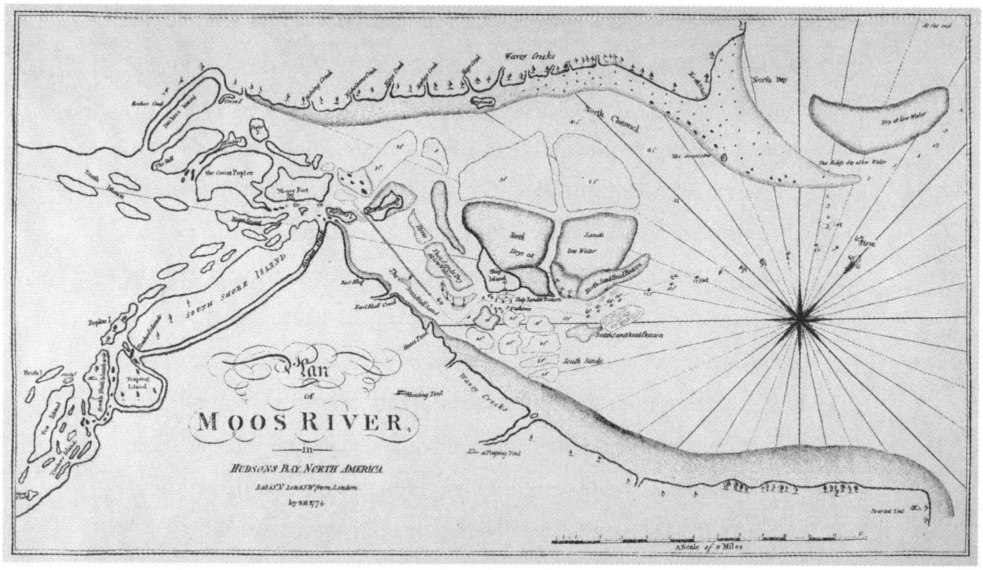

Samuel Hearne, A Plan of Moos River, 1774. *[HBCA, G. 6/10]*

1673 came to nothing, but Moose River at the bottom of James Bay offered greater initial promise. Most of Bayly's trade was coming from the Moose River basin, and he built a factory there in 1673, although it does not appear to have been continuously occupied until a year or two later.[11]

Food was running low at Charles Fort in the autumn of 1674, and the supply ships *Rupert* and *Shaftesbury* arrived too late to attempt the homeward voyage before winter. It was a particularly bitter winter for Bayly: the ships had unexpectedly brought out his replacement, former naval lieutenant William Lydall, to whom Bayly was forced to relinquish command and then to live under that command until spring. Details of that winter are incomplete, although we know it was a hungry one, and Bayly may have taken some men to Moose for the season. Spring brought relief for both body and spirit—especially Bayly's spirit, for he was one of four men left behind when the ships finally sailed, and he became governor once again after Lydall decided that Hudson Bay did not suit him. When Bayly was recalled a second time in 1679 and replaced by John

Nixon, the new governor tried to mark out a path for his successor, "leest he break his shins as Lydall did."[12]

We might perhaps understand Bayly, and the company he served, a little better if we knew exactly why he was recalled on either occasion, but the records are incomplete. Appearing before the Committee on 17 December 1679, he "hath been told wee have some things to charge him." These charges were not specified in the minutes, but Bayly was to receive a written account of the charges against him at the next meeting and was to respond in writing. Unfortunately, Bayly did not live to answer the charges against him; within a month of his arrival in London he fell ill, and died on 6 January 1680 at the home of HBC stockholder William Walker. His alleged sins were neither forgiven nor forgotten, but they were passed over in favour of a public tribute. He was buried at the company's expense in the church of St. Paul's, Covent Garden, and Nixon was sent "an Escutcheon, which wee would have you set up for the observation of the Indians, that they may be made to understand he is dead, and that the Company used him kindly."[13]

Bayly had indeed been treated kindly: in 1678 the Committee had raised his salary from fifty pounds to two hundred pounds and sent him his viol; in reporting his death to Nixon, the Committee lamented that by his "unexpected death wee lost much of the light & assistance wee expected from him." A subsequent investigation estimated that he had misapplied £828 15s. 6d. worth of the company's goods during his tenure, yet the final settlement of his account with his widow (in December 1683) included a gratuity of £175 7s. 4d. "in consideration of her husbands Good service" and to make the total £400.[14] Given the unsystematic state of the company's accounts during this period, if the Committee had planned to censure Bayly for not keeping track of incomings and outgoings, it would have been very much a case of the pot calling the kettle black.[15]

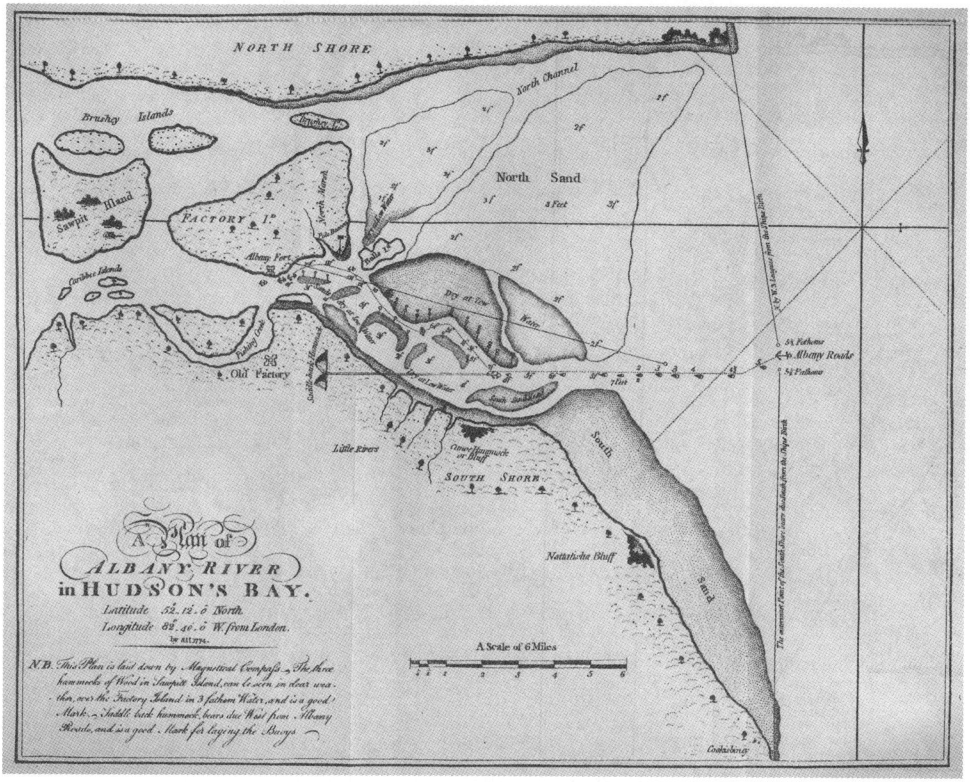

Samuel Hearne, A Plan of Albany River in Hudson's Bay, 1774.
[Rich and Johnson (eds.), Moose Fort Journals, *endpiece]*

New Horizons

Sometime in 1679 the HBC established its third permanent trading post, a "house of some strength" on Bayly's Island at the mouth of the Albany or Chichewan River.[16] It was known by the latter name until rechristened Albany Fort in 1683 in honour of the company's new governor, James, Duke of York and Albany. Followed closely by the construction of a central transshipment depot on Charlton Island in 1680 and a settlement at Port Nelson in 1682, Albany marked a turning point as the HBC entered its second decade.[17]

The company's operations were still characterized by a mix of caution and curiosity: resources were limited, and no dividends were paid to shareholders until 1684.[18] However, while the 1670s were a settling-in period, the early 1680s were years of expansion. New operations increased the numbers of men needed but also tested the limits of what those men were willing to do for their employer. Violent intervention by French forces—both military and commercial—tested those limits even further.

The Nelson River settlement was initially unsuccessful, and, for the time being, fortune seemed most likely to be had on the eastern shores of James Bay—the eastern mainland, or East Main (Eastmain). In addition to furs, company servants sought the potentially valuable mineral deposits believed to exist there, particularly mica (isinglass). Trading stations on the Eastmain (or Slude) River were wintering camps, crewed by the men of the sloop attached to Albany and commanded by the sloop master. The sloop was often accompanied by a few other servants, but only sometimes by a miner. A permanent house was built in 1719 on the north shore of the Eastmain River, near the mouth of Fishing River; before then, the men probably lived on the sloop or in tents.[19]

The Committee and its factors also considered inland operations, not so much to increase trade as to disrupt French competitors operating out of the St. Lawrence valley. An overland expedition from the south had nailed the French royal coat of arms to a tree near Charles Fort during Bayly's absence in the autumn of 1671, a deliberate ceremony of possession. (We do not know if the French obtained Cree consent before affixing the arms, but such consent was a consistent and necessary element in these French imperial ceremonies.) As elsewhere in the early modern Atlantic world, the space of Hudson Bay was more actively reconstructed by the English and the French in regard to each other than in regard to the First Nations.[20]

The French proved to be persistent adversaries. The governor was at home to receive Jesuit Father Albanel in 1674 and trader and explorer Louis Jolliet in 1679.[21] A French post was operating about one week's journey upriver from Charles Fort as early as 1673–74; five years later the

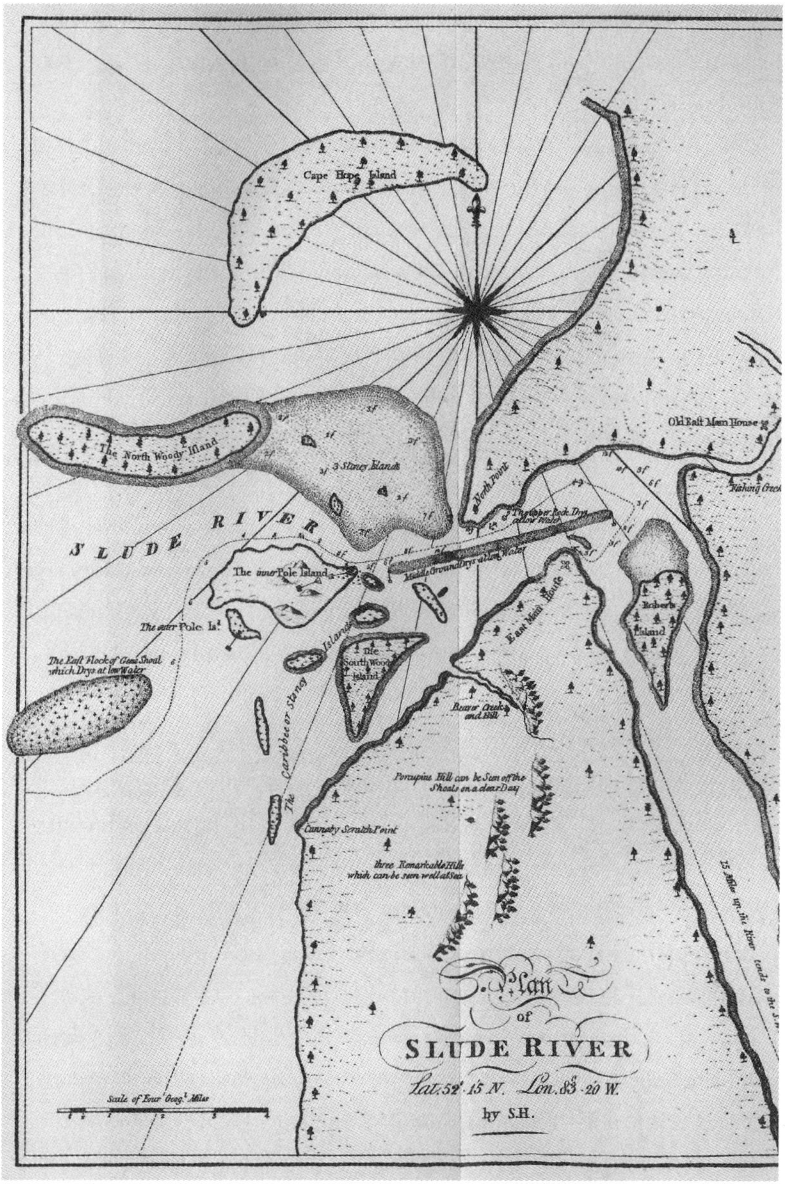

Samuel Hearne, Plan of Slude River, 1774. *[Rich and Johnson (eds.),* Moose Fort Journals, *endpiece]*

French were only one day's journey upriver, and five years after that a post on Lake Nipigon brought them within easy striking distance of the Albany River basin.[22]

It is unclear who initially proposed HBC expeditions to the headwaters of major rivers like the Rupert or the Albany "to Draw downe the Indians by fayre & gentle meanes to trade wth us." The only skills explicitly sought for such service were "strength of body" and a familiarity with the Cree language, dialects of which the Bayside men had some opportunities to learn from Upland and Eastmain Cree traders and from the emerging Homeguard Lowland peoples (who were adjusting their seasonal patterns in order to provide support services such as hunting and mail carrying).[23] However, neither Bayly nor his successors could find any men willing to undertake such an expedition. In 1683 Henry Sergeant recommended that "your Honours should give good Encouragement to those who undertake such extraordinary Service, or else I fear there will be but few that will embrace such Employment."[24] The Committee dismissed fears about the danger of such journeys and promised to reward men who brought Indigenous peoples down to the factories for trade, but it was not enough.[25] Michael Dove feels that this was just as well and suggests that an important factor in the successful move inland in the late eighteenth century was "the final appearance of an overseas maritime system that could now service the coastal factories reliably and efficiently, thus providing a base from which expansion could occur"—an element that was noticeably lacking in the 1690s and early 1700s.[26] Nevertheless, not for the last time, the company's servants identified inland service as "extraordinary," not to be undertaken as part of their contractual obligations but only with added "Encouragement"—and perhaps not even then.

Recalcitrance on the part of a few servants stood out because the company's Bayside labour force during this period was small: in 1682 only thirty men were left in the country.[27] Governor John Nixon argued that there ought to be at least fifty in permanent residence in Hudson Bay. Albany needed twenty-three: a factor, a surgeon, two tailors, "one man that hath been ane ould souldier, whose office shall be to to [*sic*] keep the men in order," "one that can look after the guns" (i.e., a gunner, or perhaps a gunsmith), an armourer, a caulker, and fifteen labourers. Moose needed twenty-two: the governor, a warehouse keeper or deputy governor, two tailors, a smith, a carpenter, two sawyers, a sergeant, a gunner, a secretary, a cooper, a sloop master, three mariners, and seven labourers and boys.[28] Nixon did not indicate where the other five men would be posted; most likely they were the crew of the sloop, which would winter on the Eastmain. By 1685–86, at the height of the HBC's early expansion, eighty-nine men were serving at five establishments. Governor James Knight, however, recommended that those eighty-nine be reduced to thirty-six in James Bay (eighteen at Albany, twelve at Moose, and six at Charles Fort) and an unspecified (though probably smaller) number at Port Nelson and Severn; he omitted the depot on Charlton Island because he believed it weakened the other posts and caused unnecessary danger and inconvenience.[29]

John Nixon, governor from 1679 through 1683, cast a long shadow over this period. He seems a more logical choice than the Quaker firebrand Charles Bayly, having previously served as a magistrate and administrator in Carolina and in some capacity in the East Indies; however, the Committee invested its authority in a man whose credentials as a gentleman are more obvious than his credentials as a man of business. The Committee found fault with Nixon's accounting (as they had with Bayly's) and criticized his handling of the trade. After he had returned home, there was considerable debate over whether to pay him the balance of his account (three hundred and five pounds); he was eventually paid, but the deputy governor, Sir Edward Dering, put his objections on record.[30]

Nixon was succeeded by Henry Sergeant, another gentleman of good standing with questionable business skills. Sergeant was unique in being allowed to bring his family (kin, servants, and clergyman) to Hudson Bay with him—a perquisite usually denied to merchants in most other English overseas companies of the period. Hugh Verner, factor at Charles Fort, was also given permission for his wife to join him there, but that permission was rescinded at the last minute with no explanation.[31] The Committee may have engaged in an internal debate similar to that among the EIC's directors in 1614, when Captain William Keeling challenged their policy of not allowing wives in their factories. Keeling had petitioned for permission to bring his wife, Anna, with him to the English post at Bantam in Java. Alison Games describes it thus:

> *Some Company members believed the presence of Anna Keeling was necessary because so much time apart from her might damage Keeling's soul and the "quiet of his minde." Others were hostile to Keeling's petition, fearing his wife's presence would keep Keeling's attention too much on her and would "soe hinder the maine busynes that hee is employed for... of passinge from porte to porte," seeking out new opportunities for the Company's country trade and unable to stay in any one place with his wife.*[32]

Be that as it may, the HBC's records do not explain why Verner was given permission in the first place. Perhaps to his contemporaries it was obvious: if Sergeant and Verner were expected to act as heads of households in Hudson Bay, they would be better able to do so with their wives at their side. However, the domestic tone that this sounded was soon drowned out by the clangour of alarm bells.

New Dangers

The expansion of the 1680s was tempered by a concern over expenses and by an awareness that the HBC faced direct competition for its Bayside trade. At Port Nelson in 1682 John Bridgar built a new trading post within a few miles of similar expeditions by a group of New England merchants and by the Canada-based Compagnie de la Baie d'Hudson—led in the field by Pierre Esprit Radisson, who had returned to French service in 1676.[33] Radisson captured both his rival groups and destroyed Bridgar's post during the winter of 1682–83 but returned to HBC service in 1684—bringing with him the French fort and the five men garrisoning it, Jean Baptiste Chouart (Groseilliers's nephew), Elias Grimard, Claude Durvall dit Bouchoir, Nicholas Eyron dit Lamottoo, and Anthony Doyon.[34] Bridgar's prospects did not suffer from his poor showing at Port Nelson, and neither did the company's presence in western Hudson Bay; a new fort (York Fort) was built at Port Nelson in 1684, followed a year later by an outpost on Severn River.

Much more damaging was the episode for which Henry Sergeant is best remembered: presiding over the company's resounding defeat by the French in 1686. Although England and France were not at war, the governor of New France, the Marquis de Denonville, sent a military expedition overland to drive the English from James Bay and thus secure dominance of the fur trade north of the Great Lakes.[35] With thirty regular soldiers and about seventy Canadien militiamen, Pierre de Troyes (commonly known as the Chevalier de Troyes) captured all three HBC posts in James Bay and the sloops *Craven* and *Hayes* with an ease that startled both de Troyes and the HBC's Committee. The factories were reasonably well fortified and might have been defensible if garrisoned by trained soldiers. Instead, they were garrisoned by English traders, artisans, clerks, and labourers, who put up little resistance, and French accounts depicted them as taken by surprise in all instances.[36] News of the victories had reached France but not Britain by November 1686, when the two countries signed the Treaty of Whitehall to resolve various points of contention in North America. Each retained possession of territories and posts controlled at the time of the treaty, and so, without knowing it, Britain relinquished James Bay to the French.[37]

It may have been just a matter of time before Hudson Bay became a theatre of military conflict. Besides the larger imperial conflict, the English were competing with New France in their proverbial backyard, a region regarded by the French as an extension of the *pays d'en haut* (Upper Country) upriver from Quebec.[38] Much of the HBC's first four decades unfolded against a backdrop of major warfare, especially the War of the League of Augsburg (King William's War, 1689–97)[39] and the War of the Spanish Succession (Queen Anne's War, 1702–13). The 1686 attacks on

James Bay surprised the English because they came from overland rather than by sea and because they came while England and France were at peace. Nevertheless, they highlighted how vulnerable the company's posts were without trained military garrisons.

The company was vulnerable in other ways too. Wartime conditions raised prices and wages, made labour scarcer, and put merchant shipping at risk. Other long-distance trading companies experienced similar difficulties.[40] In some ways, the English-French struggle for control of Hudson Bay mirrored the earlier English-Dutch struggle for control of the west African trade in the 1660s—a struggle that ruined the RAC and prompted the formation of a new RAC in 1672.[41] For almost thirty years after 1686 the French presence in Hudson Bay and the insecurity of wartime conditions were the principal factors affecting HBC strategies and tactics.

"Constant Perill from the French"

After the French captured James Bay in 1686, the conflict between French and English (specifically between the Compagnie du Nord and the HBC) dominated each side's activities in the Bay area.[42] Hudson Bay was never more than a sidelight (more commonly a footnote) to the broader imperial conflicts, but the HBC's position was made more vulnerable by William III's indifference to colonial issues and his obsession with Flanders; his naval strategy was focused in the eastern Atlantic and the Mediterranean, depriving English America of protection against French raiders and privateers during the war that now bears his name.[43] Economic competition was occasionally supplemented by military action, but generally the HBC preferred the less expensive option of peaceful coexistence. An attempt to quietly re-establish an English presence in James Bay in 1688 ended ignominiously: Governor Marsh died and "by subtle degrees our Factory shipps & goods [were] surprised [and captured], to the perpetual shame of the nation."[44]

In 1692 the Committee decided to retake Albany by force. The frigate *Royal Hudson's Bay* (Captain Michael Grimington), the fireship *Prosperous*

(Captain Henry Baley), and the frigates *Dering* (Captain Leonard Edgcombe) and *Pery* (Captain Cotesworth) sailed from Gravesend, well armed and carrying letters of marque. The expedition was under the overall command of James Knight—who delayed his acceptance and the ships' departure by attending to his own affairs.[45] The ships arrived in the Bay too late to launch an attack on Albany, so the whole expensive expedition wintered on Gilpin's Island on the East Main—minus the *Dering*, which had sailed back to London with furs from Port Nelson. When Knight's forces sailed to Fort Ste. Anne (Albany) in the early summer of 1693, they found it garrisoned by five Frenchmen and by an armourer who had gone mad, murdered two of his fellows, and been put in chains. The five men put up a brief resistance before fleeing into the woods, leaving the fort, the furs, and the armourer in English hands.[46]

Unbeknownst to the English, the French failure to resupply the James Bay posts since 1690 had resulted in starvation and mutiny, and more than twenty men had deserted Fort Ste. Anne and gone overland to Canada. Ironically, the Compagnie du Nord's vessel the *Ste Anne* arrived at the fort of the same name later in the summer of 1693, only to be met with a hostile reception from the HBC's ships; convinced that a strong English force in possession of one post made the other two untenable, the *Ste Anne* evacuated and destroyed forts St. Louis (Moose) and St. Jacques (Charles) and then sailed home. Although the Committee was jubilant at its success, the ease with which James Bay had fallen prompted some speculation whether George Geyer and a handful of men from Port Nelson could not have accomplished as much at far less expense. The point was rendered moot by the French capture of Port Nelson the following year.[47]

Nevertheless, Knight's success was immediately followed by the HBC's first—and until the nineteenth century its only—experiment with a standing military force. In 1693 Captain Philip Parsons and Lieutenant Samuel Adams received royal commissions in "an Independant Compa[ny] of foote to bee forth with Raised & Imployed in Hudsons Bay, for the Defence of the same against our enemies in those parts." Thomas Matthew received a commission as second lieutenant from the HBC but apparently not from the king.[48] The royal commissions reminded them (and us) of what was clear from the charter: notwithstanding the authority and autonomy of private companies, "Monarchy was at the legal core of the Empire."[49]

What (if any) form the independent company of foot actually took is unclear. Royal commissions notwithstanding, Parsons and Adams took orders and received wages from the HBC. Parsons was initially recommended to the Committee "as a person Qualified for accompts and otherwise" and was sent as deputy governor to York Fort—where he and Matthew were captured by the French in 1694. Adams served quietly at Albany for four years and then went home.[50]

Although Parsons's royal commission exhorted him "to take the said Compa. into your care & charge & duley exercise as well the officers as souldjers in Armes & to...Keepe them in good order & dicipline," the company's commission mentioned no such thing. The Committee told Thomas Walsh (the new governor at Port Nelson) that "we have sent over a Gentelman of Good Education for Deputy Governor One Capt. Philip Persons [*sic*] & doubt not but he will answer Expectations in executing that Charge and Trust."[51] It seems most likely that the independent company of foot was simply ordinary hands doing their duty to the company, "whose Servants they are whose Bread they eate & whose Wages they take."[52]

For a brief moment in 1696 the London Committee could see a sunny future peeking through the clouds of war. Three HBC ships and two men-of-war arrived at Fort Bourbon (York Fort) and just two hours later frightened off two small French vessels; the fort's garrison, short of food and ammunition, and disheartened by seeing its reinforcements sail away, surrendered after a three-day siege. Captain Henry Baley of the *Hudson's Bay* took command of York and sent Captain Michael Grimington home in the *Dering* with the French prisoners and the happy news that all of Hudson and James bays were back in English hands.[53]

The clouds closed in again the following year, when le Sieur d'Iberville recaptured York after a dramatic naval battle and a spirited defence by Captain Baley and his men. Honourable terms were negotiated, and the Englishmen marched out with drums beating, muskets loaded, and colours flying—but, though they carried with them their arms and baggage, they left the furs behind.[54] York Fort became Fort Bourbon once more and remained so for nearly two decades.

For most of the thirty years after 1686 the company controlled only one factory in Hudson Bay: Port Nelson (York Fort) in 1686–93, Albany in 1694–96 and 1697–1714. Port Nelson had an outpost at Severn River between 1685 and 1690, and Albany maintained regular winter camps on the Eastmain from 1693 onward. Labour needs were thus more limited than they had been earlier, even though in the interest of defence Port Nelson and then Albany in turn supported larger staffs than in peacetime. Such tenuous circumstances placed a premium on loyal and experienced servants, and the Committee generously bestowed both monetary and non-monetary favours in order to retain such men. By the time the French finally vacated the Bay, the HBC had accumulated a much larger overhead than it considered healthy.

The company's circumstances allowed a new kind of governor to emerge. Neither George Geyer at Port Nelson nor James Knight at Albany were the well-connected gentlemen that Nixon and Sergeant had been. Geyer had been in the company's service since 1672, accompanying Bayly on his explorations of James Bay for several years; he was appointed governor at Port Nelson in 1686. Knight entered the service as a shipwright in 1676 and six years later was chief of Chichewan (Albany) and Nixon's deputy governor.[55] Although both men were trading privately during their tenures, that was not enough to shake their strong relationships with the Committee, who valued their knowledge, experience, and firm leadership in the Bay.

These were dark times for the HBC. While Baley was surrendering York, wartime shortages of cash and the poor sales of beaver in a glutted market had left the company unable to find fifteen pounds for rigging for its supply ships. In 1700, 1703, 1704, 1707, and 1709, it sent out no ships at all.[56] In 1702, hemmed in by Fort Bourbon, Fort Phélipeaux (Severn River, established in 1699 or 1700), and French traders inland from James Bay, a vulnerable HBC requested the assistance of three men-of-war, a bomb-vessel, and two hundred soldiers; all they got was a royal commission for Governor Fullartine.[57]

John Fullartine was an Edinburgh tradesman who had joined the HBC in 1683; he had twice been taken prisoner at Albany, in 1686 and 1689, but returned to the company's service each time. His "fidelity & Industry" was rewarded in 1695 when James Knight chose him as deputy governor; Fullartine succeeded Knight temporarily in 1697–98 and permanently in 1700. He had much in common with his superior: he rose from tradesman to governor; he had a temper and little patience for what he considered the ignorance of his employers; his devotion to the company did not weaken his determination to trade privately; and he ended his HBC service as a member of the Committee (he and Knight being the only two to do so).

Fullartine's successor and (to some extent) protegé, Anthony Beale, illustrated even better than did Fullartine and Knight the company's determination to find its officers from within. He was apprenticed to the HBC in 1678, but his subsequent occupation was never specified. Beale was in charge of the Eastmain trade from 1698 to 1701 and was named deputy governor in 1700. He became governor in 1705, based partly on Fullartine's recommendation of him as "a very carefull honest man & knows ye affairs of this Country as well as moste men yt ever were in it & deserves encouragement as being an old Servant & one yt has been allways faithfull to his masters."[58] Unfortunately, Beale's preferment came at the expense of men equally deserving of promotion, particularly Henry Kelsey and Nathaniel Bishop, who both had to wait several years before receiving commands of their own. Such was life when the company had more faithful and deserving servants than it had positions of responsibility to offer them.[59]

Albany's complement was thirty-five men and boys in 1703–4; this had dropped to twenty-seven by 1706 and climbed to a maximum of forty-four by 1713.[60] Such limited staffing requirements did not require large-scale recruitment in specific areas. In fact, during the tense and tenuous years in which the HBC and the Compagnie du Nord shared the Bay, the

English company was less concerned with recruiting new men than with retaining old hands, despite the higher wages they commanded. Given the difficulties and expenses of wartime recruiting, it seemed more expedient to re-engage the devils they knew.

French military incursions thus quashed much of the HBC's early optimism, turning the Committee's priority from expansion to survival. However, some entrepreneurial spirit survived. In 1691, for example, the Committee expressed the hope that young men from Port Nelson would volunteer to travel inland, as Henry Kelsey had done the previous year. It also gave the Port Nelson council permission to re-establish New Severn (which Thomas Walsh had burnt down rather than surrender to the French in 1690) and/or to build a new post upriver from Port Nelson at its discretion (although it did neither). The Committee assured the council that "what with the fullnesse and encrease of our trade from year to year & the severall new Settlements which you see we designe (and may have our old ones Wee hope in time Restor'd) Wee doe not doubt but there will bee Imployment Enough to gratifie all Our Faithfull and Industrious Servants."[61]

The company's major arena for expansion remained coastal, focused particularly on the mouths of rivers: Charlton Island was not reoccupied after being destroyed by the French in 1686, but a short-lived trading post was established at the mouth of the Churchill River two years later.[62] A summer whale fishery was continued from Port Nelson, but a new trading house was not built at Churchill until 1717. On that occasion James Knight referred to "one place...where formerly the English had built one [trading post] wch they found so badd that After they had built it I believe they was so Disscouraged that they sett it a fire to Run away by the light of it."[63]

The Committee maintained its interest in trading voyages to the headwaters of major rivers as a way of combating French competition inland. Chief factor John Fullartine described one group of upland Indigenous peoples who visited Albany as being "so much Frenchified yt they ask'd for ye Goods wch: they traded in French."[64] The Committee hoped that inland expeditions could be undertaken by William Dolbey, George Holstead,

Matthew Vicary, and Nicholas Weeden—who had all been apprenticed to the company for eight years by 1689, from Christ's Hospital, London (the Blue Coat charity school)—provided they were able to learn some Cree.[65] However, none of them remained in Hudson Bay long enough. Dolbey returned to England in 1693 or 1694 and was employed in the company's office, later serving as warehouse keeper until his death in 1717. Holstead returned in 1692, and nothing more is known about him, although the Committee chastised Geyer for sending him home before his time had expired, being "a Stout Fellow & hardy lad else Would not have grown soe much since he went hence." Vicary died at York on 8 November 1696. Weedon returned to England in 1691 and was pressed into the Royal Navy at Deptford the following April.[66]

Former apprentice Henry Kelsey in 1690 was the first—and for twenty-five years the only—Englishman to travel inland from the Bay. The Committee had promised that servants who "shall shew their forwardness to go upon new discoveries" could hope to receive "upon their good success...advance of wages or gratuity for their pains." George Geyer reported: "I sent up Henry Kelsey (who chearfully undertook the journey) up into the country of the Assinae-poets [Assiniboine?], with the captain of that nation."[67] London was pleased to hear of Kelsey's inland journey: his wages were doubled (from fifteen pounds to thirty pounds) for the time he spent inland, and he afterwards received a thirty-pound gratuity. The Committee hoped that such "encouragement...will instigate other young men in the factory to follow his example."[68] However, Port Nelson was captured by the French in 1694, and the English at Albany were too aware of French traders inland from their factory to venture very far upriver. No other inland journeys were undertaken before the Utrecht restoration.

Reconstruction and Expansion

Whereas most of the thirty years before the Treaty of Utrecht (1713) had been a time of warfare and tension, the thirty years after Utrecht saw relative peace and stability in Hudson Bay. The treaty agreement removed the French presence from, and its claim to, Hudson Bay, although the HBC never succeeded in collecting the massive sum it sought in damages. French traders based in the St. Lawrence valley established themselves more firmly in the country upriver from the HBC factories, but security in the Bay allowed the company to resume the carefully optimistic expansion that the French attacks had interrupted in 1686. Defensive mentalities are not easy to change, however, and the continuing sense of vulnerability was expressed in the orders to Henry Kelsey when he succeeded as governor in Hudson Bay in 1718. Kelsey was to assemble his men:

> *in ye hearing of ym all, Cause your Comission to be openly & distinctly Read, wch when done you are to Administer to ym the Oath of Fidelity to his Majesty King George & likewise ye Oath to ye Compa[ny] You are also to Inform them the Disasters that have happen'd to ye Compa[ny] during your Memory through Cowardice & Neglect, & that they should behave themselves like faithful Subjects, for ye Honour of ye Crown & Interest of ye Compa[ny], with what Else you Shall think Convenient for their Encouragem[en]t.*[69]

The losses of the war years weighed heavily in the minds of HBC Committee members, all of them shareholders who in 1718 received their first dividend in nearly three decades.

York Fort was reoccupied in 1714 and rebuilt the following year, and trading posts at Churchill and Moose were re-established in 1717 and 1730, respectively. An increasing scale of operations required a larger and somewhat more diverse labour force, but recruitment processes remained relatively unchanged from previous years. The most conspicuous difference was a greater variety in the geographical sources of recruits, particularly the increasing number of Orkneymen. In general, the patterns apparent after 1714 were not innovations, although they may sometimes appear to be due to the greater number and variety of company documents surviving from the 1720s onward.

The management of the Bayside operations also showed considerable continuity. The venerable James Knight came out of retirement to reclaim York, and Anthony Beale did likewise in 1720 after a six-year absence. They and almost all the other factors serving between 1714 and 1740 had seen action against the French in their younger days: Henry Kelsey, Thomas McCliesh (Macklish) Jr, Richard Staunton, Nathaniel Bishop, and Joseph Myatt. Even Joseph Adams had been a very young apprentice when the men of Albany beat off a French attack in 1707. Like Beale, former apprentices Kelsey and Adams had spent their youth in an HBC household and in turn rose to be head of that household themselves. The other four men—two shipwrights, a cooper, and a gunner—had similarly graduated from journeymen subordinates to positions of authority and responsibility. Although some of them had to wait longer than they would have liked for such rewards, the cautious growth of the post-Utrecht era provided more opportunities for advancement than had been possible when Albany and Eastmain stood alone against the French.

The company's priority after the Treaty of Utrecht was regaining and maintaining a stable trading position. James Knight, returning to the Bay as governor, had more ambitious plans: he was convinced that the Churchill trade in furs and whale oil would outstrip the returns of any other HBC establishment. The Committee were not convinced, and canvassed some of his subordinate officers "whether you think yt place will Answer our Charge...& whether it may not be a means to lesson ye Trade at York Fort."[70] Knight reoccupied York and persuaded former apprentice William Stuart to travel into Dene territory with a Chipewyan known as "the Slave woman," or Thanadelthur. They were to facilitate trade by helping make peace between the Chipewyan and the Lowland Cree—keeping one eye open for copper and gold along the way. Knight predicted, "By this Success I beleive our Company may begin to be thought a rich Company."[71] He followed up his interest in the Chipewyan trade in 1717 by building a new trading house at Churchill River and by sending apprentice Richard Norton to find a group of Chipewyan traders who had already come to the mouth of the river and turned back inland before the Englishmen arrived.[72] Norton was sent north again in 1718 on a peace mission not unlike Stuart's, and the following year the Committee rewarded him for his efforts. For his having endured "great hardship" and having been "very active and diligent in endeavouring to make peace amongst" the First Nations, "we being always desirous to encourage diligent and faithful servants, upon application of his mother in his behalf, have ordered him a gratuity of fifteen pounds."[73]

Apart from these journeys made by Stuart and Norton, expansion and exploration remained coastal for nearly thirty years. From the new post at Churchill (renamed Prince of Wales Fort in 1719), regular sloop voyages were made up the coast to trade with the Chipewyan and Inuit. Northwestern Hudson Bay was also the focus of James Knight's final venture, an ill-fated search for Arctic gold, which ended in starvation and death on Marble Island in 1719. However, even service at Churchill River itself was considered more onerous than service at more southerly posts, and the advance party in 1717 included four labourers (James Miller, John Wateridge, James Callant, and Nicholas Coxworthy) who had negotiated higher wages for serving there.

In some respects, Churchill was a castle in the air on which Knight had mortgaged his considerable reputation; its trade never rivalled that of York and only began to match Albany's when French inland competition intensified north of Lake Superior after 1730.[74] Instead, Prince of Wales Fort became the biggest construction project undertaken by the HBC before the twentieth century: the building of a new stone fort consumed most of the 1730s and 1740s, and its reconstruction (to correct dramatic shortcomings) occupied most of the 1750s and 1760s. The manpower necessary for the undertaking made it the primary consumer of labour. In 1733 Richard Norton's complement there was sixty-four, and he recommended that 109 men were necessary to complete the building in six or seven years: four masons, thirty-three mason's labourers, six men "[t]o manage two clay vessels," six "[t]o manage two draught [of] cattle," thirty "[t]o draw stone etc," and thirty "to make proper provisions for men and cattle for the winter" (if the factory were provided with four teams of cattle, this total could be reduced to eighty-four men).[75] In comparison, at the new Moose River house in 1734, William Bevan asked that his complement be increased from twenty-six to thirty, observing that Moose was the factory closest to the French and therefore required a strong garrison.[76] When the men of Albany were preparing to settle Henley House in 1743, Joseph Isbister declared that he needed a total of twenty-eight men to properly staff Albany and Henley together, not including the Eastmain expeditions, but that he only had fourteen men and two boys.[77]

Considering that the company's establishments had only borne a passing resemblance to military outposts even at the height of the French menace, the peacetime construction of a stone fort along clearly military lines—it bristled with forty cannon on the ramparts, plus a battery of up to six more guns at Cape Merry across the river—demands some explanation. The Committee's minutes and correspondence are surprisingly uninformative on this point, but disgruntled former HBC engineer Joseph Robson probably hit the mark in suggesting that it was to give the appearance of the company's commitment to the region. He had in mind the rather narrow views of discouraging interlopers and fending off criticism for inactivity, and certainly the HBC wanted to impress upon prospective competitors and French military leaders alike the risk and expense of living and trading in the Bay. Only in retrospect do we know that no French military expedition would penetrate the Bay until 1782: at the time, the harbour of Churchill—by far the deepest and safest of any the HBC's harbours—seemed the best place to anchor the company's maritime presence. Of course, the fort may have looked impressive (once it was finished), but it never had any soldiers posted there or even enough servants to man all the guns.[78]

Richard Norton devoted much of his time and energy (and eccentricity) to the construction project. In case he needed reminding, the Committee pointed out:

> *Wee shall now be at a very great Charge & Expense in maintaining & paying Wages to such a Number of men, Wee hope You will Exert Yourself*

> *upon all Occasions in forwarding the work with Expedition & take all possible Care that every Persons [sic] follows his Work & performs his duty as he Ought to do & if any Person whatsoever neglects his duty & refuses to obey Your Command Wee do hereby Order You to send such Person home by the first Opportunity.*[79]

Norton acknowledged the pressure he was under, promising:

> *[A]s I cannot but be sensible that your honours' expense must...be very great to carry on such a building I do positively assure your honours that nothing shall be wanting in me promoting the same with the greatest expedition we possible [sic] can and shall be sure not to suffer any person to neglect his duty therein.*[80]

Some aspects of the building placed unusual demands on the workmen. During the 1735–36 season, labourer Robert Gawdie and carpenter Thomas Smith were injured while blowing up rocks with gunpowder, a task that Norton described as dangerous but necessary. These accidents "struck such a terror upon all our men that none will undertake to perform the same." Only Smith, though twice "grievously wounded," was willing to do the job, which he had done since 1734 "and has had ten gallons [of] brandy yearly for his encouragement therein. His time being out next year [1737] he is willing to continue longer in your honours' service and execute the said office in blowing up rocks as well as other duties provided your honours will please to raise his salary £5 per annum...for that dangerous undertaking."[81] Smith went home in 1738 with a five-pound gratuity for his dangerous work. No man was willing to take over that job for less than five pounds extra per annum, except Vincent Norton, whose apprenticeship had just expired and who had just been engaged by the Prince of Wales council as bricklayer and mason for one year at twenty pounds; he agreed to do it for four pounds extra per annum.[82]

The other major undertaking of the 1730s was the HBC's return to Moose River. Even after Utrecht, the company's trade in the whole

James Bay basin was conducted via Albany and its winter outpost on the Eastmain. These efforts alone had brought in sufficient furs to satisfy the London market, and the HBC already feared that the reoccupation of York and the new establishment at Churchill could leave them with an embarrassment of riches and a glutted market. Joseph Myatt suggested re-establishing Moose largely to save Indigenous trading captains the hazards of the journey from Moose River to Albany by canoe along the shores of the Bay—in fact, it was they who first suggested the idea to him. He knew that trade at Moose would be partially lost to Albany, but he also knew that the difficulties of reaching Albany made the French traders up Moose River a more attractive option for the Cree. It was this consideration that motivated the Committee to approve the venture.[83]

Sloop master William Bevan had surveyed Moose River and scouted out a site for a house as early as 1727.[84] Three years later, plans and orders for a fort were sent out from England. Authority at the new outpost was initially invested in a triumvirate of Albany men: sloop master Thomas Render to command the new *Moose River* sloop and to direct the men; carpenter John Jewer to direct the construction; and labourer John Bricker to direct the trade (because he could speak Cree, having come to Albany as a boy in 1726). Myatt had recently died; his second, Joseph Adams, had been promised the command of Moose but now had to stay and take charge of Albany. Prophetically, Adams felt that the most important thing Moose needed was a competent master, and in 1730 he implored the Committee to send a suitable man from England. No such man was sent, and Render—who had only entered the company's service the year before—was left in charge, until he provoked a mutiny and forced Adams to replace him with Jewer in October 1731.[85]

As soon as Moose was established, the safety of the river and the anchorage (compared to the hazards of Albany) prompted a decision to ship directly from England to Moose and thence by sloop to Albany, instead of the other way round. For the first time, senior managers were physically distanced from the unloading and loading of the supply ships in the Bay. No wonder, then, that Moose came under scrutiny in 1736, when the Committee expressed concern at the quantities of illicit brandy allegedly being landed at the factories and distributed among the servants.[86]

William Bevan and the Moose council promised vigilance in this regard, while "wondering at your honours being informed that any such practice being carried on here, it being unknown to us and almost impossible."[87] Their response seems disingenuous, appearing as it did in the same letter that informed the Committee of a major fire that had nearly destroyed Moose on Boxing Day, 1735: everyone in the fort at the time (including several Cree guests) was intoxicated. That spring, while Bevan and his council were debating how to break the bad news, their employers were composing their annual general letter to Moose, which called upon Bevan to "make a thorough Reformation in the Factory under Yr Command which Wee are very sorry to tell You [we] find by all acco[un]ts to be the worst Governed of any of our Factories in our Country and in the greatest disorder and Confusion the most Disobedient to Command and the most given to Mutiny and Sottishness." When they heard about the fire, the Committee took no notice of the hardships endured by the men left temporarily homeless in the middle of a subarctic winter, instead condemning their "Carelessness" and lamenting "that great and unhappy accident" that "is a very great loss to Us."[88] Bevan was immediately recalled, along with surgeon Robert Holliday, accountant Samuel Maidman, shipwright Jacob Anderson, mariner John Evans, and labourers John Tate, William Spence, George Robinson, and Peter Isbister Jr—nine men from a complement of just over thirty.

The fire highlighted a host of issues at Moose. Foremost in the Committee's initial reaction was the design flaw of having two cookhouses instead of just one, a "Useless" extravagance that was to be immediately eliminated at all factories—a potentially dangerous one too, considering how close one of Moose's cookrooms was to the gunpowder room! Bevan was immediately recalled (along with most of his council), and veteran factor Richard Staunton was sent to take charge and sort things out. His orders from the Committee cast the situation not just as a business problem but as a moral problem: "In the first place wee recommend to You the fear and Service of Almighty God that publick prayers, according to the Usage of the Church of England be duly p'formed...and that You punish all wicked and profane persons."[89] The injunction was a common trope in letters from London, but here it was front and centre and carried a sense of outrage that was echoed in Staunton's later reports. He discovered rampant private trade and other widespread examples of servants putting their own interests ahead of their masters'.

Staunton, James Duffield, and George Howy in turn spent the next ten years trying to reform Moose Fort. The Committee evidently felt that relative "outsiders" were best placed to correct the irregularities that had developed at Moose (and probably, to a lesser extent, at Albany and the other factories too). Staunton had served the company for thirty years but had been in England since 1732, while Duffield and Howy had both been engaged since the Boxing Day fire.

Henley, Flamborough, and Richmond

Despite the re-establishment of Moose, French traders continued to expand deep into the western interior: the James Bay posts had never been free from French competition, and even York Fort was beginning to feel the effects by the early 1730s.[90] Joseph Isbister took the struggle into Albany's hinterland in 1743, after several parties of traders arrived with few furs but well "Clothed in french Cloth": "I Asked Severall of them what they came here for as they had Traded all their goods with ye french, I was Answard that they came downe to See their friends that was hunting for us." On his own initiative he established Henley House at the junction of the Albany and Kenogami rivers, about 180 miles upriver from the factory; he intended it as "a garisson on ye fruntter"[91] to discourage French traders from settling in the area, and as a rest station for Indigenous peoples travelling to and from the Bay. The Committee restricted trade at Henley to guns, powder, shot, cloth, and tobacco, and to only when the river was frozen; trade during seasons of open water was permissible only when it was clear that the Indigenous peoples would trade with the French rather than go down to Albany.[92] Henley's first master, mariner William Isbister (Joseph's brother), asked to be on the same footing as a sloop master, presumably equating Henley with Albany's other seasonal outpost, Eastmain (where William had served before this posting).[93] Indeed, this inland venture drew upon contemporary experiences of coastal trade expansion along the shores of Hudson and James bays: the Eastmain trade had been formerly managed by Joseph Isbister himself, one of several mid-century factors and masters whose HBC service had begun on the sloops.

The Committee encouraged Isbister to push further up the Albany River in 1755, seeking to secure the company's inland trade on the eve of war with France.[94] Unbeknownst to them, the Henley experiment had met a tragic end during the previous December when a group of Lowland Cree had attacked and killed the five men stationed at Henley—master William Lamb and labourers Robert Ash, Daniel Bowland, George Gun, and James Short ("the Stoutest and best men belonging to this Fort").[95] Isbister (encouraged by the suspicions of the Lowland Cree who brought the first reports to Albany in March 1755) initially blamed the French rather than the First Nations, who he felt had been either "Seduced and Corrupted... or employd."[96] In fact, the primary instigator of the attack was Wappesiss (or Woudby), a long-time Upland Cree trading "captain" at Albany. He had enjoyed many privileges at Albany under George Spence (1747–53), including largely unrestricted access to the factory and its provisions, but when Isbister returned to command, he greatly curtailed those privileges and thus alienated Wappesiss. At Henley, William Lamb similarly denied Wappesiss easy access to the house and its food supply, even though Lamb (like Isbister at Albany) kept two Cree women in the house as his companions. These women were Wappesiss's daughter and daughter-in-law, yet Lamb failed to recognize the social obligations that these relationships entailed. After suffering what he viewed as grave insults for more than a year, Wappesiss and his extended family visited Henley in December 1754, were given one night's food and lodging by Lamb, and then were told to pitch a tent outside the walls of Henley. The next day they killed Lamb and the four men under his command.

In June 1755 Wappesiss and his sons, Shenap and Snuff the Blanket, were examined at Albany by a makeshift tribunal—Isbister and his council (surgeon George Rushworth and shipwright John Fairfowl)—in the presence of Albany's entire complement of twenty-one men. The Albany council passed a sentence of death on the three men in custody and (in absentia) on three others implicated by Wappesiss during the "trial": the sentence was signed by every man at Albany, twenty-four signatures and marks in all.[97] Isbister then waited to hear the opinion of the council at Moose, who replied that "it must be very displeasing to one of a tender & compassionate nature [by which they presumably meant Isbister], but Blood requires Blood."[98] Isbister received their approval of his decision on 21 June and proceeded with the execution the same day. Despite the precautions taken by Isbister in trying to distribute responsibility, his judicial experiment (particularly the application of capital punishment) was an important factor in his recall to Britain in 1756. The Committee expressed regret at "the loss of so many Innocent Men who fall sacrifices to Lambs great Misconduct," and concern for Isbister's safety: "As we find the Indians are greatly exasperated at the Execution of the Assassins, for which reason we have thought it necessary to Recall you, especially as your Contracted time will be expired and you seemed Desirous to return."[99]

This was the first time the English had tried to extend their own criminal law into Indigenous communities. The precedent was not followed up on for decades to come, but it is unrepresentative in a broader sense as well. Jörg Fisch and Jack P. Greene caution us against seeing European law as a tool of imperialist domination prior to about the middle of the nineteenth century: "to live under European law 'was a privilege, usually not to be granted to the indigenous people.'"[100] There is a real element of desperation in Isbister's behaviour—understandable, given that he had just been informed of the single largest number of casualties suffered at Indigenous hands in the company's entire history to that date. He and Lamb had pushed the situation beyond the capacity of the existing informal systems of resolving disputes between the household factory and neighbouring Indigenous households, and he needed to do something drastic to rectify the situation in some way. Significantly, his first thought was to blame the French "Other" rather than his Cree neighbours. Although he defended the tribunal and executions as a way "to let the Indians Know that the English will not put up with Such Villainous Treatment," that message was meant to reassure the remaining members of his household at least as much as it was meant to intimidate the First Nations.[101]

Although the murders and Isbister's heavy-handed response to them brought his HBC service to a premature end (he was only in his mid-forties), Henley marked the beginning of an increasing involvement in the interior. In 1754 James Isham at York began sending men inland to winter with Indigenous groups—as Henry Kelsey, William Stuart, and Richard Norton had once done—thus regularizing what had previously been practised only sporadically. Henley was re-established in 1759, and again in 1766. New conditions of inland travel and trade placed new demands on a small number of HBC servants, and the resulting tensions foreshadowed the developments after the construction of the first fully fledged inland trading post in 1774.

Henley House was the earliest and clearest indication that the company was taking innovative approaches to defending and expanding its trade, but it was not the only one in this period. The construction of Flamborough House on the lower Nelson River in 1749 was meant to fend off renewed interest from English interlopers.[102] James Isham had been picked to command the outpost, but the accidental drowning of chief factor John Newton required him to take charge of York instead; Isham's young kinsman, Samuel Skrimshire, was later appointed master of the house. However, Flamborough was considerably closer to York than Moose and Henley were to Albany, allowing Isham to keep it physically dependent on the factory. Skrimshire's situation was made more awkward by the failure of any interlopers to materialize and by Isham's surly

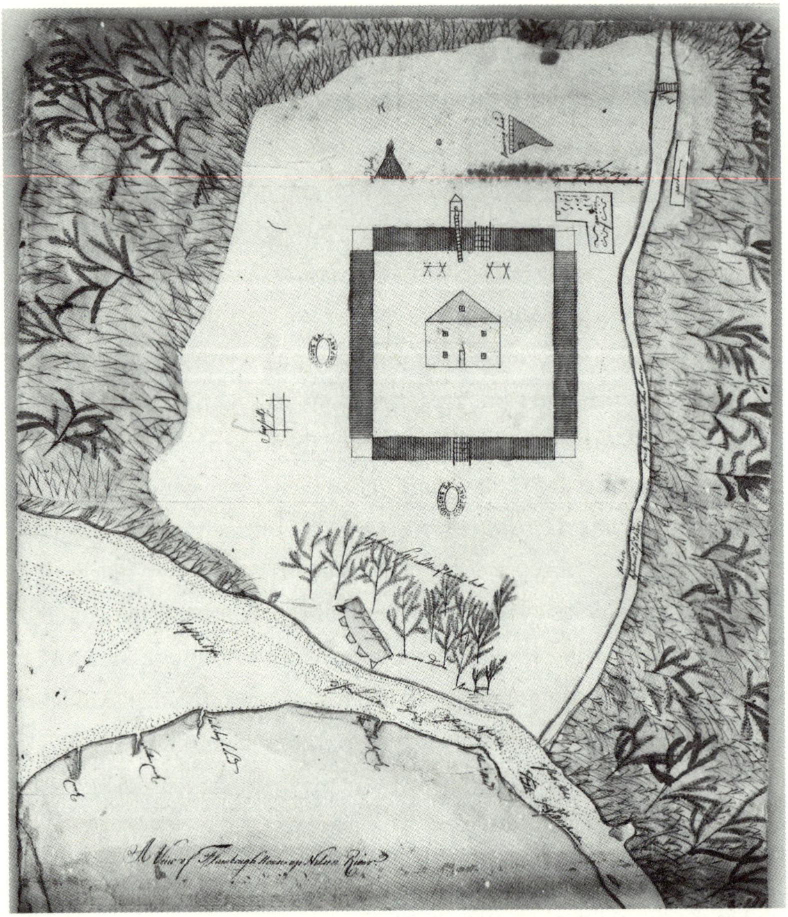

James Isham's A View of Flamborough House up Nelson River, 1754, *illustrates the traders' habit of clearing the ground around their houses for workspace and so that enemies could not sneak up on them. Note that even so small an outpost as Flamborough had a "brewing hut."* [HBCA, G. 1/100]

micro-management. Denied the right to trade for anything other than provisions, Flamborough drifted into an unsatisfactory role as a permanent goose-hunting camp and was closed in 1759.[103]

Another short-lived experiment was Fort Richmond, established on Richmond Gulf in 1750. It was part of a long-standing commitment to expanding and diversifying the company's trade on the eastern shores of

Hudson Bay; it was also (like Flamborough) a proactive response to the threat of English interlopers seeking to exploit the trade of eastern Hudson Bay. The HBC proposed a mining operation for nearby Little Whale River: the miners were primarily looking for copper or lead but explored the area around the mine for any kind of ore. Three miners were posted to Fort Richmond / Little Whale River but were sent home in 1751 because the venture was not meeting expectations.[104]

The miners were sent home by surgeon John Potts, who as the new master had recently arrived at Fort Richmond and found "a Lifeless, Spiritless, discontented crew." The first master, sloop master Thomas Mitchell, had been so busy trading privately (openly enough for the Committee to have found out about it) that he had found neither the time nor the energy to hide his pessimism about both the trading post and the mine. Potts was more optimistic, almost pathologically so: the failure of every project he attempted there never deterred him from writing hopeful but unconvincing letters to London. Well might he write such letters, for his only previous taste of command had been the 1747–48 season at Moose, and he was determined to make Richmond work, both for himself and for the company. By 1756, after a violent and unnerving episode with an Inuit group, even Potts had to admit that Richmond would never live up to his hopes: the post was closed in 1759.[105]

Pedlars

The British conquest of New France in 1760, and the confirmation of that conquest by the Treaty of Paris three years later, delighted the Hudson's Bay Company. Even before that, the French inland traders had faced major supply problems, and by 1760 their posts stood empty. Within a few years, however, merchants from England, Scotland, and New England were establishing themselves in Montreal and reclaiming New France's old trade routes, trading partners, posts, and personnel. These entrepreneurs—who would eventually coalesce into the North West Company—began reoccupying French posts west of Lake Superior in 1767 and rapidly expanded their presence after that. After only a few years' respite Albany and Moose were once again facing stiff competition.

The decline in the company's trade was precipitous. At York, Ferdinand Jacobs, the senior factor in Hudson Bay, assured his employers that it "has affected me more than anything that ever happened to me." He recommended sending winterers inland "in a body with a careful prudent man to command them, and to build a house or houses on the most convenient places to stop the pedlars from robbing you of your trade."[106] He vowed "to remove those thieves off your Land" and suggested that force might be needed to dislodge the interlopers.[107] However, the Committee feared the expense of an inland trading post and in 1769 proposed an outpost in the style of Henley. They baulked at Jacobs's request for fifteen to twenty-five men "until we see the probability of success to arise from such an inland establishment"; they voiced concern over sending a large quantity of trade goods "where they may be liable to various accidents;" and they preferred to see a seasonal post, whence the men would return to York for the winter.[108]

Jacobs's inland proposals were strongly opposed by his second at York and master of Severn, Andrew Graham.[109] Graham argued that by "lay[ing] aside fruitless undertakings about the Forts, such as building Out houses...and look[ing] sharp after the furr trade in all its branches," the Bayside factors would be able to "overturn all the schemes of the Canadian pilferers without applying to birch rind canoes, and such like wild schemes that is impracticable, and I am positive would be attended with all bad consequences to the Company."[110] Graham's opinions were probably reinforced by his dislike and distrust of Jacobs, but they were convincing because they were reasonable and carried the weight of almost twenty years of service:

> *The long knowledge I have of the affairs in Hudson's Bay makes me affirm, that however advantageous it may be to two or three poor pedlars from Canada to drive a wretched and vagabond life after a few furs, I do not*

think it is, and am certain it would not be, worth the notice of an Honourable Company of Gentlemen to follow such pitiful game.[111]

Graham's choice of words illustrated a shift in attitude. When the HBC's main competition came from French traders, company servants defined themselves as Englishmen. After Anglo-American merchants took control of the St. Lawrence fur trade in the 1760s, HBC employees placed less emphasis on national distinctions (although most of the Canadians' labour force continued to be French) and began distinguishing themselves as servants of an "Honourable Company" rather than as "pedlars."

Graham grossly underestimated the threat posed by the Canadien traders. He attributed the decline of trade at York to Cree traders "harbouring and strolling" with inland nations "for the sake of good living," and to "this game they call going to war." As late as 1771 Graham declared, "I am certain that the pilfering trade carried on [at] this present time within the limits of the Company's Charter by the English Canadians is neither with the spirit, experience, nor profit, with which it was carried on by the French before the conquest of Canada," and assured himself that, "let we Factors exert ourselves to gain the confidence of the natives, and I am certain the trade in total will not only be kept up, but may be increased."[112] Only after he had grasped the danger and came round (more or less) to Jacobs's point of view did the Committee authorize the establishment of its first fully fledged trading post inland from the Bay.[113]

That outpost, Cumberland House (built in 1774), was soon followed by others: Wapiscogamy House, about 120 miles up Moose River in 1777 (rebuilt and renamed Brunswick House four years later); Gloucester House, about 234 miles up the Albany River from Henley in 1777; a short-lived post (no more than log tents) on the shores of Lake Missinaibi between 1777 and 1780; Hudson House and Manchester House on the Saskatchewan River in 1779 and 1786, respectively; South Branch House on the lower South Saskatchewan River in 1785; Pis-quo-chag-a-ma at the mouth of the Frederick House River in the winter of 1784–85; and

Frederick House beside the lake of (eventually) the same name in 1785. From 1771, company servants began to occupy Eastmain House year-round for the first time: the sloop's crew still made up two-thirds of the twelve-man complement, but the inclusion of an armourer who could repair the guns of the Indigenous men was a major boost to trade. In 1776 a small house was built at the mouth of Rupert River after ninety years of HBC absence from that site. All of these outposts required HBC servants to spend more time away from the main factories, an experience that became increasingly common after 1774.

Expansion was fraught with anxiety. The growth of Albany's operations alarmed both the Moose Fort council (who feared that the Rupert River post would draw traders and hunters away from Moose) and the Albany council (who feared that the Committee was not assigning sufficient numbers of hands to man and supply all their outposts). In 1779 the Committee made both Eastmain House and the Rupert River outpost dependencies of Moose, leaving Albany to concentrate on its inland houses, Henley and Gloucester. In 1781 the Committee increased Eastmain's complement to sixteen because the new sloop being used on James Bay was larger and required a crew of ten rather than eight.[114]

The company's labour force steadily expanded after 1773, when the Committee "ordered 17 Men Extraordinary for the particular Service of Our Inland Expedition."[115] This was due primarily to the construction of new trading posts, because most of the Bayside posts were augmented only slightly. York grew from twenty-three men in 1725 to sixty in 1775 and had (including its dependencies) a complement of one hundred in 1782: thirty-four men at the factory itself, sixteen at Severn, and fifty men inland.[116] Prince of Wales Fort, however, was greatly reduced even before construction work had been officially completed in 1771; its complement of thirty-nine in 1782 was almost half of what it had been during the 1730s. The black-whale fishery at the mouth of the Churchill River temporarily increased the size of the garrison to sixty-six in the mid-1760s, but that venture did not answer expectations and was abandoned in 1772.[117]

This period of expansion ended with the capture and destruction of Prince of Wales Fort and York Fort by French warships in August 1782. Neither factory put up any resistance, and there is no record of any casualties.[118] However, the attacks cost the company considerably in the loss of goods and furs and left the men who were inland from York reliant on their Canadien competitors for survival until 1784.[119]

The attacks also coincided with the arrival of smallpox in the western interior. The company received the first reports of the approaching epidemic at Hudson House on 22 October 1781.[120] Although the Englishmen did not suffer much directly from "that Devouring Disorder,"[121] they were painfully aware of the high death toll among the First Nations. It was a human tragedy on a horrific scale, about which the company could do little: short of provisions and lacking any useful medicines, William Tomison at Cumberland House offered what assistance and palliative care he could. In January 1782 he lamented in his journal that "it cuts me to the Heart to see the Miserable condition they are in & not being able to Help them." A few days later he observed that "it is hard labour to keep the House in fuel and bury the Dead."[122]

The epidemic seriously disrupted trade and deprived both the Englishmen and the Canadiens of provisioners. By February 1782 Tomison could only feed his men fish and flour, while William Walker at Hudson House lacked even those basic foodstuffs. Walker observed that the epidemic was proving "very detrimental to Our Affairs" and suggested that "this will give the Canadian Traders a trial and let us know whether they be Substantial Men or No."[123] It was a trial for the HBC too, of course—but they had faced dark days before.

News of the French attacks had reached the Bottom of the Bay (i.e., James Bay) by February 1783, and the officers of Albany, Moose, and Henley met in council to debate their best course of action. Their decision to consolidate at Albany and Moose was understandably defensive, but they hoped to do so with such vigour as to impress the First Nations and (more importantly) "inspire our dejected men to Confidence." For the same reason the officers resolved to put their men in uniform in order to "Excite emulation and ambition as well as proper confidence in our men"—and hopefully to fool the French. The uniforms, of course, were simply a thin veneer of military discipline on what had always been an essentially civilian trading post community.[124]

York and Churchill were reoccupied immediately: unlike the attacks of a century earlier, this time the French did not stay to trade; they merely took the furs and ran. As the HBC tried to bounce back from this body blow as quickly as it could, it brought new strategies to bear that would draw the company away from the patterns of behaviour and expectation that had been built up over more than one hundred years. In 1786 William Tomison was promoted to the command of York, but he was given a new designation: chief inland. He would organize York's inland efforts from the outposts themselves, while the greenhorn Joseph Colen stayed by the Bay as resident chief. For decades the command of York had been considered to be one of the most senior in Hudson Bay, rivalled only by first Albany and then Moose; to post York's factor not at the factory itself but on the leading edge of inland activity was a strategic commitment to the interior trade that promised to make what had been "extraordinary" service the "new normal." The HBC's centre of gravity, of operations, and of authority in North America was relocated irrevocably.

|| The company's first forty-five or fifty years, from its founders' first voyage in 1668 until the Utrecht transition, was a foundational period that can be subdivided into an initial time of optimism and expansion and a subsequent period of drastically curtailed operations after the French attacks in 1686. In general, the primary concern of this foundational period was the establishment of trade and administrative mechanisms that could somewhat reduce the risks faced by the fledgling company. These early years represent the most crucial but most under-documented period of the company's history.

The major turning point was the period immediately after the Treaty of Utrecht, signed in 1713. In 1714 the company reoccupied its former posts that had been in French hands and in 1717 established a new post, at Churchill River; as a result, the scope of operations increased substantially from what they had been since the mid-1680s. The removal of the French presence from Hudson Bay allowed the HBC a period of stability in its trade that allowed for greater and more consistent profits than before. At the same time, the increasing French presence in the interior helped encourage the HBC to undertake various initiatives to protect and expand its trade.[125]

The decades after the Utrecht transition saw a continuation of the period of stability, compared to the company's tenuous existence prior to Utrecht and to the volatile competition that the HBC would experience in the late 1700s. This period can also be subdivided into two distinct phases. The first was a rebuilding process, in which the company reoccupied posts vacated by the French and recovered its position in the Bay; this slow process of cautious expansion is often overlooked thanks to Joseph Robson's 1752 accusation that the HBC was sleeping by the edge of a frozen sea.[126] The second phase began in 1743 with the establishment of the inland outpost of Henley House; this was followed by new outposts at Flamborough and Richmond, by the re-establishment of Severn in 1759, and by the sending of men inland to winter with Indigenous groups for the purposes of encouraging trade. Both of these phases were marked by cautious optimism. The London Committee members were buoyed by the possibilities of the post-Utrecht era, but they remembered the troubles before 1713. They also knew that the French had been removed only from the shores of the Bay, and that Canadien traders were spreading in even greater numbers into a poorly understood interior.

Stability was seriously challenged in the late 1760s when the Montreal-based fur trade came into the hands of vigorous new partnerships and a new regulatory scheme. The company's 1772 decision to build trading posts inland from Hudson Bay clearly marked the end of that stability, even though the decision was not executed until two years later. The Montreal "pedlars" came west in greater numbers than the pre-1760 French traders had been able to, a fact that changed both the nature of their competition with the HBC and the nature and variety of personnel issues within the HBC. Some of the problems of conflicting expectations faced at Henley and Flamborough, and with the company's inland winterers, foreshadowed the changes of the 1770s. The move inland and the increasingly face-to-face competition with the Canadien traders created a working environment that was fundamentally different from the one experienced by earlier generations of Bayside personnel. The resulting changes to the company's demands on its servants, and to the servants' demands on their employer, foreshadowed some of the issues of the HBC's later transcontinental operations, and thus lie beyond the scope of this study. The transitional period after 1774 was only briefly interrupted by the sudden return of French warships to Hudson Bay in 1782 and by the smallpox epidemic of 1781–82. The men at the Bottom of the Bay felt vulnerable enough to withdraw from Severn, Eastmain, Rupert River, and all inland posts for the summer of 1783 to concentrate on the defence of Albany and Moose. When the immediate danger had passed and they ventured out again, they did so with a new focus that set the stage for a new—and at times desperate—period of competition and expansion.

3 "No Certain Method for Any Thing"

Recruitment, 1670–1713

Ordered that the Secretary indeavor to gett 10 honest and able Fellows batchelors not under 20 nor above 30 yeares old to be either Bricklayers, Carpenters, Quarriers or such like and present them to the Compa. not exceeding 6. 9 or 12 li. p. Ann.

—*Minutes of the Hudson's Bay Company*, 29 March 1682

IN THE COMPANY'S EARLY DAYS recruitment needs were limited. The overseas labour force generally numbered about thirty, and even in the heady days of the mid-1680s the land service was little more than twice that size. The company needed more men stationed in the Bay than could be regularly spared from a ship's crew, but not so many men as to demand a structured recruitment policy or even a clearly defined occupational hierarchy or salary structure. In general, staffing of trading posts could be managed through a combination of volunteered applications, patronage, and other informal methods (such as the engagement of a few men from the supply ships for Bayside service). The inns and taverns through which London's news flowed probably did much of the Committee's work for them by circulating information on company ships departing for Hudson Bay and on employment opportunities for seamen and landsmen. The

Jean-François-Marie Belier's 1785 portrait of Pierre Esprit Radisson seems to hint at some dissatisfaction, or perhaps merely fatigue from Radisson's active cultivation of private and public transcripts in Britain, France, New France, and Hudson Bay. [LAC, C-15497]

Committee's 1672 complaint that their ships were being "pestered" by men looking for work on the ships or in the Bay indicates that potential employees were seeking out the company as well as the reverse.[1] However, the fitting of needs to available hands (and determining the needs in the first place) presented ongoing challenges.

Communication between London and Hudson Bay was key. In 1687, not yet aware that the French had made themselves masters of James Bay, the Committee recalled Henry Sergeant ("with the whole parcell of Women appertaineing to him") from Albany, John Bridgar from Moose, and Pierre Esprit Radisson from Port Nelson, "but such other of our men as you may have Occasion for, you must deteyne them another yeare the uncertainety of our affaires at present for want of advices from the Bottome of the Bay putting us to a Non plus how to Supply their places."[2] Seven years earlier the Committee had instructed John Nixon to send home yearly "a punctuall & particular Account of all our Servants in the Country, and how they are imployed in the severall Factories & Vessells," partly to let the Committee know "whether wee are over or understocked wth. men for our impl[o]y-ment."[3] Although none of these early lists has survived, this accounting became common practice and helped alleviate problems.

The Committee often felt that its factors were asking for too many men, but Nixon complained that he was not given enough information to reasonably predict his labour needs:

> *[O]ne of the greatest plagues that I have... [is when] the men doe pretend their tymes are out, the trooth of which I am ignorant in, for yow doe not wryt to me how longe they have served, or are to serve, but yow send order for their comeing home, and sendeth me non to supply their places, (instance), yow sent for your smith [probably gunsmith Samuel Oake], but sent me non in his roome.*[4]

Lack of information allowed Nixon's men to surprise him with wage demands, which he usually had to meet to avoid being short-handed. Problems also arose if supply ships failed to reach Hudson Bay or were obliged to winter over in the Bay; in either case, men whose contracts had expired could not go home.

HBC personnel issues were variously complicated and clarified when Hudson Bay became an arena of military conflict in 1686. On the one hand, obtaining sufficient and suitable recruits became more problematic, and the company often faced what it saw as exorbitant demands from experi-enced servants. On the other hand, the Committee became somewhat more explicit about what it expected of its employees. By 1714 a basic framework of practice and expectation had been built, on which they could expand in the more peaceful times that followed the Treaty of Utrecht.

Ship to Shore

The predominantly maritime approach to Bayside trade allowed the company to rely heavily on the crews of the supply ships to man seasonal posts in the early 1670s. However, the maintenance of year-round posts required a new approach. The kinds of men required were not significantly different from a ship's crew, but, in order for a permanent post to be secure, it required a complement equivalent in number to that of a ship. Only in the mid-1680s did any of the garrisons grow to larger than twenty men; usually there were a few officers, a few skilled tradesmen, and enough hands to man the watch and perform various tasks. Most of the company's workforce was not directly involved in trade, accounting, or management; these were reserved for the factor and his officers (usually no more than a second and a clerk).

The question of what skills or abilities were necessary for service in Hudson Bay was one that the London Committee was ill suited to answer. No Committee members had any experience of life and labour in the Bay until former shipwright and governor James Knight was elected to the board in 1700.[5] William Lydall was ordered in 1674 "to procure tenn men fitt for the Companyes Service to Stay in the Countrey," even though he himself had not yet been to Hudson Bay. However, Lydall did have some (unspecified) experience in the Russian trade: the Committee may have assumed that service in Hudson Bay was not unlike service in northern Russia. The East India Company in its early years probably drew on the experience of the Russia Company to build up its own commercial organization in Asia, but Lydall is the only example of the HBC drawing on the experience of the Muscovy merchants.[6]

Acquiring the numbers of men needed was not a problem for the HBC. Some prospective servants approached the company on their own initiative, and as early as 1671 the company's ship at Gravesend was being "pestered" by men wanting to go to Hudson Bay. To avoid this the Committee resolved in April 1672 that "no persons hereafter bee imployed to Stay in the Countrey or otherwise but by consente of the Committee," a resolution that was reaffirmed two years later. Ship's captains were allowed to recruit crews for their ships, but such men still had to be approved by the Committee. In 1684 all men wishing to go to Hudson Bay were directed to the office of notary public and long-time Committee member Nicholas Hayward, where "any two of the Committe[e] have Power to agree with them and give report thereof to the Committe[e]." Recruitment venues could be in more public places as well, such as the Amsterdam coffee house in London in the early 1690s.[7]

Little documentation of early recruitment has survived. This contrasts sharply with the EIC, whose archives preserve considerable correspondence from prospective traders. Although few were so creative as John Wright (engaged in 1609 as steward's mate on the *Dragon*), who wrote his application in verse, most men appeared formally before the EIC directors

> *either in person or through a letter, armed with the recommendations of Company members or bolstered by their own impressive trade experiences. They recited the languages (usually at least three) they spoke and explained how and where they had acquired experience in trade—generally in the Mediterranean, but also in the West Indies and occasionally in the Indian Ocean with rival trade companies.*[8]

What is known about early HBC recruitment suggests that the company was taking its servants as it found them. John Nixon chastised his employers for their unsystematic approach:

> *To think how this country hath been served would greive any man that hath a charge in it, for sometyms we have coalls, and no iron, sometyms iron, and steel, but no smith, otherwhiles no grind-stones, sometyms much of on[e] thing, and want of aneother, so that there hath been no certain method for any thing.*[9]

The Committee's surviving minute books do little to dispel this impression, providing only glimpses of the decision-making processes involved in recruitment. The company's daily business in London was carried out by members of the Committee, along with a few permanent or casual employees (primarily a secretary and a warehouse keeper). On 8 February 1672 the Committee ordered its clerk, Thomas Rastell, to record the names and addresses of men "who Shall offer themselves to Serve the Company eyther at Sea or to Stay in the Countrey...& presente the Same from time to time to the Comittee." On 21 May 1672, for instance, Mr. John Palmer offered to serve in Hudson Bay and was engaged as Governor Bayly's second; on 19 March 1674 Walter Farr successfully petitioned to go to the Bay as surgeon and apothecary; and on 25 February 1680 Mr. Conyers Fairfax offered himself as warehouse keeper in the Bay and was accepted. Men also sought employment for lesser positions in this way: on 7 May 1680 Henry George offered his services as an edge-tool maker at twenty pounds per annum.[10]

Even the process by which the first governor in Rupert's Land was recruited is opaque. Little in his personal history suggested Charles Bayly as an obvious choice for the management of any kind of commercial venture. The rocky road he had travelled from Roman Catholicism to the Society of Friends (Quakers) had taken him to France and America and back again and seemed to be ending in missionary zeal and successive prison terms. His last place of incarceration had been the most prestigious: the Tower of London, his home for five years. The charge laid against him (but on which he never seems to have been examined) was seditious practices, relating both to his repeated refusal to take the oath of allegiance and to his disruptive role within the English Quaker community.[11]

In 1669 Bayly petitioned the king for his release, and his request was granted on the condition that Bayly go to Hudson Bay, but there is no consensus regarding the reason. Bayly had corresponded with the king a few times during his imprisonment, and the two may have known each other as children. Bayly's biographer, Alice M. Johnson, speculates that

Charles II might have seen this as a way of either "ridding himself of an obstinate prisoner" or "helping an old acquaintance by making the conditions of release those of exile with dignity and remuneration." Sir John Robinson may also have been at least partly responsible: he was one of the original HBC shareholders, was lieutenant of the Tower of London during Bayly's residence there, and had tried (and released) Bayly several years earlier when he was lord mayor of London.[12]

If Bayly seems an odd choice to head up a venture of this kind, it may have been because those who engaged him were not entirely clear what kind of venture it was going to be. The Governor and Committee were vague about his particular role; though Bayly was first engaged in 1669, before the company was even chartered, the first known mention of his rank was not until 1674. The surviving records strongly suggest that Bayly possessed little or no business skill. His ultimate successor, John Nixon, told the Committee that "I desire not to stay longer in the countrie then to settle things in a good order and method, and to leave a better precident to him that shall come after me, then I found my selfe."[13]

There is no evidence, however, that Bayly was hired for business skill. No doubt, like those of the Virginia Company before them, the directors of the HBC wanted a governor who could ensure a stable and prosperous establishment as quickly as possible, but in the absence of any analogous circumstances they could only speculate on what sort of man would be best suited to accomplish this. In that instance what was ultimately deemed most important was not a gentleman's particular qualification but his ability to convince those under his command "that he understood what had gone wrong and how to fix it."[14]

In the HBC's formative days it seems likely that Bayly was being hired not as a commercial manager but with a view to governing a colony, or possibly as a kind of consul or ambassador (as was the case in the EIC's early years).[15] If that was the case, Bayly's chief qualification was that he was a gentleman.[16] As such, he would have possessed the necessary standing to act as the patriarch of the large household about to be established in James Bay and would be accepted in that role by the officers and servants under him.[17] The ships' captains were seldom deferent, though: Captain Nehemiah Walker's abusive behaviour brought Bayly to tears on several occasions, and on his homeward voyage in 1679 Bayly was similarly treated by Captain Richard Power and the ship's surgeon, Dr. Rainer.[18]

Walker and Power were heads of their own shipboard households and not subject to Bayly's terrestrial authority, but their behaviour reminds us (as it reminded Bayly and those around him) how shallow the roots of authority often were in the early modern Atlantic. Bayly, Nixon, and their peers were far from being the only English office-holders struggling to stake a claim to legitimacy in the "New World." Landed elites were rare in the early English settlements (non-existent in Hudson Bay), and middling men who were chosen to lead voyages and settlements seldom possessed social status commensurate with their office. Michael Lacombe's observation about early-seventeenth-century Jamestown applies equally well to Albany or Charles Fort:

> *Making it harder for such men to present a sufficiently authoritative self, there were few material reflections of social status in the Americas. Houses and furnishings were rough, dependents often sickly and few, and hunger was a constant concern. In this fluid context, would-be leaders seized any opportunity to stake or challenge a claim to authority by, in effect, striking a pose calculated to confirm their claim to office.*[19]

Bayly, then, like other seventeenth-century colonial governors, was expected not simply to possess social authority but to enhance his leadership by expressing that social authority. Unfortunately, he was not entirely successful in deploying his reputation (such as it was)—in being regarded by others as a person of status and power, capable of facilitating or bestowing favours.[20]

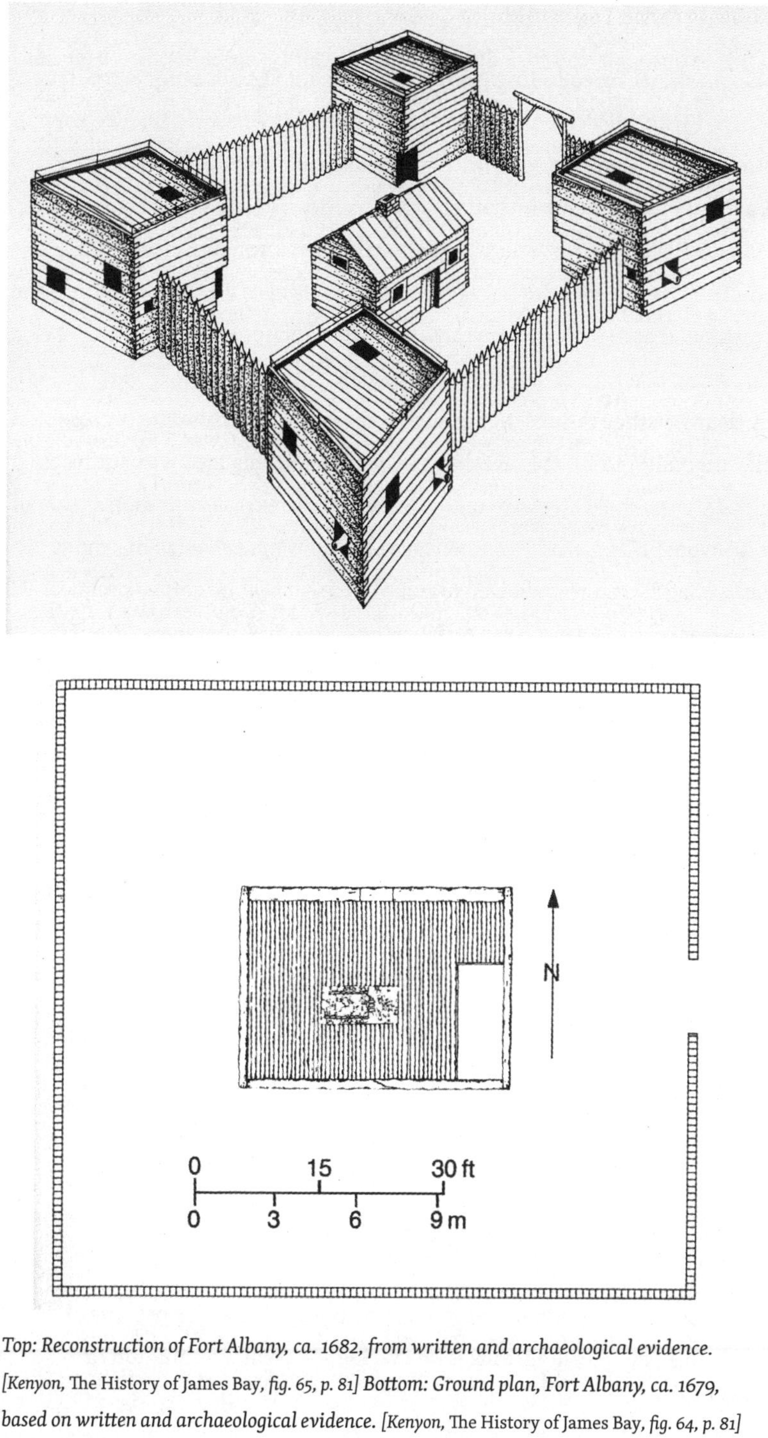

Top: Reconstruction of Fort Albany, ca. 1682, from written and archaeological evidence. [*Kenyon,* The History of James Bay, *fig. 65, p. 81*] *Bottom: Ground plan, Fort Albany, ca. 1679, based on written and archaeological evidence.* [*Kenyon,* The History of James Bay, *fig. 64, p. 81*]

Finding "Able Young Men"

The questions surrounding Bayly's engagement are not unique; most men entered HBC service without any indication of the process followed. On 16 May 1674 the Committee minutes recorded the names, occupations, and wages of eleven men who had engaged on three-year contracts to stay in Hudson Bay; only one (surgeon Walter Farr) was actually referred to elsewhere as having been so engaged. The minutes of 27 October 1683 included an order "that in future all Servants that are taken into the Company Service, those that doe recommend them be incerted in the Minute booke," but it is unclear whether the absence of such references after this date represented clerical omissions or the fact that men were being engaged without recommendations. The waters are muddied even further by a case such as that of John Woodbridge, who "went with you without his Friends Consent as his Father Sayth" and was allowed to come home early at his father's request.[21]

A few recruits were close relatives of Committee members. Thomas Phipps Jr, engaged in 1678 as a warehouse keeper at Moose, was the cousin of Thomas Phipps Sr; and James Walker, son of William Walker Sr, filled the same position at Port Nelson in 1683. Two of James's brothers were also employed by the company at this time: William Jr was the company's attorney, and Nehemiah was a ship's captain.[22] More commonly, however, Committee members brought forward nominees whose relationships to them were unclear. In 1671 Sir John Kirke recommended a gentleman named Manning, though he mentioned no specific position; in 1672 Sir John Robinson recommended edge-tool maker Thomas Wilkinson; and in 1674 Sir John Griffith recommended William Lydall, and Sir James Hayes recommended Thomas Copley, both for the post of governor in Hudson Bay (Lydall was appointed, and Copley was disappointed). In 1684 Nicholas Hayward offered the services of Benjamin Mesnard of Paris, "formerly a Soldier there"; Mesnard was engaged for four years, but his occupation was unspecified.[23]

Occasionally, company servants also appeared to act as patrons of sorts. In April 1684 long-time HBC mariner Michael Grimington Sr recommended apprentices Samuel Martin and John Allen, shipwright William Benson of Limehouse, and mariner and gunner Edward Adams of Poplar (a riverside London parish).[24] However, the roles of shareholders or servants in recruiting are not straightforward. In May 1685, a week or so before the ships were due to sail for Hudson Bay, the Committee's secretary, Onesipherous Albin, was ordered at the last minute to "hire a Bricklayer for the Bottom of the Bay at Gravesend as reasonable as he can."[25] Albin was thus actively involved in recruitment but did not necessarily act as a patron.

Connections (where they can be demonstrated) were important but not paramount. The Committee's 1680 instructions to Governor Nixon expressed a hope that "you will not be the lesse diligent, though the Earl of Shaftesbury and Sr. Peter Colleton, who first brought you into the Compa's. service, have sold themselves out [sold their stock], and some of us who are unknown to you do supply their places."[26] Nixon's connection to Shaftesbury seems to have been uninterrupted by the latter's departure from the ranks of shareholders, because he sent Shaftesbury the skin of a young beaver as a present in 1682.[27] However, Nixon did not suffer from either his continuing connection with Shaftesbury (who had lost a power struggle within the company) or from his lack of personal connections with the current Committee. Even the prospects of Thomas Phipps Jr survived the suspicions of complicity in his cousin's planned interloping expedition in 1682: the younger man's time in the Bay was ended by a wage dispute upon his promotion to the command of Port Nelson.[28]

The Committee's comment to Nixon suggests that a servant's most important connection was with the Committee as a whole or with the company as a corporate entity. This perception is encouraged by the paucity of surviving correspondence between Bayside servants and individual Committee members. Yet, against that we must place Radisson's 1684 complaint about (unnamed) men "who profess to have protection and favour" and who thus did not exert themselves very strenuously in the company's interest.[29]

Connections (where they can be demonstrated) did not always guarantee security. Henry Sergeant entered the service in 1683 described as "a very worthey & well quallified gentleman," "a person very well approved of by his Royall Highness the Duke of Yorke," the HBC's London governor, and "allso Interested in the stock with us."[30] However, the Committee was dissatisfied with his handling of the trade and recalled him from Albany in 1686 (though the orders were lost when the *Happy Return* sank en route to the Bay). His connections were less important than the Committee's perception of him as a poor husband of company goods, a perception supported by reports from returning servants.[31]

Other connections may have been useful, though records of them are often opaque. John Bridgar (deputy governor in James Bay, 1685–86) may have been related to John Bridgar of Rotherhithe, one of two coopers supplying the HBC in 1683, and/or to Charles Bridgar, who made and repaired sails for the company's ships around the same time.[32] However, there is no indication that Bridgar's entry into the company's service in 1678 was due to his connection (if any) with either or both of these London tradesmen or that their connection with him helped procure their contracts with the company. Thomas Gilpin (Gilphin), who served in the Bay from 1682 to 1685 (at £6-9-12, no occupation specified), was related to James Knight, but this was not mentioned in the surviving records until he re-engaged in 1691:

> *[H]ee hath lived in the bottome of the Bay Severall years, is related to Mr. Knight who was Deputy Governor there, & hath Fourescore pounds a yeare Land here, & yet comes upon very reasonable wages, On all which wee desire you to shew him respect and Looke upon him as you find him capable & deserveing.*[33]

Henry Chambray (engaged in 1684, no position specified) was recommended by Stephen Evance, one of the company's bankers.[34] On a more humble scale, James Blaymire, engaged in 1682 (no occupation specified), was the son of Henry Blaymire, a gunsmith who had done work for the company earlier in the year.[35]

Even where possible kin relationships can be inferred or demonstrated, there is usually no clear evidence of what role they played in recruitment. In the late 1670s Charles, Patrick, and Thomas Savage all served the company on land and at sea: Thomas appears to have entered the service first, and the Committee paid Patrick (newly engaged) one pound for recruiting four men of unspecified occupations in 1678, the same year as Charles entered the service. In the mid-1690s Albany's complement included John Fullartine and his brother Dr. George Fullartine.[36] None of these men was mentioned as playing a role in recruiting the others, but their roles may not have been formal or even known to the Committee. For instance, John Fullartine may have recommended the company to George rather than recommending George to the company; likewise, Charles and Patrick Savage may have sought employment with the HBC because they knew that Thomas was doing well in the service. Such informal (and unrecorded) participation in recruitment undoubtedly played a more important role than the surviving documents indicate.

In a few cases, non-kin may have played a greater role than kin. For instance, John Allen was a relative (probably a brother) of Albany bookkeeper Joshua Allen, but John was apprenticed to the company in 1684 on the recommendation of mariner Michael Grimington Sr.[37] In fact, the most recent research into apprenticeship (at least in London) shows little evidence that personal ties of kin or place of origin shaped apprentice recruitment in any significant way.[38] Recruitment through non-kin connections could have included recommendations from neighbours, drinking companions, shopkeepers, and fellow churchgoers. London's alehouses or public houses may have been particularly significant because they played an important role in providing (among other services) contacts and news of jobs, and by the end of the seventeenth century some were functioning as houses of call for certain trades.[39] The Committee may also have utilized one of a growing number of registry offices, employment agencies helping to place servants and other workers. The Committee could also have advertised in newspapers, put up posters, distributed handbills, or attended statute (or petty) sessions in and around London, in which local justices of the peace supervised the signing of new service contracts.[40]

The company's senior employees may have taken an active role in recruitment. Bayly, Radisson, and Groseilliers were entrusted with important tasks like procuring trade goods, but they do not seem to have been officially entrusted with recruitment.[41] There is no evidence that early company employees were sent into various parts of England and Scotland for the specific purpose of recruiting. However, men who themselves came from outside of London had opportunities to recruit new men while visiting family or running errands for the Committee.

Hugh Verner (factor at Charles Fort in the 1680s) was involved in recruiting at least four and possibly ten men for the 1683 voyage. In April of that year the Committee reimbursed him for advance money paid to John Driver (a tailor from Ipswich), James Muddy (a cooper from Leith), John Fullartine (a "tradesman" from Edinburgh), and James Sinclare (a mariner "of Scouros in Scotland"). Later that month he stood security for advance money paid to James Harrison and Calvin Oliphant (seamen of Burntisland, Fifeshire), Magnus Browne (seaman), John Couter (tradesman of Edinburgh), and George Forrest and Thomas Ballenden (seamen).[42] Verner recommended three men for the 1684 voyage: James Swan, David Cleney, and John Crooks (it is unclear if all, or only Crooks, were from Prestonpans in Scotland). He again recruited men in 1691 while purchasing "Scotch plaids" in Scotland.[43]

In 1683 Verner was also reimbursed for fifty shillings that he had paid to get John Driver out of prison. It is unknown why Driver was in prison—though debt may be a reasonable speculation—or why the company was willing to pay fifty shillings to get him out. In 1691 the company paid five shillings to get John Bringhurst out of prison so he could go to Hudson Bay. In 1705 the company paid a more substantial sum to get shipwright Alexander Thoyts out of prison, "being in Custody for Debt & his Creditors being willing to Release him upon ye Compies Advanceing some moneys the Comtte doe agree to pay him ye Sume of twelve pounds provided he goe ye voyage this present yeare. Which is to be deducted out of his wages." However, Thoyts was an old hand, having served at Port Nelson from 1689 through 1693. The size of his debt is unknown, but apparently this arrangement barely made a dent in it: one of his creditors, Mr. Benjamin Travers, later requested (through the Committee) that Thoyts pay ten pounds a year "towards his Debt."[44]

In 1683 the Committee began requiring security for advance money paid out to recruits before sailing time. Without corroborating evidence, however, it is impossible to know whether a Bayside officer's act of standing security (as in Verner's case) indicated involvement in recruiting the man concerned or any previous connection with him. Similarly, we cannot know the nature of the relationship between the Parsons family and William Haynes, Member of Parliament for Dartmouth, even though in 1693 Haynes and Edward Parsons together posted a five-hundred-pound security for Edward's son, Phillip, who had been engaged as deputy governor for Port Nelson.[45]

Verner's efforts may raise more questions than they answer, but another example of ad hoc recruiting sheds some light on what the Committee was looking for. On 3 March 1693 a Captain Simpson, who had previously commanded one of the company's ships, paid his respects to the Committee before making a short trip to Scotland for personal reasons. Although it is unknown which party took the initiative, Simpson assured the Committee that in Scotland he could find men to serve the company "at Cheape wages" (music to their ears, no doubt). At a subsequent meeting on 8 March the Committee instructed Simpson to bring back ten or twelve thick Scottish plaids as possible trade goods and to recruit "10 or 12 Able young men Twixt 20 and 30 yeares of age...or any person yt [that] has worked in ye mines who may be a Usefull hand in those parts." Simpson does not appear to have recruited anyone and in June was dismissed from the service for delaying the supply ships' departure from Gravesend for no apparent reason.[46]

Vague though they were, the Committee's instructions to Simpson are echoed elsewhere. The earliest guidelines to the recruitment process can be found in the Committee's March 1682 order "that the Secretary indeavor to gett 10 honest and able Fellows batchelors not under 20 nor above 30 yeares old to be either Bricklayers, Carpenters, Quarriers or such like and present them to the Compa. not exceeding 6. 9 or 12 *li.* p. Ann."[47] Apparently, the HBC shared the EIC's preference for "'grave staid men,' with all of their problematic experiences...[over] 'younge greene heads' who lacked sufficient maturity and probity to serve companies and merchants reliably and competently."[48] In 1684 Morgan Lodge—postmaster of Deal (Kent), who acted as the company's agent, inspecting homeward ships for evidence of private trade through much of the 1680s—was asked to find ten or fifteen men to serve the company as either seamen or landsmen for three or four years. His instructions specified the wages to be offered to sailors ("£18 p. yeare at highest") and unskilled labourers ("though they have noe trade...£6 the first £8 the second £10 the third & £12 the 4th yeare besides their Accomodation"), but not indicating how many of each sort were required or any other details.[49]

This letter to Lodge is the earliest direct evidence regarding active external recruitment of servants. It was not the start of a new policy but a necessary response to a recruitment shortfall: the supply ships were ready to sail but needed ten or fifteen more men for Bayside service. This was also the case in 1711 when Captain Richard Ward of the frigate *Pery* carried no new servants out of Gravesend (only Anthony Beale, returning to company service to command Albany). He was "to get 4 or 5 Land Men, as Cheap as you Can" when stopping in the Orkney Islands on his outward voyage, "[b]ut we hereby order you not to Stay there above eight and forty hours on any pretence whatsoever."[50]

Londoners, Scotsmen, and "Country Lads"

For its earliest expeditions the HBC relied almost exclusively on Londoners to man its ships and staff its posts, avoiding the expense and inconvenience of recruiting elsewhere. That choice was understandable. In the late seventeenth and early eighteenth centuries London was the best and most obvious place to look for men to serve on long-distance trading voyages. It contained a large and experienced seafaring community: by the beginning of the eighteenth century more than 12,000 Londoners worked in the international trades, and several thousand more worked in the English coastal trades.[51] These men would not necessarily have baulked at spending a few years in Hudson Bay at decent pay. However, the Committee began to recognize that, while sufficient numbers of men were available, the finding of suitable men presented problems. London recruits brought inconveniences that eventually prompted the Committee to cast its net more widely.

Londoners were expensive to hire: Jeremy Boulton has described the metropolis as "the high wage area *par excellence* in early modern England."[52] Labourers there received money wages as much as twice those of their counterparts in northern towns throughout the seventeenth century; regional differences decreased during the eighteenth century, but Londoners were still paid significantly more than provincial workers by 1800. This was the essence of Governor John Nixon's criticism of "London borne childring," particularly their habit of demanding higher wages with each new contract.[53] Of course, men from all parts of Britain demanded higher wages when re-signing, but a man from a low-wage area began with lower demands than did one from London.

Nixon also blamed men's urban backgrounds for licentiousness and disciplinary problems. He asked the Committee to "send me Some country lads, that are not acquainted, with stronge drink, that will woorke hard, and faire hard, and are not debauched with the voluptwousness of the city."[54] His concerns echo contemporary criticisms of the behaviour of London labourers: the image of such men working three or four days and getting drunk for the rest of the week on their earnings was frequently used by eighteenth-century opponents of higher wages. There was ample opportunity for work (of a sort), but contemporary evidence suggests that workers were not necessarily quick to take advantage of those opportunities.[55]

The geographic origins of most company servants are difficult to trace prior to the nineteenth century. The London minute books offer the most information, but even these are inconsistent. For instance, only seven of twenty-one recruits in 1682 can be connected with a parish of origin, while eighteen of thirty-seven recruits in 1683 and twenty-eight of thirty-seven recruits in 1684 can be so identified. About half of the identifiable Englishmen were Londoners, and many of the men whose abodes were not recorded probably lived in London or its environs, given the attraction of the metropolis and the lack of significant HBC recruiting outside the London area at this time. All four of the Londoners recruited in 1683 and six of the fifteen recruited in 1684 were from the East End parishes of Wapping, Deptford, Rotherhithe, and Limehouse—all notable for their high concentrations of sailors.[56] Other recruits, described simply as being from London, may also have been from those or neighbouring parishes.

Without considerable genealogical research it is impossible to determine whether the given parish of origin reflected long-term residence or the short-term abode of a man on the move. Migration was often a two-step process, involving a move to the city before the ultimate move overseas or elsewhere.[57] Improvements in roads and transport services in the sixteenth and seventeenth centuries made travel in early modern Britain less dangerous and less time-consuming than it had been in medieval times: scheduled stagecoach services to London more than doubled in the late seventeenth century, including connections to smaller towns and villages that had previously lacked direct links to the metropolis. By 1700 a man departing overland from Newcastle could be in London within a week.[58]

If Londoners were volatile in their behaviour—and many contemporary sources agreed that they were[59]—they may have reflected the volatility of London itself. The city's population was increasing rapidly, growing from approximately 375,000 in 1650 to approximately 700,000 by 1770.[60] Much of this growth was the result of immigration, so the metropolis contained a substantial number of people who had removed themselves (or had been removed) from their home community but were not yet accustomed to London traditions.[61] These newcomers were drawn from an extensive migration field that included all of England and Wales; although most came from less than two hundred kilometres away, small numbers came from Ireland, Scotland, continental Europe, and occasionally from the American colonies. As well, some migration studies have suggested that the substantial inflow was accompanied by a considerable outflow of people and that London thus acted as a "revolving door" for mobile Englishmen and women, as well as foreigners. Given that London was a community—or, rather, a community of communities—in flux, then perhaps Londoners were not good choices for isolated trading posts on Hudson Bay. They might have been more flexible, however, and thus more suitable than other recruits, although none of the company's factors recorded such an opinion. Either way, considering that so many seventeenth-century Londoners were recent arrivals there, blaming "Londoners" may be mis-stating the problem.[62]

Nixon did not entirely blame his troubles on the effects of city life. He also attributed his men's insolence to the power they had over him: at shiptime they would claim that their contracts had expired (Nixon did not know how many were telling the truth) and threaten to go home, knowing that Nixon could not replace them until the following year.[63] Estate stewards in rural England were all too familiar with these tactics, as prospective tenants and sitting tenants alike would often delay signing new leases until the last possible moment in the hope of extracting concessions in rent; even those whose leases had time to run might claim that the lord had promised certain concessions when he was last in the country or when the tenant was last in town, and some threatened to abandon their farms if their terms were not met.[64] Those stewards sometimes felt helpless, but how much more impotent must Nixon have felt: even if he had known whose terms were up, he believed he had no enforceable law, martial or civil. Knowing he could not punish them, men who wanted to go home early could simply misbehave enough to get sent home, where they would have the opportunity to clear themselves and accuse him instead.[65]

Londoners may have been undisciplined, but the Committee's failure to empower their factors with necessary information and an enforceable authority allowed latitude for these men to misbehave as Nixon claimed they did. Insufficient flow of information led to

> *bad husbandry...when you send men of great wages, and are not sensible what they can doe for their wages, (one may goe to a faire and buy a ragged horse for 40s., that will prove better then a horse of 20 pound).... Therefore my advice is that yow would send over yearly 5 lykly country lads of 17 or 18 years of age, and let their tyms be 7 years, so that before their tymes be out they will be lusty younge-men, and fit for your service both at sea, and land, and at small wages.*[66]

He assured the Committee that "good order and method" could not be established in Hudson Bay

> *untill yow purge your country of most of the ould men, (and there is great need of it) for they ar most seek of the ould disease, of licentiousness, and will corrupt others with the same distemper, yea besides that most of them have greate wages...if England can not furnish yow with men, Scotland can, for that countrie is a hard country to live in, and poore-mens wages is cheap, they are hardy people both to endure hunger, and could, and are subject to obediance, and I am sure that they will serve for 6 pound pr. yeare, and be better content, with their dyet then Englishmen will be, so that yow may better afford to allow some better sellery to petty officers, to traine the men, and see them doe their deutie.*[67]

His recommendation for "hardy" men was echoed by Pierre Esprit Radisson in 1684, when he recommended that the company hire "only robust men, competent and capable of serving," and not "those who are of a feeble constitution."[68]

Nixon's solution of seeking out men from rural areas, including Scotland, was logical because wages generally decreased with distance from major urban centres, particularly London. In recommending surgeon John Ker to the Committee, Nixon commented:

> *[H]e can informe youre honoures how yow may get men out of Scotland, who will both faire harder, and serve at cheaper rates, then our London borne childring: they goe to france for small wages and seek their fortounes up and doun the world, and doeth good service where they are, and why may not yow imploy them for youre profit.*[69]

Ker was engaged, but there is no evidence of his involvement in recruitment.

Nixon's reference to the need for petty officers—he advocated two sergeants and three corporals—suggested that he felt a military organizational model might be necessary for discipline. His goal was not to find men more suitable for life in the Bay; although he referred to Scots as "hardy people both to endure hunger, and could," neither he nor his contemporaries emphasized the harsh Hudson Bay climate as requiring a certain kind of man. Rather, he felt that the company, like any employer, should seek hard-working men at low wages as one of the basic ingredients to corporate success. Nixon was probably Scottish himself and knew that such men and such wages could be found in Scotland, but it is impossible to credit him with the creation of any kind of recruitment system or policy, as the London Committee never linked its decisions with his recommendations.

A few of the company's early employees can be identified as Scotsmen.[70] Trader Hugh Verner, who entered the service in 1678, was probably Scottish although his birthplace remains unknown; in 1682, mariners John Anderson and Alexander Baine, both of "Borresenex" in Scotland, contracted for three years' service.[71] Eight of the thirty-seven men engaged in 1683 were Scots: a man "bred up at sea" (James Sinclare of "Scouros," who deserted with his advance money before the ships sailed), two Edinburgh tradesmen (John

Fullartine and John Coalter), three seamen from Fifeshire (James Harrison, Calvin Oliphant, and David Reidie), a cooper from Leith (James Moody), and a Highland gentleman who does not appear to have made the voyage (Archibald MacArthur).[72] Although, as mentioned earlier, there is strong reason to believe that Hugh Verner was involved in the engagement of some of these men, this was not the beginning of a deliberate policy. Of the thirty-seven men recruited in the following year, only one can be definitely identified as Scottish, while three others were probably from Scotland.[73] In contrast, nine of the 1683 recruits and twenty-three of the 1684 recruits can be identified as Englishmen.

Although Verner recruited in Scotland itself, the Committee could easily find Scotsmen in the capital. In seventeenth- and eighteenth-century London and other large towns, many inns and taverns had regional connections, as did certain neighbourhoods. A Committee member looking for Scotsmen for Hudson Bay would have looked in the western suburbs of St. Martin's, the Strand, Bedfordbury, and Holborn.[74]

Recruitment in the Shadow of War

Most of the company's first fifty years unfolded against a backdrop of uncertainty, as the sunny optimism of the 1670s was increasingly obscured by the clouds of war. The London Committee sought to find the proper balance in its personnel. Too many men would be too expensive, but too few men would be vulnerable; bold men might take foolish risks, while timid men might not offer the enemy any resistance at all. The Committee criticized the passiveness of John Abraham when he was opposed by French traders at Port Nelson, declaring:

> *[W]e hope there may come a time of Retaliation [against the French], when our affaires shall be in the hands & managery of honester or at least Wiser men [than Abraham]. We have therefore tooke speciall care this yeare to put our concernes every where into the hands of the most prudent*

& discreet persons that we can pitch upon & whose courage as well as fidelity we have good reason to confide in.[75]

In 1689 they urged John Marsh at Albany to set an example for his men by showing "Courage, and a noble indignation" toward the French "when a just occasion offers but not needlessly [to] expose your Selfe and our Factory, for prudence is as necessary and as Laudable as Courage."[76]

Recruiters—whether officially connected with the company or not—become visible in the records during this period because of the premiums they were promised or paid for the men they procured. Christopher Spencer, a gunner who served the company on land and at sea from 1688 until his capture by the French at Port Nelson in 1694, was back in England in 1696; the Committee re-engaged him for three years if his services were required, and "he being now goeing into Whales," they promised him twenty shillings for every servant he could recruit there. He does not appear to have found anyone in Wales, however, as no payments were recorded to him that spring.[77] In 1693 a Captain Bennet "promised to procure servants for ye Compa[ny] at Reasonable wages"; the Committee asked him "to Raise 30 or 40 men" and promised to reward him but did not mention a particular amount. Like Spencer, Captain Bennet does not appear to have successfully recruited anyone for the HBC.[78] In the same year the Committee reimbursed Captain Philip Parsons (newly engaged as deputy governor of Port Nelson) £7 0s. 6d. for "what he shall Lay out in procureing of men," and a Colonel Thomas Eaden received £39 12s. 0d. "for ye Raising of 12 men for Comp[an]y service."[79] In 1705 Captain Michael Grimington put the Committee in touch with a crimp (recruiter) who was ready to procure servants at the rate of one pound per man.[80] In none of these examples was a distinction made between landsmen and seamen, nor do they offer any more details on recruitment than the 1684 letter to Morgan Lodge.

There is no indication that the early HBC employed permanent recruiters in the same way as it did in Stromness and other places in the nineteenth century.[81] Rather, occasional improvised searches for likely young men in various parts of Britain supplemented the largely informal approach to recruitment that was evident in the 1670s. The Committee took the process seriously enough to make some financial investment in it, but no recruitment policy was apparent. The Committee contemplated a regular approach to apprenticeship in 1689, when it apprenticed four boys from Christ's Hospital charity school in London and told George Geyer that "wee have thoughts yearely or every other yeare to take the like or a greater number from the said Hospital."[82] However, the company's limited labour needs during this period probably tempered its enthusiasm for apprentices. As well, the failure of all but one of the 1689 apprentices to complete their indentures may have suggested that Blue Coat boys were not necessarily better choices as apprentices; unfortunately, the surviving records give very few details about their experiences.

Only six boys were apprenticed to the company between 1690 and 1713, and none of them can be shown to have come from the Blue Coat or any other charity school. The actual procedures involved in recruiting apprentices remain opaque, and even the best-documented cases raise questions. The company's deputy governor Captain John Nicholson was involved in the 1705 indenture of Joseph Adams, a five-year-old pauper from Woodford (Essex), and with the 1708 indenture of nine-year-old John Henson, a pauper of the same parish. Nicholson had built a house in the neighbourhood and a pew in the local church and served as churchwarden from 1706 through 1710. According to the Committee, Adams and Henson were "Bound to Capt Nicholson...and Turn'd Over to ye Compa[ny]," but the vestry minutes of St. Mary's Church, Woodford, recorded that on 13 May 1705 Adams was to be "forthwith bound out according to due form of Law to ye Hudsons Bay Company."[83]

Englishmen remained prominent in the labour force and were particularly well represented among the ranks of apprentices. However, northern Britain became a visible source of manpower in the early eighteenth century, as Orcadian names begin to appear in the company's account books. Although some Orkneymen probably served on HBC or chartered ships in the late seventeenth century, the first man known to have been employed on land service was Adam Isbister, a sailor on the *Pery* frigate who wintered at Eastmain in 1699–1700 with Captain Henry Baley and who in 1701 agreed (along with his crewmates Samuel Sanders and Simon Simpson) to winter there again as part of the crew of the *Knight* sloop.[84] Though primarily a sailor on the supply ships, Isbister served at Albany and Eastmain on several occasions between 1699 and 1714. He was presumably an acceptable servant because in 1702 the company ship was ordered to engage ten or twelve stout young men in the Orkneys. In 1711 Captain Richard Ward (mentioned previously) was unable to procure any men there during his forty-eight hours in port. In 1714 eight of the forty-four men at Albany had Orcadian names, and all eight of them went home that year: Gunn, Flatt, Slater, Groundwater, Lisk, and three Isbisters.[85]

The Committee was clearly casting its recruiting net more widely. In the 1680s it discussed a plan for sending a Russian to direct the proposed mining operation at Slude River on the Eastmain, and between 1701 and 1712 the Saxon miner Gottlieb Augustus Lichtenberger was in charge of that venture.[86] This was partly a response to the difficulty of finding "lusty" and able young men for Bayside service at any price in wartime Britain.

A major obstacle to recruitment in Britain was competition from the armed forces, particularly the Royal Navy. As E.E. Rich observed, "[p]ress-gangs and prize-money between them made service in the Navy both difficult to evade and more attractive than in peacetime." Marcus Rediker disputed the attractiveness of wartime naval service, arguing that "low pay and mean working conditions in the king's service made seamen none too willing to serve" in the Royal Navy. However, the fact that the company was accepting pauper children as apprentices suggests that Hudson Bay was a still less attractive destination: paupers were usually apprenticed to undesirable or unprofitable trades and professions.[87]

Regardless of how attractive naval service was, it was certainly difficult to avoid. Even when sufficient numbers of men signed on with the company, some of them might not make it to the Bay: in 1691 the list of new servants sent to George Geyer at Port Nelson was accompanied by this lament: "wee wish they had been more, but we have spared noe Cost nor paines to get them & after all our trouble some we have lost pressed away after they have entred into Contract with us, soe difficult it is in these times to gett them or keep them."[88] The Committee attempted to secure protection from press gangs—even petitioning that, in view of the importance of its trade, the company itself might be granted powers of impressment—but with limited success. Sometimes the time and effort involved in procuring convoys for their ships and protection for their servants interfered with other necessary preparations. In 1692, when James Knight's expedition to re-establish the HBC in James Bay absorbed all available recruits, the Committee explained to George Geyer at Port Nelson that "this Expedition will require many Hands, & we have been hinderd by perpetuall daily attendance here in getting Protections for our Shipps & Seamen from procuring soe many Land men as otherwise we should have done."[89] Given the HBC's limited personnel needs during this period, the company's difficulty in finding sufficient recruits is a significant example of how much of the available labour supply was absorbed by the military and related services while England was at war.

Marcus Rediker's observation that whether England and its colonies were at war "was the single most powerful determinant of the seaman's life in the early modern era" can be applied to almost anyone working in long-distance trade.

> *Wartime offered the seaman substantially higher wages, prize money, greater choice of destination and captain, and looser, less violent discipline. But it also created grave perils that threatened at any moment to annihilate the benefits....Seamen felt a deep ambivalence about the gambles of wartime.*[90]

For some men, service in Hudson Bay offered a way of avoiding at least some of those perils and keeping themselves out of reach of press gangs, while reaping at least some of those benefits in the form of higher wages.[91]

Wartime conditions drove up wages at home and abroad. In 1689, for instance, the Committee observed that "the charge of Seamen, is neare double wt. it used to be."[92] The economic pressures of wartime also exacerbated the impact of subsistence crises in Britain, as in 1693 when "unseasonable weather" hampered the sowing of summer wheat, threatened "a dearth in Europe," and doubled the price of "all manner of provisions." Due in part to cool climatic conditions the 1690s was a harsh decade for much of Britain. In Orkney (which was not as badly hit as parts of Scotland) the harvests of 1693–95 were extremely poor, and in the worst year (1696) "the harvest was said to have yielded not one twentieth of the normal crop." Hundreds died in the resulting famine, and much land went out of cultivation.[93]

War also increased the already considerable risks involved in the North Atlantic trade. In 1690 the Committee explained to George Geyer at Port Nelson that the sloop he had requested had not been sent because "in these times of warr, men are not to be gotten almost at any Rates; who will adventure in soe small a vessell, which by woefull experience wee find to be too easy prey to an enemie." The "woefull experience" to which it referred was the capture of the HBC's new frigate, the *Northwest Fox* (Captain John Ford), by the French the year before.[94] The combination of higher wages, reluctant recruits, and the higher cost of trading goods and provisions all hampered the Committee's ability to staff its overseas factories precisely when it was most important not to leave those posts undermanned and vulnerable.[95]

Bayside officers in the 1690s drew a clear distinction between those suitable for the service in such times and those unsuitable for it. Responding to complaints from James Knight at Albany, the Committee expressed its hope that the 1693 recruits "might in some measure attone for those that went with you [the year before]" and described the 1694 recruits as "one & twenty stout able fellows wch. wee hope with a Little of your management & discipline will prove very serviceable hands."[96] John Fullartine chastised the Committee in 1703 for sending Albany "poor,

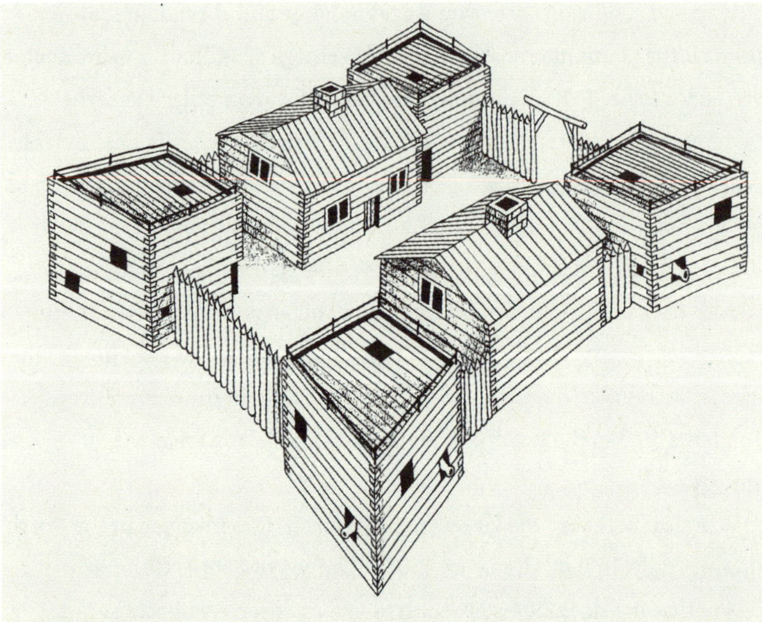

Top: Reconstruction of Fort Albany, 1686, from written and archaeological evidence. [Kenyon, The History of James Bay, *fig. 63, p. 80] Bottom: Reconstruction drawing of Fort Albany, 1686, from written and archaeological evidence. [Kenyon,* The History of James Bay, *fig. 68, p. 84]*

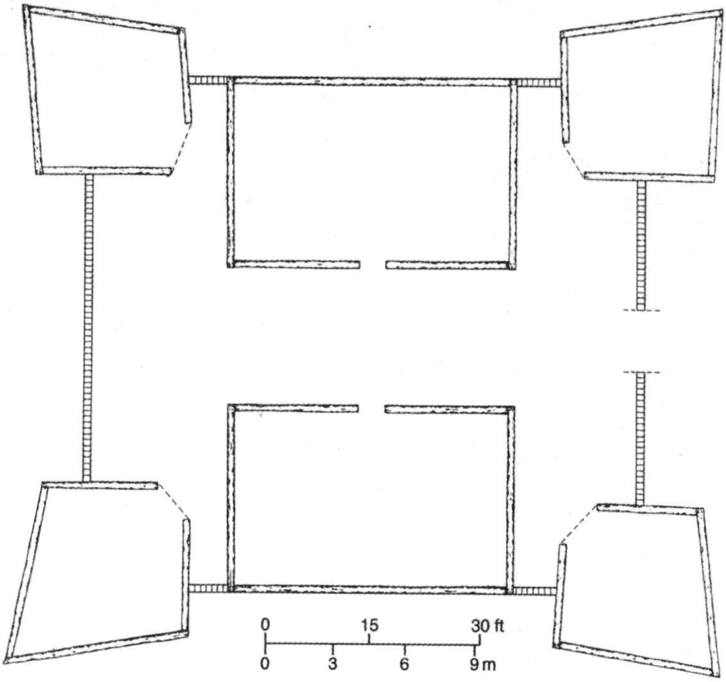

Ground plan, Fort Albany, 1686, based on written and archaeological evidence.
[Kenyon, The History of James Bay, *fig. 11, p. 21]*

Sorry, helpless Souls & no ways fitting for the Country at this juncture," and in 1705 he described the few recruits he received as "for the most part very helpless"; Anthony Beale expressed similar concerns in 1712.[97] Issues of suitability appeared defined less clearly in the minds of the Committee members, who were generally focused on obtaining a sufficient number of men, than in the minds of Bayside factors, who clearly believed that not all recruits acceptable for peacetime service were necessarily good enough "for the Country at this juncture."

The Committee and its factors wanted to strengthen their trading posts as much as possible during peace as well as war. Not only was piracy or privateering a constant threat on the open sea,[98] but peace with France did not necessarily preclude conflict with New France in Hudson Bay: Canadiens captured Port Nelson in 1683 and Albany in 1688 during periods of official

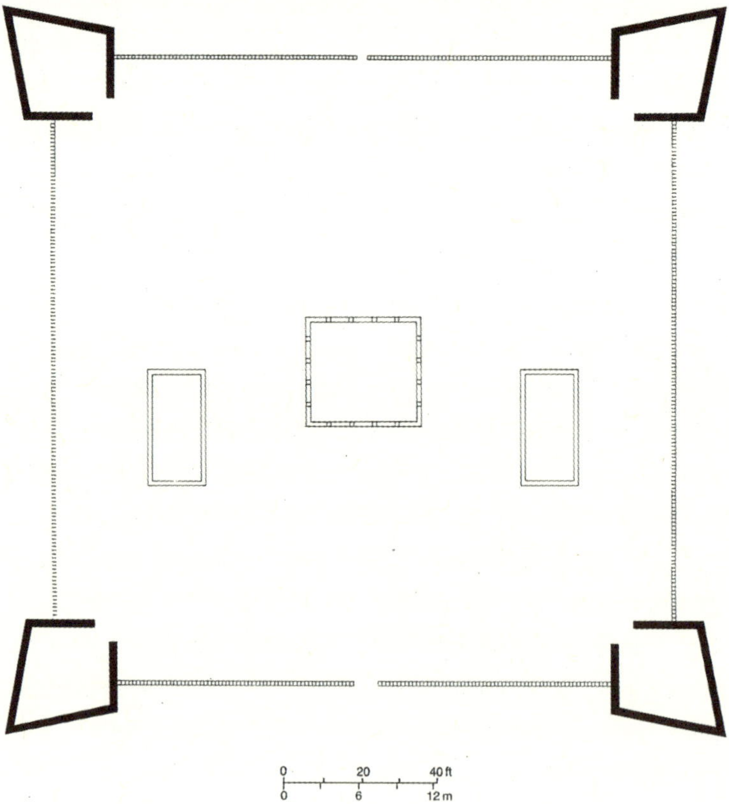

Top: Reconstruction painting of Moose Fort, 1686, from written and archaeological evidence. [*Kenyon,* The History of James Bay, *fig. 69, p. 85*] *Bottom: Ground plan, Moose Fort, 1686, based on written and archaeological evidence.* [*Kenyon,* The History of James Bay, *fig. 66, p. 82*]

peace between England and France. Furthermore, correspondence between London and Hudson Bay was annual at best, so war could break out without the men in the Bay learning about it until the Committee's next letter—or until French warships appeared on the horizon.

The company wanted to keep expenses as low as possible, but the defence of the factories was not to be compromised. In 1688 the Committee expressed concern "least New Severne should bee too Slenderly manned or ill fortified."[99] Two years later George Geyer and his council at Port Nelson were assured, "Wee would have you spare for noe Cost & paines to secure your selves & to make our Forts strong against all opposition whatsoever[;] for that end in this dangerous Juncture," they set the factory's minimum complement at fifty men, and Severn's at twenty or twenty-five. Port Nelson had between fifty and sixty men at this time, but New Severn probably had no more than a dozen. The Committee felt that John Ford (captain of the frigate *Albemarle*) and Thomas Walsh (trader and warehouse keeper) were the only men "of Sence or reason" at New Severn and had worried about the post's "Naked Condicion" should they both go to Port Nelson at shiptime.[100]

Shortfalls in recruitment put pressure on the Bayside factors to procure men from the crews of the supply ships or to convince landsmen whose contracts were expiring to re-engage. A postscript to the Committee's 1690 letter informed Geyer:

> *[F]or the more peaceable & orderly Government of our Factories in this time of Publick troubles, our express order is, that none shall Remove their posts or station wherein they are dureing this warr (unless such whose times are expired, & Cannot be prevailed upon to stay Longer or for the better service of the Compa. are Removed by the Governor) but acquiesce Cheerfully and obediently in their Respective places & Imployments...for wee Cannot but thinke emulation Ambition & discontent must bee a great prejudice to our affaires & to the Common Benefitt of the Company, at this Juncture.*[101]

Only three new men came to Hudson Bay that year—labourers Anthony Henchman and Philip Buffery and tailor George Newton—and the Committee hoped that "there will be found soe many supernumerary men out of our shipps [crews] to be left in the Countrey & yet our shipps to Returne strong enough."[102]

The following year brought more recruits, but Geyer was again authorized to engage seamen for land service if he thought it necessary. The Committee had even sent Captain Leonard Edgcombe's ship (the *Royal Hudson's Bay*) with six or seven extra seamen, whom "wee were unwilling to discharge...by reason severall of them or some of the others wee believe will be willing to stay in the Country with you."[103] All of the 1692 recruits for land service were attached to James Knight's James Bay expedition, and the Committee again instructed Geyer not to allow any servants to come home,

> *though wee desire you to recommend it to them in milde tearmes...& that for such whose times are Expired we shall take it kindly of them who stay chearfully & willingly in Our Service & not faile to remember them: In the meane time wee require them to be contented with such wages as you or Governour Knight shall thinke reasonable to give them.*[104]

By the following year the Committee apparently felt that circumstances had improved enough to instruct Geyer not to allow seamen to engage as landsmen without the Committee's approval, on the grounds of the exorbitantly high wages such fellows demanded.[105]

In 1701 and 1705 John Fullartine complained about too few men being sent out for service at Albany and the Eastmain. Two of the seven new men in 1701 (Chris Jackson and Edward Williams) were former servants re-engaging, but one (Robert Perkins) went home early in 1703 because "Sickness & indisposition has for ye most part of ye time since he has been here, rendred him a very useless & helpless hand."[106] The eight new men in 1705 also included two former servants (accountant Stephen Pitt and carpenter Alex Thoyts) but were "for the most part very helpless."[107]

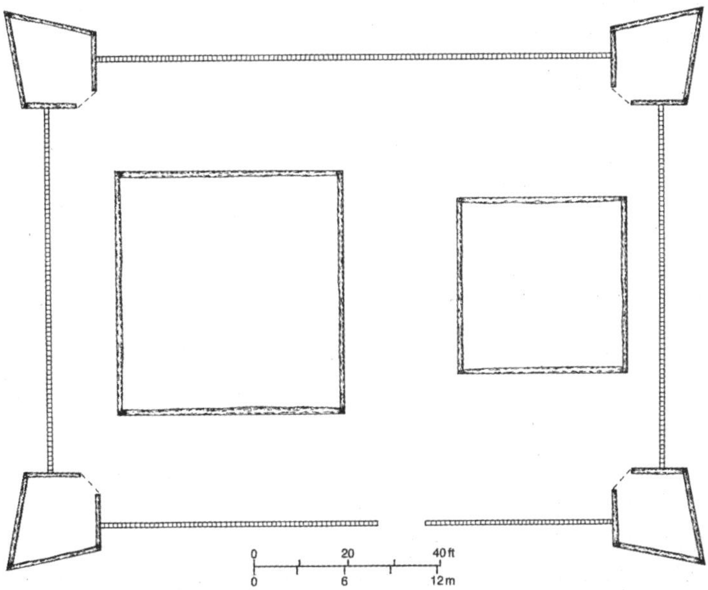

Top: Reconstruction drawing of Rupert House, 1686, from written and archaeological evidence. [Kenyon, The History of James Bay, *fig. 70, p. 85*] *Bottom: Ground plan, Rupert House, 1686, based on written and archaeological evidence.* [Kenyon, The History of James Bay, *fig. 67, p. 83*]

In 1703 Fullartine sympathized with the Committee on the difficulties of getting recruits, but of the eleven men he had been sent only one or two seemed to show any promise.[108] In all three years Fullartine felt compelled to offer several old hands exorbitant wages to renew their contracts, and in 1701 and 1705 he also engaged a few men from the crews of the *Pery* and the *Hudson's Bay*, respectively.[109]

In 1703 he engaged the *Hudson's Bay*'s gunner, Christopher Spencer, for land service at Albany, even though Spencer had demanded the same monthly wages as he had on board ship (which would have amounted to fifty-one pounds a year). Fullartine could only negotiate him down to forty-eight pounds a year in wages plus "40s to be given him in Brandy or some other thing here in ye Country, which is very extravigant wages, but was forced to comply with it by reason there was no man in ye Country yt could officiate in that poste & ye Fort could not be without a Gunner." When Spencer decided to go home in 1705, Fullartine was obliged to engage gunner Peter Farredon off the *Hudson's Bay* (at forty-eight pounds) to replace him. However, the *Hudson's Bay* was forced to winter in the Bay that year, so Spencer could not go home until the following summer; during the winter of 1705–6 Albany supported two gunners at high wages instead of just one.[110]

Fullartine's successor, Anthony Beale, reported that the recruits of 1710 were simple fools (though he felt they could be taught). No men could be recruited in 1711, and Beale described those sent out in 1712 as "verry helpless but thay are growing." The first clearly positive comment on recruits did not come until after the Treaty of Utrecht; in 1719 Thomas McCliesh Jr praised the new hands at Albany as "lusty able young men And hope will answer expectation."[111] While Britain was at war, however, the company took what men it could find.

|| The first HBC posts were relatively easy to staff, given the number of men offering their services. However, John Nixon's complaints (even if taken with a grain of salt) suggest that the Committee was not necessarily spoiled for choice. They may have preferred quantity over quality, perhaps assuming that poor recruits could be easily replaced, or they may simply

have not known how to define quality when recruiting for such an unfamiliar working environment. There was no indication of a systematic approach to recruitment; even the "Independent Company of Foot" was more of a paper tiger than a specialized body of men engaged to perform a specific task.

From the 1680s onward, the company and its servants became acutely aware of the threat (both real and perceived) from the French. In a wartime labour market the Committee sought recruits wherever it could but frequently fell short of what it and its factors considered sufficient numbers or quality. This opened the door for old hands to benefit from their masters' situation, particularly by demanding higher wages. The coming of peace in 1713, however, closed that door and shifted the balance of power back toward London.

4 "Men to Do the Business"

Recruitment, 1714–1786

Men we want Sirs, Furrs You want Gentlemen, should you please to send us the former We are confident of returning the latter.

—HUMPHREY MARTEN (York Fort) to HBC, 13 September 1780

THE PEACE OF UTRECHT restored a measure of stability and security to Hudson Bay. The HBC's garrison mentality began to ease, prices and wages began to fall, and recruits became somewhat easier to find. The Committee and its factors had always exhorted servants to get along—James Knight's orders to the men on watch at Albany included, "You are to suffer no quarrelling, fighting nor cursing or Swearing"—but this was increasingly expressed in terms of neighbourliness rather than duty.[1] Like householders in Britain, Bayside factors and the London Committee sought to maintain sobriety, industry, and decorum. Even while Prince of Wales Fort was being built as a defensive fortification, the company's establishments became more recognizable as household workplaces.

Difficulties in finding sufficient and suitable men for service in Hudson Bay were still apparent. In 1727, for instance, the Committee lamented, "We have not been able to meet with either Smith or Cooper [for Prince of Wales Fort], notwithstanding we have made diligent inquirey after them, but hope to supply you next year."[2] The primary obstacle remained the conditions of the wartime labour market, which prevailed in most of the period after 1739.

Employees who tried to use wartime conditions, however, to obtain or maintain high wages or other perquisites were still handicapped by the irregular flow of information to Hudson Bay. In 1764 a request by Albany surgeon William Richards to renew his contract for two years at forty-eight pounds a year was refused. To his surprise, the Seven Years' War had ended, and "the General Peace has lowered the price of Wages in every Instance," allowing the Committee to replace him with Eusebius Bacchus Kitchen at thirty-six pounds.[3]

The Committee consistently sought to keep labour costs as low as possible, even as operations expanded. Some factors appear to have shared this goal; for instance, Thomas Bird at Albany allowed the aging Charles Stewart (then earning fourteen pounds per annum) to leave the service in 1738 and replaced him as tailor with labourer John Whooley (then earning four pounds per annum), who "was regularly bred up unto ye Taylors Trade and is as good a Workman as any in this Countrey."[4] Likewise, when smith James Manson went home from Prince of Wales Fort in 1732, his place at the forge was taken by Evan Edwards, who had entered the service as a labourer in 1731 at £3-4-5-8-10, but was actually "a very good smith by profession." Although Edwards's wages were increased to eighteen pounds in 1732–33, he was still cheaper than Manson, who had just completed a five-year contract at £21-22-23-23-23.[5] When the Committee felt that certain factories had too many men, it chastised the factors. In 1756, for instance, James Isham was criticized for not sending some of his men home from York after failing to settle a post at Severn River.[6]

The post-Utrecht period was marked by small but important changes in recruitment practice, particularly the more regular engagement of Orkneymen from the late 1720s onward. There was still no apparent formation of an explicit recruitment policy. Although the slow but steady expansion of company operations imposed greater regularity on existing ad hoc methods, recruitment after 1714 remained very much a combination of what was possible and what was necessary.

Recruiting for Rebuilding: Orkneymen

Even in peacetime it was not always easy to staff the Bayside posts. In 1717, four years after the Treaty of Utrecht, Thomas McCliesh Jr at Albany was still waiting for wages and the labour supply to return to normal levels; he asked the Committee for an armourer and a cooper for the following year, "[b]y which time wages may be fallen: and Men Plenty."[7] In fact, the overall labour supply in Britain had been increased by approximately 157,000 men discharged from the armed forces in 1713–14,[8] but Hudson Bay may have been a relatively unattractive destination. In 1724 the Committee was unable to procure a bricklayer for York and instead engaged nineteen-year-old John Hughes, who had "workt with some Bricklayers."[9] In 1738 Captain George Spurrell was unable to engage enough mariners to serve at Prince of Wales Fort, so the council there re-engaged mariner Thomas Lovel at £18, although chief factor Richard Norton was more concerned with the fort's lack of a cooper and convinced Lovel to act in that capacity at only £16 4s. 0d.[10]

During the recent wars the HBC had turned to the Orkney Islands to make up shortages of manpower, albeit not always with success. Though geographically removed from the industrial and commercial centres of early modern Britain, Orkney was not necessarily remote; the islands' trade was strongly geared to exporting agricultural surpluses, and Kirkwall merchants had ties with Scotland, Northumberland, Norway, Germany, and Holland. Many of the Orkneymen engaged by the HBC in the early eighteenth century could have been recruited in London or elsewhere in Britain: many young Orkneymen served in the Royal Navy or in the Greenland and Iceland fisheries and thus could be found in many different British ports.[11]

The few early recruits who can be identified as coming directly from Orkney (as in 1708 and 1712) were not part of any clearly emerging pattern;

after the Treaty of Utrecht the company returned to the southern areas from which it was more accustomed to recruit. This was partly due to the Jacobite disturbances in Scotland in 1715, which prompted the company to send its ships west through the English Channel to Hudson Bay, avoiding Scotland and the Orkneys altogether. Not until 1720 were the ships' captains given the option of taking the northern route again.[12] In 1714 all eight of the Orcadians at Albany were sent home, and in 1723 only one of that factory's thirty-six men appeared to be from Orkney.[13]

Regular recruitment in Orkney began more than a decade after Utrecht. In 1726 Joseph Myatt told the Committee:

> *[I]t is my opinion if your Honrs thinks fitt to Entertain a few of the Orkney men, they would Be much fitter for your Service, when I was In the Orkneys there was severall Stout men that ofered to Serve you at 6£ p Ann, and Mr Baily Grimes Says he will procure any Number of men for you that you may have Ocation for.*[14]

The following year Myatt complained about debauched Londoners and added, "I am Glad you have Entertained a few of the Orkney men."[15] However, the Committee chose to recruit in Orkney that year only because several servants engaged in England had deserted with their advance money; Capt. George Spurrrell and Thomas McCliesh Jr (returning to York Fort after a winter in England) were ordered to "entertain 3 Hands, at the Orkneys, or in your Passage thither," and were given six pounds to pay advances, including six shillings per man as "customary allowance for bedding." McCliesh found three men for York—labourer Michael Loggin and tailor Edmund Hay (both for four years at £6-8-9-10) and James Lutitt (engaged as steward at £10-10-11-13, "being an old servant")—but "I lost three shillings by three fellows that run away, and one shilling given to a man for going six miles to acquaint James Lutit of going into your honours' service."[16]

The recruitment of Orkneymen appears to have become fairly regular (if not systematic) after this date. From 1731, HBC ships were consistently sent to Hudson Bay via the northern route, eschewing the English Channel for a stop in Stromness to top up supplies of provisions, fresh water, and (increasingly) labour.[17] The numbers of men contracted there were still not large, however: in 1732 Captain Christopher Middleton engaged five servants in Orkney, and Captain Jonathon Fowler brought six Orkney labourers to Albany in 1748.[18] The major construction project at Prince of Wales Fort was the biggest consumer of labour, Orcadian and non-Orcadian. In 1731 Richard Norton, on his return voyage to Hudson Bay after a winter in England, engaged "according to your honours' orders" sixteen servants at Stromness (all "able men" at £3-4-5-8-10); all but one were bound for Churchill River. This appears to have been a relatively large number. Captain William Coats engaged nine Orkney labourers for Prince of Wales Fort in 1733 but was unable to get four Orkney hands for York in 1735.[19]

Myatt drew the Committee's attention to the relatively low wages demanded by Orkney servants: six pounds per annum for a labourer, when wages of English hands were ranging from six to twelve pounds in their first year.[20] Yet, for the company, recruiting in Orkney was almost as convenient as recruiting in London; the hazards of the English Channel during the long wars with France had prompted the HBC's ship captains generally (though not always) to go around the north end of Britain, and Stromness (on the island of Mainland) was their last stop before Hudson Bay.[21]

Convenient, cheap, and willing they might have been, but Orkneymen did not always fulfill expectations. Joseph Myatt welcomed those sent to Albany in 1727 but observed that those engaged as mariners (Patrick Sinclair, Robert Erving, and possibly Thomas Ingleden and/or James Trumble) seemed to know very little of the matter.[22] No place in Orkney, except perhaps Kirkwall, had a surplus of tradesmen to share with the HBC. In 1694–96 nine men were listed as carpenters in the Stromness poll tax lists, but the parish of Birsay (in the northwest corner of Mainland) and the island of North Ronaldsay had none.[23] In 1727 neither Captain Christopher Middleton nor Captain George Spurrel could find a cooper, smith, or bricklayer in Orkney "or in your Passage thither."[24]

Elizabeth Gilboy, in her study of eighteenth-century English building trades, observed that London labourers and craftsmen, for all their faults (real or perceived), "possessed a distinctly higher grade of skill than those in country towns."[25] Tradesmen in Orkney often practised their skills alongside small-scale farming, although those in Kirkwall (especially smiths and carpenters) achieved wealth and prestige on par with the lower ranks of gentry through the employment of their skills and some occasional small trading. And, of course, there was no guarantee that Orkneymen would behave better than Londoners.[26]

Orkneymen could find advantages in working in the Bay. Men of all ethnic and occupational backgrounds appear to have been able to save significant portions of their earnings. Early Orkney examples include Robert Groundwater, a labourer at Moose who appears not to have purchased any goods from the company store between 1731 and 1736. Another Orcadian, William Hay, began his career in 1745 as a labourer at Albany earning £4; when he left the service in 1762, he was listed as a labourer and mariner at £20 per annum and had a final account balance of £169 4s. 11d.[27] Although these were extreme examples of men's ability to save, and men's HBC accounts did not represent the full extent of their savings or debts, Groundwater and Hay illustrate what was possible in the company's service. Given that traditional agriculture in Orkney focused on grain crops but produced no saleable surplus in one year out of three, families who had a son in HBC service—or in the new kelp industry, in linen making or straw plaiting, or on board an English fishing or whaling boat—gained a valuable supplement to their income.[28]

Orkney ministers in the 1790s complained about former HBC servants who returned home after eight or ten years of "exile" with uncivilized manners and broken constitutions but with enough money to buy or rent land; this reputation probably predated the earliest written references to it. Also, labour was often in short supply in eighteenth-century Orkney, and men going to Hudson Bay or to the fisheries physically removed themselves from the potential labour supply for kelp making, linen making, or other local industries. Saving money to buy or rent enough land to

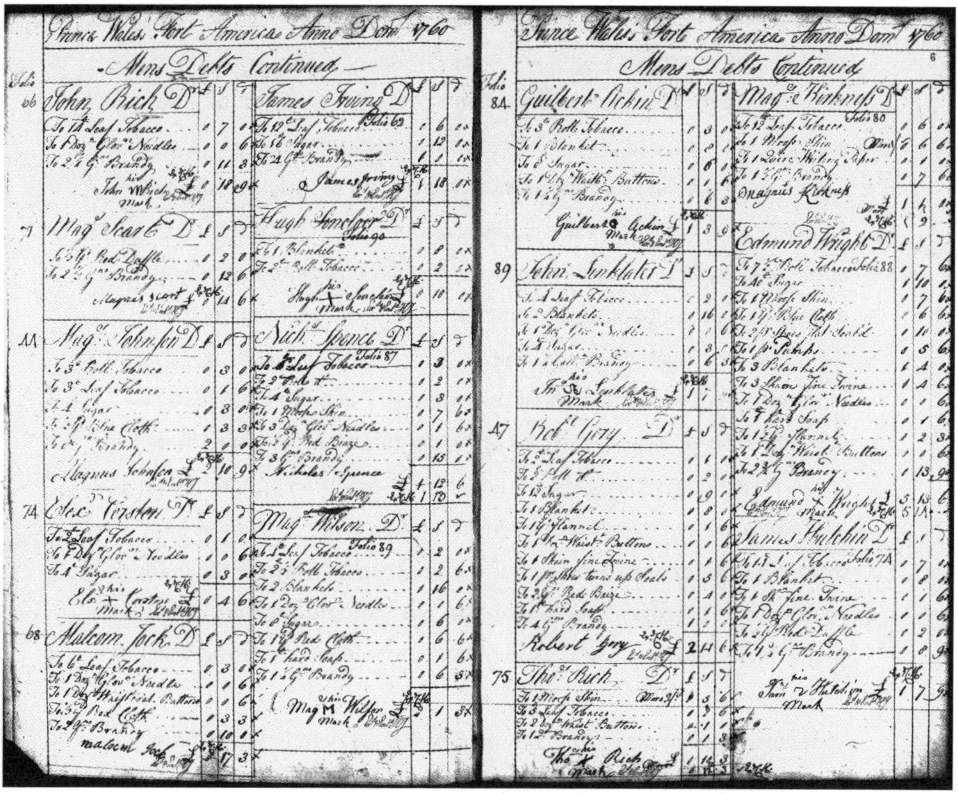

Page of "Mens Debts," Prince of Wales Fort account book, 1759–60. Every year the factory clerk compiled each man's purchases from the Company store (probably recorded in rough daybooks) and entered them in the account book, where the men signed or made their mark to verify that the clerk's list was correct. [HBCA, B. 42/d/40, fols. 5d–6]

subsist entirely on agriculture removed them from that potential labour supply for the long term, perhaps even permanently. Furthermore, former Bay men could outbid local farmers for rents (which presumably caused some jealousy and conflict), and this could lead to inflation and the over-renting of land. However, the Orkney land market had been quite active before the HBC started recruiting there; this, along with chances for even humble farmers to engage in some sort of general trade, created a greater degree of social mobility than was present in northern Scotland or the Hebrides at the time.[29] Thus, HBC service did not necessarily create new opportunities at home but rather enabled men to take better advantage of existing opportunities.

Land hunger may indeed have been a primary force driving young men out of Orkney into the HBC or other non-local employments.[30] If so, then HBC service may have seemed less attractive in the early decades of the eighteenth century because Orkney was slow to recover from the famines of the 1690s, and much land lay uncultivated. More people, however, were renting than owning land during this period: between 1660 and 1750 the number of small owner-occupiers decreased from 776 to 245. Those who owned odal-land (land held in unwritten freehold) were particularly vulnerable because the odal system of tenure came under increasing attack from Scottish lawyers and because the tradition of dividing property among all children led to intense fragmentation. Norse law had placed various restrictions on odal-land to keep it within families and to counteract these dispersive tendencies, but Scotland abolished Norse law in the northern islands in 1611, and it had probably ceased to be effective well before then.[31]

Insufficient evidence exists for as detailed an examination of the demographics of early Orkney recruitment as that undertaken by John Nicks for the late eighteenth and early nineteenth centuries, but some of his statistics suggest older patterns. Nicks's figures for 1788 showed three-quarters of Orcadian servants coming from the parish of Stromness and adjoining parishes in the western portion of Mainland (the largest island), a local concentration that later decreased. Such geographical concentration makes sense because Stromness was the Orkney port of call for company ships, as well as one of only two sizable towns on the islands (Kirkwall was the other). The decrease in this concentration suggested to Nicks either "a gradual depletion of the traditional labour pool or the expansion of interest in employment with the company—probably both."[32] Since recruitment in the Orkneys had been fairly consistent since the 1720s, the depletion of the labour pool in and around Stromness may seem the stronger argument, but the increasingly diverse parish origins of Orkneymen appear to have coincided with the period of competition and expansion after 1782, when the company's labour force was expanding more rapidly than ever before; the expansion of interest in company service would have been at least partially the result of more intensive recruitment.

Nicks's figures for recruitment levels as a percentage of population indicated to him that employment opportunities on the Bay "held a greater attraction to rural residents than to urban dwellers."[33] In an Orkney context, however, *urban* and *rural* were relative terms. Kirkwall's population had peaked at around 3,000 in 1661, but that fell sharply during the devastating famines of the 1690s. There were only thirteen houses in Stromness in 1670, and although the village expanded greatly with the growth of transatlantic trade in the eighteenth century, its population only temporarily surpassed Kirkwall's. Much of the booming trade of eighteenth-century Orkney bypassed Kirkwall; by 1742 Stromness merchants were legally challenging Kirkwall's economic dominance of Orkney, a struggle they eventually won in 1758.[34] Outside of those two towns on Mainland, however, the Orkneys were an archipelago of dispersed farms and houses, with only small and loose clusters of people and services at crossroads and other strategic points; even churches tended to stand by themselves in the countryside. The third largest trading centre in Orkney during the seventeenth and eighteenth centuries was at St. Margaret's Hope on the north coast of South Ronaldsay: there were three merchants living there in 1682, but in 1695 the total population of that settlement and neighbouring Ronaldsvoe was only twenty-three families.[35]

The specific mechanisms of recruitment in the Orkneys are no more clearly understood than they are in London. The time frame was more compact, as the ships had little time to spare if they were going to make it to the Bay and back before winter: Captain Michael Grimington Jr was instructed to "get what men you can" in the Orkneys in 1708, but he was not to stay there more than forty-eight hours "on any pretence whatsoever."[36] The fact that Stromness was the last port of call on the way to the Bay gave the captains of the company's ships a larger role in hiring men than they probably had in earlier periods. Ship captains had acted as recruiters before the 1730s, but their role is better documented after that date; for instance, some servants' accounts (which before the 1720s are less easily reconstructed in their entirety) mention cash advanced to them by ship captains upon engagement. Bayside officers returning from a season in England could also serve as recruiters on the outward voyage, as Thomas McCliesh Jr did in 1735, when he was paid £12 12s. 0d. "to Entert[ai]n Servants" and was reimbursed for cash that he had advanced them "at Orkneys."[37]

John Nicks suggested some possible methods of local recruitment in the late eighteenth and early nineteenth centuries, which may be applicable to earlier periods. Finding that company recruits from the parish of Orphir came mostly from the townships closest to the church and the parish school, he hypothesized an important role for the minister, and possibly the schoolmaster.[38] Schoolmasters would not have played a significant role in earlier recruitment, as very few schools existed outside Kirkwall before the nineteenth century.[39] Such geographic concentration as Nicks observed cannot be traced for earlier periods, but if it did exist, it could have been associated with other factors, such as the mobility of individuals, the distribution of occupational groups, or even rates of literacy.

Nicks also observed a tendency of a limited number of families to monopolize available positions.[40] Apparent geographic concentration of recruitment may have been related to extended-familial residence patterns. There is some evidence for this before 1780, though many examples only represent possible family connections, such as the large number of Isbisters serving in Hudson Bay through the eighteenth century. Some recruits had family connections through marriage. Two Irvins (Irvines, Ervins, Irwins) served in James Bay around mid-century—Robert Irvin was a mariner at Albany in the early 1750s, and John Ervin served at Moose in the early 1760s—and three labourers serving at Moose between 1756 and 1769 (John Ward, George Sinclair, and Thomas Halcro) were married to Isobel (Isabella) Ervin (Irvine), Jennett Irvin (Irwin), and Isabel Irwin, respectively.[41] Unfortunately the patchy survival of many eighteenth-century Orkney parish records presents a formidable obstacle to the tracing of family connections. Even relationships that appear straightforward at first glance prove unclear, as in the case of Peter Isbester Sr and Peter Isbester Jr, who both engaged as labourers in 1735. To the modern ear, *senior* and *junior* imply a father-son relationship, but the terms specify only that one is older than the other; for example, Thomas McCliesh Sr was the uncle of Thomas McCliesh Jr.[42]

Recruiting for Rebuilding: Londoners, "Stockton Clowns," and Slaves

Although the northern parts of the British Isles became a greater source of recruitment in the eighteenth century, they were never an exclusive labour pool for the company. The surviving correspondence suggests that hiring Orkneymen never quite lost its ad hoc flavour, a last resort when recruiting in England fell short. Writing to Moses Norton at Prince of Wales Fort in 1767, the Committee assured him that "if We can possibly procure a Brick layer We will send You one this Year, otherwise We shall direct Captain Richards to engage such a person in his Voyage Outwards."[43]

Many men were still hired in and around London, which continued to serve as a catchment basin for labour throughout Britain (especially southern England). Chief factor Joseph Myatt's complaints about unruly Londoners at Albany in 1727 echoed some of John Nixon's concerns from forty-five years earlier:

> *Some of the Servants now think it the greatest Mortification in the World by Reason I Endavour to Keep them as Sober as I can, & in short ye Londoners are so well Acquainted with the Ways and Debaucheries of the Town yt I Even Despaire Ever of Reclaiming them, for there is not one Labouring man yt Came Over the Last Year, but what are Sotts to a man, but However So Long as your Honrs take care that no Person brings Large Quantities of Brandy in the Country, I can manage them well Enough for they Can goe to no Other Shop.*[44]

Myatt was particularly sensitive to alcohol-related personnel problems because three of the four men who died at Albany during the 1725–26 season had been hastened to their graves by excessive drinking—"John Henson in Perticular, by the Little time he Lay Ill, Complained his Bowels was burned within him."[45] However, there was apparently at least some truth in Myatt's charges: one of the 1726 recruits, labourer John Murrell, had venereal disease and was sent home in 1727.[46]

Specialized work sometimes required more specialized workers than Orkney could provide. Richard Norton at Prince of Wales Fort in 1732 requested (and in due course received) "four masons that is brought up to rough laying which must be had in the country, particular near Oxford. The masons that is here are brought up to mallet and tool [i.e., more ornamental work], so are altogether strangers to the aforesaid rough laying." The one exception was John Tutty, "who is well aversed in a quarry and our sort of masonry work, he having had a great deal of experience therein and is very sufficient to supply the place of Mr Keyly."[47] To Norton's delight, his employers accepted his recommendation and procured "with some difficulty...four Masons who are all of them Extraordinary good workmen and are Capable of doing such Rough Work as You require as well as other kind of Masonry."[48] The work at Churchill also required the specialized services of a surveyor (the truculent mason Joseph Robson served in this capacity in the 1730s), as did the inland expansion of the 1770s and beyond. Englishman Philip Turnor was engaged as the company's first full-time surveyor in 1778; he was recommended by astronomer William Wales, and the value of Turnor's skills at that juncture was graphically illustrated by the five guineas' worth (£5 5s. 0d.) of books with which Wales was rewarded.[49]

Of course, the HBC was just one among many employment opportunities for tradesmen. After a spate of fires in London in 1715 and 1716, there was such "very great Imploymt" for house carpenters that the Committee was unable to persuade even two of them to sail for Hudson Bay at any price.[50] Even former servants could not always be lured back. After Albany armourer Thomas Toillier had frozen to death on 13 January 1729,

Joseph Myatt requested a replacement: "I am Tould that Mr [Meshaik] Rattonbury, who was at York Fort [1714–22], is a very Good Workman If you Aprove of him, I Should not Desire a better." However, the Committee reported that "Rattonbury" (Rattenbury) "is very Infirm and not fit for our Service, but have Sent in his Stead an Armourer [John Hancock] of whom we have a very good Character."[51]

The Inuit or Chipewyan captives of Lowland Cree war parties, occasionally purchased by or given to Bayside factors as slaves, could also be considered specialized labour. Although the factors generally portrayed the selling of such captives as the result of Indigenous entrepreneurship or greed, and their own purchasing of such captives as motivated by compassion, it is also possible that the Lowland Cree gave captives as gifts to strengthen their alliance with the English traders.[52] Sloop masters in charge of trading voyages to the Churchill River and farther north were often accompanied by Inuit boys placed in their care for one or two years to facilitate trade relations, but these boys were only temporary wards of the company and not slaves. The company wanted such boys to learn English and something of European trading customs so that they could act as linguistic and cultural interpreters after they returned to their communities. Inuit motives were probably similar, hoping that the boys would bring back useful information on English language, customs, and technology.[53]

Slaves purchased by the HBC generally appear to have been young, and most were probably intended for general work. In the 1693–94 season James Knight at Albany traded a gun, a blanket, a kettle, one pound of tobacco, and a woman's shroud [stroud?] for an Inuit "slave boy for the use of ye factory."[54] However, some were valued for their linguistic skills and/or local knowledge. Jack "Eskemay" may have been purchased by Joseph Adams as early as 1736, and worked at Albany and Eastmain until 1746; he received neither wages nor an occupational label, but the company paid for goods he took up at the factory.[55] Trolio, an Inuit man, served at Moose from 1757 until his death by drowning in 1780; he appears to have been a labourer or general hand, but in the summer of 1779 he was in

Top: Shipwright Robert Smith only served the HBC for three years (1774–77), but it was long enough for him to make his mark at Sloop's Cove near Prince of Wales Fort [Courtesy of Parks Canada]. Bottom: William Story was an early shipwright who spent some time working on the sloop at Sloop's Cove: he served a three-year contract (1757–60) and then returned to England [Courtesy of Parks Canada].

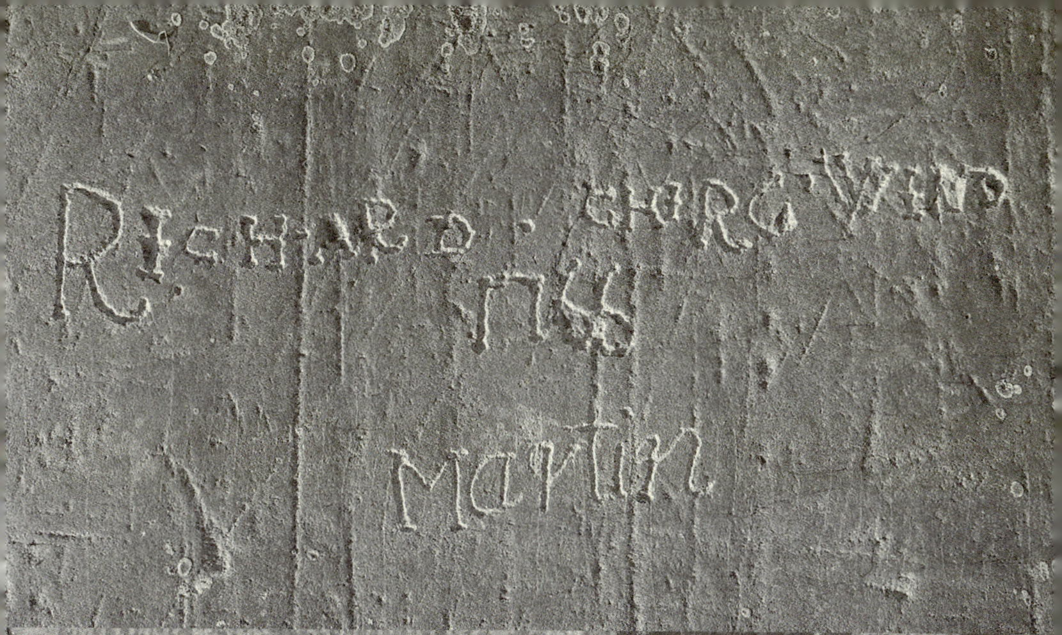

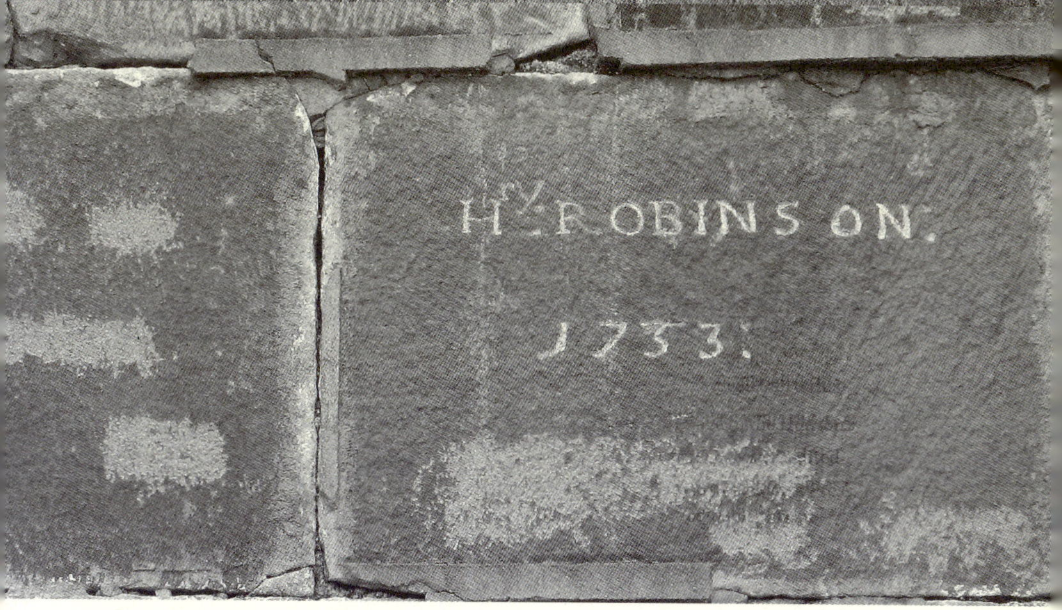

Top: When sailor Richard Chirgwind was not decorating the rocks at Sloop's Cove, he was purchasing large amounts of goods at the Prince of Wales Fort store: the 47 pounds of sugar he purchased in 1766–67 suggests either a remarkably sweet tooth or some private trading with First Nations or his factory mates [Courtesy of Parks Canada]. *Bottom: Henry Robinson signed his name on the outer wall of Prince of Wales Fort in 1753, just beside the front gate. To the left, a later* HBC *employee had signed his name in the early twentieth century, but it was subsequently erased* [Author photo].

charge of Moose's upriver outpost, Wapiscogamy House.[56] At Richmond in the 1750s the following may have been Inuit "slaves," as well: the "Duke of Richmond" (1752–59); "ye Boy Hector," later Hector Northumberland (1752–58); Caesar Northumberland (1757–58); and Dolly Northumberland (1757–59).[57]

While Inuit and Chipewyan captives were purchased by Bayside factors or sloop masters, and ship captains engaged men in the Orkneys, the Committee continued to recruit men in the London area as it had from the beginning. In fact, despite the company's expanding operations in the seventy years after Utrecht, continuity is more evident than change in its methods of finding servants. Even when men were being engaged outside London, the Committee attempted to control the process as much as possible. That they were not necessarily able to do so can be judged from their regular requests for lists of who was serving in the factories and when their contracts expired. There were also occasional surprises, such as Richard Crocket's 1717 letter from Albany informing the Committee that he had been engaged by Thomas McCliesh Jr; McCliesh had not mentioned him, however, forcing the directors to ask who he was and how much he was being paid.[58]

In 1765 the company's secretary wrote to former HBC sloop master Thomas Law, now agent for London businessman Chauncy Townsend, requesting Townsend's recommendation of "Some Artificers and Labourers" in Yorkshire (where he had business interests) for service in Hudson Bay. The occupations required and the wages and other terms of employment to be offered were strictly specified, as they were in similar letters to former Albany surgeon William Richards (in Glamorganshire, Wales) and Albany's former chief Robert Temple (in Sussex) in the same year.[59] Temple (though not Richards) was ordered not to engage anyone without consulting the London secretary.

The 1765 correspondence with Temple, Richards, and Law offers a unique snapshot of HBC recruitment: three men of different backgrounds were being asked to recruit in different parts of Britain at the same time. Richards was initially instructed to procure a house carpenter, a sawyer, a smith, a bricklayer, and seven labourers at specified wages (or lower wages, if possible). A month later he had procured six men (at least one of whom was a house carpenter) and was requested to find another thirteen. At the same time Temple was to find five tradesmen and three labourers, and Thomas Law was to obtain Townsend's recommendation for six tradesmen and seven labourers.

Relying on former servants to recruit new servants was sensible, as their knowledge of living and working conditions by the Bay would presumably have allowed them to select prospective young men best suited for the service. However, this was the only reference to Richards's particular knowledge of Bayside conditions: "As You are well acquainted with Hudsons Bay, You will inform the Persons You treat with, of their being supplied with Provisions of all kinds over and above their Wages."[60] The letters to Law and Temple made no reference to their previous service or experience.

They were not the only former officers active in this regard. In the late 1760s and early 1770s Henry Pollexfen Jr (formerly chief at Moose) was living in Kirkwall (Orkney), acting as an agent for several current and former servants. He also recommended prospective servants to the Committee. However, Pollexfen's activities seem to have been based on his own initiative rather than on orders from London.[61]

Of the thirty-seven surviving contracts signed in 1776 through 1779—the earliest in the HBC Archives—sixteen recruits came from London and its environs, three from adjacent counties, seven from the northeast of England (Durham and Yorkshire), three from Orkney, four from Suffolk, two from Scotland, and one from Portsmouth. However, only two of these thirty-seven contracts were for men engaging as labourers. Eleven of the thirty-seven men did not make the voyage to Hudson Bay, and an interesting pattern emerges in these cases: on three occasions, a pair of men of the same occupation and from the same parish (two labourers from Suffolk, two carpenters from St. Paul Shadwell in London, and two coopers from Limehouse) signed up together, accepted their advance money, and then absconded together.[62]

New recruits always received advances on their wages, usually two months' pay. These cash advances went by a variety of names over the years; "impress money" was probably the most common, though initially it seemed to be reserved for sailors. They sometimes took non-monetary forms, as in 1723 when John Churchill and John Helleker engaged as labourers and were advanced one-half of their yearly salaries (three pounds each) in clothes. The practice was generally more common at sea than on land, but craftsmen in England often received a small sum, or "God's-penny," to seal the bargain when they agreed to do a particular job.[63]

Men signed their contracts in London whenever possible, allowing the Committee to handle the disbursement of advance money as well as the negotiation of wages. The 1765 letter to Robert Temple mentioned an allowance of one guinea (twenty-one shillings) for recruits' travelling expenses to London, "but no Money is to be paid Them in part thereof until they have Signed their Contracts in London, where They are to arrive by the first of May." Not only was Temple not authorized to advance any cash, but he was not even to offer anyone employment without first consulting London.[64] The letter to William Richards also mentioned men signing contracts in London, at which point they would be paid their travel allowance.[65] Unlike Temple, Richards was allowed to offer employment without prior consultation, and a second letter stated: "The Committee consents to your paying each Person half a Guinea upon his Signing a Contract (which will be sent you...) and the remaining Half Guinea will be paid them on their arrival [in London]."[66] Ship captains recruiting in Orkney did not face the same restrictions, because Stromness was their last stop before Hudson Bay, and so sending prospective recruits to London first was impossible. However, the Committee sometimes limited captains' power when it could. In 1735, for instance, it ordered Captain William Coats to engage thirteen labourers at Orkney (he only found twelve), but the money for advances and other (unspecified) disbursements was entrusted to Thomas McCliesh Jr (returning to Albany as governor).[67]

As in earlier periods some prospective servants were proactive and communicated their desire for employment directly to the Committee or its secretary. In 1755, for instance, John Stephenson Sr wrote from Stockton (Durham), inquiring about the terms offered to the company's sloop masters. The company's secretary informed him that forty pounds per annum was usual, plus ten pounds per annum for a servant, "[o]n which terms the Committee will at your Request, Appoint you Master of their new Sloop now Building for three Years from your Arrival at the Factory Appointed, if you Agree thereto, Please send an Answer by the return of the Post." Stephenson agreed to the terms and commanded the Albany sloop from 1757 to 1763, with John Stephenson Jr as his servant.[68] In the late 1750s and early 1760s John Garbut (probably from Yorkshire), William Lockey (parish unknown), and Consett Wilson (from Stokesley, near North Allerton, Yorkshire) also entered the service as sloop mates or sloop masters in this way.[69]

This highlights a preponderance of northeasterners on the Bayside sloops at the time, partly due to recruitment by Captain William Coats in Yorkshire, Northumberland, and his native Durham. In 1741 James Duffield at Moose observed that the entire crew of the factory's sloop had been recruited by Coats, and complained that soon all of the factories would be manned by Coats's "Stockton Clowns."[70] Coats had commanded HBC supply ships since 1727, regularly sailing up the east coast of England on his outward voyage; he could also have hired Tynesiders and Teessiders in the Orkneys, as there was a fairly regular commerce between Stromness and Newcastle. Alternatively, Duffield may have meant that only Coats, and not all of his men, were from Stockton: Augustine Frost appears to have benefited from Coats's patronage, but there is no evidence that Frost was from that region. The company's maritime service attracted men from northeast England even after Coats's death in 1752. Seven of the thirty-seven surviving contracts signed in 1776 through 1779 engaged men from that region, including four from Stockton itself: mariner William Renton, harpooner Robert Robinson, and shipwrights Matthew Colling and John Claxton.[71]

Applications by post help diversify our understanding of Bayside servants' geographical origins. Men from the London area could apply to the Committee in person, while men in Orkney could apply directly to the ship's captain or an outgoing officer without any part of the application process appearing in writing. Men close to neither London nor Orkney were most likely to apply by letter, making their applications more likely to appear in the correspondence books, but those are clearly incomplete prior to the 1750s and possibly even after.

Recruiting for Competition

The menace of French competition had not disappeared with Utrecht; it had merely moved into the interior. French traders had established themselves several days upriver from Albany and kept the men of that factory on edge with occasional threats of violence.[72] From the 1730s through the 1750s the westward expansion of the Montreal-based traders seriously damaged the trade of Albany, Moose, and eventually York. As the HBC sought new responses to its old foes, it seemed to call for new kinds of servants.

In many English trading factories, traders' sons by local women often joined their fathers in their business enterprises during the seventeenth century,[73] but the possibility of hiring sons of HBC fathers and Indigenous mothers was not openly discussed until the 1750s. In 1755 James Isham reported:

> *Robt Inksiter son of Robert Inksiter taylor (formerly in your Honrs Service) Growing a Lusty Lad is Willing to be Apprentice to Your Honrs for 7 Years; He was Christned I understand in Mr Whites time, have took him in for ye present, but Referr his desire till further Orders from Your Honrs.*[74]

The Committee appears to have ignored Inkster's offer. Humphrey Marten, in successfully petitioning for his half-Cree son, John America Marten, to be allowed to go to England for an education, suggested in 1770 that "the Time may not be very farr off when Americans Born with English education may prove very usefull to the Company."[75] Earlier men (such as Joseph Waggoner and George Potts) had fur-trade fathers and may have had Indigenous mothers, but Jennifer S.H. Brown cited James Isham's son, Charles Price Isham, as "the first certain case of a native-born company son achieving a fur trade career of any note." He was apprenticed to the HBC in 1766 after receiving some education in England and was later considered one of the company's best canoemen.[76]

Around the same time, Canadiens entered the company's service, apparently for the first time since the late seventeenth century. Jean Baptiste "de Larlee" (D'Laryea), formerly master of the French house at Basquiea (The Pas), arrived at York in the early summer of 1759, seeking employment.[77] Humphrey Marten (temporarily in charge at York) sent him with Anthony Henday and Joseph Smith to winter on the northern plains, and in 1760 he sent D'Laryea to Albany. There he asked to be engaged at 1,200 livres per annum (about fifty pounds) and "promised to be greatly serviceable," but was instead taken on trial, "having no Appointment nor Salary" but "to be rewarded according to Merit."[78] Although D'Laryea appeared to win the friendship of Albany chief Robert Temple and was given some responsibility for conducting trade, his allegedly harsh treatment of the Upland Cree caused the trade at that fort to decline, and he was dismissed in 1762 with one hundred pounds for his two years of service.[79] Germain Maugenest, engaged in 1780, proved a disappointment too, although some of his advice was taken on board by the Committee.[80]

Not all Canadiens who offered their services were accepted. One unnamed Canadien deserted Peter Pangman's service in 1776 and twice sought employment with the HBC at Cumberland House; he was turned away by William Tomison in the autumn of 1776 and by Matthew Cocking in February 1777, although Cocking offered to trade for any good canoe he might bring.[81] Cocking in 1776 and Robert Longmoor in 1777 both suggested recruiting Canadiens as canoemen, but the Committee felt that such men were unreliable. Complaints of Canadien infidelity were probably influenced by the company's experience with Louis Primeau. A Quebec-born trader who had come west as early as 1749, Primeau had remained in the interior after the fall of New France and was engaged at

York for inland service in 1765; he deserted to the new Montreal-based merchants in 1773. Primeau's desertion seems to have been motivated by a personal desire or need to return to Quebec, but Cocking (a friend of Primeau's) had earlier observed that Primeau "hath a secret kindness for his old Masters." Perhaps on the basis of this episode, Cocking expressed a general fear that Canadiens could prove "very improper Persons, for they would be continually running off to the Pedlers and laying open all they know."[82] The Committee shared his anxiety, and warned Ferdinand Jacobs not to place too much trust in Canadien deserters offering their services, "lest it should appear that their Designs in applying to the Chiefs of Our Factories arise only from Measures concerted by the Original Employers to the Companys prejudice."[83]

Similar suspicions were laid on any man who switched sides. Englishman Isaac Batt entered the service in 1754 and became one of the HBC's most reliable and influential inland winterers in the 1760s. He deserted to Joseph Frobisher's service in 1775 but returned to HBC employ two years later. Beside the Cumberland House journal entry that mentioned this was a marginal comment in a contemporary but different hand (perhaps the London secretary's) wondering if Frobisher had allowed Batt to re-engage with the HBC "with a view to benefit himself by his information of our affairs whenever He shall again entice Isaac Batt into his service."[84] Batt gave the HBC good service both before and after the period in Frobisher's employ, and several company officers thought highly of him and had exerted themselves to lure him back. Nevertheless, doubts about Batt's loyalty remained and limited his opportunities for advancement after his return.[85]

Andrew Graham declared that the Canadiens "are chosen Men inured to hardships and fatigue, under which most of your present Servants would sink."[86] Cocking agreed with the Committee that most Canadien *voyageurs* were unfit for HBC service, but blamed their bad characters on the pedlars' habit of hiring reckless and improvident men who could be relied on to spend all or most of their wages in their master's store; he suggested recruiting a few specialized men (particularly canoe builders) from among those voyageurs who had fallen afoul of the pedlars for not spending enough.[87] However, there were other arguments against recruiting in Canada, particularly the problem of getting men from Montreal to Hudson Bay.

There is some evidence that in 1770 the Committee considered establishing an agency in Quebec, or even using Quebec as a starting point for trading expeditions. The scheme appears to have been proposed by former Albany factor Joseph Isbister, who had emigrated to Quebec City in 1760 and was leasing the trading post of Mingan. No details have survived, but the scheme (whatever it was) came to nothing, partly because Isbister died in October 1771.[88] By the 1780s recruiting Canadiens was no longer suggested, partly because the company's British-born servants were improving their skills with canoes.

One of the potential appeals of mixed-blood or Canadien servants was their "wilderness" skill, particularly the construction and use of birchbark canoes. On the Bay, sloops could ferry goods and personnel between factories or between the factory and the supply ship, but any settlement as far upriver as Henley or Cumberland was out of reach of the sloops. The French inland traders had adopted birchbark canoes from their Indigenous trading partners, but Captain Christopher Middleton reported in the 1740s that only five of the more than one hundred HBC men could effectively handle a canoe.[89] Although the men of James Bay had some familiarity with canoes, the canoe birch (*Betula papyrifera*) does not grow as far north as York Fort or Prince of Wales Fort; men serving there would only have seen canoes brought by upland traders, who needed their craft for the return journey.[90]

Samuel Hearne told the Committee in 1775 that there was no point in sending the large numbers of men obviously needed to contest with the pedlars for the trade of the interior until problems of supply and transport had been resolved. At Hearne's suggestion, in 1777 the Committee sent out some light timber skiffs. However, the inland servants refused to use them, arguing that there were insufficient men to operate them and that there was no shipwright inland to repair them.[91] In 1780 and 1781 chief factor

Humphrey Marten and clerk James Elphinstone both suggested assigning an Orkney boat builder to Cumberland House, where he could build boats with a much greater carrying capacity than birchbark canoes, but Marten maintained that no less than one hundred men were needed inland to support the increased trade and transport.[92] The company's inland servants, their wilderness skills, and their knowledge of Cree and other Indigenous languages were going to be vital to the success of any inland expansion. In 1780, after inland surveyor Philip Turnor had warned that York's inland settlements were short of officers, Humphrey Marten sent George Hudson and James Elphinstone inland in order "to raise a succession of officers capable of transacting your [Honours'] Inland Affairs."[93]

The difficulties faced in finding sufficient and suitable men for service in Hudson Bay became particularly acute in the late 1770s and early 1780s. The HBC was developing an inland system of transport and supply but (as Marten had warned) lacked the manpower to operate it effectively; in 1780 Marten wrote to the Committee, "Men we want Sirs, Furrs You want Gentlemen, should you please to send us the former We are confident of returning the latter."[94] Shortfalls in European labour could be partly made up by the engagement of First Nations men on a casual or seasonal basis, but this did not always prove satisfactory. That spring William Tomison complained that he had insufficient hands to bring down all the returns from Cumberland and Hudson Houses and that he was too reliant on Indigenous canoemen to bring down what furs he could: "[W]hat Indians do Consent to go down, I am under the greatest obligations immaginable by being obliged to give them what they ask for," he wrote to Marten and lamented "their Honours neglect of not sending men to do the Business."[95]

"Their Honours" chafed at Tomison's criticism. Wartime conditions had prevailed for most of the period since 1739 but had been particularly acute during the Seven Years' War (1756–63) and the American War of Independence (1775–83); the Royal Navy expanded from around 16,000 men in 1775 to almost 100,000 in 1781.[96] As in earlier years, this made "men to do the Business" hard to find and drove up wages at home and abroad, shifting the balance of power toward the company's prospective servants in contract negotiations. In 1762, late in the Seven Years' War, the Committee informed John Favell at Moose, "The scarcity of Armourers and Bricklayers is at this time so exceeding great that notwithstanding our utmost Efforts we have not been able to get either." They instructed Favell to persuade John Fleming to re-engage, with a raise or a promise of a gratuity if necessary, but "[y]ou must treat with him as from your self least he endeavour to make an Advantage of our Distress if he previously know our Wants."[97]

Factors were sometimes asked to share tradesmen, who were especially hard to come by. In 1764 the Committee instructed Moses Norton at Prince of Wales Fort, when repairs to the fort were complete, to

> *send Your Masons, or one of them at least, to York Fort or any Other of Our Factories that are out of repair, as it is so extremely difficult for us to procure Tradesmen of that sort at home. And We shall be very ready to make them a reasonable Gratuity in proportion as they shall exert themselves for Our Service.*[98]

The demands of expansion prompted a more systematic approach toward apprenticeship. Between 1766 and 1799, eleven boys were indentured from the Grey Coat Hospital (known for its mathematical school) in London, England, and seven of them were put into the land service as clerks or writers: George Charles, John Charles, George Donald, Joseph Hansom, John Hodgson, George Hudson, and David Thompson.[99] Although the company had been taking apprentices since the 1670s, the Grey Coat boys represented a more focused approach to apprenticeship than had been common in the preceding century: they had specific sets of skills that were meant to fill specific roles within the company. These boys received navigational and cartographical training, with a view to naval or maritime employment,[100] and their map-making and journal-keeping skills were expected to compensate for the perceived deficiencies of early inland winterers like Anthony Henday, Joseph Smith, and William Pink. The new "system" was not a training system, for the company sought boys

William Coats's 1749 chart of Artiwinipeck (Richmond Gulf) includes an elegy to "the amazing beauty and grandour of the place those asstonishing Mountains which border ye sound are so adorned with such beautiful verdour in such decorum and order"—two characteristics often encouraged among the company's servants as well. [HBCA, G. 1/18]

who could already read, write, and (hopefully) cast accounts—and were cheaper than adult clerks. As the company's workforce grew in the nineteenth century, apprentices became a more prominent focus of attention within that workforce, but only the beginnings of a new approach can be seen prior to 1786.

|| Both the company's operations and its labour needs had expanded and diversified considerably since 1714. In turn, sources of recruitment became more diverse, but generally the company (as it always had) simply

sought fit young men who were willing to work for particular wages. Although more systematic methods of recruitment seemed to be called for, there was no great change in the Committee's approaches to personnel issues and no emergence of recognizable policies. The Bayside factors and the masters of inland houses in 1786—trying their best to compete with Canadien traders in spite of insufficient men and supplies, and trying to build a workable inland transport system—probably would have agreed with John Nixon's complaint a century earlier that "there hath been no certain method for any thing."[101]

5 "Diligent Men" and "Idle Fellowes"

Evaluation and Retention of Personnel

[I]t shall be allwayes my care to incourrage those that are willing and able to doe yowr Honors service, let them be in whatsowever capacity...[but] there will be allways troublesome or unprofitable persons in the world, and it falls out that yow must mentaine your share of them.

—JOHN NIXON, "Report to the Governor and Committee by John Nixon, 1682," 256

SURVIVING DOCUMENTS shed at best a partial light on HBC recruitment during this period. Much of the process of engaging new servants took place beyond the purview of official documents; neither Committee minutes nor account books cared a great deal about how a man entered the service. Once he was in the service, however, some kind of evaluation was necessary, not only to judge the wisdom of the initial investment in his wages and board but also to judge whether he should be offered subsequent employment and a raise.

Factors and (to a lesser degree) the Committee frequently expressed the need to retain useful old hands to compensate for a lack of sufficient or suitable recruits, but how did they determine who was worth keeping?

These decisions were the factors' prerogative within broad guidelines. The Committee told George Geyer in 1688:

> *[I]n Generall as to men that are to Come home Wee must leave it to you, whoe can best Judge there whoe are usefull Diligent men for us, and whoe are Drones uselesse and Idle fellowes, Send home if any bee ingenious honest and Diligent, you must retaine them by faire meanes and according to their Deserts, till Wee can better Supply their places.*[1]

This set the tone for the following decades, in which the factors were generally asked to provide details of a man's character only when he left the service or (less often) when he wished to sign a new contract; seldom did the Committee inquire into a servant's skills or performance, and only from about 1730 onwards did it request regular reports on the character of all servants. Factors had a kind of standing order to send home those who "by Illness Accid[en]t or Misbehaviour [are] Render'd unfit to be Continued longer in our Service," but most men were recalled without comment when they or the Committee chose not to renew their contracts for whatever reason.[2]

The Committee in London had little more than the annual correspondence and word of mouth on which to evaluate personnel in the Bay. Incomplete information sometimes prompted the Committee to delegate to Bayside factors the authority to negotiate wages with men seeking to re-engage, a prerogative that it usually reserved for itself. In 1691, for instance, the Committee gave the council at Port Nelson permission to negotiate a new contract with John Bennett:

> *[B]ecause you can best Judge what hee is most capable of & the oppertunities that there will be to preferre him, Wee doe Leave it to you to dispose of him to his Content in our Service & to make such new agreement with him as you shall thinke reasonable or otherwise to referre himselfe to Our Favour & Pleasure if he thinks fitt.*[3]

At other times, though, incomplete information elicited frustration and impatience, as in 1737 when the Committee chastised Joseph Adams for sending them merely a list of names, "but neither their several Wages... [nor] when time out, nor Character...although You have rece'd repeated orders so to do."[4]

The adjectives used by the Committee to describe desirable (or undesirable) personnel were taken from the language of contemporary households in Britain and were not specific to the fur trade. Bayside factors drew from much the same vocabulary, partly because they were responding to their employers' expectations and partly because they had similar ideas of what a master should expect from his servants. When Robert Temple denied responsibility for the "Extravagance" of servants' wages at Albany in 1763, he assured the Committee that his men did not "Eat the Bread of Idleness." The general emphasis was on usefulness: industriousness was a moral quality that gave the individual dignity and social acceptance. Idleness, or wasting one's employment time, was sometimes characterized in early modern England as an act of robbery.[5]

The earliest data on the evaluation and retention of personnel emerges from the tense and tenuous years in which the HBC and the Compagnie du Nord shared the Bay—a period during which the HBC usually controlled only one factory. The English company was more concerned with retaining old personnel than with recruiting new men, despite the higher wages they commanded. Given the difficulties and expenses of wartime recruiting, it seemed more expedient to re-engage the devils they knew.

"Of Double Assistance in This Hazardous Juncture"

Men with some experience of Hudson Bay were valuable assets, particularly during times of war when danger always seemed to lurk just beyond the horizon. The French attacks in the 1680s interrupted many men's contracts, and most who were carried away from Hudson Bay as prisoners of war chose not to return—some never even made it back to Britain. In 1691 the Committee observed that "wee have need of an encrease of

Faithfull & Experienced Servants, & of Double assistance in this hazardous Juncture."[6] Anthony Beale in 1712 described the men who had chosen to stay in the Bay as "persons which are very Serviceable in your Countrey and Persons whom I Could not well be without."[7]

The Committee instructed John Fullartine to encourage "the most Industrious & Carefull," but utility was usually expressed in vague or general terms. Fullartine in 1701 referred simply to "some of the best hands," while Beale in 1706 tried to re-engage "most of the best men."[8] Praise for servants often referred to their moral characteristics as much as to their competence or occupation; the primary characteristics of utility were diligence, ingenuity, honesty, and (especially in wartime) courage. In 1688, for instance, the Committee described Thomas Savage as "a Stout & an honest fellow," James Bay governor John Marsh as "a Worthy person," and Captain James Young (master of the *Dering*) as "a man whome Wee believe you will finde Stout & Couragious and very usefull to you on any Occation." In other letters that year the Committee told Marsh and Thomas Walsh (master at Severn River) that they expected "proofes of your prudence fidelity & Courage."[9] Marsh's successor, James Knight, was described to Geyer in 1692 as honest, discrete, and prudent; in a letter to Knight himself the Committee claimed that it had selected him for his integrity, courage, prudence, and "Continuall faithfullness...to the [Company's] welfare & interest."[10]

Moralist William Fleetwood declared in a 1705 sermon that servants "are to be every way as useful to them [their Masters] as possible, this is the end and intention of all Masters, in entertaining Servants." He remarked that "Masters will bear with many defects of Skill and Diligence, where they are sure the Servants are exactly just and honest," adding that honest men were trusted more than skilful or insightful men.[11] Thus, general usefulness was often more valued than specific skills; the Committee told Henry Kelsey in 1710 that "wee Expect from you noe more then Dilligence & Industry to get A Trade & defend the factory to your power."[12] This would have been especially true for labourers; relatively few of them could offer a specific skill as evidence of their value to the company.

A man unwilling to be useful was more to be censured than a man unable to be useful. In 1693 the Committee instructed George Geyer:

> *[I]f any [servants are] Quarrilous or Unruly given to Faction or the like above all returne them home, tho never soe good hands for we will not Indure any factions or Grumbling p[er]sons there; Apprehending the evill Consequences that may happen by Discord & Divisions amongst you & know likewise the good frut of a good harmony & Concord.*[13]

Adding to one's inventory of skills was praised, for it allowed a man to be useful in more ways than before. The Committee applauded York's warehouse keeper, Samuel Missenden, in 1686 for trying to learn the Lowland Cree language, "whereby you will render your selfe the more capable to serve us & we upon all occasions shall be mindfull of the merits of such Persons."[14] In 1703 Fullartine reported that Samuel Goodale (his "affairs calling him home" early) had taught tailor James Norcutt how to keep the account books; Fullartine described Norcutt as "a very honest man" who "would not have Staid under ye Same wages he has now, but as it falls out it will be so much money Sav'd for I could not have been without him & now he can serve me in a double Capasity."[15]

The Committee particularly valued experienced factors in times of trouble. In 1691 it urged George Geyer to stay on at Port Nelson: "in a time of Warre & distraction Wee have Cause to feare what Effects an Innovation & Change of Government may have amongst our Owne Servants, whilst a continuance of the same in such a Juncture is allwaies most safe & prudent."[16] Continuity in government was one way that officers could set a good example for the common men—although the Committee was perhaps overly optimistic in 1693 when it declared that French competition could be undermined "by nothing more then giveing our peple due Encoragement & shewing good Example to them by theire superiours & Comanders."[17] John Fullartine felt pressured to remain longer than he wanted. In 1702 and 1703 he was "Sadly tortur'd with ye Gravel and Stone in my Kidneys" and would have gone home "but [for] the fear of some unhandsome

Reflections which might have past upon me if I had left ye Country at this juncture." He did not indicate whose "unhandsome Reflections" he feared, but a few years earlier the Committee had to assure him that it was "well Satisfied of yo[u]r Industry...[and] Integrety hopeing you will not thinke wee can listen to the Impertinances of Mercenary Men how Spetious soever their presences may be."[18]

Non-monetary issues were important in convincing old hands to remain in the country. Problems at Albany in 1703 illustrated the contention by social historian Ann Kussmaul that there was "no way better calculated to encourage servants to renew their contracts than to feed them well."[19] Fullartine informed the Committee that shortage of provisions was "the only thing that Yor: Servants complain of & not a man of them but would abate 4 or 5 lbs of their wages, if they were Sure of haveing a Reasonable quantity of good Flower."

> *[I] gott Some [men] to condescend to tarry wth: great difficulty, but was forc'd at ye Same time to prommiss them 5 lb of Flower or Meal each man a week without wch: not one of them would have tarried this year & how I shall be able to perform my prommiss God knows for I have it not in the Country for 40 men wch: is ye number I desire to keep if I can possibly procure so many.*[20]

Food was more than a mere biological necessity; it was a rich symbol and a mechanism for establishing and maintaining social relationships. As Michael Lacombe has argued for the English colonies in the Chesapeake, and as Felicity Heal has observed in England itself, the offering of food helped build distinctive bonds between the giver and the receiver(s). Sharing one's table, extending hospitality, and relieving need were all ways of "acknowledging the creditworthiness of individual members of a group through presents," in Indigenous as well as in English communities. Fullartine recognized that food—or the lack thereof—was an important element of maintaining his own and the company's legitimacy and authority.[21]

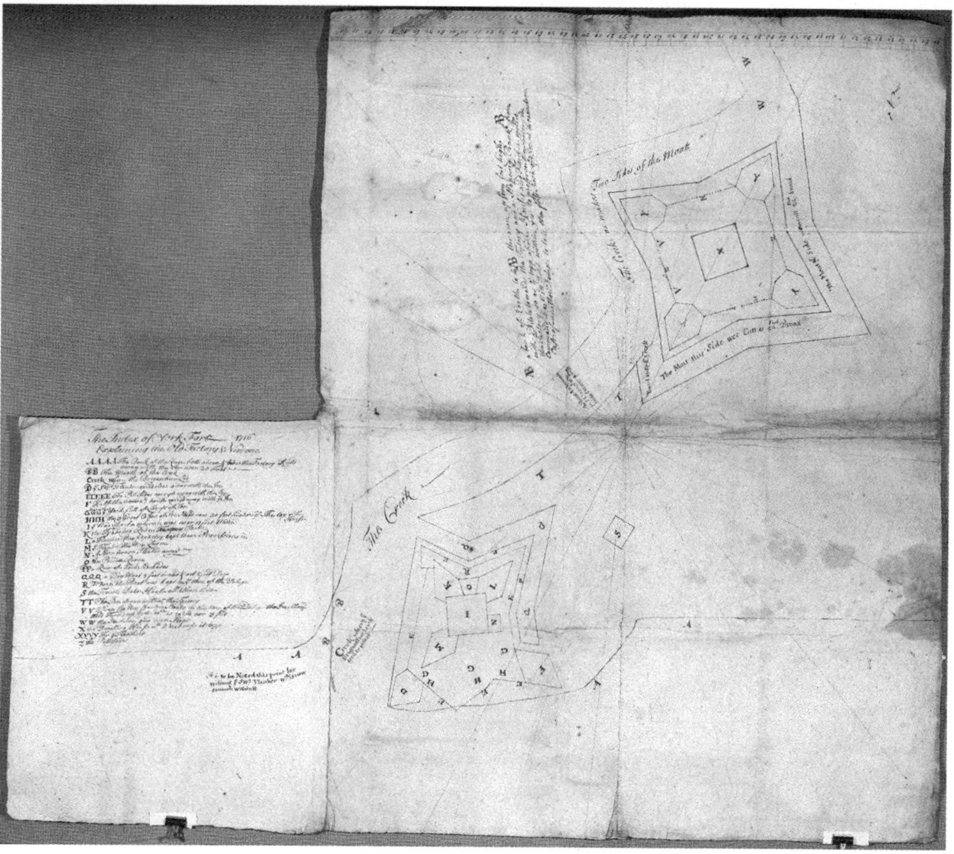

James Knight's plan of York Fort, 1716, shows both the old fort he had reclaimed from the French and the new fort he built after the great flood of 1715. Within a few years of his drawing this map, riverbank erosion caused the old fort (bottom) to fall into the water. [HBCA, G.2/29]

Fullartine added that the continual disappointments in the cargoes sent out "makes all men Seik of Yor: Country." He had been James Knight's deputy governor during a hungry season at Albany in 1695–96: despite a brisk trade in the Bay, the London fur market was sluggish, and the Committee did not have enough cash in hand to outfit the supply ships in 1695. The fear of another year with no relief from London weighed heavily on men's minds: William Filpott was charged with planning to break into the factory's storehouse, and John Cartwright was charged with mutiny

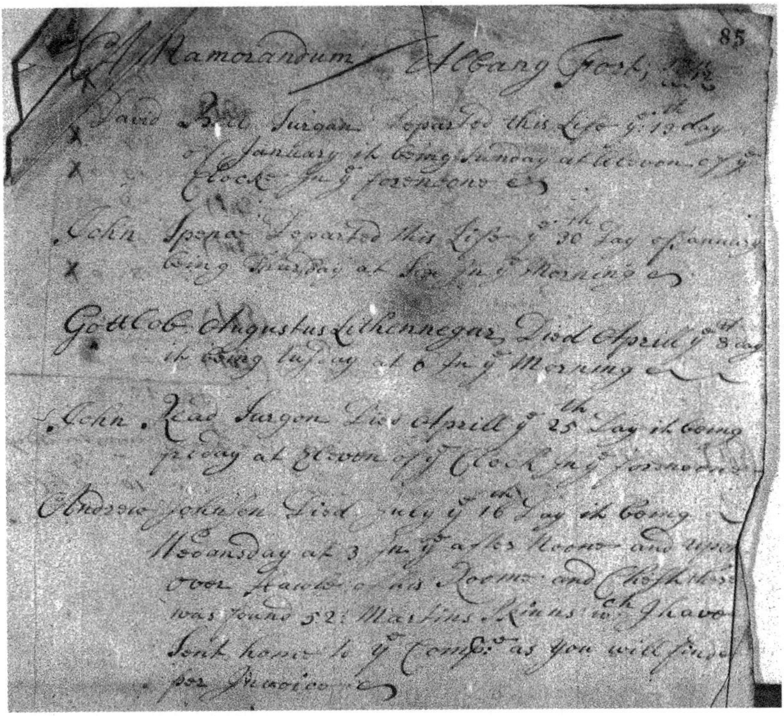

85

A Mamorandum Albany Fort, 1711/12

David Bell Surgan departed this Life ye 19th day of January it being Sunday at eleven of ye Clock in ye forenoon

John Spence departed this Life ye 30th Day of January being Thursday at Six in ye Morning

Gottlob Augustus Lithennegar Died April ye 8th day it being tuesday at 6 in ye Morning

John Read Surgon Died April ye 25th Day it being friday at Eleven of ye Clock in ye forenoon

Andrew Johnson Died July ye 16th Day it being Wednesday at 3 in ye afternoon and upon over hawling his Room and Chest there was found 52 Martins Skinns wch I have Sent home to ye Compa as you will find per Invoice

"A Mamorandum / Albany Fort, 1711/12," listed men who had died over the course of the previous year, including both surgeons. [HBCA, B.3/d/20, fol. 85]

for suggesting that the men sail for home if disappointed again. In 1717 Henry Kelsey complained that Knight had left York short of provisions but not of "Grumbling Mutinous Rascalls."[22]

Anthony Beale observed in 1706 that "the men in the Countrey whose times was out not one would stay in a long time by reason there is no sertainty of Ships comeing." No ships had been sent to Albany in 1700, 1703, or 1704, and the 1702 and 1705 ships were forced to winter in the Bay; Beale added that he himself would come home if the company could not guarantee regular shipments, decent cargoes, a sloop master, and sufficient "men to defend the Factory."[23] Sufficient personnel was also an issue in 1712, after a winter of sickness in which Albany lost smith and gunner Andrew Johnson, miner Gottlieb Augustus Lichtenberger, labourer John

Spence, and surgeons David Bell and John Read; Beale urgently requested a new surgeon, observing that it was "a Great Disincurigsment to you[r] Servants In Case of any misfortune for Such a man to be Wanting here."[24]

Sometimes men based their decisions for staying or going home on personal considerations over which neither the Committee nor the factors had control. In 1703 the personal affairs of accountant Samuel Goodale called him home, and both Henry Kelsey and John Fullartine asked to go home the following year for the recovery of their health.[25] Sometimes men's relationships became troublesome, and the factories could have acted as hothouses for germinating personal conflicts. Such conflicts were best handled by one or more parties finding another situation. In 1703 Fullartine reported that he could not prevail upon James Lynier "by reason of a foolish oath wch: he had taken not to stay in ye Country if Andw: Johnson tarried, & under 40 lb a year." Fullartine added that he "could not prevail wth: Andw: either so was forced to comply" with Johnson.[26]

Many men who (like Johnson) had been kept on at high wages became superfluous when the Treaty of Utrecht restored Hudson Bay to England; they could now be replaced more easily and more cheaply than before. Anthony Beale had forty-four men on the Albany books in 1713–14—"more hands...then is necesary"—and sent twenty-eight of them home in 1714 on the Committee's order; he made no complaints against any of the men, only remarking that "it was not in my power for to do it Before."[27] Ten of those twenty-eight men re-entered the company's service—six of them as early as the following year—although some returned at lower wages.

"Able Men for Your Honours' Service"

The easing of wartime conditions after Utrecht made the recruitment and retention of personnel somewhat less problematic. There was greater continuity in post complements, but numbers of men still returned home for a year or two and then re-entered the service. This coincided with patterns of agricultural and domestic service in Britain at that time.[28] The men's motives are not always clear, although health issues and family

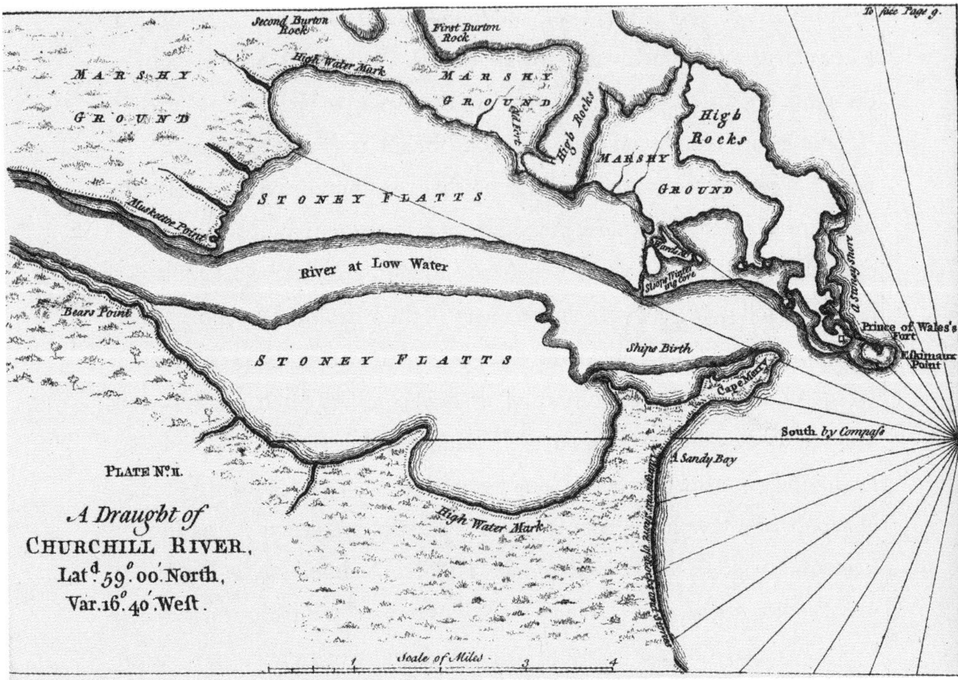

Joseph Robson, A Draught of Churchill River, *shows the location of the new stone Prince of Wales Fort on Eskimo Point, and the cove a little way upriver where the sloop wintered.* [Robson, An Account of Six Years Residence in Hudson's-Bay]

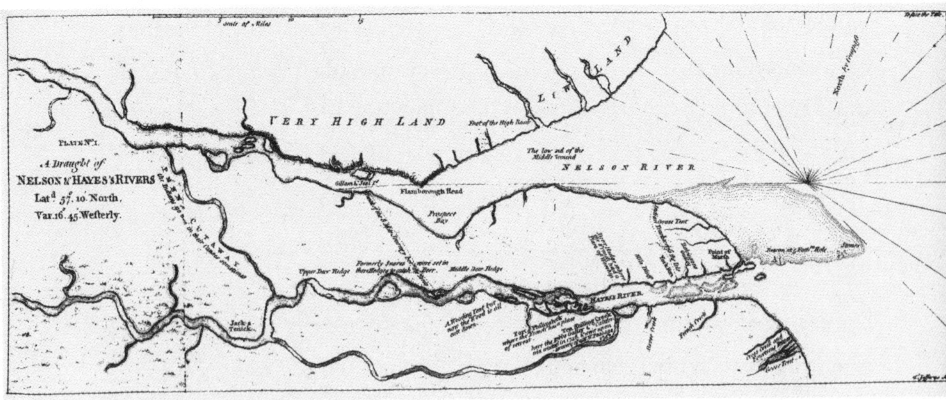

Joseph Robson, A Draught of Nelson & Hayes's Rivers, *illustrates how York Fort, unlike other Bayside posts, was set back a little from the sea. Note Flamborough Head on the Nelson River, not much further away than the Middle Deer Hedge.* [Robson, An Account of Six Years Residence in Hudson's-Bay]

emergencies were cited most often. Eastmain trader Joseph Adams in 1723 and York netmaker Anthony Henday in 1755 went home ostensibly for the recovery of their health, but each immediately re-engaged. Augustine Frost went home from Prince of Wales Fort in 1729 because his father had died, and "he has some effects left him which he is afraid he may lose if he does not go home"; whether or not he sorted out his father's estate, Frost re-engaged in 1730.[29]

In general, peacetime service in Hudson Bay was less hazardous and less demanding than wartime service. Although courage seemed a less necessary attribute than in wartime, Thomas McCliesh Jr complained in 1716 that a rumoured French post on the Severn River put him at the mercy of the Englishmen whose contracts were expiring, "[k]nowing what Treacherous next door neighbours we have to deal with."[30] The Committee continued to emphasize sobriety and industriousness, "we being desirous to Encourage all Industry & Diligence in our Servants."[31] It also encouraged the men to be neighbourly and to live together as peacefully as possible. After internal strife at Moose prompted Joseph Adams to remove sloop master Thomas Render from command, the Committee expressed its hope "that all disputes & differences amongst our Servants there have been Accommodated since the Arrival of Mr Bevan at that Place."[32] When dissension reared its ugly head again nearly forty years later, it wrote, "We are always Sorry to hear of any misunderstanding among Our Servants, as Harmony at Our Factories is a main Step towards Business being well conducted."[33] In correspondence between the Bayside posts the factors often described each other as both neighbours and friends: for example, "I Rest Yr Loving Friend & Governour"; "Yr freind Neighbour & Humble Servt."[34]

Descriptions of both "good" and "bad" servants remained much the same as before 1714. At Albany, Anthony Beale in 1714 called gunner Joseph Myatt "a Carefull young man,"[35] and in 1722 Myatt (then in charge of Albany) called Joseph Adams "a brisk Sober industrious man."[36] The new men of 1719 appeared to Thomas McCliesh Jr to be "lusty able young men."[37] In 1722 Myatt wrote from Albany:

It being your Honrs pleasure when any of your Servants are discharg'd out of your Service, that a Charector may be given of them, how they have behav'd themselves, in their Respective Stations. All persons that are Discharg'd at this time have been very dilligent in the Discharge of their duty, & Obedient to Command. Except John Upton the Armourer, whose behaviour hath been very Monstrous, which I have not fail'd to punish him for.[38]

Myatt and his successor, Richard Staunton, gave Eastmain trader John Henson "a good character," and sloop master George Gunn "a good character to be a sober and carefull man," but gave armourer Farmery Kirke "but a very Indiferent Character."[39] Staunton in 1724 wrote that he had "great hopes" that Henson "will soe be have himselfe, to be deserveinge of more of Yr Honrs favours, by beinge faithfull and dillegent, in Quallefyeinge himself for the same."[40] The Committee responded by promising both Henson and Adams "that if they are sober, and diligent, in their Business and behave themselves well, they shall receive encouragement from us, & a suitable reward, at the Expiration of their Contracts."[41]

Factors continued to praise servants in vague or general terms. In 1737 Richard Norton mentioned five labourers who were willing to sign new contracts in the following year, describing three of them (William Mackcullock, Andrew Forsythe, and Magnus Brown) as "able men for your honours' service," and two (John Elpheston and James Bartleman) as "stout able hands for many particular services"; he added that three other labourers (Alexander Garrioch, James Stinson, and John Clouston) who had signed new contracts that year were "very good and serviceable hands."[42] At Moose in 1739, labourer James Hourston was "a good hand," sawyer Richard Drover was "a very laborious servant and a good workman," and labourer Peter Isbister Sr was "a good hand and worthy of encouragement."[43] Labourer and bricklayer Thomas Austin was "a good Labouring hand and a very oblidging Servant" (1752) and "a verry usefull Man" (1754); sailor William Ward was "[a] young Man that has behaved well, and been very usefull to Us" (1759); and writer John Favell was "a good hand and behaves well" (1759). Even Thomas White's unusually emotional eulogy for Moose's sawyer William Barrow lacked detail: "With a good deal of Grief I have the unhappiness to tell you, that we have... buried one of the best & ablest Men we had William Barrow Sawyer who died on the 17th of April [1755] of a Cancer in his Mouth & Throat."[44]

In 1740 James Isham at York listed "each man's qualifications and behaviour" (not just those whose times were out) in the body of his annual letter, rather than on a separate piece of paper to be enclosed with the packet and which might be subsequently lost (see Table 1). Of his twenty-two men, Isham commented on the sobriety of eleven, including all the officers and all but one of the tradesmen. Six men were mentioned for their diverse skills, four for their honesty, two for their positive attitudes, and two for their diligence or industriousness. Isham remarked that "they do all in general behave themselves very well in the duty to my great satisfaction."[45] This echoed Thomas McCliesh Jr's 1723 praise for his men at York being "obedient and cheerful in the discharge of their duties."[46]

Sobriety—both of habits and of demeanour—was clearly seen as a positive asset. Sloop master David Vaughan lost the *Eastmain* sloop in bad weather between Albany and York in 1714, but James Knight defended him as serious and sensible: "you cannot have a soberer or a brisker man than he is" to command the new sloop *Success*.[47] Knight recognized that the need for temperance applied to himself as well, remarking to Thomas McCliesh Jr that he almost never drank any more, "so that no Man can brann[d] me to ye Compy, to Say they have [a] Drunken Governr here."[48] In 1728 McCliesh lamented the impending return of armourer Christopher Bannister to England, "which I am sorry for by reason [he is] a quiet, sober man and a prime workman, and wish heartily [I] could say as much of [Nicholas] Revilian; for when here formerly [1722–27], never sober when he could get liquor."[49]

Sobriety and industry remained part of the standard rhetoric of factors' correspondence with London throughout the eighteenth century; a representative example is the Albany council's 1757 promise to "take particular care to encourage Virtue, Diligence and Sobriety in the

TABLE 1. *Comments by James Isham on "Each Man's Qualifications and Behaviour," York, 1740*

Name	*Occupation*	*Comments by James Isham*
John Bricker		"a sober man and very fit for your honours' service in trading with Indians etc."
John Potts	surgeon	"a very sober, honest and industrious young man, and I believe very capable of the station he is under in your honours' service."
Samuel Skrimshire	warehouse keeper	"a sober lad and I hope will merit your honours' favours."
John Russell	armourer	"a sober man, a good workman at his business, and handy in some cases about the factory."
John Spur'l (Spurle, Spurrel)	shipwright	"handy in his trade but not extraordinary handy in house carpenter's work, he is a willing man in anything to be done."
Evan Edwards	blacksmith	"a sober, honest man and a good workman."
Robert Inksetter (Inkster)	tailor	"has sobriety and good honesty, a good workman for this country, and very handy in anything that is to be done."
Michael Loggin (Logan)	steward	"a sober, honest, good-natured man and one that is fit or that can turn his hand to anything in the country."
Arnold Cosshe and Charles Pulley	mariners	"sober men, performs their business as required and handy in several cases."
William Miller	blacksmith's mate	"very good for that purpose and an able man in labouring work."
John Hughes	labourer	"a sober man and very diligent in his duty."
James Luittit, James Manson, Thomas Sclater, John Luittit, James Virtue, Robert Moode (Moodie?), and William Alson (Oldson?)	labourers	"all able strong men, and fit to carry a log or any other labouring work."
Robert Edison	labourer	"an indifferent good hand in labouring work."

Name	Occupation	Comments by James Isham
Henry Inksetter (Inkster)	labourer	"a good hand in labouring work, and one we employ as fisherman."
John Dymock	labourer	"a sober man, a good hand in squaring and sawing timber."

Servants and discountenance the Contrary."[50] In 1758 it described sailor William Allen as "a Sober deserving young Man," labourer James Inkster as "a Sober young fellow and a good Pitman [bottom man on a two-man pit-saw team], who will be very useful at Henley," and sailor Hugh Slater as "a Sober Industrious young Man"; in 1760 they eulogized carpenter George Clark as "a Sober discrete Man and a good workman, and no doubt if he had lived...he wou'd [have] given Satisfaction."[51] Conversely, in 1752 George Spence sent home sailor Daniel Mackoler (a former servant who had just re-engaged for three years), "on Account of his intolerable bad Behaviour while in the Country before being both a Drunkard & a Thief."[52] In 1768 Humphrey Marten described Albany's homeward-bound smith, John Pittway, as "a good Workman, but a very bad man for Liquor."[53]

Knowledge of Cree (either the Lowland or Eastmain dialects)[54] was frequently mentioned as an asset. During the war years Henry Kelsey was praised for his efforts "to Educate the men in Literature but Especially in the [Cree] Language that in time wee may send them to Travell."[55] Upon being promoted from mate to master of the *Beaver* sloop, William Bevan was encouraged to learn Cree, for both the company's interest and his own.[56] In 1728 Joseph Myatt felt that carpenter and shipwright Alexander Thoyts would not be as useful an assistant as Joseph Adams, "for a man that hath Less Language then my self, will be of but Little Service to me."[57] In 1730 Adams (then chief at Albany) gave sloop master Thomas Render the initial charge of Moose partly because "he has more of the Language then any I can think on, which can be conveniently parted with."[58] At Albany in 1738 Thomas Bird promised to encourage apprentices William Clowes and John Dingley to learn Cree.[59] The importance of knowing an Indigenous language increased in the 1770s. Labourer Edward Loutit in

1777 was at eighteen pounds (high wages, even for an old hand) because for three years (1766–69) he had wintered with an Assiniboine trader named Ka'na'put'a'po'e'tuck. Humphrey Marten explained Loutit's high wages: "he is known by most of them [the Assiniboine], and understands their language, better than any Man in your Service."[60]

After the establishment of Cumberland House in 1774 the surest means for any man to endear himself to his superiors was to familiarize himself with the use and construction of birchbark canoes. Humphrey Marten instructed William Tomison at Cumberland House in 1776 to promise a ten-shilling gratuity "for every good large Canoe built by Englishmen."[61] Scottish labourer Robert Longmoor offered to learn how to build such craft in 1776, and by the following spring had produced two, for which he received twenty shillings worth of goods from the York Fort warehouse. Humphrey Marten called Longmoor "the first Canoe Man in your Service" and "very deserving" of encouragement for having thus improved himself and advanced the company's interest.[62] As the HBC moved inland, however, few men were as apparently straightforward in their commitment to their master's interests as was Longmoor.

"Handy at Any Thinge"

General usefulness was valued at least as much as specific skills, and diversity of ability often served men (and the company) better than did specialization. Thomas McCliesh Jr at York seemed uncertain about John Wateridge's qualifications as a gunner ("we presume him to be qualified for gunner of the factory") but in 1723 spoke of him as "a very serviceable man both in winter and summer in getting of provisions."[63] Richard Staunton praised surgeon Charles Napper for also acting as Albany's accountant, and recommended mason Samuel Wolfe as "a very good man for yr Honrs Service and Handy at any thinge."[64] A later Albany surgeon, George Spence, also "very seasonably offer'd his Service to take upon him ye Business of the Accomptant" in 1739.[65]

Some men were able to turn their hand to many different tasks. Labourer John Hughes was initially engaged as a makeshift bricklayer but was also "very serviceable to us in attending and making our nets"; in 1752 he was even repairing guns after armourer Joseph Russell froze his fingers and toes the previous winter.[66] In 1756 the Albany council recommended for "your Honours Consideration" tailor George Harvey, who "is Usefull as Taylor and Mason, and is a Sober Man."[67] James Irvin served as cooper, carpenter, sawyer, and sloop mate at various stations in Hudson Bay before going home from Albany in 1744 because of a dispute with one of the sloop masters.[68]

Rowland Waggoner was equally diverse. When "Rowley" asked for a new contract and a raise in 1728, Myatt commented that "Justice Oblidges me to give him that Just Carractor of one of the Best Servts that I Ever Saw in his Station, he Being a Good Sa[w]yer & as handy with a broad Ax as Some Carpenters, & Shoots as Well as most of the Ind[ian]s, and he will Supply the place of a Cooper if your Honrs think well of it."[69] Although officially categorized as a sawyer for most of his career (he entered the service in 1714), Waggoner became second to Thomas Bird at Albany in 1737 and succeeded Bird as chief when he died in 1739. Waggoner never learned to write; on the official 1739 letter from Albany he took a pen and traced over his signature written by someone else (probably George Spence) in pencil. Another indication that literacy was not essential for success in the early HBC can be found in 1722. The Committee encouraged pauper apprentice Joseph Adams (indentured to the company in 1705 at the age of five) to learn to write, "whereby you may be capable of Preferment," although Adams had already served the winter of 1721–22 as trader on the Eastmain.[70]

Diverse skills were valued in specialized tradesmen as well. Richard Norton praised cooper James Worrall as "a very handy man in the country for any manner of business as well as at his trade."[71] Thomas McCliesh Jr recommended York Fort smith Francis Cheeseman to the Committee as "a very good workman and very serviceable in getting provisions, and peradventure as stout [a] man as ever came into your country."[72] In 1733 Moose was not sent the armourer it had requested, because "Mr Jones who Surveys Our Guns" informed the Committee that blacksmith Anthony Brush (already at Moose) "is Capable of Performing the Armourers business as well as the Smiths"; Brush was given the extra duties and a significant wage increase (from sixteen to twenty-five pounds).[73] Tradesmen were often expected to pitch in whenever and wherever necessary, particularly at outposts with small complements. William Lamb at Henley was told in 1751 "that ye Handicraft men & others with you are not to be Confin'd to theire own perticuler trades, but to be absolutely under your Command & to do all other affaires as you shall think proper...& be sure not to let them be Idle & lazy but keep them Constantly at work."[74]

Not all tradesmen were willingly so versatile. Bricklayer James Norton (Richard's brother) almost consistently refused to work at anything but his trade after his transfer from Prince of Wales Fort to Moose in 1734, and he was seen as a bad influence on other men. He may have been "an Extraordinary good Bricklayer," as the Committee claimed, but William Bevan remarked that he would "whip and pickle him if it was not on his brothers & Govr. Macklishes Families Acct."[75] Carpenter John Halcro was sent home from Albany in 1752 before his contract had expired "for denying to assist loading & unloading the Sloop, getting of Firewood on Condition he doth not wet himself, & doing Labouring work." His truculence contrasted with that of armourer Joseph Staton: "its true he is no Extraordinary Workman but he is Sober and capable of doing the Business of the Country and is always willing to do any other work when required."[76]

Competence in one's trade was expected. Cheeseman went on hunting and woodcutting expeditions, but his activities beyond the factory walls did not detract from his skill at the forge, "he being one of the best of his employ as ever served your honours."[77] Shipwright David Peters was engaged from the *Hudson's Bay* for land service at Albany in 1727 but seems not to have been worth the thirty-six pounds he received per annum. In 1729 Joseph Myatt requested that Peters be recalled upon the expiration of his contract in 1730, "he being a very Weakly man" and unable to do his job properly. Peters did go home in 1730, accompanied by Joseph Adams's description of him as "Deficient in his Buisness [*sic*] and not fit for your Honours Service."[78] Some tradesmen's skills may have been poorly matched to "the Business of the Country," prompting chief factor Joseph Isbister to roll up his own sleeves during renovations at Albany in 1743:

> *Set John Heather to pripaire boards & Stuff fit to build a paire of Stairs withal beliving that he would be more Expedeitious with his plaine than he was with ye Axe for he Maks no hand of laing logs, so I fell to work my Self in order to Carie up ye wals I found that I Could [cut?] two logs to his one & observe that a house yt a house [*sic*] Carpenter is no fitt person to build factorys as not being Usd to ye Ax nor line a pice of timber which Maks factorys So long abuilding when they have ye Managment thereoff.*[79]

Other tradesmen may simply have been incompetent or inadequately trained. Thomas McCliesh Jr complained in 1732 that his carpenter, John Taylor, "understands but little of the carpenter's trade."[80] Richard Norton requested a new shipwright for Prince of Wales Fort in 1737 because the newly arrived John Spurle "is not only a weakly person but...ignorant and unqualified for...the...repairs of our craft."[81] Norton's criticism might have been overly harsh: three years later, Spurle was giving satisfaction at York.

Diversity of skill was not always rewarded. The Albany council recommended labourer George Taylor to London in 1756 as "a handy Man...who can do all our Cooper work very well and is worthy of Notice, he acts in Several Capacitys and is a Sober Man," but he remained at six pounds per annum until his contract expired in 1760. The council supported his request for a two-year contract at eighteen pounds, adding that he was also "a good Sawyer," but the Committee refused (without explanation). Taylor came home in 1760 with the council's recommendation as "a very usefull Servant" deserving a gratuity, but none was forthcoming.[82]

"Though All Names and Eaters, They Are Not All Workers"

Negative comments, like positive ones, more often focused on attitude or behaviour than on skill or ability. James Knight sailed for Hudson Bay in 1714 with orders to "Punish all Disolute and Profane Persons," and a few years later he complained that his work at Churchill was being hampered "by the folly & Neglect of Men for want of Doeing thare Duty."[83] At Albany in the mid-1720s armourer Farmery Kirke was "very lazy," mariner John Byers was "a very Turbulent & Contentious Person," and homeward-bound labourers Richard Millechamp, William Gutteridge, Henry Doughty, John Cox, and John Page were "not wourthy to come any More into your Country." The Committee's reply echoed this language: "Wee take notice of the List of Servants...whom you mention as indiff[er]ent hands, not worthy to be again entertained in our Service, which we shall take care to prevent, and to send over such Persons as we shall judge most fit for Our purpose."[84] Later in the decade Joseph Myatt asked the Committee to call home mariner James Miller for being "Monsterous Wiked and Disobediant to Comm[an]ds," and complained about the "Monstrouse" behaviour of former apprentice Allen Fox at Eastmain: "its Certain he was as Stout Strong man as any we had in the Country, but to take him Otherways, a Surly, Sottish, Ill Natured Fellow."[85] In 1734 Moose surgeon John Edwards was dismissed for being "a Turbulent man and disobedient to Command" and replaced by Robert Holliday, "who is recommended to Us as a sober quiet man and very Capable of performing his business as a Surgeon."[86]

Unsuitable and undesirable men had also been a problem in wartime, but the Committee and its factors felt more at liberty to cull them from the labour force after Utrecht. Richard Staunton blamed criticisms of Joseph Myatt's management of Albany on "Envey, from men of an uneasie temper and turbulant Spirit wch will not be Easy under any command, here being some of the same temper still Remaining wch your Honrs will be pleased to Remove In Due time."[87] John Fullartine sent home Samuel Thomas Langley after only one year at Albany: Langley had requested it with some "fervency & [he] can do me little or no Servis &...I've better be without than keep him, for whereas he will at home be counted to me for a man, here he can only eat a mans allowance."[88]

Factors wanted to rid themselves of troublemakers and malcontents, but they did not want to be left short-handed. In 1728 Thomas McCliesh Jr asked the Committee to replace labourers Robert Chambers and Robert Blackburn—"I am persuaded that many honester men than [them]...has been hanged at Tyburn"—and explained that he would have sent them home that year, but there was so much work to be done that he needed all the hands he could get.[89] In 1736 mariner John Evans was engaged for the northern slooping voyages, but as he was "discontented, and we apprehend may prove a seditious, troublesome fellow," Richard Norton sent him home from Prince of Wales Fort in the same year.[90] Sometimes men once considered desirable came to be seen as troublemakers: in 1726 Myatt and Staunton sent home four men who "are noways fitt for yr Service being turbelent Sottish Men," including Charles Napper and Samuel Wolfe, both of whom Myatt and Staunton had earlier praised for their usefulness.[91]

While "unfit" men could be removed from the labour force before their contracts were complete, Bayside factors cautioned the Committee against using this tactic too often. Joseph Myatt did not complain when Allen Fox was recalled after only two years of his contract, but he feared that it might "Encourage other Sorry fellows to to [*sic*] persue the Same Measures."[92] He may have been remembering tailor William Mackay, whose entreaties to go home grew so troublesome that York governor Thomas McCliesh Jr let him go in 1727.[93]

Another reason for the Committee to hesitate before recalling men was the incomplete information at its disposal. As in earlier periods, the paths along which information flowed back and forth across the Atlantic could be used to misrepresent men for good or for ill. James Knight complained from York in 1716 that the Committee "have had some misinformation against me, or have conceived some groundless opinion of my extravagancy."[94] Throughout the 1720s Joseph Myatt at Albany tried to defend himself against charges of harshness made against him in London; despite the support of senior officers like Richard Staunton, complaints about his behaviour seem to have dogged him to the end of his days. In his last letter to London, Myatt assured the Committee that the new recruits "[s]hall find nothing but Civil Usage from me, it being Contrary to my Nature to Treat any man with Morrossness or Ill manners."[95] Myatt's own experiences probably influenced his sympathy for former carpenter and shipwright Walter Long, who left Albany in 1721 after seven years of service; Myatt later observed that James Bay had not seen a better workman than Long, "and who Ever he was that Callumnized [Long]...did him Great Injustice, for I Know him to be a very Sober Honest Man and Scorns to be Guilty of those Little Pittifull Actions which he was Charged with."[96]

Likewise, in 1742 Joseph Isbister expressed his surprise at the

> *false Informations you have received, charging us with detestable Crimes, which we do abhor and shall never be guilty of, and doubt not but that all such scandalous and malicious Informations, which arise from their being keept strickt to their Work and knowing their Masters, will not find any access to your Cares for the future.*[97]

The following year Isbister and his council defended themselves against an accusation that they had murdered a Cree woman whom Albany had been supporting for several years "as an Object of Charity." They declared:

> *[W]e are extremely concerned, Yr Honrs should receive Impressions, so unnatural and cruel, so inconsistent with our former Characters, from Persons so avowed, so discontented att our Conduct, as make it very difficult to serve Yr Honrs with that Ardour & Integrity that we had prescribed to ourselves as a Rule.*[98]

Luckily for Isbister and Myatt, the company's factors were valued by their employers in spite of their faults (real or alleged). Like good estate stewards in England, "[m]en who were experienced, knowledgeable, with a head of business as well as conscientious and honest...were hard to find, and thus worth holding onto." Both groups of men generally "found their masters swift to chide and slow to bless but for all their grumbles very reluctant to dismiss them."[99]

"Old Norwesters"

The premium on "Faithfull & Experienced Servants" during the dark days of war was not reduced by the Utrecht restoration; if anything, rebuilding and then expanding the company's position in Hudson Bay relied even more heavily on "old hands."[100] In 1716 James Knight encouraged the Committee "to send as many old Norwesters over as you can" for the proposed new trading post at Churchill River.[101] In 1742 Joseph Isbister at Albany offered increased wages to sawyer Richard Drover and labourers Peter Isbister Sr and John Greenwood; he later justified his action to the Committee by explaining that the council "found them usefull Men, and could not do the Business of this Factory without such Hands, for one of them being as good as two green hands."[102] In the 1730s Richard Norton warned the Committee against high turnover of personnel, preferring to have "men inured to their several stations," and James Isham urged his masters not to call "too many old hands home in one year in so small a number of men."[103]

As demonstrated, servants (collectively and individually) were consistently evaluated in terms of their general usefulness to their masters rather than on the basis of skills specific to Hudson Bay. Honesty and fidelity were key elements of that utility, both in war and in peace. In 1703 John Fullartine recommended former apprentice Anthony Beale (then his deputy) to the Committee, calling him "a very carefull honest man" who knew the company's affairs well and who "deserves encouragement as being an old Servant & one yt has been allways faithfull to his masters."[104] In 1714 Beale (then in charge of Albany) informed the Committee that he hoped to maintain discipline and prevent "Clandestine Dooings" by "incurageing those I finde faithfull and Just to your Honours."[105] In 1764 Humphrey Marten suggested writer George Humble for the charge of Henley House (if it could be re-established), observing that he "is diligent and obliging."[106] In 1767 Marten recommended surgeon Eusebius Bacchus

Kitchen to the Committee: "he has Assisted me three Years in the Trading Room and has behaved himself in such a manner as to Shew that he has Your Honours Interest greatly at heart."[107]

The Committee promised "encouragement" to servants they perceived as "faithfull." For instance, in 1688, they assured George Geyer of their resolution "to Stand by and encourage our Old & Faithfull Servants And... Wee shall never Send New Raw & unexperienced men to put over the heads of such as have Served us Longe & faithfully."[108] The Committee lived up to that commitment in 1691, when Stephen Sinclair (formerly warehouse keeper at Albany) and Hugh Verner (formerly factor at Rupert's River) returned to Hudson Bay; they had been members of John Marsh's ill-fated Albany expedition (1688) and had only just returned to England from their French captivity. The Committee immediately re-engaged them and sent them to Port Nelson:

> *being both well experienced in our affaires & trade, tho' we could not assigne them a particular Post yet we know they will be of a great advantage to our Interest & help to you, & we doe accordingly recommend them to your favour & Care to make them as usefull to Our Service as you can, & wee doe appoynt them both to be admitted of your Councell.*[109]

Another old servant, former Albany accountant Thomas Hall, was sent to York in 1719 "to Suply the place of any Post that shall be Vacant, wherein he Can be serviceable to ye Compa[ny]." The Committee even used this as an opportunity to elicit gratitude from another "Old Servt," Nathaniel Bishop; it agreed that he serve another two years as second at Albany, "[n]otwithstanding wee have Likewise an Old Servant now Going Over, That would be Glad of Your Post and at Cheaper Wages."[110]

The case of Thomas Walsh illustrates how troubled times gave servants opportunities to demonstrate their loyalty and fidelity. In 1690 the Committee assured Walsh of its resolution "to Leave noe merritt unrewarded" and granted him a fifty-pound gratuity "for [his] further encouragement in the Preservation of our Rights and Encrease of the trade." In the following year it rewarded his "fidelity as well as ability in our Service" by continuing him as Geyer's second after he burned down his post at Severn River to keep it out of French hands.[111] The Committee approved of his choice to destroy his house rather than attempt a futile defence of such a vulnerable outpost, and declared:

> *[W]e have a Just sense & value of your fidelity in having discharged your Trust as well as any man could have done in those Circumstances...& considering the Trade Wee received thence the last year by your managemt. & the good conduct you Showed in the utmost extremity, together with the hazard you did runn in Our Service, & private Losses which must necessarily have ensued to you, Wee would not be wanting in a due encouragement & to Consider you as much as if you were still in that Station.*

They maintained his current wages (fifty pounds per annum, a master's salary) and granted him a sixty-pound gratuity.[112]

Although a detailed analysis of HBC wage levels is outside the scope of the current study, it is worth noting that there appears to have been a recognized level of remuneration that experienced labourers ("old hands") could expect in recognition of their age and experience. In 1730 steward James Loutit and labourer Michael Loggin were willing to sign on for another year if they could have "old servants' wages." Their superior at York, Thomas McCliesh Jr, called them "extraordinary common men, and...deserving as much as any old common servant." In 1731 they and tailor Edmund Hay signed two-year contracts at fourteen pounds, "being what your honours allows to good old servants"; henceforth, however, "they would contract for no time but from year to year."[113] Although Loutit had served the company between 1710 and 1718, Loggin and Hay had only entered the service in 1727. Other examples of old hands re-engaging at fourteen pounds include Albany labourers Joseph Adams (1724–26), John

Bricker (1731–34), Thomas Low (1734–36), William Macklin (1740–42), John Greenwood (1742–43), Andrew Anderson (1747–48), and Joseph Downs (1763–65).[114]

Notwithstanding the consistent rhetoric of the Committee about rewarding valuable servants of any rank, and its evident willingness to do so, wages represented a considerable expense. Just as the Committee encouraged its factors to economize on such things as provisions,[115] it also encouraged them to economize on wages when circumstances permitted. In 1694, when Knight had established himself at Albany, the Committee instructed him to "send home as many as you can spare of the men with you at the highest wages that soe the Comp[an]ies. charge may be eased, still Regarding the safety of the Factory."[116] This appears to have been the same motive behind recalling nineteen men (including the experienced trader Hugh Verner) from Port Nelson that year, for no complaints were registered against any of them.[117] Even the multi-faceted James Irvin, who acted as cooper, carpenter, sawyer, and sloop mate at various periods of his service, was sent home in 1744 "both on account of his great Wages, and att his own Request": he was earning twenty-seven pounds and was replaced by cooper and labourer John Dikes at ten pounds.[118] At one point in the relatively peaceful 1720s, the Committee grew so tired of servants in the Bay "endeavouring to impose upon you, by demanding extravegant wages" that they directed all servants to be sent home at the expiration of their contracts.[119]

Factors themselves were included in the general desire for economy. Thomas Phipps replaced John Abraham as governor of Port Nelson in 1685, but the following year the Committee complained that he had taken up his new position "with so much unsteadiness & irresolution" that he demanded two hundred pounds per annum—twice the salary that other governors had received there—"wch. we doe not take well from him," as the company's payroll "is already to[o] great." They resolved "to retrench what we can possibley of it, & the necessity of our affaires obligeth us to it."[120] This was particularly important when wartime pressures on recruitment left the company vulnerable to its servants' demands.

Pensions and Charity

The encouragement of "good" servants did not always end with the period of employment. Pensions were rare and consisted of a final one-time gratuity paid at the end of a man's service (or life) as reward for extraordinary performance, or as compensation for extraordinary loss (of limb or life) in the line of duty. This was unusual in the early modern period; few British workers injured on the job could expect much (if any) financial assistance from their employers.[121] The Committee gave a "bounty" of £2 8s. 7d. to George Newton, who "hath lost the use of some of his fingers" and came home in 1679.[122] John Bridgar was captured by Radisson at Port Nelson in 1683 and taken to Quebec, where he was released; in 1684 he arrived back in England and appeared before the Committee, which paid him £41 19s. 0d. to cover expenses incurred while he was at Quebec and on his way home from New England, and offered him a gratuity of £69 3s. 7d. for his sufferings in the company's service.[123] In January 1685 John Brownson (formerly chief mate on the *Colleton* yacht) asked "to have some adition to his former service"; the Committee, "considering he has lost his Right hand by some accident Ordered he shall have a gratuety in lieu of all sattisfaction of £5."[124] In 1690 Elizabeth Marsh received a twenty-pound gratuity "in Consideration of the Loss of her husband," John (governor of James Bay, 1688–89).[125]

During times of war with France men could argue that defending the company's possession of Hudson Bay was equivalent to defending England's possession of Hudson Bay. The Committee members themselves made this connection when exhorting their officers and servants and were willing to put their money where their collective mouth was. A 1711 order "[f]or the Encouragement of...Seamen and Servants" declared that, "although their Duty obliges them to Defend the Interest of the Said Company being in their pay, yet for their Satisfaction" the Committee promised that "any Man Behaving himself Manfully and Bravely in the Defence of their Ship Goods and Factory Shall Happen to be wounded or Killed," they may be assured of "Such Reparation and Subsistance to them and theirs as Shall be Equivalent to the Queens Gracious Proclamation in Such cases."[126] A similar promise was made in 1756 when war broke out with France once again.[127]

Such "Effectual care" was offered during times of peace as well. In 1755 the Committee ordered the accounts of each of the hands killed at Henley the previous winter to be credited with a gratuity of twenty pounds, a significant amount considering that, for example, James Shoart and George Gunn were earning six pounds per annum, and Robert Ash and Daniel Bowland were at ten pounds per annum. The administratrix of their late master, William Lamb, received thirty pounds (one year's salary).[128]

Perhaps more commonly, men maimed or injured in the company's service were retained longer than their practical usefulness may have warranted. Workplace accidents and weather-related misfortune could be a fact of life in Hudson Bay, as George Mace discovered: he suffered frostbite from exposure during his first winter at York and had all his fingers and toes amputated in March 1715. However, he did not return to England until 1720 and was then re-engaged in 1721 for four years at ten pounds; he was to be "Imploy'd in what he is capable of" at Albany, the Committee "considering him as an Object of our Charity." His superior at Albany, Richard Staunton, appeared to think poorly of Mace—he described him in 1724 as "of noe manner of service" and in 1725 as "goode for notheinge at all" and "not wourthy to come any More into your Country"—but the Committee was willing to keep Mace on had he not earnestly wished to go home in 1725.[129] At York in 1738 James Isham disobeyed the Committee's order to send home sawyer Henry Sacheveral Eastwick, "who as before we [the York council] recommend as a very useful hand in every respect as well as that he is maimed in your honours' service."[130]

There was a consistent and shared expectation that old hands deserved encouragement, "justice," and even charity. John Fullartine's praise for Anthony Beale as honest, faithful, and deserving "encouragement as being an old Servant" has already been noted. Former apprentice and bookkeeper Samuel Hopkins, who ran away from Albany in 1722 and was dismissed the following year, was re-engaged "out of Charity" in 1724.[131]

Another former apprentice, Richard Norton, was relieved of his command at Churchill in 1727; instead of being dismissed, he was sent to York to improve his knowledge and understanding of the company's trading and accounting methods. In 1730 his mentor there (and future father-in-law), Thomas McCliesh Jr, told the Committee that Norton "has behaved himself with honesty and fidelity to the best of my knowledge since he has been here, and is deserving of your honours' favour."[132]

Such expectations flowed from membership in one of the company's household factories. Contractual and temporary though that membership was—as, indeed, membership in any household often was—the master-servant relationship still relied greatly on trust, particularly when that relationship spanned a very large ocean. Trust was a precious commodity, which occasionally needed to be bought (or at least rented) at a price; the public transcript of mutual obligations required that servants' loyalty and trustworthiness be rewarded, and sometimes those benefits needed to be extended beyond their physical presence in the household factories. In addition to the material benefits discussed here, there existed a range of potential non-material gifts that by their nature are much less apparent in the surviving archival record: advice, information, connections with traders, and recommendation to other masters and employers.[133]

|| Although new recruits were cheaper to employ than experienced men, retention of personnel was very important to the Committee and to the Bayside factors. New recruits were unknown quantities; veterans who had demonstrated their value were necessary for both security and expansion. The Committee felt particularly vulnerable when England was at war with France, and tried to use the French threat to bolster the courage and fidelity of their Bayside employees. Servants were willing to face the threat, but invocations of duty could not replace regular deliveries of supplies or ample provisions. During peacetime the Committee used occasional high turnovers to jettison servants with high wages, but green hands needed at least a few "old Norwesters" to teach them the ropes. Joseph Isbister assured the Committee in 1743 that the servants to

whom he had promised higher wages were "usefull Men, and [I] could not do the Business of this Factory without such Hands, one of them being as good as two green hands."[134]

The language in which good and useful servants were defined echoed that used in contemporary households in Britain, sometimes modified to reflect the physical dangers of wartime. When Anthony Beale returned to Albany for his second spell as governor there, the Committee highlighted "your Integrity to the Hudsons Bay Company, for whom we are Intrusted, and the Good opinion we have of your Courage as well as prudence and Continuall faithfulness upon all occasions to the Welfare and Interest of the Said Company."[135] Fifteen years later Joseph Myatt's second term in charge of Albany began with the Committee praising his past "ability and conduct in the management of our affairs" and anticipating his "Prudence, Courage, & Fidelity" in the years to come.[136] The language reflected the public transcripts of household service, which were easily adapted for Bayside household factories. The particular challenges and opportunities of wartime might test those transcripts by placing unusual demands on servants, but the transcipts provided a framework within which masters and servants could negotiate or argue.

Although the demands of physical distance made HBC service unique in some respects (such as the length of service), HBC contracts were typical of early modern employment agreements. They stipulated a basic economic transaction—monetary and non-monetary wages in return for services rendered over a specified period of time—but they also acted as social and moral covenants, binding master and servant in a network of reciprocal (but often undefined) obligations. The renewal of contracts provided opportunities to emphasize those obligations, by both workers (through deferential behaviour) and by the Committee (through paternalistic behaviour). However, opportunities for conflict and tension also existed, and servants seeking better terms risked being seen as ungrateful or disingenuous. In wartime, or at other moments when the company seemed vulnerable, deferential and paternalistic behaviours could be reinforced by the invocation of courage and national duty, but they could also be undermined if servants were perceived as putting their own interests ahead of the company's. In fact, deferential behaviour could also be perceived as pursuing individual rather than corporate interests; the short-term deferment of the former, allegedly in favour of the latter, could potentially reap more long-term benefits than could straightforward wage demands.

Beginning in the 1740s and 1750s, however, new circumstances arose that seemed to push the public transcript to its limits and, in so doing, brought some private transcripts into the light of day. The HBC's slow but steady move away from the shores of the Bay and into the hitherto unfamiliar interior of the continent brought with it a new set of demands and thus entailed new sets of relationships. The established public transcript would eventually be renegotiated, but not before a great deal of blood, sweat, and tears had been shed.

6 The Inland Experience

Indeed Sir it is no wonder the Company's Servants in general is unwilling to come Inland, their usage in many particulars, not being equal to their Servitude.

—WILLIAM TOMISON (CH) to Humphrey Marten (YF), 5 June 1781, *CHJ Second Series*, 154

THE 1720S AND 1730S were decades of cautious consolidation and rebuilding, reminiscent of the company's beginnings fifty years earlier. Joseph Isbister's establishment of Henley House in 1743 marked a transition toward more energetic experimentation and inland expansion. However, service inland was not the same as service on Hudson Bay. The new demands placed on servants—particularly the transport of goods and furs up and down the Albany and Hayes rivers, and the long periods spent away from the familiar shores of the Bay—required that "extraordinary" labour become "ordinary." The Committee discovered that this could only be done with encouragement, the slow pace of which hampered the company's inland ventures into the 1780s.

The interplay of corporate agendas and personal priorities was certainly not new to the mid-eighteenth century; throughout the company's history its employees had made decisions based on the balance or imbalance of those two forces. What set the 1750s, 1760s, and 1770s apart from earlier decades were the changing circumstances in the company's operations that were upsetting the balance in an unfamiliar way. An employee of 1690 or 1720 was able to count on a relatively stable and predictable relationship with his factor and with his London masters. Ventures such as Henley House and inland wintering directly affected a minority of employees but introduced a new series of possible demands that influenced everyone's experiences and perceptions.

When the Committee turned its collective eye toward the interior of the continent, although it kept its feet planted firmly on the shoreline, it abandoned (in a sense) the established patterns of movement and labour that had prevailed for almost seventy-five years. Travelling up the Albany or the Hayes River was fundamentally different from slooping along the coast of James Bay. Spending eleven or twelve months at a time in the unfamiliar interior (whether "alone" with a group of Indigenous peoples or in a small house with a handful of fellows) was fundamentally different from living at York with a few dozen Englishmen and Orkneymen; and any kind of life or work away from the relatively comfortable factories nestled by the Bay was fundamentally different from being able to look out the window of even the smallest and most isolated coastal outpost upon the waters of an inland sea that represented a real connection with the world from which these men came.[1]

Of course, fear of isolation and fear of the unknown were not characteristic of men willing to sign multi-year contracts with a long-distance trading company. Reports of men petitioning to winter inland suggest that isolation of a sort—particularly isolation from managerial authority—could be quite desirable; also, inland wintering offered different opportunities for adventure, companionship, and personal profit. However, the company's inability to re-establish Henley in 1757 and 1764—attempts that highlighted customary expectations and attitudes as much as they challenged them—clearly demonstrated that every man had his limits.

Inland experiments after 1743 began to change the nature of company employment, its demands, its risks, and its opportunities. They were also changing the way servants were responding to those demands, risks, and opportunities. The establishment of Cumberland House and other inland trading posts exposed more men to the changing circumstances of the HBC working environment. These changes became more drastic as competition intensified in the late 1780s and beyond. Even before that, however, they influenced the way master, factor, and servant interacted, and illuminated established practices and assumptions.

Henley House

The company's experiences with Henley House shed light on many common assumptions and expectations. The attacks on the post by groups of Lowland Cree in 1754 and 1759, as well as the aftermath of those attacks, set Henley apart from other HBC establishments of the period. The destruction of Henley and the company's attempts to re-establish it generated two divergent responses on the part of the servants at Albany. While some men publicly declared their devotion to the company and its interests, others took the occasion to openly place their own interests ahead of the company's. The resultant jockeying for position, favour, and advancement was complex and not always clear, but the records of it reveal much more than most Bayside documents about what company servants believed was appropriate behaviour toward (and from) their master.

The deaths at Henley were a real shock to the men of Albany and to all Bayside servants. The fact that William Lamb's behaviour had precipitated this violence was not lost on other factors. When Joseph Smith and Joseph Waggoner departed York in 1756 to winter inland with a band of "Sturgeon" Upland Cree, James Isham warned them to "take particular Care not to be too Busy with the Indians Wives, so as to Create a misunderstanding, the contrary may be Your Own Ruin, and a great detriment to the Design You'r sent upon."[2] Upon hearing of Henley's destruction and of violent conflict with Inuit at Little Whale River the previous winter, Ferdinand Jacobs reported from Prince of Wales Fort:

> *The Mellancholy Accounts from ye Other Factorys, has caused a general Grief at this place, Their troubles are of a Dangerous consequence to the Company Interest, and particularly their own Safety, therefore I hartily wish there may be no more Ill Consequences attend them, and that they may make all Matters up in a Friendly manner, for their own Safety, and the Preservation of the Companys Trade.*[3]

Not since the French attacks of the late seventeenth century had so many HBC servants met violent death at the hands of other men; for the first time in living memory the company's employees as a group felt at risk. For some the risk was too great, and five Albany men—described by Isbister and his council as "disorderly resolute persons"—chose to abandon their contracts and return home immediately, despite being charged five pounds each for the passage.[4] Of these five, three (labourer John Meyrick, smith Patrick Mulvey, and cooper James Cutmore) had only engaged the year before, while two (labourer Thomas Stephens and sawyer Thomas Eldridge Seddon) had engaged in 1753; for Stephens and Meyrick, the five-pound charge for their passage home represented half a year's wages.

In the autumn of 1755 Albany surgeon George Rushworth wrote directly to the London Committee, explaining what had led to the destruction of Henley and using the rhetoric of a humble servant convinced of his moral superiority over many of his fellow servants. He spoke very ill of Wappesiss, calling him a pirate (as Isbister had done), but also chastised William Lamb for incautiously keeping two Indigenous women in his quarters. Rushworth reported that he had recommended to Lamb casual rather than long-term relations with Indigenous women and then advised Lamb "to consider he was in a Enemies country, and not to set his door open to every Bunter [low, vulgar woman] but do justly in his dealings, Love Mercy and call upon his god. these things Wou'd inable him to Make a good Servant to the Company." Lamb (as reported by Rushworth) had excused his behaviour by observing that Isbister kept two women at Albany. Lamb's justification echoed that of surgeon and former Albany chief George Spence, who said (according to Rushworth) that the Committee would not mind so long as trade remained strong. Rushworth also implicated sloop master John Yarrow and other unnamed men in this disregard for company expectations of chastity.

Isbister fared no better in the letter: Rushworth used Lamb to mention Isbister's two female companions as providing a justification for lower-ranking men's eschewing of the chastity ideally expected of servants in early modern households. Rushworth presented himself as defending Isbister, while doing the chief more harm than good by saying that he could not explain why Isbister was so unpopular with the Indigenous peoples as he was always very kind to them. Rushworth then forestalled possible criticisms of his own behaviour by saying: "I hope for the future All Englishmen will take this for a warning; And that your Honours will put a Total Stop to that Way of Proseedings [harbouring women] how can I, or aney Man Chastise aney person for a folt When at the same time I am Guilty of that Error My Self." He concluded by urging the Committee to send him to rebuild Henley—having cast aspersions on almost every other man who might have been considered for such an assignment—and promising to protect both the company's and the nation's interests by driving the French from the field.[5]

The Committee had every intention of re-establishing Henley House—indeed, it suggested that Isbister's failure to do so immediately after the killings must have given the Cree "a very slender Opinion of either your Conduct or Courage."[6] The following year, 1756, it responded directly to Rushworth, offering him the command of the new Henley (once he had rebuilt it), but also mentioning that "we saw plainly you were not very Conversant" in keeping accounts.[7] Rushworth thanked his employers by promising to attack any French trading posts that might be built on the Albany River: "give Me a power I will not leave one french dog upon this River as fur [far], above Henley, as to it."[8] The Albany council remarked sourly that Isbister had been the only man at Albany to propose reoccupying Henley,[9] implying that Rushworth had deliberately bypassed his commanding officer in an effort to advance his own prospects and/or that Isbister was trying to protect his own prospects at the expense of

Rushworth's. Albany's complement was increased from twenty-four to forty to allow for the resettlement of Henley, but the supply ship was late that year and the essential provisions had not been prepared.

In 1757 a new expedition to the interior was prepared but encountered almost universal resistance from the servants. Robert Temple, who succeeded Isbister in command of Albany, had anticipated in 1756 that men would be reluctant to resettle Henley,[10] and this was precisely what he found. As he recorded in detail each servant's response to his orders to go upriver, it is possible to compare those responses and what they reveal about the men's expectations. He also recorded the steps he took to try to overcome their reluctance.

His official efforts at persuading his men began on 30 May 1757, when Temple "thought it necessary to call them up one by one"—before shipwright John Fairfowl, carpenter George Clark, and himself—to find out which men had resolved not to go to Henley "and what reasons they can give for such denial of Duty."

> *The men was called one by one & we proceeded, first of all I read part of the fourteenth Paragraph of your General Letter beginning at that part; And we strictly order that ten or twelve men under the Command of Mr Rushworth & so on, then they told their Resolutions for or against & their reasons which you have below, Then I took the Contract & read to them beginning at I do oblige my Self to Stay according to the aforesaid limited time & so on.*[11]

Twenty-four men were questioned, mostly labourers; the fort's tradesmen (except the two tailors) were exempt, but writer John Favell was not. Seventeen of the twenty-four refused to go to Henley, all but one of them citing as their primary motivation a fear of being killed (labourer George Taylor simply said he would not go on any account). The most remarkable of these responses was that of labourer and bricklayer Thomas Austin, who "[s]ays he will not Serve under Mr Rushworth & that Mr Rushworth has said that Annussett one of the Murderers [convicted in absentia in

1755] lay fourteen nights in ambush with intention to shoot the aforesaid Thos Austin, this was before that unfortunate affair att Henley." No reason was given for Annussett's allegedly murderous intentions toward Austin.

Of the eight men who expressed a willingness to go upriver, three (labourer Thomas Halcro, writer John Favell, and John Butler) said that they would comply with the company's orders, possibly implying a reluctance to do so but a greater reluctance to disobey. This may also have been the motivation of former apprentice Guy Warwick in his agreeing only to help with the boats to and from Henley. One man (mariner John Banks) simply said he was willing to go; one (labourer Thomas Joplin) was willing to go but would not serve under Rushworth; and one (labourer James Stinson) ostentatiously declared that "he will do any thing for the Company's Interest."

Another council was called on 6 June, at which each man was asked again if he would comply with the company's orders to resettle Henley. At least some of the men had evidently spent the intervening week discussing their options. This time only labourer George Ballentine still refused to go under any conditions, claiming that he had served at Henley under Lamb and "was very nigh loosing his life by the late ill Management at Henley and is afraid it will be the Same." Several other men's responses remained largely unchanged: Banks, Butler, Favell, and Stinson were still willing to go; Joplin still had no objection to Henley but refused to serve under Rushworth; and Warwick was still interested only in helping with the boats.

Most men, however, were now willing to go upriver under certain conditions. Six men besides Joplin were willing to serve at Henley but not under Rushworth, while labourer Thomas Clouston was willing to serve for twenty pounds per annum under Rushworth or for ten pounds per annum under any other master. Four men demanded at least twenty pounds per annum, and eight demanded at least twenty pounds per annum plus a pension of some kind for their families in case they were killed. Thomas Halcro agreed to go if at least five hands were assigned to Henley.

The men's dislike of Rushworth was much more noticeable on 6 June than it had been a week earlier. The men's responses suggest that Rushworth sabotaged his own chances for command with some ill-judged comments to several servants. Three men reported that Rushworth had expressed the opinion that any man going to Henley for less than twenty pounds per annum "ought to be hang'd"; three reported that Rushworth had claimed that Temple planned to turn any men refusing to go to Henley out of the factory without provisions; and two reported that Rushworth declared his willingness to shoot a man for cowardice. Whatever the reason for Rushworth's injudicious comments, they discouraged men who were already reluctant to go to Henley (especially if under his command), and they undermined his own prospects for advancement. They also call to mind the Committee's earlier opinion that "such fears [of returning to Henley] was inculcated by those who Ought to have Inspired contrary Sentiments." Temple decided to pass over Rushworth in favour of George Clark, to whom the men assented, though without reducing their demands. However, Temple had no authority to agree to wage increases or pensions, so the resettlement of Henley was postponed again.[12]

Little changed after the council of 6 June. A third council, held on 15 August, recommended that the men with wage and/or pension demands go to Henley and trust the Committee to consider their conditions and possibly offer them gratuities; Temple assured them that "when it Was left in Such a Manner...Your Honours had allways Considered, & rewarded handsomely." The suggestion was not well received, however, and two men (Butler and Joplin, both of whom had previously expressed a willingness to go to Henley) announced their intentions of going home at the expiration of their contracts the following year.[13] A fourth council three days later reported that labourer and sawyer Joseph Downs and labourer and netmaker John Farrant (both just returned from the Eastmain) and three men from the supply ship (which had just arrived) were willing to go to Henley. However, the council's plan to send them upriver with Banks, Favell, Halcro, and Stinson (who had never objected to going to Henley) under Rushworth's command was unfeasible because the river was too low to accommodate the boats so late in the summer. It is unclear when or why Clark was dropped from consideration, but he had made it clear at the fourth council that he refused to serve under Rushworth. A weary council postponed the resettlement of Henley until the following year and recommended (unsuccessfully) that the company hire men specifically for inland service.[14]

If Temple's aim in recording his efforts in such detail had been to demonstrate to his employers that he had done his utmost in trying to carry out their instructions, he was not very successful. The Committee had always considered the attack an isolated incident, and its initial response had downplayed the ongoing danger from either Indigenous or French foes—despite rumours reaching Albany that French traders were offering rewards worth thirty made beaver (prime winter skins) or five pounds for the scalp of an HBC trader.[15] The 1758 letter from London expressed deep disappointment that Henley had not been reoccupied

> *notwithstanding the full and positive Orders we gave on that head in 1756 which we think you ought to have Compelled a thorough Compliance with the danger pretended…is not real but imaginary…and whomsoever shall refuse to obey your Orders on this head or shall instigate any of our Servants there to, will incur Our highest displeasure and most certainly be punished for so Notorious a breach of their Contract.*[16]

Four men (labourers Robert Lisk, William Linklater, and Peter Knight and tailor Nichol Spence) had indeed been sent home in 1757 for denial of duty in refusing to go to Henley, while three others (Butler, Joplin, and George Ballentine) chose not to renew their contracts.[17]

It is not clear whether some or all of the men who refused to go upriver at the first council in 1757 did so to seek better terms, or if the second council prompted some of the men to make the most of an unpleasant opportunity. Demands for higher wages and for pensions indicated that the men viewed service at Henley, an isolated and clearly vulnerable outpost, as extraordinary, that is, as going beyond the accepted terms of their engagement. Service there was seen as fundamentally different from service in a Bayside factory, and the men required a guarantee of extra compensation for this, rather than trusting the company to make it worth their while.

Henley House was not re-established until May 1759, when George Clark, mariner William Ward, thirteen other servants, and two Homeguard Cree set off upriver from Albany. Clark was no stranger to service in isolated and vulnerable outposts; he had been serving at Whale River in February 1754 when Inuit raided the house.[18] The summer went smoothly, but in September came news of fresh disaster. Two "Henly Boats" had set out with supplies for the outpost but returned the next day, "having met with James Inkster, and John Cromartie who told them that Mr Clark was Shot Dead and John Spence wounded in the Thigh, who they had left at a place called the fishing Creek about half way to Henly."[19] The house had been attacked by as many as forty unidentified Indigenous peoples (probably allied with the French), apparently intent on plunder, and English casualties would have been higher were it not for warning and assistance from local Lowland Cree.[20] In early October two Homeguard Cree ("Chubby" and "old Capucheen") brought Clark's body back to Albany, and he was buried with ceremony: "hoisted the Colours; Read the funeral Service, and fired five Guns over the Grave."[21]

The negotiations of 1757 were repeated in 1764, when Humphrey Marten (newly installed at Albany) was instructed to resettle Henley. His task was not made any easier by the arrival in August of a band of Cree

> *continualy dancing and singing the Warr and beging Songs, and [they] are so impudent in their demands that I know not what to do, the green scalps of the unhappy wretches [four Frenchmen and three "Englishmen"] they murder'd, are presented as a trophy of their valour to every Person they come near, at the same time they demand a reward for killing those they call our Enemys.*[22]

Again, most of the men refused to go, but this time there were no wage demands or complaints about who was going to be in charge. Of the twenty-three men asked by Marten and members of his council (outgoing chief factor Robert Temple and supply-ship captain John Horner), eight refused to go, and ten declared that they would never go to Henley under any circumstances. Labourer (and former apprentice) William Allen and sloop man John Farrant agreed to assist with the boats but refused to stay at Henley; Farrant had been willing to stay inland in 1757, but in 1765 he was willing to sign a three-year contract at his current wages if he could serve at Moose. Carpenter Thomas Pope was prepared to help construct a new building "to oblige your Honors" but would not remain inland; labourer John Stone (who had just arrived in Hudson Bay) would go if ordered; and labourer David Ross only agreed to go "after much Perswation & threatning." The only unreservedly positive response was that of sawyer John Reeves, who "Says tho' he is Fifty Eight Years of age he will Venture his Life, to saw the Wood."[23]

Robert Temple probably informed Marten of his own experiences in 1757 and the chastisement that had followed. The 1764 Albany mail packet included a brief letter from the Albany council, including Temple, Captain John Horner, and surgeon William Richards: "We whose Names are under written do declare that Mr Humphrey Marten, in Our hearing, has endeavoured by Perswation, by Entreaty, and by Threats, to get a sufficient Number of Hands to go to Henly...but notwithstanding his utmost Efforts could not prevail."[24] Marten's own letter to the Committee also lamented their failure to gather enough men for Henley.

> *I tould them the disobeying orders, was a breach of Contract...I tould them it was Your Honours firm intention to reward each Man according to his Merrit by rewarding the Obedient, and punishing the disobedient I tould them it was now greatly in their Power to continue me in Your Honours Esteem, and that in case my well being had any sway with them, it would raise my Gratitude to such a pitch as would induce me rather to pinch my self rather than they s[h]ould want for any thing, I promised each Man*

that would go to Henly a Blanket, a pair of Cloth Stockings and a Leather Toggee [winter coat]...and now Gentlemen permit me humbly to throw my self on your Humanity and permit me to hope You will not be angry with me for the Falts of others.[25]

Here in one paragraph was the whole range of managerial approaches to personnel issues in the HBC: enforcing the legal and moral authority of the service contract; promising both monetary and non-monetary rewards; threatening punishment for misbehaviour; emphasizing reciprocal obligations; and ultimately appealing to the employer as a client appeals to a patron or as a child to a father.

The dangers of transport to and from Henley were emphasized on 15 September 1766: labourers John Stone and Daniel Bryan drowned while tracking the boats up to Henley, which had just been re-established.[26] Such supply trips, however, removed men from the watchful eyes of their factors and gave the men of Albany greater opportunities to appropriate company goods for their own purposes (as Bryan had done before his death).[27] There were other potential hazards too, some not unique to inland service: on the night of 12 January 1782, Henley was destroyed by an accidental fire. John Luitit, James Rowland, and Robert Cromartie died in the blaze, and three others nearly froze to death, having escaped from the house with only minimal clothing. In reporting the accident to Matthew Cocking at York, Thomas Hutchins at Albany called Henley "the most unfortunate place in the Country."[28]

The most significant difference between Henley and Albany was the element of physical danger at human hands. Only after the first violent incident at Henley did service there become a major issue between the chief factor and the servants. In 1764, after another death had increased the perceived danger (danger that the Committee insisted in 1758 was only perceived and not real), the strength of men's determination not to go inland seemed to have increased. In 1757 tailor George Harvey had said "he will not go up to Henley on any account Whatsoever by reason of the five mens death & does not know but he may meet with the Same Fate," and labourer Robert Miller and others refused, "being afraid of being killed by the Indians."[29] Labourer Charles Sinclear had been at Henley when Clark was killed, and declared in 1764 that he "[p]ositively will not go, to Henly to run his head into the hands of the Enemy" (it was unclear whether the enemy was Indigenous or French, or perhaps both). Labourer James Thomson Sr "[s]ays Positively he will not go, that you may as well tye him to a post and Shoot him."[30]

The attitudes of labourer James Sabiston and others who in 1757 refused to go upriver for less than twenty pounds per annum and a pension for their widows were probably not much different from men who took advantage of recruitment shortfalls or wartime conditions to re-engage for higher salaries. In 1764 the workers' statements were stronger. Labourer John Cromartie's declaration that "his Life is dearer to him than all the Money in the Country" (he too had been at Henley in 1759) was echoed by others. Labourer William Shurie Jr and mariner and sawyer (and former apprentice) Joseph Downs knew first-hand the hardships to be endured at Henley; labourer John Spence had been wounded in the attack on Clark in 1759 and proclaimed that "no Money in England should cause him to go to Henly." Carpenter William Isbister "[s]ays positively he will not go, he says had he known that he was to go to Henly, he would not have come to the Country." Of the six men whose times were up the following year, only mariner George Lisk—who appears to have served primarily on the Eastmain—was willing to sign a new contract, and labourer Thomas Tate refused to sign the new contract he had been offered "for fere he should be sent to Henly." Tate claimed that the sight of Clark's body being brought home had frightened him too severely. Labourer Robert Gaudy described Henley as having a bad character; tailor George Corner and labourer James Angusson pleaded age and infirmity; and labourer James Thomson Jr refused "because the Old hands are afraid to go."[31]

In both 1757 and 1764 the Albany servants clearly recognized the vulnerability of their master and of the factors who were dependent on the Committee's good opinion. Marten acknowledged their bargaining power when he complained in 1765 that his further entreaties for men to go to Henley met with no greater success than before and indeed made him the target of unspecified abuse by some of his men (particularly labourer Andrew Atkins).[32] This abuse counterbalanced the threats that Marten and his council admitted they had used to try to persuade men the previous summer. It also indicated, however, that the men could probably have made the same kinds of demands as had been made in 1757 if they had wanted to (none of the 1764 men had been at Albany during the first two councils of 1757).

Henley was not re-established until 1766, under the management of surgeon William Richards—whose ambition and fractiousness echoed that of his predecessor, Rushworth. The choice of leadership remained important, however, as did the necessity for encouragement. In 1766 Marten had to send boats and supplies to supplement what Richards had taken upriver with him; Albany clerk George Humble "Offer'd his service with the greatest Cheerfullness or I should have had much ado to get the men to go again, but when I told them, I would give each a Duffle waistcoat, & a pair of Stockings, & that Mr Humble was to go, they made but few words about it."[33]

By the 1760s the perceived demands of service at Henley had moved beyond the limits of what was generally considered appropriate by the men of Albany. Nor were they alone. The Prince of Wales Fort journal for 1758–59 recorded a conversation between chief factor Ferdinand Jacobs, surgeon Thomas Robertson, and sloop master James Wood:

> *[I]n taulking about the men at Albany Refusing to go to settle Henley I [Jacobs] said if any of the men under my command was to Refuse going upon such an affair (under a good officer) they should not stay another year with me and that there should be some work between us, but I should have it done.... [Robertson and Wood] both said the men was in the right to object against going & that they have no business with an Enemy, Especially the wood runners without the factory walls, I replyed to them both that those officers that was of that opinion & would taulk so against*

the men did not Deserve to be of the council, to which Robertson Portly [pertly?] answered he would say so to the committies.[34]

At Albany, none of the customary tools of negotiation used by the factors or by the Committee could change the men's minds. The attempts to re-establish Henley generated the most detailed evidence that we have for this period, concerning negotiations between the company and its servants on the terms and issues of employment. Although the circumstances were atypical, especially in the men's opportunity to negotiate more or less as a single group, the assumptions and expectations that they brought to those negotiations were representative of those prevalent in this period.

Inland Wintering

Henley House was never intended to be a distinct inland trading post, as Cumberland House would be in 1774. Of greater immediate importance for the company's trade was the 1754–55 journey to the Saskatchewan River valley undertaken by HBC labourer and netmaker Anthony Henday and a Homeguard Cree man named Connawappa, accompanying a group of Upland Cree led by Attickasish. This revived the company's late-seventeenth-century efforts to send servants (singly or in pairs) to winter in the interior with groups of upland traders and to encourage all Indigenous peoples whom they met to trap furs, to trade at the Bay, and not to go to war.

James Isham's *Observations on Hudson's Bay*, written at Prince of Wales Fort in 1743, helped revive interest in inland travel and expansion. Isham suggested that an inland trading house at the head of Nelson River, or on the lower Saskatchewan River, might dislodge the French from the Lake Winnipeg basin. By the end of the decade he had become less optimistic and more defensive in the face of public criticism of the HBC and argued that the French could not be dislodged from Lake Winnipeg while Canada was still in their possession. Ironically, French traders in the 1750s complained that their western posts could never flourish while the

English were on the Bay—perhaps an exaggerated complaint as part of their appeals to the state for an increase in the price of beaver.[35]

When Isham was in charge of York, he sent Henday and Connawappa inland to winter on the northern prairies in 1754–55. Henday went inland again in 1759–60, this time accompanied by Joseph Smith and Jean Baptiste D'Laryea. Henday was the first of a series of travelling trade representatives, wintering in different areas and with different groups of Cree and Assiniboine. Although these men had a fundamentally different experience of Rupert's Land than did their Bayside colleagues, they were no more than an influential minority during this period. Only fourteen men embarked on inland expeditions between 1754 and 1770, all from York Fort, and no more than six were in the interior at the same time. In contrast to the more literate post-1770 winterers, such as Matthew Cocking and Peter Fidler, the early winterers were almost all labourers; they left behind few journals or other records and were more noteworthy because of the Indigenous people who accompanied them down to the Bay in the spring to trade than for anything they did at the factories.

The Bayside factors and the London Committee were pleased with the new inland policy, and Isham was pleased to take the credit.[36] He emphasized (among other things) Henday's devotion to his employer's interests and his ability to promote those interests effectively; and he praised Henday for undergoing "not a little hardship...yet he proceeded on his Journey with a Resolution suitable to ye design he was Sent upon."[37] In doing so, Isham could portray Henday's success as representative of his own efforts to advance the company's interests. For instance, Henday attempted another inland journey in 1755 but returned when his English companion, apprentice William Grover, became "Jaded"; Isham called this "a great disappointment in our proceedings, Captn Hendey being no Less Concerned than Myself being disappointed of an Undertaking he had so Good a prospect of success in."[38] Just as Isham's disappointment probably had as much to do with the setback to his own ambitious plans as to the potential consequences for trade, Henday's disappointment may have been multi-faceted. He may have been upset about what it would mean for the company's trade; he may have been upset about what his failure to return inland would mean for his own ambitions; and/or he may have regretted not getting to see friends or even a Cree wife. Overlapping interests and motivations made men's behaviour difficult to interpret.

The efforts of Henday and his fellows coincided with the beginning of the Seven Years' War (1756–63), which interrupted the Montreal-based fur trade for several years: although a few French traders remained in the western interior, they received no shipments of goods and supplies from Montreal after the fall of New France in 1760. British traders followed British troops into Montreal, and the trade of Albany and York fell dramatically in 1768, but Ferdinand Jacobs hesitated to send his men inland from York that year. He doubted their influence with inland First Nations (doubts reinforced by their own reports),[39] and he felt that he had been deceived in 1767 when Cree traders and his own men had told him there were no pedlars inland from York—although they had probably been telling the truth.[40]

Jacobs and his second, Andrew Graham, suggested that most men went inland to serve their own interests rather than the company's; the servants' reputations and prospects suffered without any officers defending them against such charges. Graham called the winterers of the 1760s "ignorant poor labouring men of no abilities, who likes to go for no other reason but to lead an idle and vagrant life amongst the natives, and to get a few furs for themselves....I sent most of those men myself," he admitted, "but what can I or any Factor do otherwise?" He complained that officers were unwilling to go inland, while labourers were petitioning to go.[41] When he was in charge of Cumberland House in the winter of 1776–77, Cocking reported that men whom he had sent to live with Indigenous families (principally to save on the house's provisions) complained of being neglected or mistreated by their hosts, but he blamed his men for "not being affable and otherwise endeavouring to make themselves agreable, seeming frequently displeased and unwilling to render little Assistances....[S]ome of them like very well to go off at first with the Indians, as they are removed from under the Eye of a Master and expect to have nothing to do."[42]

The "few furs" to which Graham referred were probably a major motivation for going inland, as they could significantly add to men's incomes; for instance, Anthony Henday (earning ten pounds per annum) received £8 18s. 5d. for the furs he brought back from his 1754–55 journey.[43] This was still the case after Cumberland had been established: recalcitrant sawyer William Taylor wanted his wages more than doubled for him to serve inland again, yet he offered to winter with a group of Assiniboine (with whom Edward Loutit had spent three years). Humphrey Marten was not disposed to do Taylor any favours and refused the offer, calling him "too great a Coward, to manage Indians of this stamp."[44]

When Cocking himself went inland in 1772, he believed that he both benefited and suffered from the precedents set by those who had gone before him. He reported:

> *I find the Natives consider an Englishman's going with them, as a Person sent to Collect Furrs, and not as an encouragement to them to trap &c. from the Company's Servants who came with them Inland trading the chief part of the Goods they were furnished with at the Forts [to give as gifts]: and notwithstanding all I can say to the contrary, will hardly believe but I shall also collect Furrs in their Season.*[45]

> *As to sending Servants Inland, in the manner that has been already pursued, to encourage Trade. I am of Opinion it will Answer no end; For the Persons who have been upon this Service, only like to continue as it skreened them from Duty at the Fort: And they were most of them disliked; as they never endeavoured to gain the Affections of the Natives, and converted the Goods they were furnished with to the Purpose of Collecting Furrs for their own private Emolument.*[46]

Ferdinand Jacobs complained that some or all of the men he was sending inland in the late 1760s were using company goods for private trade, and the Committee in 1771 instructed him to reduce the amount of goods issued to those men (particularly Louis Primeau).[47]

In the winterers' defence, the Indigneous peoples whom they met inland were probably familiar with the itinerant (*en derouine*) style of trading employed by Montreal-based traders, and the HBC men probably felt great pressure to trade the goods they had taken with them. The winterers probably also had difficulty convincing the Indigenous peoples of the interior to spend more time and effort trapping furs, when they could demonstrate no particular benefit and when increased trapping took time and effort away from other things those peoples wanted or needed to do.[48] As well, the Englishmen's Indigenous companions saw hosting a winterer as an opportunity for various benefits. Jacobs objected to the Committee's 1769 suggestion of discontinuing the practice of wintering, on the grounds that the Indigenous families with whom these men travelled took great pride in hosting a winterer and would feel offended if the practice ceased suddenly.[49] He could have also mentioned the gifts from the factors and the other benefits that they derived for acting as hosts and guides. William Pink reported in one of his inland journals that "i had Got me a horse to Cary my thinges, thinking that i Should Get it alonge without being Troblesome to the Indaines for the[y] think a Great deal of Carriing aney thing for an English man un less he pay them well for it."[50]

Pink and his superiors all recognized that inland travel created new opportunities for both the English and the First Nations, opportunities that would be further enhanced when inland trading posts were constructed. As the logistics of the company's operations changed, so too did the public and private relationships. Furthermore, the transfer of inland competition from French to Anglo-American merchants created new threats, some more explicit and others more insidious.

Inland Expansion: Taking the Fight to "the Cursed Pedlars Up Country"

The HBC presence in the western interior waned during the 1760s. Veteran winterers Joseph Smith and Isaac Batt went inland in 1763, but Henry Pressick (of whom much had been expected) returned home in ill health, as had Anthony Henday the year before. Smith and Batt went inland again in 1764, as did John Taylor, but Smith died on his return journey, and Taylor refused to go inland again. Another experienced inland traveller, Joseph Waggoner (probably the son of Rowland Waggoner), drowned in 1766. In 1766–67, however, six HBC men wintered with Cree or Assiniboine groups on the Churchill River (Louis Primeau), the Red Deer River (James Dearing), the North Saskatchewan River (Edward Loutit and James Allen), the South Saskatchewan River (William Pink), and the Sturgeon River (Isaac Batt).[51]

In the autumn of 1767 Montreal-based British traders began to reoccupy former French posts in the Lake Winnipeg basin that had been largely abandoned around 1760. William Tomison brought to Andrew Graham depressing reports of his winters inland in 1769–70 and 1771–72.[52] Then, in 1772, New Englander John Cole deserted Canadien service and went to York, where he gave Graham (temporarily in charge) information and advice that convinced him to discard all his previous arguments against inland posts. Graham engaged Cole for three years at twelve pounds per annum and sent him inland to bring down a fellow servant named Bove (or Beauvais), "a Canadian, a good able Man who resides amongst the Natives." Graham proposed to establish an inland post with a complement of fourteen young and able-bodied new men under a master who "must be a Young lively Person, that will continue some Years in your Service" (he recommended either Samuel Hearne or Thomas Hutchins).[53] From his post at Cedar Lake, Cole's former master Thomas Corry wrote to York, warning that Bove and Cole were deserters and thieves, and asking that the company ship them to England for trial (for which they would be reimbursed by Corry).[54] Graham ignored this letter. He was impressed by

Cole: "He is a tall, able man, speaks English, French and Indian languages, was formerly one of the batteau men under Sir William Johnston, and has travelled from Albany Town and all over French and British Canada, talks very sensibly, and can write a little, and is much regarded by the Indians."[55] Cole returned to York in 1773, without Bove and the two large cargo canoes he had promised; Graham sent him inland again, but Cole returned to Corry's service that year.[56]

Cole's desertion shook the faith of the Committee in Canadiens, but its newfound resolution to expand into the interior was not derailed. Orders to that effect had already been issued. The Committee's quick and positive response to Graham's about-face annoyed Ferdinand Jacobs, whose earlier pro-inland arguments had fallen on deaf ears thanks in part to Graham's opposition. Yet it speaks well of the Committee's determination to grapple with a problem (once recognized), especially as its other big piece of business in 1772 was writing off as a loss roughly twenty thousand pounds spent on the Churchill River black-whale fishery over the previous seven years.[57]

In the spring of 1774 Samuel Hearne and six men went upriver from York to establish Cumberland House. Having been unable to procure canoes of their own, they travelled as passengers in the canoes of upland traders: Hearne, Robert Longmoor, and Andrew Garret with one group; and William Flatt, Magnus Sclater, James Banks, and Robert Davey with other groups. Matthew Cocking, Isaac Batt, and Charles Price Isham also embarked but did not make it to Cumberland that year and ended up wintering on God's Lake. Not only had these three men had more inland experience than anyone else in the group except Hearne, but their share of the equipment and goods for Cumberland included the pit-saw and the medicine chest. Thus, the whole of Hearne's small complement was completely unacquainted with any "duty that is not Emediatly Preform'd at the Factory, none of them ever having been farther from the Forts than a Wooding or hunting tent." They were understandably anxious about what they had gotten themselves into, and they might well have abandoned the project had Hearne's leadership not been infused with his experiences under much more severe conditions.[58]

Company men also moved inland to the south and east of James Bay. In 1776 surgeon Thomas Atkinson with four hands and two Cree families established Wapiscogamy House about 120 miles up Moose River (on its western branch, the Missinaibi River, half a mile above the mouth of Wapiscogamy Creek); this was rebuilt and renamed Brunswick House in 1781.[59] Labourer James Robertson went inland from Eastmain House in 1778 and 1779, wintering in a log tent on or near Lake Mistassini. However, inland trading from Eastmain ceased after Thomas Buchan "died from real want of Victuals in crossing a Lake" (possibly Mistassini) in January 1781; Robertson had been appointed master of Rupert House, and Buchan's death left George Atkinson at Eastmain without anyone experienced in inland travel.[60]

York's inland operations expanded in 1779 when William Tomison sent Robert Longmoor with fifteen hands to build Hudson House up the Saskatchewan River. Longmoor's men included Charles Isham (whose father, James, was English and whose mother was Cree), two Englishmen (Isaac Batt and William Gray), and possibly a Welshman (Robert Davey), but the rest of his hands were Orkneymen (James Spence Jr, Magnus Twatt, Malchom Ross, Nichol Wishart, Edward Wishart, James Tate, William Copeland, James Sanderson, William Oman, Mitchell Oman, and William Lutit). When Tomison (an Orkneyman himself) took command of Hudson House that autumn, he reported that "I never see better Servant[s] in Hudson's Bay then what is here at present nor better behaved men."[61]

The new outpost, strategically placed on the edge of the "buffalo country," was intended to procure provisions as well as furs. This provoked the local Cree: in 1780 they used prairie fires to drive the bison out of the reach of Englishmen, hoping to keep the latter reliant on the Cree for the bulk of their meat. Longmoor's warehouse was ill equipped to trade for both furs and meat, so he sent five men back to Cumberland and put the remaining seventeen (including himself) on half-rations. This provoked his men: fifteen of them wrote a letter to Tomison in May 1781 in which they blamed Longmoor for the shortage of provisions, accused him of drunkenness, and refused to serve inland under him again (only writer James Elphinstone appears to have supported Longmoor).[62]

The petition against Longmoor came to nothing. Tomison investigated the men's claims of "Starving" under Longmoor's command but considered them ill founded; he did not respond to the charge that Longmoor was habitually drunk at trading time. Humphrey Marten and the York council defended Longmoor to the Committee, although they admitted that the petition was one reason they decided to send Longmoor to winter in or near the Athabasca country and put William Walker in charge of Hudson House.[63]

Nevertheless, this petition was just one example of a general dissatisfaction among inland servants. In 1775 Samuel Hearne reported from Cumberland House that "the People have not got the prosperity of the Expedition at heart...[M]any of them will rather be sent home then [*sic*] continue to go inland at their present wages and...only move in Proportion as they think they are payd."[64] In the spring of 1775 Samuel Hearne could only find three volunteers to stay at Cumberland for the summer while most of the men took the winter's returns down to York. His successor, Matthew Cocking, took seven men with him to York in 1776 (including Magnus Sclater and William Flatt "on Account of their having been here the Year before") and left William Walker in charge of three men: carpenter Andrew Garret and labourers James Batt and James Spence, the latter two chosen by the drawing of lots.[65]

Labourer John Driver was strongly suspected by the York council in 1775 of feigning illness to avoid being sent inland that year. Although he did go inland in 1776 and even expressed a willingness to re-engage for inland service at ten pounds per annum, at Cumberland House in May 1777 Matthew Cocking strongly suspected him of feigning illness again to avoid being sent farther up the Saskatchewan River. Cocking admitted that he had no proof of Driver's alleged deception and so "treated him with Tenderness and indulged him," although he refused to allow Driver to go down to York. Driver was yet again suspected of feigning or exaggerating illness at Cumberland in the spring of 1782, when William Tomison called him "a Deceitful Villain."[66]

In 1776 Humphrey Marten repeated that hands sent inland felt themselves inadequately rewarded for the hardships they endured, and mentioned Orkneymen in particular as "very remiss in protecting your [Honours'] Goods, or in making themselves acquainted with the management of a Canoe; by which means they hope to be kept at the Fort, as unfit for inland duties."[67] In order to persuade his men to go inland "Cheerfully and have your [Honours'] Interest at heart," Marten promised each man an advance or gratuity of two pounds—three months' wages for most of them. He was informed that his predecessor, Ferdinand Jacobs, had made a similar promise that the Committee had not honoured, so Marten gave each man "my note of hand" for two pounds if London did not honour his promise.[68] In fact, the Committee's approval of Jacobs's promise was en route, and Marten's promise was approved the following year—the catch, of course, being that gratuities would only be paid to those "whom You shall represent to Us as worthy of such Encouragement for that Purpose."[69]

In 1777, however, Marten became aware of "a kind of Combination" among some of York's Orkney servants: sawyer William Taylor, who had come down to York in July, "absolutely refused to return Inland, and gave several broad hints" that he and his fellows planned to "stick up for" fifteen pounds per annum (Taylor was currently on six pounds per annum). Marten asked him a second time to go inland as ordered, but "he said he would not, 'till he had conferred with his country Men"; Marten relieved Taylor of his duties, put him on one pound of bread a day, and threatened him with forfeiture of wages until Taylor relented and agreed to go inland.[70] Marten instructed William Tomison at Cumberland to inform his men of the Committee's resolve not to advance inland hands above ten pounds per annum, as well as his own resolution that servants refusing to go inland (or anywhere else they were ordered to go) would forfeit any gratuities or wage advances that he had promised them.[71] Some of the surviving contracts signed in 1777–79 contained the handwritten clause, "I will be ready to Travel from the Factory to any parts inland for the better Discovery of the Country and improving the Trade of the said Company whenever I shall be commanded so to do by the Governor or Chief Factor there without claiming any additional Wages or Gratification for the same." In 1780 the surviving contracts began specifically mentioning extra wages of forty shillings per annum for men serving inland.[72]

The Committee took some time to reach that point. It initially offered a forty-shilling per annum gratuity for servants who went inland in 1774 and 1775 and whose wages did not exceed six pounds.[73] It only approved Marten's promised gratuity retroactively in 1779, by which time Marten's men inland were demanding even more "encouragement." At the same time, the Committee instituted a schedule of premiums: for each score of furs traded at an inland house the master received one shilling, his assistant six pence, and each labourer three pence.[74] However, in 1780 Marten again warned the Committee that "[n]ot one of your Inland Servants think they are properly encouraged...they say that the wages you offer them is not proportionate to the Services they render to the Company."[75] The servants were complaining not about hardship but about not being adequately compensated for enduring more hardship than was normal at the Bayside factories and houses. As Hearne had explained in 1775, "their whole complaint is for want of encouragement."[76]

|| Expansion and experimentation were nothing new, but the construction of permanent trading posts in the interior gradually reoriented the company's focus away from Hudson and James bays. Less gradual was the change in working conditions and the nature of the work men were expected to perform. Humphrey Marten summarized inland conditions in 1780: servants' "lives frequently threat[e]ned by the Canadians who's numbers are as 15 to 1; Frequent hungry bellys; wet and cold lodgings are amongst the many other hardships they undergo."[77] When Joseph Isbister and his men were slogging up the Albany River to build Henley House in 1743, he consoled himself with the thought that "time & Experience may

render it more Easey to us, & that ye present fatigues will redound to ye Companys intrest & our Credit."[78] Whether he shared these comforting thoughts with his companions was not recorded.

Inland service redirected the Committee's expectations of its officers and servants, placing new demands on all of the parties concerned—and thus on the prevailing public transcript. Isbister realized how far he was pushing his men, noting with some sympathy that the distance from Albany to Henley was "a little to[o] Great Considering ye Capacity of our men who are but Covenanted Servants & Comonly old before they Come into this Countrey & that they are intirely Unhandy in Cannoes & unfitt for this way of life it requiring Such as can hunt & provide for them selves as ye french men doe."[79] The men's responses to those demands were foreshadowed in the establishment and re-establishments of Henley House and were developed more fully later in the century. Many of them obviously agreed with William Tomison's 1781 lament: "it is no wonder the Company's Servants in general is unwilling to come Inland, their usage in many particulars, not being equal to their Servitude."[80]

7 Master-Servant Relationships

> *[W]ee shall never be wanting to reward those yt Serve Us faithfully & honestly*
>
> —HBC to James Knight & Council (Albany Fort), 20 May 1699, HBCA, A. 6/3, fol. 43d

CONSCIOUSLY OR NOT, Tomison had summarized the dominant public transcript of the company's first century: the expectation that the "usage" men received would be equal to their "Servitude." This worked both ways, of course. The 1725 hope of the Committee that York's new gunner, mariner John Wateridge, "will faithfully discharge his duty suitable to ye incouragement we have given him" applied to all of its servants. The Committee had assured the penitent Joseph Myatt the year before that "if your diligence & Zeal for ye Comp[any']s service continue as much to our Satisfaction as your past Service you will not fail in receiving that justice from us which you will have very great reason to expect."[1]

This sense of equity was not simply expressed in monetary terms. L.D. Schwarz's examination of English wages and workplace customs found that "the phrase 'a fair day's work' was used initially in the 1770s and more freely from the 1790s, but combining this with 'a fair day's pay' started in the 1830s and was not widespread in the economic literature until the 1840s." Service—whether domestic, farm, or apprenticeship—was still undertaken primarily in families, where non-monetary considerations loomed large. Although the relationship itself was contracted, the servant's time was not; hours of work were not generally specified, because all the hours in the day belonged to his or her master.[2]

HBC servants worked within a hierarchy based primarily not on class or connections but on service. Moses Norton was tartly reminded of this in 1771 when some of his "Friends" in Britain tried to put in a good word for him should the command of York Fort become available: "We are by no means pleased that any of your Friends should personally interest themselves on your behalf upon a presumed Vacancy to happen at York Fort, for as We have always paid A just regard to Merit and long Services Sollicitations of every kind are very disagreeable."[3] This contrasted with most other long-distance trading companies, where such lobbying was common. Lord Egmont tried to obtain for his cousin a situation with the East India Company in 1733 but was told by one of the directors that "there are so many noblemen's relations already in the service that it could not be."[4]

The main body of EIC servants came from mercantile (especially Scottish) families, which entailed social and kinship networks of their own. Neither nobility nor prominent mercantile families were well represented in the HBC's workforce at this time. A well-placed patron, whether within or outside the company, could be an advantage but was not a prerequisite, nor was it a guarantee of long-term success in the service. Whereas patience and perseverance were key to success within the EIC's hierarchy, which relied on a deliberate process of promotion based largely (though not entirely) on seniority, access to the upper ranks of the HBC hierarchy was directly connected to a man's willingness and ability to behave according to expected standards.[5]

To a certain extent, behaviour (or expected behaviour) was linked to position or occupation. The Committee expected more of tradesmen and officers than of labourers and mariners (the "common men"), and factors relied on tradesmen and old hands to provide them with information and advice and to set good examples for the "green" hands.[6] When Henry

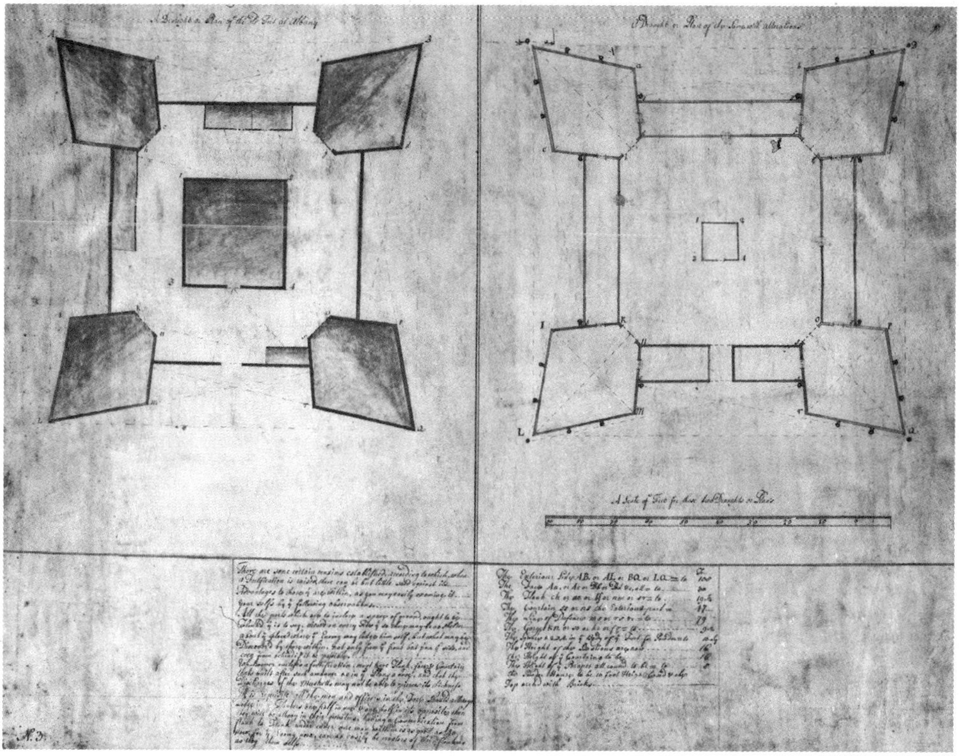

This undated plan of mid-eighteenth-century alterations to Albany shows men and goods being moved out of a house in the centre of the courtyard into the flankers and into buildings positioned along the walls. The move was made to make the post more defensible rather than to make the men more comfortable. [HBCA, G.1/75]

Kelsey was a rising star at York, the Committee encouraged him to "keepe a good understanding wth the Govr & good Decorum a Mongst the Men." When Richard Staunton took charge of Albany in 1723, he "Examined Several of the most sober men and Espitially the traides men in private" to ascertain the character of his predecessor, Joseph Myatt.[7] Tradesmen and senior labourers were often appointed to factory councils, advisory bodies with whom factors could consult and on whom rested responsibility for a smooth transition in the event of a factor's death or incapacity; for example, bricklayer Augustine Frost served on the councils of Moose in the 1730s and York in the 1750s. In 1733 the Committee even made provision for council members to take command "in Joint Commission" if factors (and seconds, if present) should die or be absent from the post.[8]

TABLE 2. *Factors and Councils, 1733*

	Albany Fort	*Moose Fort*	*York Fort*	*Prince of Wales Fort*
Chief factor	Joseph Adams	William Bevan	Thomas McCliesh Jr	Richard Norton
Second (to succeed)	None	None	Thomas White	James Napper
Council / Joint commission	William Moncrief *(surgeon)*	George Green *(sloop master)*	William Roberts *(surgeon)*	Thomas Render* *(sloop master)*
	Samuel Walker *(bookkeeper)*	John Edwards *(surgeon)*	John Morris *(shipwright)*	John Dale *(surgeon)*
	John Hancock *(armourer)*	Samuel Maidman *(bookkeeper)*	Richard Myncin *(bricklayer)*	Alex Light *(shipwright)*
	Thomas Wilson *(house carpenter)*	Thomas Gregory *(carpenter)*		*if absent, then Thomas Gittins *(labourer/foreman)*
	Richard Willis *(labourer)*	Augustine Frost *(bricklayer)*		

Sources: HBC *to J. Adams & Council (AF), 12 May 1733,* HBCA, A. *6/5, fol. 71;* HBC *to T. McCliesh Jr & Council (YF), 12 May 1733,* HBCA, A. *6/5, fol. 74;* HBC *to R. Norton & Council (PWF), 12 May 1733,* HBCA, A. *6/5, fol. 77d;* HBC *to W. Bevan & Council (MF), 12 May 1733,* HBCA, A. *6/5, fol. 81.*

In the spring of 1762 Humphrey Marten (in charge of York following James Isham's death) experienced some disciplinary problems with a few of his men—principally the accountant, Hugh Jones, who insulted Marten and demanded to be sent inland to winter with an unidentified group of Indigenous peoples. Upon receipt of this demand Marten "called up Stairs, Christopher Atkinson [sloop master], Anthony Henday [labourer and netmaker] and George Richardson [shipwright], that they might hear his (Hugh Jones's) reasons for sending me the above Letter, they being the properest Men I could think of." Marten interviewed Jones in their presence; Jones was less than co-operative, and Marten threatened to hold him in chains until the supply ship arrived if Jones did not sign a document agreeing not to leave the factory without his permission. The agreement was copied into the post journal and witnessed by Henday and Richardson, along with a statement that Jones had signed the agreement of his own will and had not been coerced in any way. Marten added that "this in Justice I must declare that Christopher Atkinson has behaved in the best manner, his whole study as well as Anthony Hendays being to keep peace below Stairs."[9]

Nevertheless, there are many examples of men attaining high rank and/or enjoying long service despite frequent bickering with their employers over a variety of issues; the Committee even overlooked private trading by George Geyer, James Knight, Robert Pilgrim, Humphrey Marten, Ferdinand Jacobs, Moses Norton, and others who had charge of the company's trading posts. Thus, an analysis of behaviour and misbehaviour cannot entirely explain men's experiences within the company. Less visible factors were also playing a critical role in shaping HBC service. Although there is no evidence that the London Committee sought to make its business anything more than just a business, in early modern Europe even "just a business" had social dimensions. Commercial firms were (and still are) social systems, encouraging appropriate behaviour and discouraging inappropriate behaviour.[10] These were not explicitly constructed mechanisms but rather were intrinsic to the nature of early modern business and to the broader cultural and social values of the times.

Master-Servant Rhetoric in the HBC

As we have already seen, the rhetoric employed by the Bayside factors and by the London Committee reflected contemporary understandings of the proper relationship between master and servant. Abundant and inexpensive advice manuals emphasized the proper behaviours and attitudes to adopt toward one's superiors and inferiors. Servants and apprentices were expected to have regard for their master's profit and reputation,[11] as well as for their own future prospects, while masters were expected to behave with paternal firmness and condescension (graciousness and affability to one's inferiors).

Both inward and outward HBC correspondence was consistently couched in the terms of the master-servant relationship.[12] James Knight—himself a shareholder and former Committee member, as well as a long-time servant—signed his 1714 letter to the Committee, "I rest your honours' most faithful and obedient servant to command." Thomas McCliesh Jr concluded a 1723 letter, "wishing your honours health and prosperity both at home and abroad is the earnest desire of your honours' most humble and obedient servant." James Isham concluded a 1739 letter by promising to "use my uttermost endeavours in the performance of all such orders I have received from your honours to the uttermost of my power which is the eternal desire of, Honourable Sirs, your honours' most dutiful and obedient humble servant to command." Even the French-Canadian Jean Baptiste D'Laryea described himself in 1761 as "Vortes [*sic*] humble et votres avbeisat [obeissant] Serviteur Larlée."[13]

Deference was the predominant tone. Knight expressed the hope that his handling of the transfer of power at York in 1714 was satisfactory: "Sir, if I have done anything amiss as may not be taken well by you and the rest of the committee [of which he had so recently been a member], pray pardon me...I beg the favour of a little correction rather than to be far condemned."[14] This was precisely the approach taken by the Committee when Richard Norton's management of Prince of Wales Fort fell short of expectations. It demoted him and transferred him to York,

> *to be under the direction of Governr Macklish, which we are certain will be very much to your advantage and improvement in the knowledge of our Trade and Accounts, for we do not think that you have converted any of our goods to your own use, with any design to defraud the Company, but believe that what we observed...hath been for want of your knowing perfectly the method of Trade, used at our other Factories, and our design*

in removing of you, is only to give you an opportunity, to qualify your Self, for farther advancement in our Service which you will not fail to do, by observing and following the instructions you will receive from Capt Thomas Macklish, We wish you success, and remain Your Loving Friends.[15]

According to McCliesh, Norton accepted his demotion with good grace, anticipating author Samuel Richardson's advice "that you shew no Impatience of being told of your Faults; but that you think every one your Friend who informs you of any thing for your Good."[16]

When Richard Staunton was trying to reform Moose in the late 1730s, he hoped that the Committee would "cast a favourable construction upon my endeavours, and if I have erred from your honours' expectation I faithfully promise an amendment when in my power." The following year, however, he was feeling his age more; he had entered the service in 1694, so he was probably at least in his late sixties in 1739. "I humbly beg pardon if I have acted or said anything contrary to your honours' interest and intentions that I have used my utmost endeavours and skill, and if it does not please your honours I shall be glad that your honours can have one to manage your affairs with more prudence and advantage for I am advanced in years."[17] McCliesh responded to the Committee's disapproval of a suggestion he made in 1723 by assuring the Committee that "what I have done was out of a real concern I had for a public interest without the least regard to a private one."[18] Their language echoes that of estate stewards back home, defending themselves in tones of reproachful dismay against allegations of carelessness or negligence; for example, Richard Pollard wrote to his mistress, Rachel, Countess of Bath, in 1644: "I hope what I have done shall not give you cause of discontent, but if I have done amiss herein it is the error of my judgment and not my want of any good affection to serve your honour were it to the effusion of the last drop of blood that warms my veins."[19]

Even complaints could be expressed in deferential terms. In 1723 McCliesh complained about the poor physical condition of York Fort compared to Albany but assured the Committee, "I am mighty well satisfied in all respects, this being a place of greater profit to your honours." Five years later he concluded a long paragraph about the poor quality of recent trade goods and supplies: "I hope what I have above written will give offence to none of your honours, having no other meaning nor ends than a hearty goodwill towards your honours' interest, and be assured of my best endeavours towards the same."[20] A 1739 letter from James Isham at York was a litany of complaints about, and recommendations for, goods and supplies of all sorts. He explained that he and his council "thought [it] our duty" to mention these things, and he was "heartily sorry to trouble your honours with such a long petition. But I do humbly assure your honours I have gave your honours a true and exact account of every particular aforementioned to the best of my knowledge, hoping your honours' pardon for the same if anyways taken amiss."[21] When Joseph Isbister lamented the French penetration of the Albany River valley in the early 1740s, he expressed his loyalty in his usual ostentatious style but also inserted a jibe at his employers:

> *I heartly Could wish that Somthing Expiedient in Conjunction with Mr Duffield [at Moose] could be don or thought of to prevent this great trespas & incroachment, I would undertake any thing that Could in Any measure preserve ye Companys Trade Even to ye hazard of my life...it is no Small griff to me that it is not in my poure to prevent this incroachment on ye Companys territories, iff ye factory was but well maned as it ought to be at all times then could I a have Sent 10 or 12 men & a take these pedlers whilst they are but few in number brought them downe & Sent them home [as prisoners].*[22]

Most men were careful not to criticize the Committee directly, deflecting blame in the same way that they might have criticized the king's ministers rather than the king himself. In 1733 William Bevan complained about the quality of meat sent out that year but claimed to be certain "that our being served in so shameful a manner by your butcher has escaped your observation hitherto."[23]

That decidedly domestic note, containing though it does the implicit charge of carelessness against the Committee, treads a fine line between censure and commiseration. In so doing, it highlights the extent to which the company's servants in North America expressed in long-distance annual correspondence what most servants in Britain were able to express face to face to their masters on a daily basis. Scholar James Carey has helpfully distinguished communication as *transmission* (the dissemination of information) from communication as *ritual* (the sharing and legitimizing of belief systems).

> *A ritual view of communication is directed not toward the extension of messages in space but toward the maintenance of society in time; not the act of imparting information but the representation of shared beliefs. If the archetypal case of communication under a transmission view is the extension of messages across geography for the purpose of control, the archetypal case under a ritual view is the sacred ceremony that draws persons together in fellowship and commonality.*[24]

At the same time as both the Committee and its servants were imparting information to each other, they couched that information in the ritual sentiments of the public transcript—even, or especially, when the information they were imparting was going to be unwelcome.

Factors and other servants employed deference and accompanying expressions of loyalty to gain the Committee's friendship. Such friendship could be valuable in protecting a servant from attacks by rivals on his reputation or position; like English ambassadors, consuls, and governors elsewhere in the Atlantic world, factors in North America were somewhat removed from the social and political contexts within which their reputations had been built and had meaning.[25] The Committee's friendship could also result in advancement within the company. These expectations were

The depot building at York Factory National Historic Site was built in the 1830s with some materials taken from the Octagon, which had previously occupied that location. One set of shelves was found to contain boards that had been painted by one of York's residents in the late eighteenth or early nineteenth century. A fiddler—a detail from York Factory painted boards. [Courtesy of Parks Canada]

A goose hunter—a detail from York Factory painted boards. [Courtesy of Parks Canada]

A couple dining—a detail from York Factory painted boards. [Courtesy of Parks Canada]

consistently encouraged by the Committee, who signed its letters "Your loving Friends" and promised gratitude and favours to those who served "your honours' interest" well.[26] As long as the rhetoric was backed up with actual benefits, such words and phrases carried power, and the same patterns can be seen in EIC correspondence from the period.[27]

Relationships within early modern households, even relationships of submission and duty, were commonly expressed in terms of "love." In 1682 the Committee offered John Nixon much advice on "meanes to draw our Servants to Love & obey you." In 1719 Henry Kelsey signed his letters to his subordinate at Churchill, Richard Staunton, "Your Real Loveing Frind to Serve You" (to his other subordinates he was merely "Your Frind"), and sent "[m]y love to Mr Hancock & the Doctor unknown with all other Acquaintance." In 1761 Jean Baptiste D'Laryea declared that he loved Robert Temple (chief factor at Albany), and the men at Severn River sent "[l]ove to [their] Factory Mates" at York. Humphrey Marten spoke of gaining "the Love of the Natives" and told Thomas Kitchin at Albany, "I love and esteem the Men [of York], and in return they love and revere me." The Committee consistently signed its correspondence to its servants

"Your Loveing Friends"—although an interesting exception is found in a 1720 letter to apprentice Richard Norton, which it signed "Yr Love[in]g Masters."[28]

Such usages of the term *love* are probably best understood as formal or ritualized expressions of sentiment.[29] The word *affection* usually characterized more spontaneous and emotive relationships but was used in HBC correspondence in much the same way as *love*. In 1682 the Committee informed Nixon that Captain William Bond's "last ill carriage hath begott So great a Reputation amongst us, that there is nothing but your recomendation can resettle him firme in our affections."[30] In 1686 it appointed John Bridgar governor at Albany, "knowing well your Direction and moderation & how well you are affectioned to our service and Interest." In the same year, they assured Pierre Esprit Radisson

> *that your particuler Interest is fixed & safe here at home. And...you must doe your Faith great violence if you beleeve that there is any one [on the Committee] but who is intirely your friend & will in all occations be ready upon your good Success in our affaires to embrace you with all respect, affection & gratitude.*[31]

In 1756 the Albany council described its chief, Joseph Isbister, as "a man so well affected to your Honrs Interests that no fatigue nor hazard wou'd deter him from Serving you to the Utmost peril."[32]

"Your Own Creditt" and "the Comp[an]ys Profitt"

So eagerly were these rhetorical themes pursued—indeed, more eagerly by the servants of the company than by its directors—that men sometimes appeared to deny their own interests. At York in 1723 Thomas McCliesh Jr promised "my best endeavours in promoting of your interest to the best of my knowledge," and in 1732 he declared, "I hope without offence no man as ever served your honours has your interest more at heart."[33] Richard Norton declared, "I shall make it my whole care and study to find by what means I may promote your honours' interest" and promised to "entertain none but such as are diligent in your honours' business." Norton's successor at Churchill, Anthony Beale, expressed himself in similar terms in 1729: "Your honours will find this year by the trade that whilst I serve you it is my whole study and endeavours to increase the trade for your honours' interest and always shall during the continuance of my staying here."[34]

Servants' deference did not indicate that they subsumed their own interests in the company's interests; the role of company man was just that, a role to be played at particular times for particular purposes. Deference was often conditional and sometimes calculating, and public and private transcripts sometimes intersected and sometimes did not.[35] The latent cynicism that the modern eye might detect within this rhetorical tapestry was not perceived as such by those who were actively weaving those threads together (from both ends of the loom, as it were) to create a single, cohesive, and even idyllic portrait of life and labour in HBC factory households. It was how the world—their world—worked.

All parties knew that idyllic portraits were seldom a case of art imitating life, but the idyll gave them a framework within which to make sense of disordered reality. For instance, crises such as very poor trading seasons or military defeat prompted the Committee to apportion blame, while its servants tried to deflect it. The terms in which Henry Sergeant and his men negotiated who was to blame for the fall of James Bay in 1686 reveal much about the reciprocal expectations that were already establishing themselves within the company. Appearing before the Committee in November 1687, Sergeant accused not only Deputy Governor John Bridgar at Moose of negligence but also some of his own men at Albany—labourers William Arrington and Frederick Johnson, sawyers William Folder and John Meacham, shipwrights Edward Coles and Phillip Scovell, tailor Hugh Mitchell, gunsmith and edge-tool maker John Stevens, and surgeon Edward Evans—of "Mutinous Caballs amongst themselves" and of being unwilling to defend the factory. Cooper James Moodie, Thomas Bannatine, and apprentice Anthony Beale also appeared before the

Committee that month; they challenged Sergeant's claims against the men of Albany and hinted darkly at "severall Remarkeable faileings in Governor Sergeant."[36]

The Committee was inclined to lay much of the blame at Sergeant's door, prompting him to write "The Answere of Henry Sergeant...to the Charge against him by the Hon[oura]ble Hudson's Bay Company," in which he repeated his earlier claim that mutiny among his men forced him to surrender Albany to the French.[37] Coles, Mitchell, Meacham, Stevens, Folder, and Arrington replied to Sergeant's accusations in two documents, in which they claimed:

> *Wee urged the Governor that Wee might fire upon them [the French] to prevent their proceedeing further against us, but hee utterly denyed us yett neverthelesse* soe zealously affected wee were to your honors interest *that some of us fired 3 Gun's against the French, at which Governor Sergeant was soe displeased that hee threatened to punish us for it that were Concerned in it, this Caused much dissatisfaccion amongst us (tho noe mutiny as hee hath Declar'd.) for it was observed that after that Factory was beseiged all animosityes Ceased amongst us and* Wee united firmely against the Enemy, and remained every man in his respective quarter's *untill such tyme as the Governor Comanded us to Surrendr. by which it may appeare to your honors* how Willing wee were to maintaine your rights, *and Mr. Sergeant was pleased to say that wee behaved our Selves like men and thanked us for it and told us hee would report the same to your honors.*[38]

These men, whom John Oldmixon described as "the most considerable among" Albany's hands, and who described themselves as "your Honors humble Servants," were among the twenty-two men left by the French to winter near Moose, while Sergeant and the rest (including most or all of the officers) wintered somewhat more comfortably at either Port Nelson or New Severn. As evidence of Sergeant's maliciousness, Coles and his companions observed that "hee alledges nothing against the men that were at Albany River with us, and Came home with him, but onely reflects upon us whoe hee Supposed Dead among the French."[39]

Much was at stake: the Committee's legal counsel argued that Sergeant's wages (two hundred pounds per annum since 1683) were forfeit if it could be proven that he had been at fault "either by neglect or cowardize." The company brought legal action against Sergeant in the Court of King's Bench for twenty thousand pounds in 1688, but the case was settled out of court, and Sergeant received his full wages up until his capture.[40] The company's dispute with Sergeant stands out as unique in the history of HBC. This is in stark contrast to its trading contemporaries, particularly the Royal African and East India companies, whose relations with their overseas factors and merchants were characterized by an almost continuous series of suits and prosecutions—prompting Thomas Phipps Sr to remark to his son, James, in Africa in 1712, "Companies are always ungrateful."[41]

HBC servants understood that, if they wanted the company to be grateful, they would have to earn that gratitude through good and appropriate behaviour. They could serve their own interests by serving the company's interests, and what threatened the company's interests also threatened their own. In 1717 James Knight advised William Stuart (newly appointed second to Henry Kelsey at York) "to behave Your Self as You ought to doe, to be Dilligent & Carefull in Whatsoever You are Intrusted with or Employd in." Knight concluded by reminding Stuart of the several obligations that he had to consider: "So hopeing you will be Mindfull of the Trust & Confidence as is Reposed in You, for Your own Creditt, the Comp[an]ys profitt, & to my Satisfaction—This Dureing Pleasure—I Rest Yo[u]r Loveing Friend & Govern[o]r to Serve, James Knight."[42] Stuart was expected to advance his own interests (his own "Creditt" or reputation) and those of his master (the company), while satisfying his patron (Knight). Knight expressed his relationship to Stuart in both sentimental and instrumental terms and portrayed his role as governor in terms of sentimentality (*love*) and reciprocity (the amphibious phrase *Governor to Serve*); he used the same rhetorical tactic in letters to another former apprentice, Henry Kelsey.[43] At the same time, Stuart was reminded that his worldly success depended on the "Pleasure" of his patron(s)—although Knight was ambiguous about whether Stuart's principal patron was his immediate master (Knight as governor-in-chief) or his corporate master (the company).

In 1716 the aging Knight, upset at what he perceived as suspicion and interference from the Committee, declared, "I thank God he has given me more sense and I know my duty too well to do anything that may be prejudicial to the Company, I would sooner die first." A few years later Thomas McCliesh Jr wrote from Albany to assure the Committee that he had "more value for my Reason then to forfeit it to the prejudice of your Honrs: my Wife and Children." In 1722 Joseph Myatt praised the "Generosity" of the Committee in raising his salary and appointing him chief of Albany, "for all which Manifold favours I Return your Honrs my hearty & Unfeigned thanks," and he promised to "promote your Interest to the Utmost of my Power & Ability, in every thing that is just and honest." At the same time, he defended himself against complaints that he expected the homeward-bound armourer John Upton to make: "Assuring you that I ever had a greater Value for my Reputation then to forfeit it to the Disprejudice of your Honours." He noted that Upton's behaviour "hath been very Monstrous, which I have not fail'd to punish him for. Therefore if the said Upton should Endeavour to disprejudice my Name, I hope Your Honrs will be pleas'd to cast a favourable Construction upon it." Myatt's successor, Richard Staunton, found Albany and its trade in good condition in 1723, "at wch I am glad, hopeing it will prove very Sattisfactory to your Honrs Proffit and his [Myatt's] credit & Interest."[44]

Myatt's 1722 letter set out the boundaries of his participation in the public transcript to which his masters were asking him to subscribe. He (publicly) refused to go beyond the limits of "every thing that is just and honest," limits beyond which the Committee would (it was hoped) not ask him to go. The success and reputation of the company and that of its servants were clearly connected, and Myatt refused to pursue either one at the expense of the other. As Faramerz Dabhoiwala has remarked, "honour and reputation...were part and parcel of how individuals in this society conceived of the relationship between the personal and the public, and between the projection and the perception of one's character."[45] A study by D.R. Hainsworth of estate stewards quoted chief steward Reverend Charles Usher's 1672 remonstrations with his employer (Sir Richard Grahame of Netherby) regarding what he perceived as a callous and unjust policy on Grahame's Cumberland estates: "Your honour is so dear to me as I cannot but desire you to be just in all your doings." Hainsworth commented, "This was by the standards of this deferential and formal society a blistering rebuke."[46] Myatt, like Knight and McCliesh before him, was expressing the hope that his employers would never force him to register such a rebuke to them.

Commanding one of the company's factories or houses was seen as a position of great trust. Joseph Isbister and his council wrote from Albany in 1741: "We humbly assure Yr Honrs we are very sensible of ye great Trust and Confidence Yr Honrs have reposed in us, and we shall make use of all Opportunities, to give Yr Honrs proof of our Diligence & Care, and we shall always exert our utmost Endeavours to promote ye true Interest of ye Compy." Andrew Graham, having taken charge of York after James Isham's death in 1761, promised to faithfully discharge "this valuable trust that is now unhappily fallen upon me for the company's Interest, & mine own honour." Ferdinand Jacobs at Prince of Wales Fort (now the senior officer in Hudson Bay) replied to Graham, "The Trust that has fallen upon you is valuable Indeed, & ought to be Discharged with the greatest prudence, care, and frugality."[47] Even seemingly lesser tasks could involve considerable responsibility: when George Humble's party was stymied by low water en route to Henley with supplies in 1766, an exasperated Humphrey Marten tried to rouse Humble with these words: "Remember Sir Your Character is at stake, and that nothing but the Clearest Demonstration will Convince the Company You have done your duty."[48]

In 1767 Marten and his council members (Captain John Horner and surgeons William Richards and Eusebius Bacchus Kitchen) outlined their understanding of their duties:

> *Lastly We Promise a dutifull observance and Performance of all the Orders and Instructions now Given us, as well as in Your Honors former General Letters, we will endeavour to Extend the Company's Trade by all Lawfull means...We will Continue to treat the Natives with Civility and deal Justly with them...Virtue, Diligence & Sobriety is, and shall be Encouraged in Your Servants, and the Contrary is Discountenanced to the Utmost of our power, and in all things we will Endeavour to behave, so to merit Your Esteem, To Conclude We Sincerely wish Your Honours Health and Happiness, and that Success may attend You both at Home and Abroad, is the Hearty Prayers of / Honrble Gentlemen Your most Obliged and Obedient Servants.*[49]

Thomas White employed more personal, but no less showy, rhetoric in 1736. The Committee had offered him a two-year contract in charge of York at fifty pounds, with a retroactive wage increase (from thirty to fifty pounds for the last two years) and a fifty guinea (£52 10s. 0d.) gratuity at the end of the new contract.

> *Your honours' proposals for my continuance in the management of your honours' affairs at York Fort seems to have so much respect to my weak endeavours that, had your honours made no advances on account of wages, I must and should have thought myself a very ungrateful wretch to [have] left your affairs at such an unfortunate crisis as this, notwithstanding my very earnest inclinations to have seen my native country; and as your honours has been pleased to lay a conditional obligation on me for a term of two years, which notwithstanding the sweetness of a gratuity seems to me after so long a vacation from even the innocent and necessary pleasures of life, an age, I cannot determine with myself really what to say, but wholly leave it to your honours' pleasure whether to suffer me to come home the next year or stay your conditional time, my life and service being wholly devoted to your honours' interest to the uttermost of my capacity.*[50]

White came home in 1737 and, presumably, went on to devote his life and service to the interest of another master.

Joseph Isbister informed the Committee in 1755 that he intended to come home unless Henley House was re-established: "I shall be Extremely Concerned to leave Your affairs in a bad way, but be pleased to permit me to say, I have this for my Comfort—that I have Keept up to the rules of Justice and integrity, fidelity without breach of Trust."[51] In 1768 Humphrey Marten spoke highly of his "Old Factory Mate," Thomas Hopkins, "knowing him to be a Worthy Man, and doubt not of his performing the dutys of his Station, with success to Your Honours; and consequently Honour to himself." Hopkins took command at Albany while Marten was on leave in 1768–69. He assured the Committee that he would be willing to stay another year if Marten did not recover his health or otherwise proved unable to return to his charge, but added, "I hope Your Honours will not think that I want to Supplant Mr Marten, far from it, for I have the highest opinion of him, and know him to be Capable of managing any of Your Honours affairs in this Country—and none more so."[52]

Company servants recognized what the contemporary advice manuals and conduct books preached, that good conduct in service was often linked to future prosperity: men "subsist by Credit and good Fame, and nothing gives it, or secures it, like the being Diligent and Careful, Industrious and Laborious in their Service." Such advice was also found outside of conduct books. In 1789 Sussex mercer Thomas Turner advised his son Philip, who was a servant at Brighton: "do be always careful to perform to the very utmost of your Power that is to be a good Servant, as it is not only a duty you owe your Employers but your own Interest will likewise result from it, for a prudent Sober, industrious Servant is a Character valuable and will always recommend itself to the esteem of worthy & sensible people."[53] Henry Kelsey put it even more strongly when he faced accusations of misconduct in Hudson Bay: "it is a great Dolor to be represented so Odiously to our Masters and tuched in ye most Sensable part (yt is) A Mans reputation wch is more Valuable yn Life itself."[54]

Kelsey and Turner, though separated by nearly seventy years, shared the dominant business ideal of the period: the person of "credit" and "reputation." Keith Wrightson has described this ideal as "an amalgam of private and public virtues which coalesced in a model of both personal and commercial integrity."[55] As Fleetwood, Richardson, and other guides to proper behaviour emphasized, credit and reputation were built through good and appropriate behaviour, especially toward one's superiors who were in a position to act as patrons or benefactors. And a vital component of the search for benefits and preferments was the expression of gratitude when they were achieved.

The Committee emphasized gratitude as an important part of its relationship with its servants. In 1690 the Committee referred to Captain John Ford (who was captured by the French in 1689 and defected to their service) and the servants-turned-interlopers John Abraham and Captain John Outlaw as "ungratefull perfidious men, who have eate of our Bread & turne Renegadoes, towards us afterwards." The Committee took "Notice of ye Satisfaction" that Thomas White expressed at being given the charge of York Fort in 1734 "and are perswaded You have Used Your Utmost Endeavours to discharge the Trust Wee reposed in You." His reward has been noted previously.[56]

In turn, HBC servants incorporated the expected gratitude into their rhetoric. For example, William Bevan at Moose wrote in 1734, "I humbly beg leave to return your honours my most hearty thanks for all your favours which so fully calls for my utmost care and attention for your interest." Gratitude was offered not just for specific favours or encouragement but for the Committee's general treatment of the men in Hudson Bay. In the same 1734 letter Bevan and his council wrote, "We return your honours thanks for your care of all your servants in sending us a good supply of provisions as well as other goods."[57] Their complaint about the company's butcher the previous year had been taken on board, despite a notable lack of complaint from Churchill and the supply ships, which had received beef and pork from the source. "Wee have this Year taken particular care abt it and hope what Wee have now sent You will give Satisfaction," the Committee wrote, adding that it had just built a new and larger supply vessel (*Sea Horse*), "being desireous that our Servts should not want for any thing necessary for their Support & comfortable Subsistence."[58]

No eighteenth-century factor offered more words of gratitude than did Humphrey Marten. In 1766 he offered (through the collective voice of his council) "the Sincere thanks of a Heart glowing with the warmest Gratitude" for his confirmation as chief factor at Albany, and "doth Promise, He will on all Occasions at the Utmost hazard and Perrill of his Life, defend Your rights, and will use every means in his Power to advance Your Trade." In 1768, when the Committee granted him leave to come home for a year to recover his health, the council replied that "this fresh mark of Your Goodness to him doth in some measure distress Him as he hath it not in his power to shew his Gratitude according to the full extent of his wishes." In 1771 Marten promised that "Inclination, Duty and Gratitude, all strongly prompt me to exert my self in suppressing the Evils of Private Trade."[59]

Marten also portrayed gratitude as part of other relationships. In 1764 he wrote to London that he had told the Albany hands (whom he was trying to persuade to go to Henley) "that in case my well being had any sway with them, it would raise my Gratitude to such a pitch as would induce me rather to pinch my self rather than they should want for any thing." There was an element of desperation in his efforts, but they were based on the fundamental concept that loyal and active service should be rewarded. A few years later he told the Committee that "Justice and Gratitude Force me most humbly to recommend...to Your Notice" surgeon Eusebius Bacchus Kitchen, who "has Assisted me three Years in the Trading Room and has behaved himself in such a manner as to Shew that he has Your Honours Interest greatly at heart." And in 1768 he wrote, "We are fully Convinced by the tender Concern Your Honors shew for the loss of Your Servants how much You have their Preservation at Heart, such Goodness we hope will meet with a sutible return of Gratitude, by a

Diligent and Faithfull Discharge of the Dutys of each of us in our Several Stations."[60]

Although neither God nor religion was strongly invoked, they were never absent from the rhetoric of HBC correspondence. The Committee asked for God's "Blessings upon the diligent care and prudence" of James Knight and his council at Albany and told John Fullartine and his council "to prevent and discountenance all drunkenness, Curseing & Profane Sweareing, & all Imorality & Ireligion & to promote & Encourage Vertue & good Religion" by reading morning and evening prayers every day.[61] This was a common injunction among long-distance traders, as in Istanbul merchant Philip Williams's 1639 advice to a Livorno-bound colleague: "to remember his duty to God by beginning each day with prayer, to behave himself in a civil and orderly fashion aboard ship and in port, to keep the company of men from whom he might learn, and, most particularly, to listen, and not to speak."[62]

Factors and servants invoked God in their correspondence too. Thomas McCliesh Jr refuted allegations of private trade in 1719 by declaring, "As God is my Sole Judge I never Defrauded your Honrs In Skin nor Skins directly or Indirectly by Converting them to my own use, or to the use of any person or persons." Thomas White concluded a letter to Joseph Isbister by "heartily wishing you health and that God may be your Guide & conduct you in all your proceedings for the benefit of the Company & your own Safety." George Rushworth claimed that he told William Lamb at Henley to "do justly in his dealings, Love Mercy and call upon his god. [T]hese things Wou'd inable him to Make a good Servant to the Company and that he Might Expect the Smiles of Mr Merry [deputy governor in London] at all times." Joseph Isbister claimed that performing divine service was "our Greatest delight; otherwise should not have put You to the Expence of those Sermons now sent out."[63]

In many cases the injunctions of God or religion were implicit in the rhetoric of company correspondence. Many of the adjectives consistently used to characterize good servants—*faithful, diligent, honest, sober*—appeared in contemporary advice manuals in more overtly spiritual contexts. In *The Apprentice's Vade Mecum* (1734) Samuel Richardson urged application, industry, and diligence:

> *[Y]ou will reap the Benefit...to the End of your Life, and, in all Probability, to the End of Time, and for ever: for 'tis a very great Chance, if the same Motives which influence you to do your Duty in one Part of Life, will not have due Weight with you in all the rest; since to do your Duty to Man is a fair Step in the Way of doing what is required of you by God Almighty.*[64]

While advising apprentices of the earthly rewards of good service and good behaviour, Richardson declared that "Your Duty to God" was of paramount importance.[65] Earlier in the century William Fleetwood assured his readers, "The Service and Obedience of Servants, shall not go unrewarded in the *other* World, however it fare with them in *this*." He considered the promise of heavenly reward "sufficient encouragement" for their faithfulness, diligence, and honesty. To become a servant was not a sign of God's displeasure:

> *He only commands them, that whilst they continue so, they should behave themselves as becomes their Condition, with all Submission and Humility, with all Obedience, Diligence, and Industry, with Truth, and Justice, Faithfulness and Honesty; which will make their Condition easie to themselves, and cause them to be well serv'd by others, when-ever they emerge and get above it.*[66]

Here again, we see the light at the end of the tunnel of servitude, the reasonable hope that emerging into independence was more a question of "when" than "if"—provided one behaved oneself along the way.

Communication and Negotiation

The Committee's rhetoric kept before its servants the idea that they were all valuable to the company and its activities. Factors had regular opportunities to communicate with the Committee, but literate servants regularly wrote directly to the Committee and almost always received some kind of response; illiterate servants could ask someone else to write on their behalf.[67] Theoretically, this allowed men to bypass their superior officer as intermediary or broker, although it was usually possible for factors to read any private correspondence included in the official packet.

Unfortunately little private correspondence has survived in the archives, and we can only guess at the contents of many of the private letters referred to in the official correspondence. In 1711 both Henry Kelsey and Thomas McCliesh Jr wrote from Albany, seeking promotion—although, with Anthony Beale and Nathaniel Bishop returning to the Bay as governor and deputy governor, respectively, Kelsey and McCliesh had to content themselves with managing the Eastmain River trade. In 1727 former apprentice Samuel Hopkins was promoted from steward to bookkeeper but signed a contract "for one year only for he designs to write to your honours of his further intentions." In the 1730s Churchill bookkeeper Thomas Bird and York steward Mitchell Logan both wrote to the Committee about their futures.[68] In 1752 labourer Joseph Roach and mariner William Trinaway both went home from Albany after only two years of their five-year contracts for reasons explained in private letters to the Committee, and sailor Robert Irwin sent a similar "Petition" to come home the following year. Labourer John Hughes, however, "wrote to his mother last year [1731] to acquaint your honours that he designed to continue longer in your service."[69]

The opportunity to correspond (or, if in London, to speak) directly with the Committee was open to all servants but seems to have been particularly valuable to ambitious younger men seeking avenues of advancement. In 1724 Thomas McCliesh Jr advised mariner John Wateridge to write directly to the Committee about his aspirations to become York's gunner. In 1732 Albany accountant Richard White felt that he was being held back at Albany, despite enjoying the friendship and patronage of his superior, Joseph Adams. White refused to sign a four-year contract because of what he perceived to be small wages (twenty-five pounds) and wrote to London on that account—although the Committee considered his demands extravagant and recalled him.[70] The Committee had been in a similarly unsympathetic mood in the cost-cutting years immediately following the Treaty of Utrecht:

> *Acquaint Jos. Myatt that Wee received his Letter, but do not think fit to Comply with his Demands so [he] may return Home, & whereas Geo. Lisk has like wise wrote to Succeed Jos. Myatt as Gunner he very well knows his Contracted time is not Expired, nor will be till next year, So that you may acquaint him also, that if he be not Satisfied in ye Station he is in, when his time is out may return home Likewise. As to Richd Crockett who Contracted with you for 2 years at £15-12 p Ann & whose time is out this year, you may inform him that wee are not willing to give him £26 for another year, so may also return home by ye Ship that Comes to you.*[71]

In the same letter the Committee expressed its willingness "to Encourage our Servts that they may promote our Interest in hopes the Compa[ny] may in time reap some Benefitt for their Cost & Labour, Who have not receiv'd one penny Dividend almost these thirty Years." This, of course, was the proverbial bottom line of the public transcript from the Committee's point of view; officers and servants needed to keep it in mind if they wanted the "Cost & Labour" of their own investment in the public transcript to pay them any dividends.

In September 1755 Albany surgeon George Rushworth wrote privately to the Committee after the first Henley House incident as a means of advancing himself in the service ahead of his peers. In doing so, he employed many of the tropes expected from a humble and loyal servant, wrapping his words in deference and piety. He portrayed himself as deeply attached to his employers' interests, particularly in the case of Henley, and apologized for the strength of his opinions: "Please Honble Gentlemen to forgive these, as I have a feeling Compassion for Those our fellow Servants, and the Loss of Your Honours Trade has given me inexpressible Concern." Surgeon William Richards also tried to profit from other men's reluctance to serve at Henley, but the Committee was less receptive to his overtures. He applied to his superior, Humphrey Marten, several times in 1765 and 1766 for permission to return to England but was refused; Marten believed Richards was anxious because he had not received a private letter from the Committee.[72] Rushworth and Richards each saw Henley House as a place to be master of one's own house. As surgeons, they had a high social standing within the household factories, yet generally remained outside the formal chain of command and succession. Command of Henley thus also offered them a point of entry into that chain, with the possibility of subsequent advancement.

That is probably how Albany's sloop masters saw Eastmain House, although the satisfaction of being the master of a seasonal or temporary household, such as a sloop's crew, could be offset by the frustrating subordination expected when one was back at the factory.[73] Upon his return to Hudson Bay in 1751 as master of Flamborough House, Samuel Skrimshire wrote to the Committee in some dismay:

> *Hon'ble Sirs*
>
> *I make bould to trouble Your Honours with these few lines thinking it a duty becoming all Such persons Your Honours may think proper to Nominate as master of wone of your out Houses as well as wone of Your Cheif factory's, to acquaint Your Honours we Arriv'd with in heiring [hearing] of the factory Guns on the 24th of July and on the 25th I went oup to the Fort ware I found every body well and was Receiv'd with a Great deal of Joy and hope that my Conduck will all way be Deserving of Your Honours preferment.*
>
> *Gentellmen I cant but Say I was Very much Surprised at the opening of Your Honours Packquait in not Receiving Sum orders how to prosead when at flamboury House, but more in perticular on in Quiry I was tould Your Honours did Never desine I Should Carray on Eney Trade their only for Provisions allways under Standing Your Hon's I was Sent on the Same*

Acc'tt as Mr Isham Came over the Last Year [as master of Flamborough] wht I under Stoud at that time was to have bean Supploy'd from YF with Such Quantity's of Goods as mite be Requasite to Supploy Such Ind's as freaquantly Come Down that Riv'r as well with Goods as Provisions Everay Summer that thay mite not have the trouble and feateague yt Sum times attends them in Going Round the Point of Marsh or Carrying their Goods &c across the Island having freaquantly none [known?] their Goods so much Damaged that they could not trade them for Sum time or at Least be four we could Pack them their four incase enay thing of that Natour Should happen I hope Your Honours will not Eneway's Sencer my Condouck for I do a Shour Your Honours nothing Shall be wanting on my Side in promoting Your Honours Interest as far as my orders may Run.

Gentellmen I humble ask Your Honours parden in Case You Should think I have enay ways bean too frea in Expresing my Self in the manner I have, being nothing more then the Reall trouth. I'm to prosead to the North Riv'r as Sune as posable the Sloop Can be spar'd Having not to inlarge but wishing Your Honours ahappey Site of all Your Ships with a Good Trade from their Respective forts and am Gentellmen Your Honours most Obedient

And Humble Servt
At Command
Saml Skrimsher[74]

Skrimshire's humble rhetoric clearly expressed his hope and expectation that the command of Flamborough House would prove to be a significant promotion, despite its being an "out House" rather than a "Cheif factory." His deferential tone could not hide his frustration; his references to promoting the company's interests and facilitating trade were also references to the ways in which an independent command could promote his own interests and facilitate future favours from the Committee. He probably feared that Flamborough would fail and that he would be blamed;

he had already been recalled once—and as a result apparently lost James Isham's friendship and patronage—and now he sought to avoid future censure.

Only rarely did servants address themselves to individual Committee members. In 1765 Humphrey Marten humbly offered each member a "Nest of Roggins" (birchbark baskets, probably made by his Cree wife, Pawpitch) and commented that, "had I not been fearful of apearing too Free I should have Addressed a Letter to each of the Gentlemen to crave his Protection."[75] Significantly, Marten offered gifts to all Committee men equally, seeking the "Protection" of all rather than the patronage of any one in particular. Marten's gift was exotic (in a London boardroom, at least), which in some respects made it a more intimate gift than something more commonplace; he was thus positioning himself as a member of the Committee's collective household family, rather than as an ordinary subordinate. The language of giving in early modern England characteristically minimized the value of the gift in order to underline the spirit in which it was given, part of a repertoire of gift exchange that incidentally linked well (though not perfectly) with Indigenous concepts of gift exchange.[76]

James Knight wrote private letters to Governor Sir Bibye Lake and Deputy Governor Captain John Merry after taking possession of York in 1714, but Knight had sat on the Committee before he returned to Hudson Bay and knew both men personally. The letters were deferential, offering "my most due respects" to both men and promising Lake that "I never shall be wanting in my duty to serve you to the utmost of my power," but he also promised Merry that "I will make it my business to serve the Company in every respect" and "I will take all the care I can for the Company's interest." In his next letter home, however, Knight "chose rather to write by way of journal all the information I have had of the northern country for fear I should write in a letter to one Committee man more than another and so give a disgust."[77]

In turn, the Committee always portrayed itself as a collective entity or individual when addressing its servants, an image doubtlessly encouraged by a high degree of stability in Committee membership.[78] Servants owed their loyalty, deference, and gratitude to "your honours" rather than to any particular Committee member; the Committee as a whole was their master. In theory, this prevented Committee members from competing with each other for influence and patronage. Whether it did is difficult to judge, given the abbreviated and impersonal tone of the Committee's minute books, but the surviving correspondence certainly gives no indication of such competition. Even those who owed their initial employment to a particular Committee member (or members) were assured that they could rely on the friendship of all.[79] This stands in stark contrast to the EIC, where the opportunities for bestowing patronage were arguably the chief attraction of serving on the court of directors. Every year, each director was allowed to nominate (according to seniority) a certain number of applicants to the positions of writer, cadet, surgeon, chaplain, home officer, and even warehouse labourer, as well as licensing free merchants, allocating voyages to the commanders of privately owned ships, and granting passage for individuals wishing to travel to the East.[80]

HBC servants could not take the Committee's friendship for granted. In 1688 the Committee called Governor George Geyer (at Port Nelson) its "Cheife usefull man...haveing been soe many yeares in our Service and are soe well experienced in all our affaires and in our true interest." It denied Geyer's request to come home that year, claiming to know "that you will never desert our imploymt. as long as wee think fitt to Continue you in it," but approved of "your Modesty" in making the request "with a Submission & Resignation to our pleasure & Service." It assured him that "as Wee see our Trade increase and a larger Cargoe Come home every yeare, soe you shall find our Favour & kindnesse increase towards you." The implied threat—that failure to increase trade would result in the loss of the Committee's favour—picked up on a similarly double-edged promise made earlier in the letter, assuring Geyer of "our Continued Favour unlesse Wee should see extraordinary Miscarriages Committeed by you." The Committee's 1686 letter to Pierre Esprit Radisson when he was in charge of the trade at Port Nelson was blunter: "as we will have none to blame if we faile of a glorious trade but your selfe, so in the happey success of it, you will not only finde your owne account & advantage together with us, but we shall alwaies enlarge our selves towards you in such waies of acknowlidgment as shall be fitting & Due to your prudence & Industrey."[81]

Both servants and officers were concerned with the ways in which they were being portrayed to their masters. It is often difficult for scholars (as it was for the Committee) to judge the extent to which complaints and criticisms about individuals were valid and to evaluate the reputations that certain posts occasionally acquired as dens of various iniquities. Factors usually tried to deflect blame from themselves, commonly (and conveniently) condemning their predecessors. At Albany, for instance, Thomas McCliesh Jr in 1716 and Joseph Myatt in 1727 both attributed servants' complaints about their management to the fact that men had been able to do as they pleased under Richard Staunton (who had been in charge in 1714–15 and again in 1723–26); in 1741 James Duffield made a similar complaint about Staunton's management of Moose.[82]

McCliesh and Myatt may have been less concerned with challenging Staunton's favourable reports of his own behaviour than with emphasizing their own strengths in maintaining order and promoting the company's interests. Their comments were made in self-defence against complaints made to the Committee by the men of Albany. McCliesh referred in 1716 to a petition sent to London by "severall of our men...Concerning my being severe, & som'what Tyrannical as they term'd it."

> *At first I was Oblidged to be somewhat severe; for the men was grown to yt Degree of ill Manners; that they Did what they pleas'd with Mr Staunton; & thought to have used me with ye same so yt I took 5 of the greatest Transgressors & Whipt them; Ever since they have been Obedient and willing In ye Discharge of their Duty; neither have I beat, a man since: nor have I had any Occassion, for it is not in my Nature to use any man with Morossness; or ill manners and by yt same rule, I will be treated.*[83]

Myatt's defence eleven years later was expressed in much the same words:

> *I am Informed there is Some Complaints a comeing home against me, but I Do ashure your Honrs it is not in my Nature to treat any man with Morrossness or Ill manners, and I think it is but Reasonable I Should be Treated with the Same, Some of the Men are grown to such a Pitch of Ill manners yt they Did what they pleased wth Mr Staunton & they thought to a Served me after the same manner, but I Punished 3 or four of ye Greatest Trancegressors & they have ben very Obidiant to Commd Ever Since.*[84]

Myatt's criticism of Staunton contrasted with Staunton's defence of Myatt in 1723. Staunton had replaced him that year following both a drop in trade and complaints from some of Myatt's men. Staunton, however, reported that Myatt's management had been very prudent, and assured the Committee that "w[ha]t Ever hath been Represented as prejuditiall to him hath been out of Envey, from men of an uneasie temper and turbulant Spirit wch will not be Easy under any command."[85]

Drunkenness and Sobriety

Alcohol was a frequent point of contention between masters and men, both in Britain and in Hudson Bay. Drink played an important role in the early modern workplace. At Prince of Wales Fort on 3 June 1732, Richard Norton "laid ye first stone in ye foundation of our new fort & gave our people some liquor in wch wee all drank a health to our masters success to ye building."[86] When the main residence was completed a long eight years later,

> *I gave our men liquor for housewarming with which wee all drank the following healths, and discharged a vollie of small arms and 3 pieces of cannon at each health vizt. to church and king, to the Prince of Wales and the Royal family, to the Honble Hudson Bay Compy, to success to the fort against all Enemies, to all the Comp. as servants in genll and concluded*

the Evening with Repeating ye Honble Y Govr ye Depty Govrs and Committees healths separately.[87]

In the context of both work and leisure, such strategic use of alcohol encouraged workplace conviviality, harmony, and fellowship. John Nixon had advised that "yow aught to send us a litle more liquors for indeed the couldness requereth it, which would cause your business to goe one cheerfully that the men might have a dram now and then, when occasion serveth, for if it be well applied it is a soveraigne remedy to all their melancholic distempers."[88]

The Committee certainly took this advice to heart and was understandably hurt and concerned when it discovered that the beer and brandy sent out for the servants' "Refreshment" was being sold "amongst Them selves at Extravagant Prises."[89] The gentlemen's mess at every factory was particularly well supplied with alcohol, and homeward-bound factors often received gifts of wine or brandy for the voyage. The Committee was usually quite blunt about its motives, as in 1770, when it sent "the Chiefs Table" at Moose forty gallons of French brandy "[a]s a farther encouragement for Our Council at Moose Fort to prevent all Private Trade and the more earnestly to comply with Our present Orders." Ferdinand Jacobs at York and Andrew Graham at Severn received thirty-six and twenty gallons respectively in 1773, "in full expectation that these Encouragements will induce all Our Officers to consider the Companys and their own Interest to be jointly united."[90]

Like other employers, however, the HBC drew a connection between drink and idleness (or worse).[91] When the *Eastmain* sloop was lost in the ice near York in October 1714, the crew placed the blame entirely on Captain Michael Grimington Jr of the *Prosperous* hoy for delaying their departure from Albany: "he neglected his Business...he & his men were all Drunk, broaching the Compies Liquors." As well, James Knight was told "that he has deny'd to to go to Winter at the Eastmain wth the Hoy, if all these things be true, pray Send him home...for no Man shall stay here, that fails in his Duty to Serve the Company."[92] At Albany in 1732

Joseph Adams chose Jeremiah Coppage as Thomas Render's mate on the *Moose River* sloop (recently renamed the *Churchill*) over Martin Fowler, "by reason yt Fowler is not capable to Effeciate in that station, he being a man Inclineable to Liquor." In the following year Adams called accountant and assistant trader John Walker "as helpless as a Child and very much Adicted to Liquor which Gives me a Great uneasiness and may prove very Prejudicial to your Interest in Case of my Decease." The Committee sent Thomas Bird to serve as Adams's second instead of Walker.[93] Joseph Isbister succeeded George Gunn as master of the *Beaver* sloop after the Albany council revealed that Gunn "hath for the last two Years been very Sottish and hath given offence to the Indians at the Eastmain, to the disadvantage and lessening of the Company's Trade at that Place."[94]

Alcohol was a factor in the 1735 Boxing Day fire that almost completely destroyed Moose Fort. Former sloop master William Bevan had been in charge since 1732 but apparently did little to hinder his men's drinking (of which he may have been too fond himself). Bevan's replacement, the veteran Richard Staunton, later reported to the Committee:

> *[D]runkenness and debauchery have been the causes of all your honours' misfortunes, for if there had been but one discreet person [the fire could have been prevented]...But I may with justice say they were all stupefied or else some one man would a endeavoured before the flames broke out to a found from whence that smoke should proceed for so many hours together.*[95]

Not surprisingly, the fire at Moose focused the attention of the Committee on the issue of drunk and disorderly behaviour in its factories; it also forced the factors to defend themselves and their men. James Isham assured the Committee, "No Gang of men Can behave soberer, than has been here [at York Fort], and which your honours may be assured we shall discourage anything to the contrary: the consequence is so dreadful." The Prince of Wales Fort council suggested that reports of drunkenness at its factory were false, and "asserted for an undoubted truth that our people have behaved in a very sober and orderly manner, there being a particular

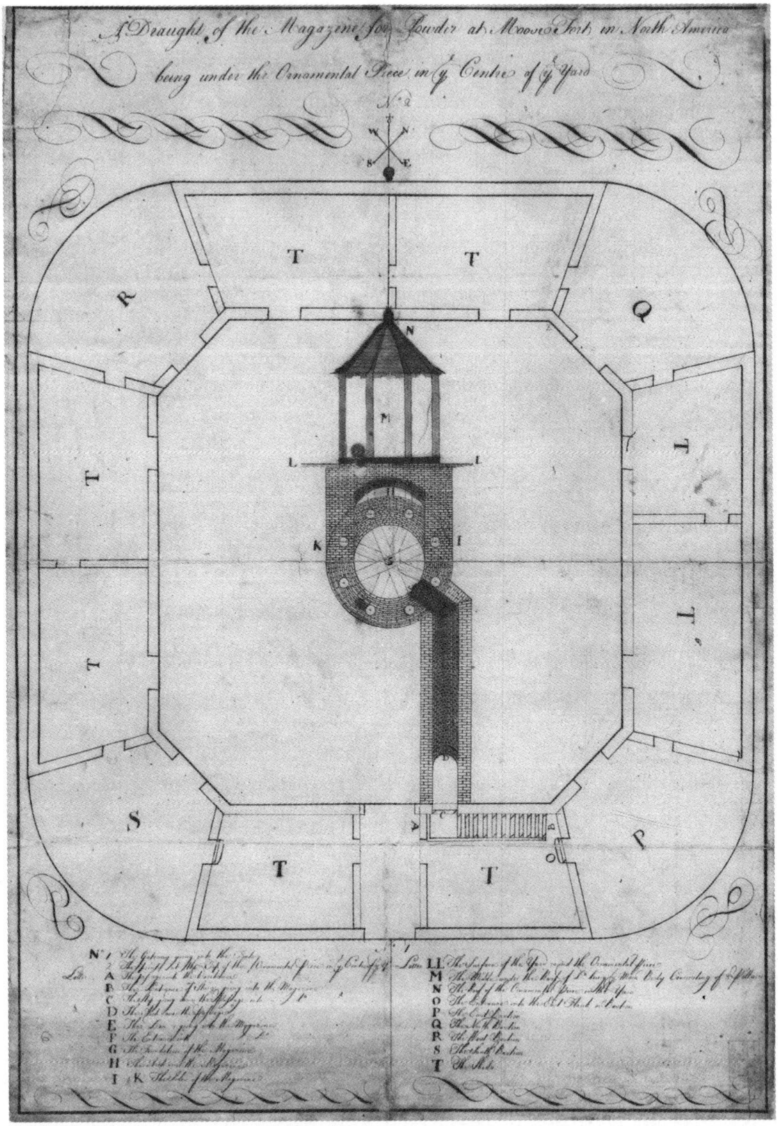

This undated plan of Moose Fort (probably ca. 1746) shows men and goods located along the walls and in the corner bastions, while the centre of the courtyard is occupied by a charming ornamental piece. [HBCA, G.1/101]

regard had to suppress all indecencies." Likewise, Thomas Bird promised vigilance in keeping Albany's men from drunkenness, although he himself was posthumously accused of "that vice."[96]

These factors—particularly Isham—were juxtaposing the sobriety allegedly prevailing at their posts against the disorder at Moose, where Richard Staunton roundly condemned the men's "drunkenness and debauchery."

> *[I]f there was any one that had any spark of honesty or modesty remaining in them, it was become a custom here, and I am afraid in other parts of your country, to abolish those principles of honesty and virtue, and to endeavour to get them into the same scrape with themselves, that there should not be any one to accuse the guilty...or...left to impeach them, nor boy not so much as the very Company's apprentices but what have been debauched, insomuch in a few years more your honours would a had no occasion neither for a warehouse nor any trading room, only for your honours to a provided a ship, trading goods and provisions, to a paid your servants wages, and I may with justice say that every servant here in your country would a been very officious and double diligent to a taken vigilant care your honours should not a been overburdened with too much profit if any.*[97]

Staunton referred to the servants' diligence, vigilance, and care for "your honours" but turned those desirable qualities on their heads by using them to describe the servants working for their own interests rather than for the company's. His vivid portrayal of Moose as "a dismal ruinated place" began with alcohol and ended in vaguely defined "vice" and "ignorance" (i.e., offences or sins caused by ignorance).[98] He singled out labourer Thomas Carr as "one that is so corrupted with evil examples that he is not at all fit for your honours' service," and sailor John Smith, "his brother...as he calls him...[who] has twice as I am informed been sent home for misdemeanours, once from Churchill and once from hence, he being a vile man and...any one that shall speak in his behalf must have had a feeling in some of his evil practices." Staunton predicted that Carr and Smith would meet a bad end: "I wish they do not both go up Holbourn Hill in a cart."[99]

Factors strongly believed that a wicked man could corrupt those around him. In 1739 James Isham sent home bricklayer Richard Mincyn, "not thinking it convenient to keep him with sober men, he being continually drunk and corrupting other men from doing their duty." In 1726 Albany chief Joseph Myatt complained that mariner James Miller was "So Monsterous Wiked and Disobediant to Commds, that I Desire he may be recall'd home the next year for I fear he will Currupt all ye young Men in ye factory." In 1766 the Committee recalled three of Moose's tradesmen "in expectation that the rest of Our Servants will not be corrupted by their bad Examples." Richard Staunton sent carpenter John Booth home from Moose in 1737 for "being a very fractious man and one that is enough to corrupt the whole country."[100] In 1738 Richard Staunton and accountant George Howy (the only man at Moose whom Staunton trusted enough to have on his council) suggested that this moral corruption affected their colleague's health:

> *And now I do not at all wonder at Mr Macklish [Thomas McCliesh Jr] return home the second time [in 1736], he having the first time found how your honours' affairs was managed amongst the natives in the country. I am of the opinion it then made him sick which made him return, but coming a second time and finding the factory quite demolished and the state of affairs in all respects worse and worse, it then made him bad indeed if not right down ill, for to think he had so much encumbrances to manage or such a sea of difficulties to go through that he rather chose to return and quit your honours' service than to plunge himself into so many difficulties in his old days, where he was sure he should get no credit.*[101]

Moose Fort itself seemed to be tainted by the evil men within it: "For some time after my arrival I was really ashamed to find such a dismal ruinated place as I did then find it to be and so very much corrupted."[102] Robert

Pilgrim at Prince of Wales Fort would have sympathized: in February 1748 mason John Davenport spent a Saturday night and all day Sunday drunk and then was found dead in his bed on Monday morning. "I was Going to Say that this way of Dying is a Natural Death for a Northwester, but I will Venture to Say itt is a Norwest Death, for sure I am this is the 4th man has Gone this way since I have Knowne this place, by the force of good Liquor as they call itt."[103]

Penitence, Forgiveness, and Reconciliation

Most miscreants left the company's service. Albany armourer Peter Stephens, "a good workman (and tolerable Sober)," offered to serve as blacksmith too after Patrick Mulvey went home early in 1755. Stephens was only one year into a five-year contract at twenty pounds per annum with a ten-pound gratuity at the end; the Committee offered him a thirty-pound gratuity for his extra efforts, "provided he does the Smiths Work also, and behaves to Our Satisfaction," but Stephens rejected that offer and demanded thirty pounds per annum. Isbister chose to send him home:

> *It is remarkable & well Known to us all that this Peter Stephens has behaved much worse Since the Ships departure then he did all last year, by reason he thinks we cannot do without him & takes advantage of our being without a Smith & has been frequently drunk & disorderly notwithstanding what he promised to me last shiptime when I write in his behalf for better encouragement as he was to Act in two Capacitys as Armourer & Smith.*[104]

Although "as to the first he behaved so tolerable well that he deceived us all," in 1755–56 Stephens and his "Accomplice," labourer Thomas Jopling, were frequently guilty of drunk and disorderly behaviour, and insubordination. On one occasion they attempted to defraud surgeon George Rushworth of his gun, and they may have been involved in private trade as well. Isbister took Stephens's misbehaviour personally, not only as a threat to "the peace and Safety of this Place" but also as rank ingratitude for Isbister's writing on his behalf. After soliciting that support in 1755, Stephens had repeatedly challenged Isbister's authority within the factory. Too late he recognized how impolitic this was. On 1 September 1756, the day after the arrival of the supply ship, Stephens tried to dip into that well of support once more.

> *Petter Stephens Came to me this morning Seemingly Sorry for his ill behavour & beg that I would do him no injury to which I replied that if he did himself no injury I would not, at ye Same time he wanted his wages fixt at £30 p Ann, which I told Could not be Complied with & that he ought to Submit to ye Companys Generosity if he thought to do himself any Service, & to be more sircumspect in his behavour.*[105]

Stephens was not "more sircumspect in his behavour," and a few nights later he "behaved in a most Audacious manner by Absenting himself from this Fort, & going Amongest ye Indians & Scaling the wales at an unseasonable time of ye Night." This was the final straw for Isbister, who gave Stephens twenty-four hours to pack his belongings, and then bundled him onto the homeward-bound ship. Stephens's presence was deemed more damaging to the household factory than the absence of both a smith and an armourer.[106]

Some other men, however, found mercy and forgiveness. Former Blue Coat boy Samuel Hopkins was apprenticed for seven years in 1714 and was keeping (or at least copying) the accounts in his second season at Albany, but he apparently found Joseph Myatt's management too confining and left Albany without leave on 3 October 1722. Hopkins wintered away from the factory (the precise location is unknown) with an unnamed Home Guard Cree and returned to Albany on 1 May 1723; he left again on 17 May, but the Upland Cree whom he followed upriver did not want him, and he was quickly apprehended by two of his factory mates.[107] Hopkins went home in disgrace that year, but the Committee re-engaged him in 1724 "out of charity." He served at York, where he was once again under the command of Thomas McCliesh Jr (as he had been through almost all of his apprenticeship); McCliesh reported in 1725 that "Samuel Hopkins has behaved himself very handsomely, and [I] have made him steward this year, by reason believe he is naturally honest." The Committee made it clear to Hopkins that "according to your behavior you shall receive encouragement from us" and that "the only way to continue our favour, and to incline us to advance you" was to "be carefull and diligent in your Business, and to the utmost of your Power, endeavour to promote our Interest." Hopkins served as steward until 1727, and then as book-keeper, before returning home with Thomas McCliesh Jr's praise in 1731: "he has been very diligent and honest in the discharge of his duty, and is deserving of your honours' favour."[108]

Myatt himself was the recipient of some gentle correction from the Committee, which was alarmed by a 50 per cent drop in Albany's trade for 1721–22 and suspected "some mismanagement" (although French competition may have been nearer the mark).[109] Myatt was demoted to second in 1723 and replaced with Richard Staunton, who rehabilitated Myatt's commercial reputation and brought about a rebounding trade. The Committee's concerns ran deeper than the trade, however:

> *We have Several Accounts from too good hands to be disbeliev'd, that many Iregularities, & debaucheries are crept into ye Factory, where you are, ye certain consequence of which must be disgusting & terrifying ye Natives from coming to Trade with us, & ye ruining & Spoiling our own Servants, & making them uncapable of doing us any Service, besides ye great Scandal this will be to our religion in General & a very great disgrace to us all who have ye power to prevent these Mishiefs & do not make use of it, to prevent these disorders we hope these cautions will put you upon yr Guard, & remove these grievance, that we may have no further Complaints, who wish you Health & Happiness, & are Yr Loving Friends.*[110]

Without more details we cannot judge how disgusted or terrified the Indigenous traders might have been, but the Committee certainly seems to have been nauseated by what was happening. Yet the letter ended with a caution, a friendly farewell, and a chance at redemption for both Myatt and Albany.[111]

McCliesh considered Hopkins's "misbehaviour" representative of the general state of affairs at Albany after his own departure from thence in 1721—"I think that most of them turned fools and madmen"—but more important in Hopkins's return to favour was that he was "very obliging, and appears now to be mighty sorry for his former misbehaviour." In 1734, when surgeon John Edwards went home from Moose, his superior, William Bevan, commented that Edwards was "wonderfully reformed and has behaved in a very dutiful and obedient manner this last year, his whole deportment being the reverse to his former conduct." In 1739 the Albany council mentioned that labourer William Macklin and mariner William Fosset "were called before ye Councill and examined, who both made their Submission, and begg'd Mercy, wherefore we thought it not necessary to continue their Punishment."[112] Even Joseph Isbister—noted for his robust approach to discipline—observed that "it was in my power both to pardon and to punish, the first is preferable to the last, Especially when the Criminal acknowledges his fault, & promises better behavior for the future."[113]

Factors and other senior servants were sometimes explicitly offered opportunities either to clear their names or to beg forgiveness. In 1719 the Committee sent Henry Kelsey a copy of unspecified "Accusations [which] had been Said Before us, Concerning Yr Conduct which wee hope you will Clear Your Self of...being very Unwiling to think that a Person wee had so Good an Opinion of as your self should forfeit their Estimes, who are Yr Love[in]g Friends."[114] Even Thomas Hall, who was accused of abusing his position as warehouse keeper by embezzling trade goods and furs, was offered a faint hope of reprieve: Governor Kelsey was ordered to investigate and send Hall home immediately, but if "he Clears himself to Yr Satisfaction," Hall could be transferred to Prince of Wales Fort for the final year of his contract.[115] Others took the initiative themselves and confessed their sins to the Committee. Accountant Hugh Jones, who had clashed so seriously with Humphrey Marten at York, wrote such a letter (which has not survived) in 1762 and received this reply:

> *We...are sorry to find, from your self as well as others, an Acknowledgement of your ill Behaviour. But as you have promised an entire Amendment of your Conduct for the future, we shall at present Desist from treating you according to your Merit: But if we hear any more Complaints of your Conduct, you must not expect further favour from / your Loving Friends.*[116]

William Falconer, master of the *Severn* sloop in the late 1760s, also failed to show his Bayside superiors proper deference but avoided punishment by showing a humble and contrite heart to his superiors in London.[117]

Themes of reconciliation in HBC documents reflect similar patterns in the resolution of master-servant conflicts in contemporary Britain at the time. Authorities there often used example and public display to communicate their expectations of appropriate behaviour, especially among young people. They used the language of friendship, submission, amendment, and forgiveness to preserve the relationship that "disorderly" servants challenged; the suitably chastened miscreant was in turn expected to submit to authority, ask forgiveness, and promise future amendment.[118] When employed by the HBC, such themes were powerful because they exhibited the best aspects of paternalism, namely the rhetorical figures of the compassionate master and the obedient servant.

Factors claimed to set a good example for their men to follow. In 1741 Joseph Isbister and his council referred to the many "Vices" of which the men of Albany were guilty: "we have not only promised to rectify [such behaviour], but shall be carefull to show a virtuous Example in ourselves." In 1738 Richard Staunton lamented that "I cannot do as formerly show both good examples and precepts, only now good precepts and dictate, for I cannot go abroad as formerly, age hindering my speed." He and Howy also hoped to "reclaim" the "Captain" of the Moose River Lowland Cree (who had learned "so much villainy" from the English) "if possible...by showing him good examples and kind usage."[119]

The value placed on good and proper behaviour was highlighted by references to *decorum*. In 1728 Joseph Myatt recommended engaging a mate for sloop master William Bevan "by Reason Mr Bevan is Oblidged to be on Shore as Soon as he Arrives at his Winter Quarters [Eastmain], In order to trade with the Indians, and his men Standing all upon a Footing, there is no Decorum kept on Board the S[ai]d Vessell when Ever his Back is turn'd." In 1732 Joseph Adams praised his second, Thomas White, who had recently acted as chief while Adams was at Moose: "at my return I found that he had Acted with a Great Deal of prudence & Delligence both in Treating the Natives well and Carr[y]ing a Good Decorum." Richard Staunton promised "to keep a good decorum in your factory" at Moose in 1739, and John Potts promised to severely punish any "breach of Decorum" at Richmond in 1750.[120]

|| In wartime, factors were expected to maintain a more military-style discipline but also neighbourliness and decorum. The latter focus increased in peacetime, as befitted the households that their factories resembled. Henry Kelsey warned the men of Prince of Wales Fort "not to let any animossety arise or breed any disturbance wich may be any ways prejudiceale to the Compy, or disquiet the Govermt."[121] The rhetoric of deference, love, and affection fit well with contemporary expectations of the master-servant relationship and served to gloss over the cracks in the everyday realities of such relationships. Cracks there were, especially in Hudson Bay, where physical isolation and the peculiar circumstances of trading-post environments placed unfamiliar constraints on the household model.

8 Tensions within the Household Model

As to your own Conscience in Relation to the Indian Woman and Family, we agree with you that we have no power over that but Certainly the Company ought not to be put to any Charge, or their affairs be Damaged thereby.

— HBC to Richard Norton (PWF), 17 May 1739, *Letters*, 292n

THE RHETORIC OF SOCIAL COHESION sought to reiterate the content of the public transcript. It was also intended to convince other parties that the rhetoric accurately reflected reality. Sometimes this could be transparently false or at least suspect. The men of Moose Fort in 1736 were wasting their ink when they tried to impress the Committee by how, "with heart and hand," they were assiduously rebuilding the factory that they had inadvertently burned down the year before. Yet, to omit such rhetoric cast doubt on the cohesion it portrayed: after a period of weak leadership at Albany in the late 1730s, new factor Joseph Isbister sought to curb "the height of Insolence that threatens to Demolish all forms of Government."[1]

Most of the time, the public transcript offered a framework within which master and servant could converse, negotiate, argue, and (when necessary) heal social wounds. Behind the actual exchanges lay the expectations—some of which were frustrated—among members of the household. Early modern households were imperfect creations inhabited by imperfect people in an imperfect world and as such could act as hothouses of tension and conflict.[2] In Hudson Bay, multi-year contracts and geographic distance deprived men of the opportunity to change masters on a regular basis or at short notice and thus deprived the household factories of an important safety valve.

This is not to suggest that the household factories were closed societies. The distance between Hudson Bay and Britain did not prevent the men from corresponding regularly and privately with people back home. In 1715, for instance, the Committee required that men sending letters home from the Bay had to include them in the official mail packet, "that they may first come to us, whereby others may not know & be acquainted wth our Concerns before our selves as they have heitherto been."[3] Also, the much nearer communities of Lowland and Homeguard Cree, and of Upland Cree and Assiniboine traders, offered new social connections. Both sets of relationships, Indigenous and European, caused the Committee many sleepless nights: social networks could become (or begin as) economic networks, and these could potentially threaten the company's business that these men were supposed to be conducting and protecting.

The Issue of Private Trade

Private trade came to be perceived as the most serious internal threat to the company. In May 1672 the Committee ordered that "all persons to be imployed Shall enter into articles or otherwise oblige themselves not to trade in beaver upon forfeiture of theyr goods & wages." In 1674 the Committee was quite active on this front. Carpenter Solomon Soles's account was charged with nineteen private skins. James Tottenham's wages were withheld until his wife delivered up thirty-four beaver skins that he had traded privately. More of Tottenham's illicit trade was subsequently discovered. Tottenham did not feel that he had done anything wrong, however, and in February 1674 he tried to secure the arrest of the man (a Mr. Powers) who had impounded his furs; in turn, the Committee ordered that if he succeeded, it would post bail for Powers and pay the costs of his suit. The company's sailors appear to have been instrumental in revealing these cases of private trade, just as they were probably instrumental in facilitating those cases that the Committee did not discover: the Committee received its information about Soles from seaman Mathew Trim, and about Tottenham from Tottenham's accomplice, seaman Cuthbert Winter.[4]

The Committee itself showed some conflicting attitudes on private trade. In early 1674 seamen Thomas Wakefield and Nicholas Adams were charged for illicit skins (five pounds and eight pounds, respectively), but in each case "the rest of his trade [was] allowed [to] him." Surgeon Walter Farr successfully petitioned to go to Hudson Bay "as Chirurgeon & Apothecary" for three years and to be allowed some private trade, and newly engaged governor William Lydall was allowed to trade privately in all things except beaver skins, provided it was done openly. The Committee seemed to clarify its position in May when it directed that "no private trade bee allowed in any kinde of furres, &...all other private trade which may be allowed in any other comodityes, Shall bee by publicke License & brought into the Companyes warehouse to the ende that they may have cognisance thereof."[5]

Overall, the energy with which restrictions on private trade were enforced varied from year to year. At times even defining private trade could be a problem. In 1681, when trade goods ran low, John Nixon allowed his men to trade their blankets and clothing to the Indigenous peoples rather than turn away the furs being offered. The Committee initially intended to keep the furs thus acquired, arguing that the men had been trading as agents and servants of the company, though they would be compensated. Eventually the Committee changed its mind and allowed certain men to reclaim at least some of their furs.[6]

By this time the Committee was taking a stricter attitude toward private trade. In that year, it reluctantly agreed to "the application of severall persons" to send necessaries to their friends in Hudson Bay but directed that such packages be inspected and approved by the Sub-Committee for Shipping; it also ordered that all private letters to men in the Bay "shall be publickly communicated to the Committee before they are sent." In 1681 the Committee "viewed" private chests being sent out to Walter Farr and Brian Norbury; thirty years later they instructed chief factor John Fullartine to "take care" that the "severall necessaries" sent to Alexander Thoyts from home were "[e]xpended for his owne Use & not Sold as merchandises to our prejudice, & to an Evill Example." Similar tactics were also employed by the Royal African and Muscovy companies to combat illicit trade.[7]

In 1682 the HBC commissioned Morgan Lodge, postmaster of Deal (Kent), to put three waiters (i.e., customs officers) upon the *Diligence* when it arrived at Gravesend. Jean Baptiste Chouart and the other Frenchmen engaged in 1685 were allegedly reluctant to take the oath of fidelity, partly because of its prohibition on private trade.[8] A 1685 plan for allowing servants to trap and to trade, provided they declared their takings and shipped them home openly, was discontinued in the following year when the Committee declared that "what ever comes to our servants hands, whither by the one way or the other, it ought to be esteemed as our owne, for we are at great and vast charges there."[9]

This argument was common in early modern England, although exceptions to the rule are easy to find.[10] Samuel Richardson's 1734 manual, *The Apprentice's Vade Mecum: or, Young Man's Pocket-Companion*, considered it "very reasonable" that a servant or apprentice "should be restrained from trading or dealing for himself" because "an Apprentice has no Time that he can properly call his own." Besides the risk of the master being "robbed of the Profits of his Business" by "a clandestine Trade...carry'd on in his Name, and at his Expence," Richardson warned against "the Damage that may accrue to him by Loss of Time, and by that want of Attention to his Master's Business which *Self-Love* and *Self-Interest* must beget in the Servant, when he has one of *his own* to mind."[11]

Although generally frowned upon in domestic commerce, private trade was common in early modern long-distance commerce, where it has generated considerable debate, both then and now. In at least some cases it was considered a justified perquisite; the right to carry private cargo without freight charges (for mariners to sell privately, sometimes in lieu of wages) on board vessels was variously known as *privilege, venture,* or *portage*. Aspiring young merchants apprenticed to Levant Company traders in the early seventeenth century frequently engaged in personal trade apart from their masters' business while serving the last half of their indenture in the East, but the Virginia Company expressly forbade private trade in 1606.[12] There has been some uncertainty about whether the practice persisted into the eighteenth century, but Peter Pope has found convincing evidence of it in the colonial New England trades to the West Indies, Isle Royale, and Newfoundland.[13]

The motivations for the system of portage were varied. One 1693 Admiralty Court case suggested that portage was allowed in the Bristol (Virginia) trade specifically to offset risk, while portage in the Newfoundland trade was justified as a reward for honest and faithful service.[14] The RAC used opportunities for private trade (along with high remuneration) to attract talented men to serve as its agents in the West Indies, and there seemed to be enough available trade that private trade did not necessarily damage corporate profitability. Such was not the case in Africa, where the RAC initially allowed a modest scale of private trade—ranging from £300 of goods for the agent-general down to £30 for a junior factor—but discontinued this in 1680, offering higher salaries instead. Thus, the remuneration received by the agent-general rose from £400 per annum to £1,100 per annum plus a £200 gratuity after three years' service in lieu of private trade.[15]

India, however, presented many opportunities for private trade that were not necessarily at the East India Company's expense. At first, the EIC officially prohibited private trade and compensated its factors for this loss of privilege by granting them a sort of commission, based on the profits of a certain share of each voyage's (or year's) trade. In practice, however, they were allowed a specific amount of private trade each year, not to include spices or drugs. For instance, a factor of the first grade received a hundred pounds plus the profits on two hundred pounds' worth of "adventure," while a factor of the fourth (lowest) grade received twenty pounds plus the profits on forty pounds' worth of "adventure." Like the RAC, the EIC began raising the salaries of factors in order to discourage them from illicit trade, and by 1633 a new president (the highest rank) received five hundred pounds per annum. Private trade continued, despite the company's efforts to restrain it: almost all of the EIC's seventeenth-century factors were accused of private trade. The directors in London often tried to use legal proceedings against offenders but were just as often thwarted in such legal action by factors' influential patrons. In 1620 the Surat Council (responsible for the EIC's trade in India and Persia) warned London against stern punishment for private trade, arguing that "if some tolleration for private trade be not permitted none but desperate men will sail our ships."[16]

By the eighteenth century most restrictions on private trade had been lifted, and the granting of this freedom became an important attraction of serving in the East.[17] It was largely confined to—and, indeed, came to dominate—the "country trade" (i.e., trade within the region, rather than with Europe).[18] Scholarly debate over whether or not this was a good thing forms part of the larger debate over the modernity of these early modern long-distance trading companies. Emily Erikson has recently argued that "private trade allowances both contributed to and were a part of a larger pattern of decentralized decision making in the English [East India] Company…[which] encouraged employees to stay longer in the East, exploring new ports and linking existing English settlements into a tighter network of communications." This "decentralized organizational structure—constructed through the combination of private and Company trade—was the central pillar of the English East India Company's continued expansion and adaptability over nearly two centuries."[19]

Private trade certainly decentralized the structure of the EIC, but its directors explicitly tried to restrain or limit that development. A 1785 outline of the EIC's London administration shows a Committee for Private Trade and a Committee for Preventing the Growth of Private Trade; the latter, at least, persisted until the company's India trade monopoly ended in 1813.[20] Regardless of the question of corporate profits, illicit actions by overseas servants were a challenge to the directors' authority and ultimately entangled the EIC in a series of political conflicts that led to colonial rule. That company's pivotal victory in Bengal in 1757 was prompted by private trade interests aiming to curtail the growing private trade by French merchants.[21] As the EIC began moving into political administration and revenue collection in the 1760s, some directors believed that they had almost entirely lost control of their overseas servants.[22]

In Erikson's narrative, "the adoption of private trade allowances...institutionalized a pattern in which agents' and principals' interests were independent but aligned."[23] A generation ago, Holden Furber felt that the EIC had been so eroded by its servants' private concerns as to be little more than a façade. More recently, Sanjay Subrahmanyam and H.V. Bowen preferred the term *carapace*, an institution pursuing its corporate aims while at the same time being "used by other actors for their own ends."[24] During the eighteenth century the EIC "was sometimes portrayed as a powerful monolith," but "it could also be described as a loose collection of individuals who operated under a flag of convenience and exhibited very little allegiance to any higher form of authority or interest."[25] The overlap and tension between political and business activity by corporate interests and by private interests meant that the institutional boundaries of the company were never fixed.[26]

The HBC Committee never lifted restrictions on private trade, compensating for this prohibition by allowing servants to trap their own furs and send them home with the company's furs for sale; the men received one-half of the proceeds from the sale of their skins, while the company took the other half. This scheme was introduced in 1700 to increase the harvest of small furs like marten, which in England at the time were selling much better than beaver. Private furs had to be handed in to the warehouse by the end of February, before the men were needed for the serious work of the trading season. In 1701 the scheme was modified so that they could keep feathers (from hunting waterfowl) for their own bedding. At Albany in 1715 Thomas McCliesh Jr sent eight men marten hunting and "[l]ikewise

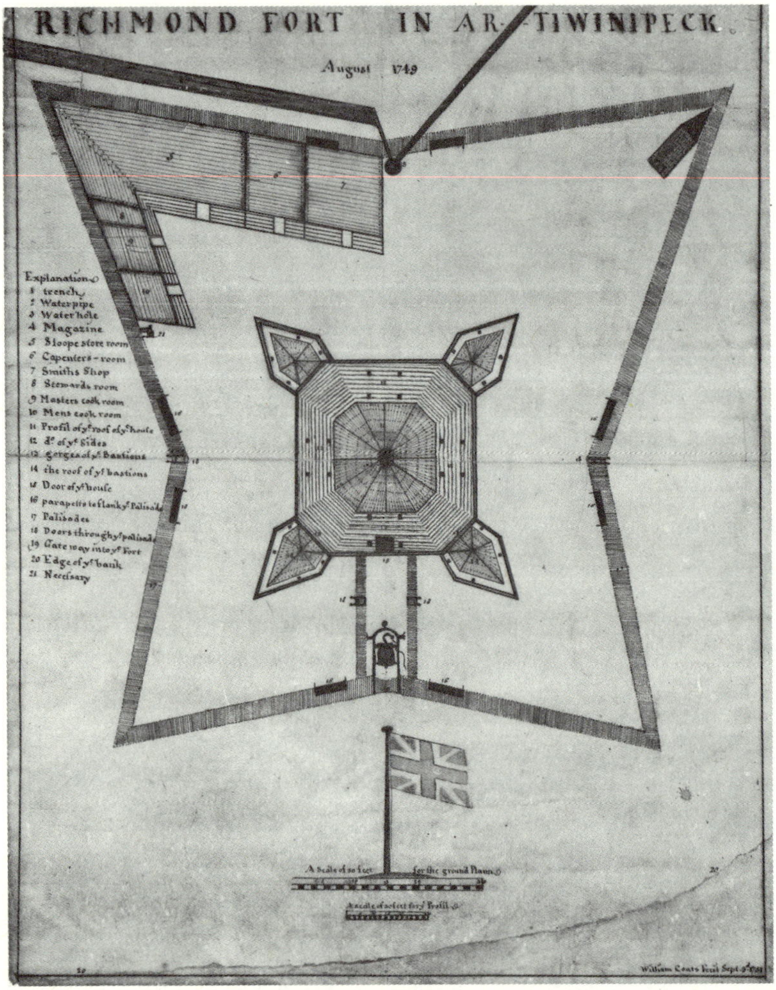

William Coats's 1749 drawing of the future Richmond Fort shows workshops and cookrooms (one for the master, one for the men) clustered in the top left corner, while the bedrooms and trading rooms were located in the central building. The washroom or "Necessary" was along the west wall (top right). [HBCA, G.1/104]

gave Liberty to all the men Att home to goe Att times a Marten Catching" when winter set in, "being A safe time of the Year." When the men returned from hunting, he searched them for concealed furs before they entered the gates.[27]

Of course, private trappings could disguise or encourage private trade or even theft. In 1719 the Committee complained about "a very Great Quantity of Martins as well as Other sorts of Furrs" that were brought home privately on HBC ships and sold in London for hundreds of pounds sterling before the company's own furs made it to market. In 1721 York warehouse keeper Thomas Hall was accused of taking the best of the company's furs and replacing them with the worst of his own private trappings, for which he was dismissed. Those who concealed their furs and tried to sell them clandestinely forfeited both the furs and their wages if caught. In 1751 the Albany council promised to "putt an entire Stop to lying out a Trapping, in Order to prevent the Abuses Made thereof," but nothing much seems to have come from that.[28]

In 1715 and again in the 1720s the Committee authorized factors to purchase the servants' furs on the spot, offering a bottle of brandy and half a pound of sugar for each marten skin.[29] In general, though, the men preferred cash or credit over payment in kind—in February 1716, for instance, eleven Albany men traded 65 marten skins for brandy and sugar and sent 881 marten skins home as private trappings—and the account books indicate that this policy allowed many of them to substantially supplement their wages.[30] The profit was uneven, as higher-ranking men tended to send home many skins, and many men sent home no skins at all. Although the common hands tended to earn less from their furs in absolute terms than their superiors did, the value of the furs relative to their respective salaries was significant—significant enough that Albany labourer Matthew Sargent wrote the Committee to complain that he was kept too busy in the factory to enjoy the "liberty" of going out "a trapping as other servants do." The not altogether unsympathetic reply was "to follow the Governors orders and you may depend the Company will consider your services at the end of your contract which will be more to your advantage than if you had that liberty." The reply may not have been sympathetic enough, for Sargent immediately asked to be released from his contract.[31] Some factors appear to have employed the company's labourers in trapping for them.[32] Some of the men's furs may have been trapped by Indigenous wives or companions, and women probably would have done the cleaning, stretching, drying, and so on to make the furs saleable.

The line between private trapping and private trading was never clear. In 1737 the Committee (already in a foul mood after hearing of the major fire at Moose) chastised the Albany council for not including in the official homeward cargo several "Scraps of Beaver" found among the effects of five men who had drowned in a boat accident—"no man being intituled to any sort of Furr's the Compa deal in."[33] A bylaw from 1739 stated that "every Member Agent Factor Officer or Servant" trading privately would forfeit their wages and their stock and dividends (if any) and receive a fine of three times the value of the goods traded, as well as the possibility of further penalties being imposed by the company's general court of stockholders.[34] The earliest surviving contracts (late 1770s) included a clause by which a servant guilty of private trade forfeited two years' wages.[35] Yet surprisingly few men were actually dismissed for private trade. While commanding York in the late 1720s, Thomas McCliesh Jr sent home four men for such an offence, all of them labourers: Benjamin Harding in 1727, James Broadbent in 1728, and Robert Chambers and Robert Blackburn in 1729. However, their private trade may not have been as great a sin as their theft of goods and furs from the warehouse: McCliesh claimed that Chambers and Blackburn had each been "a thief at all opportunities" and that "many honester men" than they and Broadbent "has been hanged at Tyburn."[36]

Geographic and logistical considerations made private trade less of a problem for the HBC than it was for its contemporaries. The Royal African Company, like the HBC, used oaths of loyalty in conjunction with direct incentives, direct monitoring (when possible), substantial bonds, and rewards for good conduct to control private trade. However, the RAC was in a poorer position to monitor its ships' captains, as the coast of Africa and the islands of the West Indies offered far more locations suitable for illegal activities than did Hudson Bay.[37]

Nevertheless, in 1736 the Committee expressed concern at the quantities of illicit brandy that (it was informed) were being landed at the factories and distributed among the servants. It felt that such quantities, added to the large amount of liquor it officially sent out each year, were more than was good for its servants' health; it was also aware that excess liquor could be traded privately with the Indigenous peoples. The Committee instructed its servants to keep a watch for illicit liquor, defined as that being landed without written permission from at least one Committee member. If found, it was to be confiscated and a report sent to London (so that guilty parties could be prosecuted). Informers were promised a 2s. 6d. reward for every illicit gallon they discovered.[38] Moose came under particular scrutiny, especially after the Boxing Day fire. Richard Staunton reported in 1738 that "according to the best information I have had there has been some hundreds of gallons landed [illicitly] at this place [Moose] as well as at others in one year contrary to your punctual orders," and warned the Committee that "so long as there is any one person permitted or winked at, it will be...impossible for any one man in your country to quite abolish underhand dealings."[39]

Perhaps the greatest concern was that factors were trading privately or facilitating such activity by their men, for instance, by allowing them to take up large quantities of goods from the store. At Moose in 1738, for example, a bundle of uninvoiced fox skins, labelled as the property of former factor William Bevan, was found in a cask of small furs. In 1770 the Committee acidly remarked to Humphrey Marten at Albany, "We think it very extraordinary that there Should be any hiding places in Our Factory, wherein Our Servants could conceal any Furrs from the Knowledge of Our Chief, as in the case of [John] Newman last year." It ordered him to immediately search the entire establishment ("as privately as possible to prevent Clamour"), "especially...the South Shed up Stairs, where it is apprehended a Box lies concealed wherein are 200 Otters and Catts besides, Beaver Coats."[40]

Company servants on land and at sea also exchanged furs among themselves. In 1738 James Isham referred to "an old custom of [factors] giving to the captains and officers a present of furs," but assured the Committee that it "is much more sparingly now than formerly." In the following year Richard Norton tried to persuade the Committee that the information it had received on this issue was "in a great measure groundless."[41] In 1771, however, Andrew Graham described an elaborate system of exchange, by which factors distributed furs to the men under their command and to the captain and crew of the supply ships; at York these gifts ranged from eighty martens and two beaver coats for the second, to one beaver skin and one moose skin for each common hand. The factors and their men then sold these and other private furs to the ship captains (at a fraction of their market value) for resale in Europe. Graham observed that this practice had been going on for some time at all of the company's establishments, and it was probably partly what Joseph Robson was referring to in 1752 when he complained of factors giving "bribes to skreen their faults and continue them in their command." Taken in conjunction with Isham's comment, this suggests a well-established custom of redistribution, perhaps originating in the same redistribution of harvests and/or profits commonly found in the early modern European fisheries.[42]

Graham mentioned these practices in the context of a new wage structure for officers, which was instituted in 1770 after "manifest proofs of Imposition by some [servants] of a higher Class in whom Our Confidence was placed." Almost two thousand illicit marten skins were seized in 1769, along with dozens of beaver, otter, and muskrat furs. "The very remarkable Attempts of Our Servants [at private trade] which have been discovered this last year strike at the Existence of the Company," so the Committee eliminated payments for private trappings but increased officers' salaries and offered commissions on the value of company furs sent home. Commissions were extended to lower ranks in 1779, when the Committee initiated a schedule of premiums whereby, for every score of furs traded at a post, its master received one shilling, his assistant six pence, and the hands three pence.[43]

Graham estimated that the new system promised to almost double factors' incomes; he suggested that any man who complained (as Ferdinand Jacobs did) must have been involved with significant private trade. Humphrey Marten at Albany declared to Graham, "I am heartily glad that we now have it in our power to save a little money, without either being obliged to impose on others, or be imposed on ourselves."[44] Marten also took this opportunity to profit from his past behaviour in a non-monetary way.

> *And Now let me own somewhat in regard to my self (for I want not to make my Self appear more Righteous than I am,) Be it known therefore to Your Honors that it was my Constant Custom to put by from 250 to 300 Marten skins every Year many of which Skins were my trappings according to the Plenty or Scarcity of such Goods; Part of those Skins went to purchase a little French Brandy, to Eke out 7 ½ Gallons for 12 Months, for four Persons (for the Cag [keg] seldom ran more) and the remainder was a lift to my then low Wages...But as Your Honors generosity hath rendered us capable of doing very well without any Sinister help, the above said 300, are packed up with those found in the Box [i.e., they are being sent back with the confiscated furs].*

He also mentioned that he had made up a little parcel of marten skins for each Committee member "as a small token of my Gratitude" and was sending those with the rest.[45]

Marten's tactic was particularly audacious, considering that later in the same letter he asked permission to bring his half-Cree son, John America Marten, to England.[46] That Marten was able to turn his past misconduct to serve his future prospects in this way, by baring his conscience to his employers and praising their generosity, was partly due to the contrast between his gratitude (and platitudes) and the complaints of his colleague at Prince of Wales Fort, Moses Norton, whose entire service was overshadowed by concerns over his private trade. To reinforce Marten's promise of future honesty, the Albany council that year assured the Committee:

> *What impositions were carried on with regard to Trappings last Winter We know not, But this some of Us know, that Mr Marten hath frequently*

thrown into Your Trade more than half the Marten Skins he might justly have sent home as his Trappings, Contenting himself with the Number that Mr Temple Constantly sent home.[47]

Although Marten did maintain a trapline to keep himself physically active, it seems unlikely that a chief factor would have had enough time to do as much trapping as he claimed; presumably at least some of his furs were trapped by his Cree wife, Pawpitch, or by their son.

The Committee's reorganization of its officers' pay in 1770 was similar to the Royal African Company's pay restructuring in 1680. As profits declined in the face of increasing competition, the directors had to clamp down on private trade: there was no longer enough trade to "share" with its servants. The two companies responded the same way, by increasing salaries and perquisites to compensate officers for the loss of their illicit gains. As late-seventeenth-century French trader Jean Barbot had advised all European companies trading in Africa, "grant them such competent salaries, and perquisites, as may content them, and they may not be tempted to commit perpetual breaches of trust, and contrary to their most solemn oaths, and all the ties of conscience, *to make hay, while the sun shines*; as is too notoriously and generally practised."[48]

As noted, it has been suggested that private trade in India represented a system of decentralized property rights, wherein the company explicitly connected private opportunities with corporate opportunities. As shipping and trading capital was allocated by the central office on the basis of rates of return, a high rate of return meant more such resources and in turn meant more opportunities for both the company and the private individual to expand their trade. Private cargo space on the company's ships was also allocated on the basis of performance, so that factors who had exerted themselves on the company's behalf were able to bring out more goods with which to trade on their private accounts.[49] The HBC's factors might have agreed with this argument, but the Committee almost certainly would have sided with Jean Barbot, who blamed "want of virtue enough to withstand the temptations of opportunity and importunity of bad example" for the RAC servants' breaking of their oaths against private trade.[50]

When the Committee came face to face with private trade in 1769–70, it immediately sacked Captain John Horner of the maritime service and recalled several servants who had previously been implicated in private trade. Yet the factors—who, like Horner, were guilty not only of breaking the rules themselves but also of aiding and abetting other scofflaws—received a slap on the wrist and a substantial pay raise "in hopes of securing the Fidelity of Our Chiefs...and encouraging their Diligence and Industry."[51] As Hainsworth observed of estate stewards in England, they "bobbed up and down on the waves of [their] master's wrath until the storm blew itself out. It was probably as rare for a lord to sack his steward as it was for him to disinherit his eldest son."[52]

Not unlike the EIC at around the same time, the Committee chose to forgive (though not to forget) their wayward servants' "want of virtue" in the face of temptation. It explicitly modified the public transcript (as expressed through salaries and perquisites) to make it more competitive with private transcripts, thus reducing the allure of future temptation—and increasing the potential costs (in lost income) of servants succumbing to temptation again. When the *Prince Rupert* was discovered bringing illicit furs home from Albany in 1771, her captain and mates forfeited their bounties, as did Marten, chief factor John Garbut of Moose, and Eastmain trader Thomas Moore—although they were offered a reprieve "upon a due Submission and promise...of more Diligence and Attention to Our Interest for the future....But We do give You this Notice that the like Indulgence will never be Shewn again, You must therefore for your Own Interest be more attentive to Ours."[53]

Conflicting Households

The ongoing conflicts over private trade highlight the major source of tension within the HBC's overarching master-servant relationship. Intimately connected with it was the ongoing—but usually less explicit—debate over sexual relations and marriage. This, too, was seen as both an economic issue and a moral one. Although the Committee pontificated on these questions less frequently, it arguably posed a more serious threat to the cohesion and effective operation of the HBC's household factories.

The ideal model of the early modern household family called upon all members of that household except the patriarch and his wife to be celibate. While premarital sexual relations undoubtedly took place, getting married was associated with starting a household of one's own and thus was incompatible with a state of subservience in the household of another. In late-seventeenth-century Newcastle, for instance, an apprentice joiner and three bricklayers were each fined two pounds for marrying while they were apprentices, and two of them were fined for having children while they were apprentices (at the rate of two pounds per child); in comparison, the bricklayers' guild in Newcastle in the late seventeenth century charged two pounds for entry into the membership.[54] Samuel Richardson's 1734 advice manual for apprentices explained that marriage, "tho' a lawful Engagement, in a Person who is his own Master, and has a Right to dispose of himself, is often of very fatal Consequence to a young Man, who is an Apprentice."[55] For company servants, wives in Britain were not usually a concern in this regard, as the physical distance between husband and wife created a pseudo-bachelorhood. However, forming long-term connections with Indigenous women challenged the implicit structure of the household factory in the Bay.

The Committee seems to have preferred bachelors, as suggested by their 1682 order "that the Secretary indeavor to gett 10 honest and able Fellows batchelors not under 20 nor above 30 yeares old."[56] There is no evidence, however, that married men were excluded from company service, and many men who entered the service as bachelors married while home on leave or between contracts. It is impossible to know exactly how many men had wives back home, nor is it easy to determine how many married men were already married when they first entered the company's service, and how many men married while in Britain between periods of service. An employee's spouse (or other family) usually only appeared in the

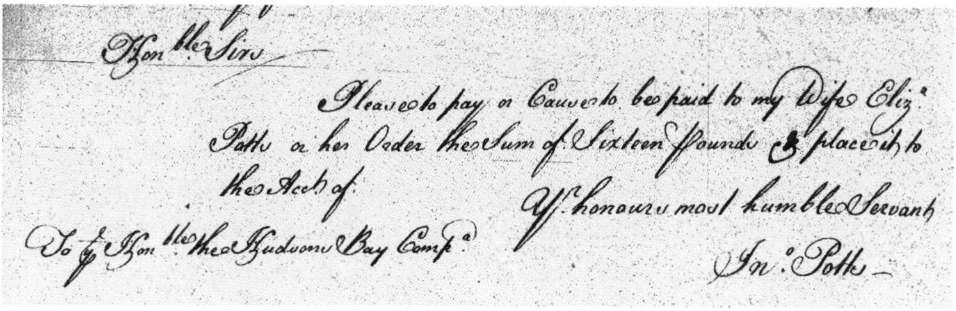

Hon.ble Sirs

Please to pay or Cause to bee paid to my Wife Eliz.a Potts or her Order the Sum of Sixteen Pounds & place it to the Acct of

Yr honours most humble Servant

Jn.o Potts

To ye Hon.ble the Hudsons Bay Comp.a

John Potts's bill to his wife, Elizabeth, 1746. The bills copied into account books at an outpost provide a small glimpse of family connections back in Britain. [HBCA, B.135/d/15, fol. 66d]

company's records when she requested permission for him to come home early or when she received money paid out from his account. References in men's accounts to women sharing their surname may refer to wives but might equally refer to mothers, aunts, or unmarried sisters. The available evidence only allows the statement that a significant minority of company employees had wives in Britain, without allowing any quantification of how much of a minority they were. It was not uncommon for couples in early modern Britain to separate (temporarily or permanently) in order to find work.[57]

There are several instances in the early London minute books of wives petitioning the company to allow their husbands to return home. Such requests were habitually granted "if hee desire it."[58] In 1728 Thomas McCliesh Jr complained about the "importunities" of Mrs. Christopher Bannister, the wife of York's armourer, clamouring for her husband to come home. McCliesh claimed that Bannister never mentioned to him any plans of going home, but homeward-bound servants had told the Committee otherwise. McCliesh's apparent failure to write on Bannister's behalf (as "you had promised him so to do"), plus Mrs. Bannister's petitions, prompted the Committee to release the armourer from his contractual obligations.[59]

Having a wife in Britain could affect a man's service in Hudson Bay in other ways. In 1723 tailor James Fettus was "crazy" to come home from York Fort before his time was out because his wife had broken her leg;

he did go home in 1724 (one year early) but re-engaged in 1725 and served for another twelve years.[60] In 1730 York cooper Henry Lewins requested (and received) permission to come home the following year; his time was not yet out, but his wife had died the previous winter and he had been informed "that he shall be utterly ruined in case he does not come home next year."[61] For Thomas McCliesh Jr the presence of a large family in England may have been an incentive to stay in the company's service. Although he had come home from Albany in 1721, being "very Desireous of haveing the Happiness to see my wife & children," he returned to Hudson Bay the following year; in 1724 he asked the Committee "to pay this last year's wages by giving my wife a bond for a £150 and to pay her the other fifty pounds this ensuing March. The interest of the above-mentioned £150 will be a great help to my family, having no less than eight in number, whose daily maintenance depends upon my industry." However, in 1733 he again expressed a desire to come home, "that I may have the happiness of seeing my family."[62] Thomas Hopkins hinted at the strain that his absence was placing on his family in Britain, when he asked the Committee, "I hope that you'll be so kind as not to mention to any Body that I want to stay a year longer, for in case Mrs Hopkins was to know that I wanted to stay another year it wod make her very unhappy."[63]

Domestic problems may have been a motivation for some men to enter the service in the first place. English parishes—or, at least, tax-paying parishioners—were often concerned when a man left town or the country in search of employment because they could not be certain he would return: the wife and children a man left behind might become a charge on the parish. The term *widow* was sometimes used in parish accounts as a courtesy title for a deserted wife.[64] We can only speculate on the marital situation of Albany labourer George Lisk, who appears to have married in Britain between contracts in 1721–22; after making payments to his wife in 1722 and 1723, he then seems to have cut her off, prompting the Committee to intervene. The company's secretary wrote to Lisk in 1726:

> *[Y]ou may be satisfied ye Committee will not Order any part of your Wages to be paid to any Person without your consent or desire, but they think it reasonable and require, you will allow something Yearly for the Maintenance of your Wife, which they will take care shall be laid out for Her use and Support, therefore as the Gentlemen are so kind to give themselves that trouble, and your Wife in so much want thereof hope you will not refuse to allow her something out of your Wages.*[65]

It sounds very much as if Mrs. Lisk had been unable to obtain satisfaction from her absent husband and therefore had brought the situation to the Committee's attention.

The Committee also intervened in the case of mariner Nicholas Coxworthy, who had sent home two letters of attorney in 1725: one directed that seven pounds of his wages be paid to his sister, and the other directed that all of his wages be paid to his wife. Having previously ordered that no man be allowed to draw more than half of his wages, the Committee could hardly comply with both requests. However, "[t]hey Expect you will send an Order for your Sister to receive what is her due, otherwise will give them reason to think you deal very unjustly by Her."[66]

There is a growing body of literature examining the ways in which transatlantic emigrants maintained contact and relationships through letter writing. Elizabeth Jane Errington sees such letters as "a way both to sustain familial webs of affection and to invoke obligation; and by asserting their continuing place in the family circle, letter writers also sought to confirm their own identity and place in the world."[67] Whether people were together or apart, their familial relationships were constantly being negotiated to accommodate changing circumstances.

Nevertheless, long absence in the Bay could certainly strain marital and other relationships. In November 1681 Elizabeth Noldridge applied to the Committee for her husband Richard's wages but was denied (despite having a letter of attorney) on the grounds of a report from Thomas Wilkinson. Wilkinson, a gunsmith and edge-tool maker recently returned from Albany, told the Committee that Mrs. Noldridge "hath had several

Bastards since her said Husband went away" in 1674 and that Mr. Noldridge (a bricklayer at Albany) had instructed Wilkinson to request the Committee not to pay her any of his wages.[68] Noldridge came home in 1682 but re-engaged two years later. The Noldridges may have reached some kind of reconciliation, because she later received his wages and the proceeds from the sale of his effects after his death in 1686.[69]

Noldridge's case highlights an important way in which service in Hudson Bay could challenge and even reshape a man's identity. A man's definition of himself involved his occupation and his position within the household family, both of which (but especially the latter) could be strained by the physical distance between Britain and the Bay. Noldridge was a husband, and possibly a father, but for eight years (1674–82) his company service removed him from the daily affirmation of being a householder. His wife apparently felt his absence during this time and sought another man to fill at least some of the roles that her husband was unable to fill. (Noldridge was still providing for Elizabeth to at least some extent: the company's secretary paid her money from Richard's account in 1676, 1679, and 1680.) When Noldridge returned to England in 1682, he probably found that his household family had successfully adapted to his absence and that he was no longer the important link he had once been. His bricklayer contacts with former workmates and customers may have suffered as much from his long absence as his marriage had. His re-engagement with the company in 1684 may have represented his desire to return to a place where his occupation and household position were less problematic than they had become in England.[70]

Of course, hiring bachelors did not necessarily remove the possibility that family concerns might bring a man home before his contracted time was up or might prevent him from signing a second or third contract. In 1680 the return of Samuel Oakes was requested by his sister, that of Samuel Huxford by his mother, and that of John Dew by his father.[71] In 1696 John Todd at Albany was informed that the Committee had granted his mother's request for him to be allowed to come home, "his Mother alleadging he hath a right to an Estate wch. is in Controvercey, his father being dead." However, no ship sailed home from Albany that year, so Todd could not return to England until 1697.[72]

Potentially more problematic were family connections formed in the Bay. From the first days of the company through the early nineteenth century the Committee strongly discouraged their servants and officers from fraternizing with Indigenous women.[73] Nevertheless, Jennifer S.H. Brown has documented at least fifteen instances of company men taking Indigenous companions prior to 1770, although she observed that none of these women was apparently designated by her European companion as *wife* in the European sense.[74] Although this kind of socialization contravened company expectations of celibacy, few men were disciplined for such behaviour. A greater deterrent (at least against promiscuity) may have been the custom of a man paying the surgeon a month's wages for curing venereal disease, "as an encouragement to the surgeon, and to make men more careful that they avoid such vice for the future." When the Committee ordered factors to discontinue that custom in 1738, the councils at Prince of Wales Fort and York urged them to rescind the order. James Isham actually refused to publish the order at York, explaining "with submission to your honours we humbly conceive this will be in some measure opening a door for licentiousness and debauchery."[75]

The mid-eighteenth century saw something of a public debate in England about the nature of marriage. The Clandestine Marriages Act of 1753 was meant to put an end to marriages outside the established Church of England, but there was (and is) no consensus about the extent and nature of clandestine marriages either before or after this Act. Rebecca Probert and Liam D'arcy Brown argue that (among other things) this debate addresses questions about the very nature of marriage in that period: "Was it perceived as a personal and private relationship, to be conducted outside the control of the state, or was it a public commitment whereby the parties assumed legally enforceable rights and responsibilities?" Their studies suggest that the latter was the case, although Richard Norton (referred to earlier in this chapter) may have disagreed. In the context of Hudson Bay, men might have seen the "state" (a.k.a. the company) as a less important arbiter of marriage and of the concomitant rights and responsibilities than were the Indigenous communities from which their partners came—although the tragic events at Henley suggest that they did not always pay enough attention to those either. Certainly the circumstances of Hudson Bay made it easy to marry clandestinely (i.e., without prior notification and outside the usual place of residence), much as London was famous (or infamous) for being an easy place to be privately married. Despite scholarly emphasis on the scandals and irregularities of such unions, clandestine marriages in England before 1753 were still legal and carried no contemporary stigma, and Scottish law required neither banns nor licence.[76]

What we know of the patterns of who married in HBC country (as opposed to already having wives in Britain) followed the expectations suggested by the household model. Charles Bayly was married, but there is no evidence of any suggestion that his wife join him in the Bay. An early experiment allowing officers to bring their wives from Britain was soon ended. In 1683 the newly appointed governor Henry Sergeant sailed for James Bay with his son (Henry Jr), his wife, her companion (Mrs. Maurice), a maidservant, and a clergyman (John French).[77] In the following year Elinor Verner received permission to join her husband, Hugh, at Rupert's River (where he was chief factor) on the understanding that he would pay her passage and twelve pounds per annum for provisions, but permission was rescinded before she sailed. The minute books recorded no reason for this decision, only mentioning that "upon divers good Considerations it is the opinion of this Committee She Shall not goe this expedition nor any other woman."[78] The advisability of sending women into an area that could be vulnerable to French attack was probably foremost in the directors' minds. The Committee recalled Sergeant and "all your Family" (referred to elsewhere as the "whole parcell of women appertaining to him") in 1687, and no more white women were allowed passage to Hudson Bay until the nineteenth century.[79]

Despite company expectations to the contrary, factors (as surrogate patriarchs) could justify to themselves selecting long-term partners from the Lowland or Upland Cree and were under pressure from the Cree to do so. Besides establishing a kin connection upon the foundation of which an economic relationship could be built, the women could serve important roles as cultural mediators and interpreters. English traders around the early modern world took local women as partners for the same reasons; to the examples analyzed by Jennifer S.H. Brown and Sylvia Van Kirk, we may add examples from Japan, Africa, Batavia, and elsewhere.[80] There is a great deal about these relationships that we do not know, but we should refrain from being overly cynical about them. Naomi Tadmor's shrewd comment about marriage in Britain in this period could apply equally to Hudson Bay: "Between strategic marriage and love at first sight lay a broad terrain in which prudence and affection interplayed."[81]

It is not always clear whether relationships were casual or long term. In 1686, for instance, the French who captured Moose found a Cree woman in the apartment of tailor Anthony Dowridge (who was in charge during John Bridgar's absence), and another in the apartment of carpenter John Fortnam, but there is no way of knowing the status or nature of these relationships from this snapshot alone.[82] Joseph Adams had a relationship with a Cree woman of "ye blood Royal" and returned to England in 1737 with a half-Cree daughter, Mary, who received most of his estate in trust when he died later that year.[83] The will of Rowland Waggoner instructed his executor, James Duffield, to take his son (perhaps future company servant Joseph Waggoner) back to England.[84] When Robert Pilgrim retired from his command at Moose in 1750, he brought his son to England, along with a Cree woman named Ruehegan (Thu a higon); after Pilgrim's death she returned to Hudson Bay (probably the Churchill River area). Pilgrim's attachment to Ruehegan dated from sometime before 1748 until his death in 1750, but in 1747 he was apparently keeping two Indigenous women and their children in his apartments at Prince of Wales Fort.[85] Richard Norton and his son, Moses, each kept Indigenous companions when they were in charge of Prince of Wales Fort (Richard also appears to have formed attachments in his youth); James Isham, Joseph Isbister, Humphrey Marten, and Ferdinand Jacobs also had Indigenous companions while they were serving as chief factors, as did inland officers of the late eighteenth century like William Tomison, Robert Longmoor, Malchom Ross, and William Walker.[86] As well, Isham, Isbister, Pilgrim, and possibly Moses Norton were polygamous, keeping more than one Indigenous wife—a practice outside the privileges of a British householder but quite feasible within Indigenous concepts of marriage.[87]

The Committee deplored such breaches of decorum by men in positions of responsibility but took few steps to actively restrain them. James Isham returned to his command at York on the understanding "that you do not harbour or Entertain any Indian Woman or Women in our Factory or permit others under you so to do," but his successor Ferdinand Jacobs later described York under Isham as worse than "the worst Brothel House in London."[88] Richard Norton clashed with the Committee over his choice of companionship, and the Committee eventually backed down; in 1739 it admitted to him that, "[a]s to your own Conscience in Relation to the Indian Woman and Family, we agree with you that we have no power over that but Certainly the Company ought not to be put to any Charge, or their affairs be Damaged thereby."[89]

Humphrey Marten's long-term companion was Pawpitch, daughter of the "Captain of the Goose Hunters" at Albany. He successfully forestalled the Committee's criticism of this attachment by calling upon the same Christian concepts that the Committee expected him to demonstrate in his management of its business affairs. In 1770—in the same letter in which he admitted to private trade—Marten made a personal request of the Committee.

> *And now Gentlemen I hope to have your Pardon for what I am going to say, You have taken the Wisest and most generous methods to have a set of Honest Men in your employe, but I cannot be good by halves, Your regulations have easied my Conscience greatly, but yet there is a Load hangs on it that it is in Your Honors Power to remove, We are told by God and Nature that it is Our Duty to take care of Our Offspring, and that we shall be severely punished if we do not. If so how can I forbear to Petition Your*

Mr Samuel Hearne, Late Chief at Prince of Wales's Fort, Hudson's Bay, 1796, *by an unknown artist, depicts Hearne as a fine old English gentleman, but the fanciful modern viewer may wonder if his tired-looking eyes are remembering the hardships and hard work of his years in Hudson Bay.* [HBCA, P-167]

Honors once more that my Son, John America Marten may be permitted his passage to England, where he may have a Christian and European education and become an usefull member of Society, I will gladly pay for his Passage, and make a Deposite of 50 Pounds as a Security to the Honble Company against any Expence...the Time may not be very farr off when Americans Born with English education may prove very usefull to the Company.[90]

Marten used his duty to God to win the official approval that he needed in order to send his country-born child home on the company's ship. The Committee authorized Captain Joseph Richards to take on board "an Indian Boy called John America Marten...provided Mr Marten orders him to be delivered to some of his Friends in London, but not otherwise."[91]

Jacobs's complaints about Isham notwithstanding, lower-ranking men were not allowed the same conjugal privileges that their superiors allowed themselves. Andrew Graham explained that "the Factors keeps a bedfellow within the Fort at all times," but junior officers were only allowed to entertain their companions in their apartments "at proper times" (and never overnight), and common men could only fraternize outside the factory walls.[92] Isham's men were allowed to keep women in their apartments, but they were the exception; more commonly, men had to socialize during hunting trips or go "over the Works in the Night."[93] The latter option, however, was a challenge to domestic security, and men could be punished for it. The external perimeter of the house was a frontier in custom and law, not to be breached after dark.[94]

Thus, servants who formed long-term attachments in the country were pushed toward the edge of the household factory. As the Committee forbade men from settling in the country, these servants could not leave the old household and form a new one of their own in Hudson Bay like they could in Britain. As already noted, Hudson Bay lacked the institutional frameworks of colonial governance (such as parishes, courts, and assemblies) that would make such settlement possible in a British context. The absence of such institutions—particularly the absence of courts, considering that the English "system of law and liberty...was the very essence of their national identity" in the early modern period[95]—emphasized the fact that the areas outside the fort walls had not been structured or imagined as British space, and thus that settlement could only take place according to Indigenous frameworks. HBC servants could only form what John Foster and Gerhard Ens called a "sub-household," which was unstable both in itself (as the man was unable to fully adopt the patriarchal role) and as an element within the principal household factory.[96]

One of the clearest examples of such tensions involved Augustine Frost at Moose in the 1730s and early 1740s. In 1742 chief factor James Duffield stated that Frost had several wives and numerous family members among the Moose River Homeguard Cree and that Frost was considered "so much an Indian himself that he has no concern for either his native country or the Company's interest."[97] This was perhaps an exaggeration and probably represented Duffield's opinion more than the Cree's. However, Frost had served at Moose since 1730 and was a member of the council there; thus, though classified only as a bricklayer, he had a clear social standing within the factory that could have made him a desirable marriage partner. He was certainly a son-in-law of both Old Muccatoon ("father of the rabbit skin guard") and Old Nimitihige, and his brothers-in-law included Pasqueyo and Messhaeopway.[98] Hunting trips and other tasks away from the factory allowed Frost to maintain a presence in his Indigenous family.

Duffield criticized Frost for being the vital link in the local network of private trade; for connecting supply-ship captain William Coats and the crew of Moose's sloop (who had all been recruited by Coats) with the Moose River Homeguard Cree. Frost's connections with the Homeguard were based on marital ties, and so his involvement in private trade was an expression of his conflicting loyalties: he was bound by contract to protect the interests of his company household but socially obligated by marriage to advance the interests of his Indigenous household. His attempts to act as a father and a husband strained the stability of the household factory.[99] However, his "sub-household" was itself unstable because Frost's ability to function as patron and patriarch in a British sense was limited by his reliance on Coats (in providing the link with Britain that was necessary for private trade) and by Duffield's ability to send him home. Yet he could not act as a Lowland Cree "patriarch" (a very different role) because his fathers-in-law were still alive and active.[100] Humphrey Marten might have sympathized, on a personal if not a professional level:

> *[T]his morning departed this life, the Indian woman called Pawpitch... by whose Death my poor Child becomes Motherless, and should Your Honours not Consent to his going to England (which O my God forbid) he will be a poor helpless Orphan indeed his Grandfather being deep in Years and having a numerous family, cannot provide for him hard if the Son is debarr'd from reaping the fruits of the Father honest industry.*[101]

Even a chief factor lacked the independence to perform his paternal role as completely as he would have wished.

Homeguard Cree—especially those with an HBC father or grandfather—also came to see themselves as components of the household factory.[102] Although their understanding of the household and of the role of the patriarch was different from the English understanding, they clearly felt an attachment to the English establishments. One former servant told a parliamentary select committee in 1749 that "the Indians near the Factories Consider their Factories as their Home. The Company relieves their distresses, keep their Families for several Months together."[103] The Homeguard Cree played instrumental roles as hunters, fishermen, guides, and messengers for the household factory, and in return company officers were generally willing to act in a paternal role toward the Cree; in the autumn of 1769, for instance, a Cree man left his "exceeding Ill" wife and three children at Albany for the winter, and by the spring they were "hearty and well" thanks to the care of surgeon E.B. Kitchen and "the nourishment afforded them from Your Honors Fort."[104] This partly explains why factors frequently identified Indigenous peoples by possessive phrases (such as *our Indians* or *Albany Indians*); such phrases expressed the expectations of where certain families and groups were to trade and hunt, by identifying to which household factory they were connected.

The Committee demanded celibacy, but both the Homeguard Cree and upland traders found such an attitude anti-social. Indigenous peoples consistently encouraged the formation of marriage alliances between their women and HBC men in order to create reciprocal social connections between the two groups.[105] Building and using kin networks in order to minimize risk or obtain relief in times of need was very familiar to the HBC men of this period, so they should not have been surprised by the negative consequences of denying the obligations arising from such networks.[106] When Thomas McCliesh Jr took command at York in 1722, he "had sufficient trouble with some of our home Indians by reason I turned them all out of the factory."[107] Augustine Frost warned James Duffield that denying the Homeguard Cree regular access to Moose Fort would antagonize them, but Duffield believed the warning to be a ruse to reunite Frost with his Indigenous kin and make Moose "an Indian Factory, with his own wives & Numerous family both in & about it as was ye Custom before."[108] The killings at Henley House in 1754–55 illustrated the potential cost of violating Indigenous expectations of social behaviour. James Isham was told about a similar incident at the French post of Fort Phélipeaux (Severn River) in the early eighteenth century. The French had forced some Cree women into the post against their will, but the women were liberated by their husbands one night after the women had urinated on the French gunpowder; according to Isham's account, eight Frenchmen were killed.[109]

Restrictions on women could also arouse the resentment of the men who were being deprived of their companions. Isham's successor at York (Jacobs) expelled servants' wives from the factory, and several men responded by feigning illness and refusing to work.[110] In 1753 armourer Joseph Statton threatened to run away from Albany when Joseph Isbister barred his "Indian Mistress" from the factory. Despite Isbister's dismissive terminology, Statton took the relationship seriously enough to spend more than one year's salary on her.[111] This dispute was also work related. On 10 September 1753 Statton stopped work at four o'clock in the afternoon because his wife

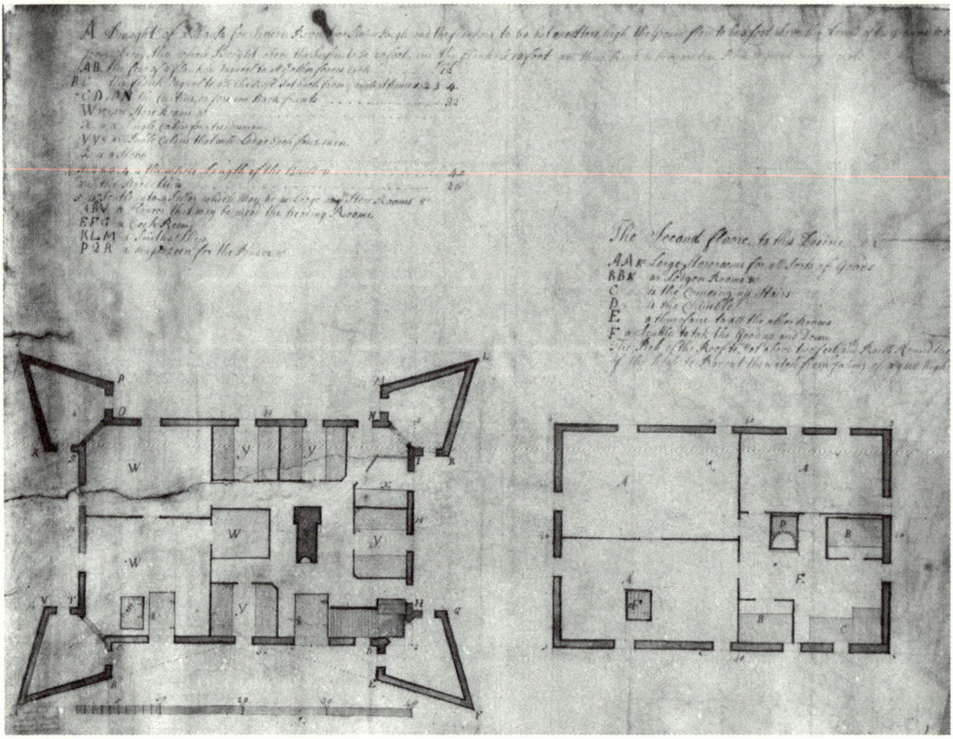

In this anonymous A Draught of a House for Severn River, *ca. 1759, the common hands share four-man cabins, while the blacksmith has a single cabin to himself. It is unclear where the master sleeps, although there are two unallocated "Lodgen Rooms" on the second floor among the storerooms.* [HBCA, G.1/105]

"wanted his Company"; seeing Statton cross the courtyard in his great-coat, Isbister angrily inquired "where he was going & why he had left work before other men or before he was Cal'd off from work...[Statton] replied & said if they have a mind to be made Neagors [i.e., "niggers" or "negros"] of, that was no reason he should be so, & plainly told me that he would work no longer nor would he be confined to hours." Isbister took Statton by the collar into his shop (to avoid a public confrontation) and pointed out "ye Ill Consequence of Such his ill behaviour & Example, he rud[e]ly Ansured & said he did not Care."[112] Statton, like many other servants, found himself in an impossible situation. Company regulations prevented him from fully expressing his sentimental and familial attachment: he could neither bring "his woman" to Britain nor could he live independently with her in Hudson Bay (though he apparently contemplated the attempt). His efforts to protect his privilege of cohabitation only got him sent home and thus separated forever from "his woman."

Officers' social and sexual lives are difficult to reconstruct, and those of the "common men" even more so. In 1755 James Isham reported from York that Robert Inkster,

> *son of Robert Inksiter taylor (formerly in your Honrs Service) Growing a Lusty Lad is Willing to be Apprentice to your Honrs for 7 Years; He was Christned I understand in Mr Whites time [1734–37 or 1741–46], have took him in for ye present, but Referr his desire till further Orders from Your Honrs.*

When labourer and bricklayer John Hughes was going to return to England the following year, Isham complained of "having had some trouble concerning of John Hughs Daughter, who wants her for to go on board for England." Hughes appears to have claimed that the Committee had authorized his daughter's passage to England ("saying it was yr honrs Desire"). Isham "having no such orders, nor yet the captain, and in Looking back to your honor's [letter] of 16 May 1751 (parh 27) find a strict order to the contrary... therefore stopd her returning to England, Referring such to yr honours."[113] Neither request seems to have received an official response from the Committee.

|| Men arrived in Hudson Bay with preconceptions about the proper relationships between masters and servants. Most, if not all, had previously spent time in apprenticeship or service (domestic, craft, or agricultural), and their personal experiences were reinforced by the conduct manuals so prevalent in the contemporary popular literature. Humphrey Marten's 1771 assurance that "Inclination, Duty and Gratitude, all strongly prompt me to exert my self in suppressing the Evils of Private Trade"[114] summed

William Richards painted A South View of Albany Factory, a Winter View, *sometime after entering* HBC *service in 1800 and before his premature death in 1811. He was born in Rupert's Land, probably somewhere in the Albany River valley, to John Richards, the half-Cree son of surgeon William Richards.* [HBCA, P-118]

up the major elements of the contemporary ideal of a servant's relationship to his master. Ten years later he informed the Committee of his intention to leave the service (which he had entered in 1750) due to ill health:

> *[T]he return of an inviterate billious disorder hath too often deprived me of the use of my Limbs, and, what is worse, at particular periods deprived me of that Vigour of mind, that is really necessary to the well conducting [of] your affairs; on this Account Gentlemen I must decline the honour of being employed by you any longer; why should I fill a station I find myself unfit for?*[115]

Marten's predecessor, Robert Temple, assured the Committee that "nothing gives me so much pleasure as giving satisfaction to those that employ me."[116] These men internalized and practised the expected values of deference and submission, and they could do so without abandoning or deferring their own self-interest; indeed, they could use their mastery of the language to advance themselves. As the Committee once told Marten, "You must...for your Own Interest be more attentive to Ours."[117]

Labourer and bricklayer Augustine Frost illustrates the possibilities and the limitations of such logic, as well as a sense of the ideal and the reality of company service in the post-Utrecht period. As a labourer at Prince of Wales Fort in the early 1720s, Frost distinguished himself as "a very good hand for the country" and very useful as a bricklayer; his wages rose from ten pounds to sixteen pounds in 1724. He was to go home in 1725, but in light of the deaths of mariner William Manning (d. 30 November 1724) and labourer George Hicks (d. 27 May 1725), Frost agreed with chief factor Richard Norton "to tarry in the country for the same wages as George Hicks had [fourteen pounds]." Norton observed that he was "a very serviceable hand for the country as fishing, fowling or any other employ." Frost was again set to go home in 1726, when newly engaged bricklayer Thomas Haws, "being a very sickly man," returned home after only one year in the Bay; in his place the council re-engaged Frost for one year at twenty pounds.[118] The Committee wanted to move Frost to York in 1729—and York would have been glad to have him—but Frost preferred to return home, "having been in the country ten years and his father being deceased this last year, he has some effects left him which he is afraid he may lose if he does not go home."[119]

It is not known whether Frost was able to secure his portion of his father's estate. Whether or not he was able to sort out his affairs in England, he re-entered HBC service the following year, this time being sent to Moose as a bricklayer at sixteen pounds. In 1733 William Bevan reported that Frost was no longer able to undertake bricklayer's work (not saying the reason), but in 1735 Bevan re-engaged him for two years at twenty pounds, "he being a very useful man and we having no bricklayer."[120] As mentioned earlier, Frost married into local Homeguard Cree families and became a member of the council at Moose. He was the only member of that council not recalled after news of the Boxing Day fire

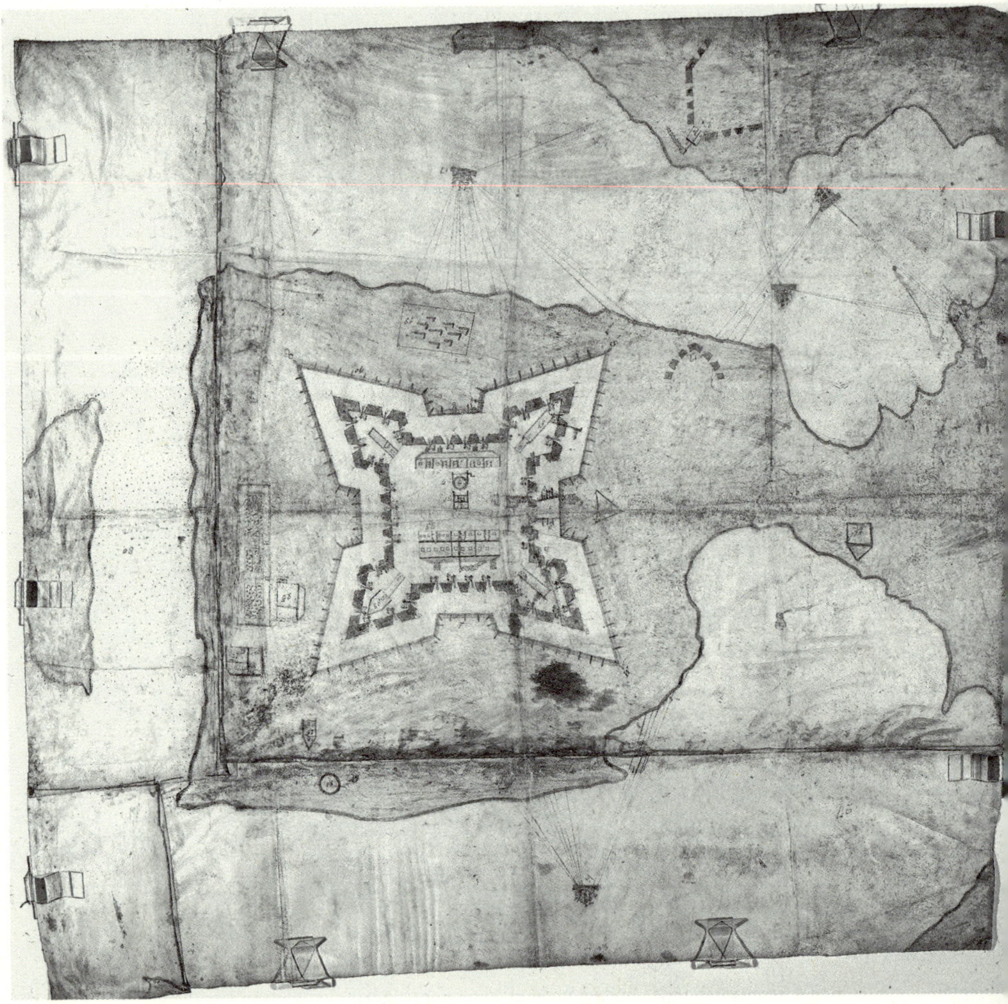

James Isham's plan of Prince of Wales Fort, ca. 1740s, bristles with cannon but contains no more space for men and goods than did other factories—though here most of the men did not have to sleep in the bastions. [HBCA, G.2/26]

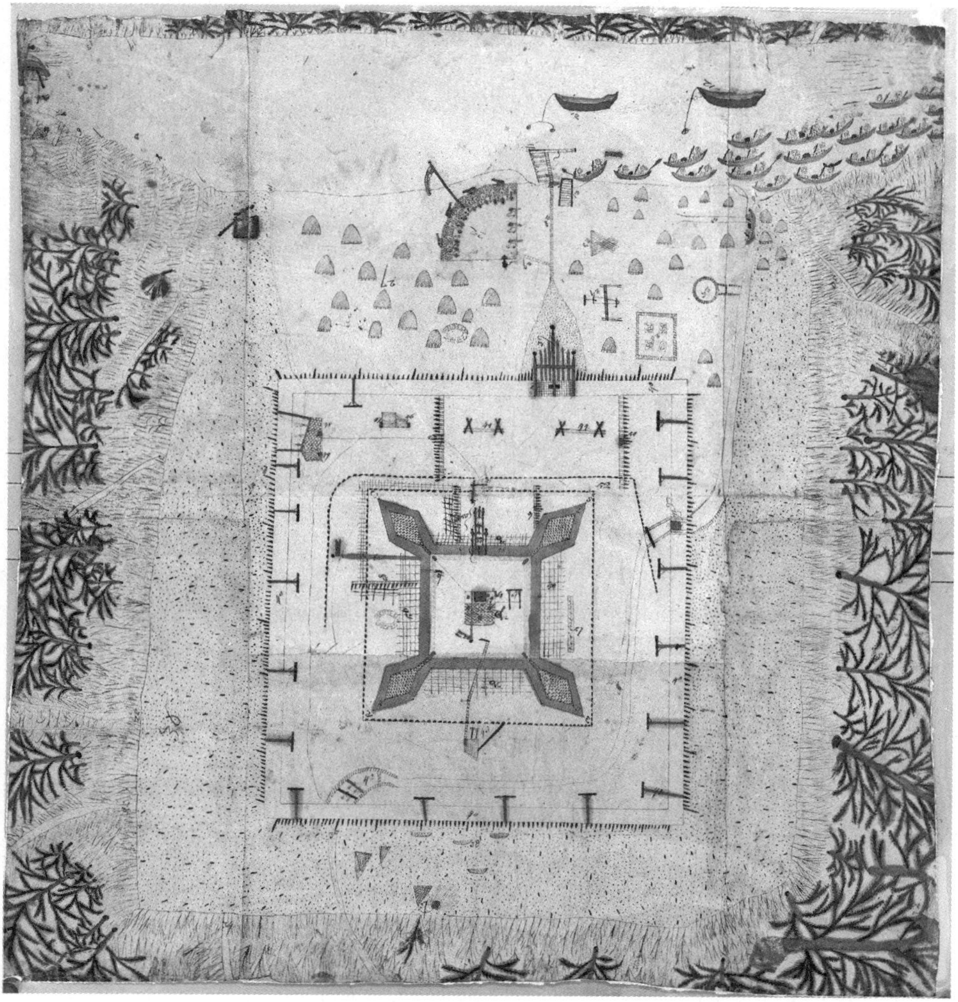

James Isham's plan of York Fort, probably drafted around the same time as his plan of Prince of Wales Fort, fairly bustles with life, including the arrival of many canoes of Indigenous (probably Cree) traders and visitors. [HBCA, G.2/5]

reached London, but chief factor James Duffield sent him home in 1742 as "incompatable to the Company's interest."[121] However, he re-entered the service again in 1746 and served at York, where he was a member of the council from 1748, and where he died in 1759.[122]

Frost's thirty-five years in Hudson Bay were unusual, but otherwise his service illustrates the trends among his contemporaries, as well as among men who came before and after him. He was consistently described as "serviceable" and "useful" (except by Duffield), and his utility was enhanced by his versatility. In 1729 Thomas McCliesh Jr commented that "the good character given of Augustin Frost is what I have been informed by all that is competent judges."[123] The language used by factors to describe Frost was the language used throughout the company's long first century to describe the best and most valued servants.

Like many HBC servants, Frost maintained ties with home, and, like him, some men briefly interrupted their company service to attend to personal or family matters in Britain. Even after ten years away Frost maintained contact with friends and family in England, although those ties may have weakened after his father's death. Despite James Duffield's claim that Frost had become "so much an Indian himself that he has no concern for either his native country or the Company's interest,"[124] there is no clear evidence that he had abandoned England for Hudson Bay. Indeed, there is a hint of fatigue in Beale's comment that Frost had been ten years in the Bay and was ready to see home again. He had been about to leave the Bay on at least two occasions (1725, 1726, and probably 1735) but re-engaged when opportunity presented itself.

Those opportunities, which helped keep Frost in service for so long, were twofold. On the one hand, he had opportunities to serve his corporate master and to step up in a time of need in the way that all good servants were expected to do; this was probably the case in 1725 when he took a pay cut to remain in the country in George Hicks's stead. On the other hand, he had opportunities to advance his own interests, particularly in 1726 when his reward was a significant wage increase. These two motivations were so intertwined in Frost's mind (and his contemporaries' minds) that scholars two-and-a-half centuries away could never disentangle them.

Long service represented at least a certain degree of accommodation between master and servant, but it does not necessarily indicate that the servant had subsumed his own interests in his master's interests. Even if we do not take Duffield's accusations at face value, there is no doubt that Frost's Indigenous family connections caused some friction within the household factory of Moose. Although he was trying to do what most servants wanted to do—become a householder in his own right—the restrictions of Bayside life did not allow him the luxury of acting both as a servant and as a husband. Those restrictions discouraged men from spending more than a small portion of their working lives in Hudson Bay; before 1786, HBC service offered limited internal opportunities to move away from subordination in the household of another toward becoming a master of one's own household.

Conclusion

> *[W]e very well remember what we promised you, which was that if you behaved to our Satisfaction during your Contracted time, you should meet with proper Encouragement...therefore it entirely rests with you to Behave in such manner as to make your self deserving of our further Regard.*
>
> — HBC to Henry Pollexfen Jr (RF), private, 22 May 1754, HBCA, A. 5/1, fol. 2

> *[I]t is only by your Industry in all our Affairs, and properly Acquitting your self of everything entrusted to your Charge, that you will be Entitled to our future favours and preserve the Esteem of / Your Lov[in]g Friends*
>
> — HBC to Samuel Skrimshire (FH), private, 27 May 1755, HBCA, A. 5/1, fol. 10

THIS STUDY approaches early modern personnel issues in a way that is more systematic than the way in which contemporaries approached the same issues. Even the specialized commercial academies emerging in Britain by the end of the eighteenth century did not teach concepts of labour management.[1] This is not to say that recruitment and retension of workers lacked rhyme or reason but rather that such decisions were not seen as a distinct sphere of business activity; early modern companies did not have a human resources department.

In general, pre-1786 evidence indicates that the HBC selected recruits on the basis of their (presumed) competence at a particular occupation and their willingness to serve overseas at a specific wage for a specific period of time, rather than trying to predict their suitability for Bayside service. Notwithstanding descriptions of men as "useful for the Country," there is little evidence that specialized skills were needed or sought. If such skills were needed, the Committee apparently felt that they could not be learned or acquired anywhere other than the Bay. Without the Committee's ability to pre-determine suitability for the service, selection criteria for recruitment remained generic, no different from those of an ordinary householder seeking servants. The only way of knowing for certain whether a man would do well in the Bay was to send him there and watch his progress.

In the evaluation, "good" personnel were defined and described in terms drawn from the contemporary ideals of master-servant relationships in British households. Sobriety, industry, diligence, honesty, and diversity were valued characteristics for men in all ranks of the corporate hierarchy. Higher-ranking men had a responsibility to lead by example; this applied to officers, of course, but also to skilled tradesmen and old hands. Failure to live up to these expectations could significantly hamper a man's prospects. Although a capable servant was worth hanging on to, in the long run a stable servant was more valuable to the company.[2]

After the Treaty of Utrecht the creation of new trading posts and other ventures required a gradual increase in the size of the company's workforce, and this growth quickened from the 1770s onward. Expanding operations were accompanied by an expanding pool of recruitment. London remained the principal catchment area until the last quarter of the century, but Stromness became an increasingly important supplement. Yet the greater numbers and geographic diversity of recruits were not accompanied by a greater system in the process of recruitment until after 1786.

Slow but steady expansion also provided new opportunities for men of all ranks to demonstrate their value to the company.[3] The promise of such opportunities was part of the public transcript, a vertical consciousness that connected masters and men even as they were separated horizontally by consciousness of relative status and rank. The public transcript was most visible (it is to us, at least) in questions of upward mobility and of encouragement. From the earliest days of the company, its servants expressed the hope that those already in the service would be preferred over newcomers. The Committee responded positively, fulfilling its 1688 promise that "[w]ee shall never Send New Raw & unexperienced men to put over the heads of such as have Served us Longe & faithfully."[4] In the hundred years after the end of Henry Sergeant's tenure as Bayside governor (1686), John Newton (factor at York, 1748–50) stands out as the only "outsider" parachuted into a senior position in Hudson Bay. Although potential candidates always outnumbered available positions, the practice of promoting from within was firmly entrenched.

Mobility and encouragement took on new aspects when expansion reached into the interior of the as yet little-known continent. The company's mid-eighteenth-century servants were apparently not discouraged from inland travel by fear for their lives, even though several of them made their journeys during the war with France, and all of them were aware of the events at Henley House. Why were so many men in the 1750s and 1760s willing to go inland, when so few had been reported willing in the 1680s and 1690s? Early slooping expeditions and trading voyages (even in wartime) attest to the bravery of those who served the company in its early years. Allegations of dishonesty among the eighteenth-century winterers suggest that at least some of the men had personal motivations, but possibilities for personal aggrandizement existed in the early decades as well. Factors had no way of proving that winterers were using company goods to trade on their private account, so the winterers could claim a large amount of furs as their own trappings and receive good market value for them without appearing to cheat the company (an option not officially available to the earlier men). Acting as an agent of the company's interests among the First Nations of the interior thus paid personal dividends and demonstrated how private considerations influenced worker behaviour on (and away from) the shores of Hudson Bay.

Probably the greatest difference between the men of Anthony Henday's generation and those of Henry Kelsey's was their familiarity with Hudson Bay. When Kelsey went inland from York, the English presence there was less than a decade old. By Henday's time, relationships with both Lowland and Upland Cree were more established and more intimate. Although Henday himself had only been in Hudson Bay for four years when he embarked on his inland journey, he benefited from the long-standing relationships that the household factory of York Fort had with Homeguard Cree and Upland Cree households. Once inland, he and other winterers could build their own relationships, including marriage with Indigenous women—which the Englishmen would have seen as an important step toward forming households of their own.

This also explains why wintering inland was more popular with servants than employment at an inland outpost. At Henley or Cumberland, men were still under the command of another, whereas wintering with an Indigenous group (even for a few weeks or months, to save on the house's provisions) removed them from managerial supervision. Many men had difficulty integrating even temporarily into their host Indigenous communities: Matthew Cocking claimed that the winterers "only like to continue as it skreened them from Duty at the Fort: And they were most of them disliked; as they never endeavoured to gain the Affections of the Natives, and converted the Goods they were furnished with to the Purpose of Collecting Furrs for their own private Emolument."[5] These "private" men relished the prospect of independence and objected to trading a subordinate role in an HBC household for an equally subordinate role in an Indigenous one. Those who did make that transition could potentially begin building sub-households of their own, although clear evidence of this was unlikely to appear in official records. In this way, inland journeys could stray from the company's expectations: the objections to wintering made by Andrew Graham and Ferdinand Jacobs in the late 1760s were reactions against the interests of Indigenous "households" and of the HBC's "private" men impinging on those of the factors and of the Committee.

The patriarch of the household factory (like the household family) may or may not have been married, but the dependent members of the household were expected to be celibate. Those with wives in Britain could look forward to returning to their positions as householders in their own right, although (as Richard Noldridge found) the long separation may have strained those relationships beyond repair. Servants who became husbands and fathers in Hudson Bay, like Augustine Frost and Joseph Statton, had no option of becoming independent householders; they had to either restrict their relationships with Indigenous women to casual or intermittent contact or strain the relationship with their employers by trying to act as dependents in one household and as husbands and fathers in another. Only regular inland winterers like Joseph Smith and Isaac Batt had any real opportunity to establish themselves beyond the factory walls, and even their freedom was only temporary and limited, being confined by the orders of the Committee and of their factors and by the expectations of the senior members of their Indigenous families.

Samuel Hopkins in 1722 showed how easy it was to physically leave the household factory. One fine day in early October he simply put his gun over his shoulder and walked out the front door; the sentry watched him go but made no attempt to stop him or even question him. But even this prodigal son eventually returned to his corporate father's home and had to demonstrate a humble and contrite heart before the fatted calf was put on the grill. There simply was no viable option in this period for the creation of independent households outside of HBC or Indigenous contexts; for these British servants, labour, land, and authority all remained focused on the factor and the household factory.

Despite the obvious strains and limitations, the civilian household factory was thus the fundamental social unit on the shores of Hudson Bay, clearly recognizable despite the constraints of geography and the parameters of historical precedent. As the basic unit of social and political life in early modern Britain, the household was a fundamental influence on the way in which men viewed their workplaces, and this was reflected in men's behaviour and rhetoric on both sides of the Atlantic. Although membership changed, the institution maintained continuity over time, throughout this period, and well beyond. Furthermore, each household factory was internally held together, and bound to other household factories and to the London Committee, by ties of patronage, brokerage, and friendship. These ties mediated the network of horizontal and vertical relationships and helped inject an element of sentimentality to soften the instrumental nature of labour relationships.

Both private and public interests were at work in Hudson Bay, but the tension that this sometimes created was far from inevitable, nor did the former need to be abandoned in favour of the latter. Although vertical ties within household factories seemed to subordinate individual men to the community, deferential words and behaviours could advance the interests of servants as well as those of their masters. Deference was based on a reasonable expectation of future benefits, implicitly (and occasionally explicitly) promised in the negotiated public transcript. A subordinate position in a household was tolerable partly because there existed a real possibility of social mobility, even to the point of one's actually becoming a householder.

Social mobility carried a few men to the upper ranks of the company's hierarchy, and they achieved householder status through the charge of a factory or a house. However, before the rapid expansion of operations from the 1780s onward, during which the HBC labour force grew from under two hundred to over nine hundred men,[6] Hudson Bay offered only a handful of such opportunities. For most men in company service, their options for social mobility were similar to those in contemporary British households.

The specific reasons for which men departed service in Britain and in Hudson Bay are as opaque as their reasons for entering service in the first place, but the public transcripts prevailing in early modern Britain were constructed upon a framework of reciprocal expectations and obligations. Men were willing to remain in a subordinate position as long as they felt they had access to the social and economic benefits implicit in the publicly accepted hierarchy of paternalism and deference—such as increasing wages and status, the accumulation of savings, or a sense of community and security. If they perceived those benefits as being placed beyond their reach, they were more likely to strain or even abandon the behaviours expected of them by their superiors.

Those superiors, including the HBC Committee, sought to maintain orderly and effective households by recruiting and retaining servants who were sober, honest, and diligent. Frequent turnover among those servants was common, as it was in Britain; the public transcript did not promise progressive advancement within a single household but assumed that people would move from one household to another during their lives. Turnover was a useful way for the Committee to control the wage bill and was not a cause for concern so long as good servants could be found to replace the homeward-bound men.

Household factories, like household families in contemporary Britain, were flexible institutions predicated on long-established conceptions of master-servant relationships. This foundation was not static. In Hudson Bay those relationships were changing under pressure from the new demands of inland activity after 1743. By 1786 both the Committee and its servants were revising their expectations of each other in the context of a changing working environment on the shores of Hudson Bay and in the interior of Rupert's Land.

The HBC's long first century stands distinct from the company's later periods, with its own social dynamics and contexts, both in England and in Hudson Bay. Yet the structure of household factories, and many of the expectations that such a structure entailed, persisted for another century or more after that. While there is still much to be learned about this early period, the trials and tribulations (and successes) of this civilian household model through the often volatile, more than one hundred years that followed need to be explored in greater detail. We should build on the work already done in examining how the behaviour of the Hudson's Bay Company and its servants shaped the colonial world that, in 1870, would be taken over and reshaped by the Dominion of Canada.

The patterns established in the earliest days of the HBC shaped the way in which the company interacted with its workforce, its trading partners, and the world around it. They help us understand that world and the influences of the company and its men on it; they also help us understand the perplexities of those who came later as missionaries, explorers, and government agents. Most importantly, they help us understand the men who served at those factories—whether as factor or labourer, tradesman or apprentice, old hand or green hand—and give us a better sense of how they were navigating the social, economic, and other contexts within which they lived their lives and strove for better things ahead.

Appendix

Choosing Our Words Carefully

THE VOCABULARY OF THIS STUDY intersects with both early modern terminology and the vocabulary of current scholarly discourse. The language used in the HBC's early records provides significant insight into the perceptions and understandings behind the words—hence the liberal quotations from primary sources used here. My own choice of language stems mostly from these sources but is also drawn from the larger contexts of ongoing scholarly debates. To borrow D.R. Hainsworth's observation, "[t]he historian...has to define his terms yet remain well aware that the definitions he is using would not necessarily have been recognized by the men he is writing about, although the distinctions he draws between degrees of status and responsibility undoubtedly would."[1]

Some men in the company's service, especially in the seventeenth century, were not given occupational labels in the records. This is remarkable because seventeenth-century English society was very conscious of rank and status, and a status or occupational term (formally known as an "addition") was typically attached to a person's name for legal purposes. A similar situation existed among indentured servants bound for colonial America: three-fifths of the male servants recorded in the Middlesex registrations of 1683–84, and more than one-third in the London registrations of 1718–59, were not identified by trade or occupation. The absence of additions may indicate the lack of an occupation; that is, those without additions were lower in occupational and economic status than those with recorded trades and tended to be younger and less literate. Some of these men could have been apprentices who had not yet completed their indentures and thus had not yet gained the additions of their trade; some could have been vagrants unattached to either a household or an occupation; and some could have been servants in husbandry without specialized skills.[2]

Occupational labels in the Hudson's Bay Company (when they occurred) were sometimes vague, particularly in the late seventeenth century. The dividing lines were not always clear between carpenter, ship carpenter, and shipwright; blacksmith, gunsmith, and edge-tool maker; and mason and bricklayer. Generally, the HBC seemed to be less exact with its occupational labels than was common for tradesmen in Britain. This may reflect the men's incomplete training in a specific skill or simply the fact that some recruits were journeymen who had not served an apprenticeship in a trade; for instance, many journeymen employed in towns in northern England were not drawn from the ranks of town apprentices. Alternatively, it may reflect a multiplicity of occupations, which was both common and necessary given the high unemployment of the early modern period.[3] There is very little evidence on which to base an evaluation of the skill and experience of tradesmen in HBC service, just as it is almost impossible to make such judgements about most contemporary craftsmen in Britain.[4]

Overall, most men in HBC service were identified by occupational labels, but the significance of those labels is not always clear to modern readers. For instance, seventeenth-century surgeons were often barbers as well, and they separated from the barbers' guild in London only in 1746; they were characterized by their emphasis on manual skill rather than on medical theory and were not held in particularly high regard.[5] Internal medicine was the field of physicians, while pharmacy was in the hands of apothecaries; only the Royal Navy seems to have expected its surgeons to have knowledge of pharmacy.[6] It would be reasonable to expect the HBC to make similar demands, given that company surgeons were the only source of European medical care in the Bayside factories.

In terms of social status, blacksmiths were among the upper ranks of Britain's skilled artisans at the end of the seventeenth century, but their status seems to have declined through the eighteenth century.[7] R. Campbell's *The London Tradesman* (1747), a detailed guide to various occupations for parents and guardians looking to apprentice their children, characterized the specialized craft of edge-tool making as a "country" trade, but whether Campbell was referring to rural areas or to provincial tool-making centres like Sheffield and Birmingham is unclear. He also described a gunsmith as both a joiner and a smith but cast doubt on how much of the latter skill was required by mentioning that the ironwork (especially the barrel) was often bought already made.[8] The term *armourer* had by the eighteenth century become a relatively meaningless label: the armourers' guild in London included brasiers, founders, copper-smiths, and many other kinds of metalworkers.[9] In the HBC records, *armourer* appears to have been used more or less as a synonym for *gunsmith.*

House carpenters and bricklayers were occupations of a lower status than blacksmithing, primarily because fewer of them were able to become relatively large-scale independent masters: in 1696 there were only twenty-one master bricklayers in London.[10] Masons—who before the nineteenth century also acted as architects—enjoyed status equal to or surpassing that of blacksmiths. Their superiority to bricklayers was reflected in the higher premiums that parents and guardians were willing to pay to apprentice their sons to master masons: between ten and twenty pounds in London, compared to between six and ten pounds to apprentice as a bricklayer. A stonemason required knowledge of geometry, designing, drawing, and architecture and was "among the first Rank of Tradesmen," while bricklayers had less training, less knowledge, and less status.[11]

The relationship between masons and bricklayers was similar to that between carpenters and sawyers. The Carpenters' Company (i.e., guild) of London characterized sawyers as mere labourers and successfully maintained the social and economic distance between them until at least the middle of the eighteenth century. Highly specialized woodworkers such as ship carpenters and coopers commanded higher wages than house carpenters, but the social distance between them was less obvious.[12]

Tailors had the lowest status of the skilled tradesmen employed by the HBC, and this was reflected in their lower wages compared to those of blacksmiths and carpenters. Tailoring was a highly traditional craft, but one that was overstocked and subject to great seasonal fluctuations. In the mid-eighteenth century Campbell distinguished master tailors from "the mere working Taylor"; most of the latter were employed "only to sew the Seam, to cast the Button Holes, and prepare the Work for the Finisher." He claimed that "not one in ten of them know how to cut out a Pair of Breeches."[13] HBC tailors presumably possessed a greater degree of skill than that, although they were almost certainly not master tailors. Little is known about the roles played by Homeguard Cree women in preparing clothes for the company's servants; possibly they collaborated to an extent with the factories' tailors. A tailor's employment prospects in Britain were generally not good in the 1700s—Campbell called them "as numerous as Locusts...and generally as poor as Rats"—and by the middle of the century pauper boys made up the majority of boys apprenticed to the trade in England.[14]

Labels applied to men employed afloat are sometimes confusing. The term *sailor* was often used for the crew members of Bayside sloop and transatlantic supply ship alike. It was not uncommon for men to shift between the two types of vessels as need dictated, and the sloops themselves made occasional transatlantic voyages. Where such distinctions can be made, this study refers to men on the supply ships as *sailors* and those on the sloops as *mariners*; as a group, *seamen* may be distinguished from *landsmen*, although men sometimes crossed those lines as well.[15]

It is particularly difficult to discern the qualities and skills encompassed by the term *labourer*. The *Farmer's Magazine* in 1779 defined *labourer* as "a man hired to work by the day or week, or employed by the acre, rod, pole, etc"; this was the sense in which it was used in most wage assessments and other British sources from the sixteenth through the eighteenth century. During this period, labour was perceived as a general and fairly abstract social activity, usually associated with drudgery. Labourers worked in gangs, large and small, on myriad tasks that did not require specialized skills. Of course, as Donald Woodward rightly points out, "even the use of a spade or shovel involves some skill," but the skills possessed by "unskilled" workers were so common as not to command any kind of premium.[16] Only in the nineteenth century did labour become a measurable component in discussions of political economy, as an element of production, and as a pool of workers available to be hired; at that time it also began appearing as an adjective in phrases like *labour costs*, *labour market*, and *labour relations*. These phrases—however useful—have an anachronistic ring when applied to the seventeenth and eighteenth centuries, as does the more general term *personnel*.[17]

In Hudson Bay, *labourer* was used as a fairly general label. Men who were given no occupational label, or described simply as *hands*, can probably be considered in the same category as labourers. However, *hand* was also used more generally. This study uses *hands*—along with *servants*—to refer to all company employees not in possession of command over others (officers). The word *employee* is slightly anachronistic, being a nineteenth-century American word, but *employer* (or *imployer*) and *employ* (or *imploy*) were current in eighteenth-century Britain.[18]

Officers in the HBC were not military ranks but positions of responsibility within a corporate hierarchy. Officers included the factors (or chiefs) of the major posts, which were thus called factories (a term quite common elsewhere in England's early modern commercial empire).[19] HBC factories were not places of manufacture but trading establishments in the charge of a factor. A factor was an agent or representative, particularly one who bought and/or sold for another (perhaps working on commission), or one who had the charge and managed the affairs of an estate (thus a bailiff or land steward). HBC officers also included the masters of smaller outposts or "outhouses" (referred to here as *houses*), and men serving as a second or a deputy.

Some factors were granted or used the term *governor*, a term derived from Tudor military usage: governors were initially men who commanded military garrisons within conquered regions, first in France and then in England and Ireland (where the governzor was also given responsibilities for agriculture and civil society). When first transposed to North America, colonial officers and governors came almost exclusively from military backgrounds, which imposed a particular kind of order on these early settlements.[20] HBC usage was almost entirely civilian, sometimes referring to a specific factory but usually encompassing several posts in a region such as the "Bottom of the Bay" (James Bay). This reflects the language of the company's charter, which empowered it to appoint governors and councils in its territories, who served as both executive and judicial bodies. After 1714 the governor of all of Hudson and James bays usually resided at York Fort, but geographical distance left the chief factor of Albany (sometimes styled *deputy governor*) a fair amount of autonomy at the Bottom of the Bay.[21]

The term *factor* (which is also used in the charter) is preferable to *manager*. The verb *manage* originally referred to the handling of horses and men in a military context, but by the end of the seventeenth century *manager* could mean a trainer and director or a careful housekeeper.[22] Both of these senses could apply to HBC factors. Contemporary documents sometimes referred to *management*, but never to *managers*. Although factors of long-distance trading companies have been convincingly portrayed as managers in modern business enterprises,[23] this emphasis on modernity risks obscuring older elements of HBC factors' roles and workplace relationships. They more closely resembled both estate stewards and waged foremen in contemporary Britain—two groups that have not been sufficiently investigated by scholars—and played complex roles as heads of workplace households ("household factories"). The HBC's overseas governor was comparable to the stewards of some English estates that "were very large, comprising several different manors, and required the watchful care of a chief steward with several understewards and a small army of estate servants to carry out his orders."[24]

Likewise, the company's employees were servants in household factories. Partly for this reason, I prefer the term *service* over *career* to describe the time span of a man's employment. Men in Hudson Bay would not have thought of their time with the company as a career: the predominant seventeenth- and eighteenth-century sense of that word was of rapid, unrestrained activity. Only in the mid-nineteenth century did it lose its derogatory implication and indicate progress in a vocation.[25] Even in the modern sense, the word *career* does not apply to most of the company's employees, because their times in Hudson Bay were not as long term as the word usually implies.

Notes

INTRODUCTION

1. E.E. Rich and A.M. Johnson, eds., *Hudson's Bay Copy Booke of Letters Commissions Instructions Outward, 1688–1696*, with an introduction by K.G. Davies (London: Hudson's Bay Record Society, 1957) (hereafter cited as *L.O. 1688–1696*), 139.
2. The East India Company (EIC) was more self-consciously systematic in its organization and operations. H.V. Bowen, *The Business of Empire* (Cambridge: Cambridge University Press, 2006), 184–85, observed "an extraordinary degree of permanence and continuity… [in] the management of the Company's affairs" through the seventeenth and eighteenth centuries.
3. The Royal African Company (RAC) experimented with agriculture at some of its trading posts in Guinea in the late seventeenth century, but these came to nothing and were abandoned by the middle of the eighteenth century. P.E.H. Hair and Robin Law, "The English in West Africa to 1700," in *The Oxford History of the British Empire*, vol. 1, ed. Nicholas Canny (Oxford: Oxford University Press, 1998), 260–61.
4. See Elizabeth Mancke, "Another British America," *Journal of Imperial and Commonwealth History* 25, no. 1 (1997): 25–26.
5. Patrick K. O'Brien, "Inseparable Connections," in *The Oxford History of the British Empire*, vol. 2, ed. P.J. Marshall and Alaine Low (Oxford: Oxford University Press, 1998), 60.
6. See, for instance, Elizabeth Mancke, *A Company of Businessmen* (Winnipeg, MB: Rupert's Land Research Centre, 1988), 10; Harold Innis, *The Fur Trade in Canada*, rev. ed. (Toronto: University of Toronto Press, 1999), 142. For parallels with the EIC, see H.V. Bowen, *Business of Empire*, 184–85. The most complete discussion of the HBC's organizational structure is in E.E. Rich's two-volume *History of the Hudson's Bay Company, 1670–1870*. As Vere Harmsworth Professor of Imperial and Naval History at St. Catherine's College, Cambridge, and as General Editor of the Hudson's Bay Record Society in the 1940s and 1950s, he construed HBC history more broadly than most other scholars have.
7. "Their fixed assets such as warehouses or wharves can be important, but in essence trading companies trade with other people's technologies, processes, and brands. They

add value to such technologies and brands through their knowledge about markets and relationships and contacts with other firms, suppliers, and consumers." Geoffrey Jones, *Merchants to Multinationals* (Oxford: Oxford University Press, 2000), 6.

8. H.V. Bowen, *Business of Empire*, 24, 29–52. Good historiographical surveys of these debates are Joseph E. Inikori, *Africans and the Industrial Revolution in England* (Cambridge: Cambridge University Press, 2002), chap. 3; Kenneth Morgan, *Slavery, Atlantic Trade and the British Economy, 1660–1800* (Cambridge: Cambridge University Press, 2000).
9. G. Jones, *Merchants to Multinationals*, 3.
10. In particular, see Ann Carlos and Stephen Nicholas, "Theory and History," *Journal of Economic History* 56, no. 4 (December 1996): 916–24; and Ann Carlos and Stephen Nicholas, "'Giants of an Earlier Capitalism,'" in *Trade in the Pre-Modern Era, 1400–1700*, ed. Douglas A. Irwin (Cheltenham, UK: Elgar, 1996), vol. 1, 118–39. For the EIC, see Margaret Makepeace, *The East India Company's London Workers* (Woodbridge, UK: Boydell Press, 2010), 7, 198–99; Emily Erikson, *Between Monopoly and Free Trade* (Princeton, NJ: Princeton University Press, 2014). For a dissenting view, see H.V. Bowen, *Business of Empire*, 21–23.
11. Erikson, *Between Monopoly and Free Trade*, 19. Analyses of the EIC by Erikson and Makepeace illustrate how business history and organizational theory have not yet caught up to the social historians in revising previous understandings of the role of early modern social structures in facilitating entrepreneurial endeavour and economic development. See, for instance, Erikson's discussion of "the limitations of patrimonialism" in Dutch and English commerce (19–20).
12. Craig Muldrew, "Interpreting the Market," *Social History* 18, no. 2 (May 1993): 164.
13. See Richard Whipp, "Labour Markets and Communities," *Sociological Review* 33, no. 4 (1985): 777–78; also Makepeace, *East India Company's London Workers*, 197. For the HBC, see, for example, Michael O'Leary, Wanda Orlikowski, and JoAnne Yates, "Distributed Work over the Centuries," in *Distributed Work*, ed. Pamela Hinds and Sara Kiesler (Cambridge, MA: MIT Press, 2002), 27–54.
14. John Rule, *The Experience of Labour in Eighteenth-Century English Industry* (New York: St. Martin's Press, 1981), 208–9, 211; J. Jean Hecht, *The Domestic Servant Class in Eighteenth-Century England* (London: Routledge & Kegan Paul, 1956), 74–75, 77, 80, 206; Peter Laslett, *The World We Have Lost*, 3rd ed. (London: Methuen, 1983), 51. However, also see Ilana Krausman Ben-Amos, *Adolescence and Youth in Early Modern England* (New Haven, CT: Yale University Press, 1994), 85, 173–74; Margaret Pelling, "Apprenticeship, Health and Social Cohesion in Early Modern London," *History Workshop* 37 (Spring 1994): 41; Paul Griffiths, *Youth and Authority* (Oxford: Clarendon Press, 1996), 294; Glen Makahonuk, "Wage-Labour in the Northwest Fur Trade Economy, 1760–1849," *Saskatchewan History* 41, no. 1 (Winter 1988): 2.
15. Richard Price, "The Labour Process and Labour History," *Social History* 8, no. 1 (January 1983): 62, 64; Patrick Joyce, "Labour, Capital and Compromise: A Response to Richard Price," *Social History* 9, no. 1 (January 1984): 70, 73. Also see Richard Price, "Conflict and Co-operation: A Reply to Patrick Joyce," *Social History* 9, no. 2 (May 1984): 217–24; Patrick Joyce, "Languages of Reciprocity and Conflict: A Further Response to Richard Price,"

Social History 9, no. 2 (May 1984): 225–31; E.P. Thompson, "The Patricians and the Plebs," in *Customs in Common: Studies in Traditional Popular Culture* (New York: New Press, 1993), 71–72. Very little of this ongoing debate has been incorporated into the work of Canadian scholars; see, for instance, Robert C.H. Sweeny, "Understanding Work Historically," *Labour / Le Travail* 41 (Spring 1997): 246–47.

16. Keith Wrightson, "The Social Order of Early Modern England," in *The World We Have Gained: Histories of Population and Social Structures*, ed. Lloyd Bonfield, Richard M. Smith, and Keith Wrightson (Oxford: Basil Blackwell, 1986), 198.

17. E.P. Thompson, "The Moral Economy of the English Crowd in the Eighteenth Century," *Past & Present* 50 (1971): 76–136. Also see E.P. Thompson, "The Moral Economy Reviewed," in *Customs in Common*, 259–351; John Stevenson, "The 'Moral Economy' of the English Crowd: Myth and Reality," in *Order and Disorder in Early Modern England*, ed. Anthony Fletcher and John Stevenson (Cambridge: Cambridge University Press, 1985), 218–38; Patrick Joyce, "The Historical Meanings of Work: An Introduction," in *The Historical Meanings of Work* (Cambridge: Cambridge University Press, 1987), 26.

18. Donald Woodward, *Men at Work* (Cambridge: Cambridge University Press, 1995), 181, 205–7. Also see Stephen D. White and Richard T. Vann, "The Invention of English Individualism," *Social History* 8, no. 3 (October 1983): 361.

19. This juxtaposition has been challenged recently; see, for instance, Maxine Berg, "Women's Work, Mechanisation and the Early Phases of Industrialisation in England," in *The Historical Meanings of Work*, ed. Patrick Joyce (Cambridge: Cambridge University Press, 1987), 64–98; Hans-Joachim Voth, *Time and Work in England, 1750–1820* (Oxford: Clarendon Press, 2000), esp. 5–11, 72–76, 154–59.

20. John Elliott, quoted in Philip D. Morgan and Jack P. Greene, "Introduction: The Present State of Atlantic History," in *Atlantic History*, ed. Greene and Morgan (Oxford: Oxford University Press, 2009), 3.

21. Carole Shammas, introduction to *The Creation of the British Atlantic World*, ed. Elizabeth Mancke and Carole Shammas (Baltimore, MD: Johns Hopkins University Press, 2005), 4.

22. Useful overviews of the field include Shammas, introduction, 1–16; Morgan and Greene, "Introduction," 3–33; also see Joyce E. Chaplin, "The Atlantic Ocean and Its Contemporary Meanings, 1492–1808," in *Atlantic History*, ed. Greene and Morgan, 35–51. Limited work has been done to incorporate the HBC into its Atlantic contexts, but even less has been done to incorporate its Indigenous trading partners into those contexts; as an introduction to such an undertaking, see Amy Turner Bushnell, "Indigenous America and the Limits of the Atlantic World, 1493–1825," in *Atlantic History*, ed. Greene and Morgan, 191–221.

23. T.S. Ashton, *Economic Fluctuations in England, 1700–1800* (Oxford: Clarendon Press, 1959), 173–74; Robert W. Malcolmson, *Life and Labour in England, 1700–1780* (New York: St. Martin's Press, 1981), 37; Woodward, *Men at Work*, 4, 12, 13, 133, 135; John Burnett, *A History of the Cost of Living* (Harmondsworth, UK: Penguin, 1969), 181; L.D. Schwarz, *London in the Age of Industrialization* (Cambridge: Cambridge University Press, 1992), 49. Keith Wrightson, *Earthly Necessities* (New Haven, CT: Yale University Press, 2000), 308–9,

describes early modern England as a series of geographically overlapping regional, sub-regional, and local labour markets.

24. Richard S. Dunn, "Servants and Slaves," in *Colonial British America*, ed. Jack P. Greene and J.R. Pole (Baltimore, MD: Johns Hopkins University Press, 1984), 161.
25. See Bernard Bailyn, "Introduction: Europeans on the Move, 1500–1800," in *Europeans on the Move*, ed. Nicholas Canny (Oxford: Clarendon Press, 1994), 1; Michael Bliss, *Northern Enterprise* (Toronto: McClelland & Stewart, 1987), 101.
26. Mancke, "Canadian Model," 7.
27. See James Horn and Philip D. Morgan, "Settlers and Slaves," in *The Creation of the British Atlantic World*, ed. Elizabeth Mancke and Carole Shammas (Baltimore, MD: Johns Hopkins University Press, 2005), 24 (table 1.2), 27.
28. Sean T. Cadigan, "Merchant Capital, the State, and Labour in a British Colony," *Journal of the Canadian Historical Association* 2, no. 1 (1991): 41, makes a similar point regarding the Newfoundland fishery.
29. Peter Clark and David Souden, introduction to *Migration and Society in Early Modern England* (Totowa, NJ: Barnes & Noble, 1987), 26; Peter Clark, "Migrants in the City," in *Migration and Society in Early Modern England*, ed. Clark and Souden, 267–68; Peter Clark, "Migration in England during the Late Seventeenth and Early Eighteenth Centuries," *Past & Present* 83 (May 1979): 59. For circular mobility in the Orkney Islands, see William P.L. Thomson, *History of Orkney* (Edinburgh: Mercat Press, 1987), 207. Also see Philip Goldring, "Labour Records of the Hudson's Bay Company, 1821–1870," *Archivaria* 11 (Winter 1980/81): 54.
30. Horn and Morgan, "Settlers and Slaves," 27 (including quotation from Bailyn); also see Horn, "British Diaspora: Emigration from Britain, 1680–1815," in *The Oxford History of the British Empire*, vol. 2, ed. P.J. Marshall and Alaine Low (Oxford: Oxford University Press, 1998), 35–46.
31. Peter Laslett, "Mean Household Size in England since the Sixteenth Century," in *Household and Family in Past Times*, ed. Peter Laslett and Richard Wall (Cambridge: Cambridge University Press, 1972), 127; Patrick Joyce, "Work," in *The Cambridge Social History of Britain, 1750–1950*, vol. 2, ed. F.M.L. Thompson (Cambridge: Cambridge University Press, 1990), 132, 144; Joyce, "Historical Meanings of Work," 5, 10, 25. Also see E.P. Thompson, "Eighteenth-Century English Society: Class Struggle without Class?," *Social History* 3, no. 2 (1978): 133; E.P. Thompson, "Time, Work-Discipline, and Industrial Capitalism," in *Customs in Common*, 382; Wrightson, *Earthly Necessities*, 20.
32. Joyce, "Historical Meanings of Work," 4, 6–7. Wrightson, *Earthly Necessities*, was concerned that postwar studies of early modern England portrayed the period simply as a prelude to late-eighteenth-century industrialization, "less a dividing range in historical experience than a landscape of gently rising foothills" (20). White and Vann, "The Invention of English Individualism," felt that empirical research by social historians in the late 1970s and early 1980s was outrunning scholars' ability to fit that research into a comprehensive conceptual scheme (345).
33. Raymond Williams, *Keywords* (New York: Oxford University Press, 1976), 66, 76; Phil Withington and Alexandra Shepard, introduction to *Communities in Early Modern*

England, ed. Alexandra Shepard and Phil Withington (Manchester, UK: Manchester University Press, 2000), 3–4; John Rule, *The Labouring Classes in Early Industrial England, 1750–1850* (London: Longman, 1986), 155–56. For a critical analysis of developing perceptions of community and some of the connotations that they carry, see C.J. Calhoun, "Community: Toward a Variable Conceptualization for Comparative Research," *Social History* 5, no. 1 (January 1980), 105–10.

34. But see Dipesh Chakrabarty, "The Muddle of Modernity," *American Historical Review* 116, no. 3 (2011): 663–75.
35. Muldrew, "Interpreting the Market," 169.
36. Rule, *Experience of Labour*, 208–9.
37. Naomi Tadmor, *Family and Friends in Eighteenth-Century England* (Cambridge: Cambridge University Press, 2001), 42–43; Griffiths, *Youth and Authority*, 291.
38. For useful historiographical context see John Smolenski, "Introduction: The Ordering of Authority in the Colonial Americas," in *New World Orders*, ed. John Smolenski and Thomas J. Humphrey (Philadelphia: University of Pennsylvania Press, 2005), 1–16.
39. Mark L. Thompson, "'The Predicament of Ubi,'" in *The Creation of the British Atlantic World*, ed. Mancke and Shammas, 72. Also see Jack P. Greene, "Empire and Identity from the Glorious Revolution to the American Revolution," in *The Oxford History of the British Empire*, vol. 2, ed. P.J. Marshall and Alaine Low (Oxford: Oxford University Press, 1998), 220–21.
40. Mark Thompson, "The Predicament of Ubi," 72–73, 335n3.
41. Alison Games, *The Web of Empire* (Oxford: Oxford University Press, 2008), 7–8.
42. Elizabeth Mancke, "Chartered Enterprises and the Evolution of the British Atlantic World," in *The Creation of the British Atlantic World*, ed. Elizabeth Mancke and Carole Shammas (Baltimore, MD: Johns Hopkins University Press, 2005), 256–57.
43. "It was the classic responsibility of the head of household to patrol the boundaries and lock up fast at night. 'Shutting in' was a universally recognised hour, after sunset, but before bedtime, a fateful moment that set in motion a ritual ceremony of fortification.... Bells, trip wires, servants sleeping across the doorway and nasty guard dogs were all expected to rouse the household. Defensive weapons including firearms were common." Amanda Vickery, *Behind Closed Doors* (New Haven, CT: Yale University Press, 2009), 29, 30, 31. Also see D.R. Hainsworth, *Stewards, Lords, and People* (Cambridge: Cambridge University Press, 1992), 186–204, especially 186: "The steward of a seventeenth-century estate was a man perpetually on guard." Paul C. Nigol accepts the household as the basic unit of organization but places more emphasis on what he designates military-style discipline in the factories. Nigol, "Discipline and Discretion in the Mid-Eighteenth-Century Hudson's Bay Company Private Justice System," in *Laws and Societies in the Canadian Prairie West, 1670–1940*, ed. Louis A. Knafla and Jonathon Swainger (Vancouver: University of British Columbia Press, 2005), 153–56.
44. Mark Thompson, "The Predicament of Ubi," 80.
45. Games, *Web of Empire*, 52–53.
46. Muldrew, "Interpreting the Market," 177–78; also Wrightson, *Earthly Necessities*, 301.
47. Wrightson, *Earthly Necessities*, 75, 77–78.

48. Almost no correspondence between the Bayside posts has survived from before 1745, but after that time the factors often described each other as neighbours as well as friends; for example: "Yr freind Neighbour & Humble Servt." James Isham (York Fort) to Robert Pilgrim (Prince of Wales Fort), 3 January 1747, Hudson's Bay Company Archives at the Archives of Manitoba (hereafter cited as HBCA), B. 239/b/4, fol. 4d. All archival references will be to the Hudson's Bay Company Archives at the Manitoba Archives unless otherwise specified.
49. See Patricia Seed, *Ceremonies of Possession in Europe's Conquest of the New World, 1492–1640* (Cambridge: Cambridge University Press, 1995), 20; Mancke, "Chartered Enterprises," 240–48. It is worth noting that the HBC held its territories through the sovereign (according to its charter), whereas the RAC and EIC generally held their overseas settlements by agreement with Indigenous authorities, to whom they often paid rent or tribute. Hair and Law, "The English in West Africa," 261.
50. Greene, "Empire and Identity," notes that English migrants considered "the English system of law and liberty...crucial to their ability to maintain their identity as English people," and they viewed "English legal arrangements as the best way to preserve the properties they hoped to acquire" (222).
51. See, for instance, April Lee Hatfield, "Mariners, Merchants, and Colonists in Seventeenth-Century English America," in *The Creation of the British Atlantic World*, ed. Mancke and Shammas (Baltimore, MD: Johns Hopkins University Press, 2005), 141–46.
52. This legislation allowed the continuation of French civil law in Quebec and extended that colony's boundaries south to the Ohio River and west to the Mississippi (at the expense of other colonies such as Virginia). In essence, this confirmed the Proclamation of 1763 in placing the Trans-Appalachian West under the jurisdictional authority of the British imperial state rather than of the colonies.
53. This gave the courts of Lower Canada jurisdiction over cases in the far west, although it did not include Rupert's Land. Also, it excluded civil cases concerning land, which had to be tried in Britain.
54. Most of the work done on the legal history of the HBC has been focused on the nineteenth century, but see Paul C. Nigol, "Discipline, Discretion and Control" (PHD diss., History, University of Calgary, 2001); and Nigol, "Discipline and Discretion," 150–82; Russell Smandych and Rick Linden, "Administering Justice without the State," *Canadian Journal of Law and Society* 11 (1996): 21–61. More generally, see Hamar Foster, "Law and Necessity in Western Rupert's Land and Beyond, 1670–1870," in *Laws and Societies in the Canadian Prairie West, 1670–1940*, ed. Louis A. Knafla and Jonathon Swainger (Vancouver: University of British Columbia Press, 2005), 57–91.
55. Greene, "Empire and Identity," 221; William M. Offutt, "The Atlantic Rules," in *The Creation of the British Atlantic World*, ed. Mancke and Shammas (Baltimore, MD: Johns Hopkins University Press, 2005), 160. Also see Mancke, "Chartered Enteprises," 251–53. For an example of the impact of such extensions of English law into the Newfoundland fisheries, see Cadigan, "Merchant Capital," 17–42. Ian K. Steele observes more generally, "However hegemonic the legal system may have been in structure, it functioned primarily as a local vehicle of negotiated dispute settlement" in the late-seventeenth-

and the early-eighteenth-century empire. Steele, "The Anointed, the Appointed, and the Elected," in *The Oxford History of the British Empire*, vol. 2, ed. P.J. Marshall and Alaine Low (Oxford: Oxford University Press, 1998), 113.

1 EARLY MODERN CONTEXTS

1. HBCA, A. 11/116, fol. 42, quoted in E.E. Rich and A.M. Johnson, eds., *Cumberland House Journals and Inland Journal, 1775–82: First Series, 1775–79* (London: Hudson's Bay Record Society, 1951) (hereafter cited as *CHJ First Series*), 309n. Also in Rich and Johnson, eds., *Cumberland House Journals and Inland Journal, 1775–82: Second Series, 1779–82* (London: Hudson's Bay Record Society, 1952) (hereafter cited as *CHJ Second Series*), xxiv–xxv.
2. Games, *Web of Empire*, 14.
3. Games, 82–83.
4. K.G. Davies, *The Royal African Company* (London: Longmans, Green, 1957), 163n, 378–81, 383, 386, 390; Carlos and Nicholas, "Giants of an Earlier Capitalism," 128. Prince Rupert and James, Duke of York, were also involved in both the HBC and the RAC, but there is little evidence that they played active roles in governing either company.
5. Rich, *History of the Hudson's Bay Company*, vol. 1, 25, also 30–31. Also see Robert M. Weir, "Shaftesbury's Darling," in *The Oxford History of the British Empire*, vol. 1, ed. Nicholas Canny (Oxford: Oxford University Press, 1998), 379.
6. Hudson's Bay Company Archives Biographical Sheet, s.v. "Baker, William (Sir)," http://www.gov.mb.ca/chc/archives/HBCA/biographical/b/baker_william.pdf.
7. Games, *Web of Empire*, 10–11.
8. Games, 137, made a similar observation about the Jamestown colony in Virginia, where "the English who sought lessons in other European endeavors in America had only their reading and some largely irrelevant lessons from the Caribbean, Roanoke, or the fisheries to rely on."
9. The chronology of various incarnations of the RAC and of other chartered companies trading to Africa can be confusing. For clarification, see Davies, *Royal African Company*, 39–44, 97–101, 125–26, 349; David Richardson, "The British Empire and the Atlantic Slave Trade, 1660–1807," in *The Oxford History of the British Empire*, vol. 2, ed. P.J. Marshall and Alaine Low (Oxford: Oxford University Press, 1998), 444–45.
10. For the RAC, see Davies, *Royal African Company*, 252; Hair and Law, "The English in West Africa," 256; K.G. Davies, "The Living and the Dead," in *Race and Slavery in the Western Hemisphere: Quantitative Studies*, ed. Stanley L. Engerman and Eugene D. Genovese (Princeton NJ: Princeton University Press, 1975), 86. For the EIC, see K.N. Chaudhuri, *The English East India Company* (London: Frank Cass, 1965), 21. To be fair, the EIC's early success was followed by some losing voyages and declining political support, from the 1620s through the 1650s, before commercial and political prospects rebounded in the 1660s and 1670s.
11. For the EIC, see Nicholas Canny, "In Search of a Better Home?," in *Europeans on the Move* (Oxford: Clarendon Press, 1994), 274; Holden Furber, *John Company at Work* (Cambridge, MA: Harvard University Press, 1948), 23, 27; H.V. Bowen, *Business of Empire*, 139, 264; Makepeace, *East India Company's London Workers*, 94–95. For the HBC, see E.E. Rich,

ed., *Minutes of the Hudson's Bay Company, 1671–1674* (Toronto: Champlain Society for the Hudson's Bay Record Society, 1942) (hereafter cited as *Minutes*), liv–lv, 19, 22; E.E. Rich, ed., *Minutes of the Hudson's Bay Company, 1679–1684: First Part, 1679–1682* (Toronto: Champlain Society for the Hudson's Bay Record Society, 1945) (hereafter cited as *Minutes, First Part*), xviii; Rich, *History*, vol. 1, 183; A. Beale (Albany Fort, AF) to HBC, 23 July 1706, HBCA, A. 11/2, fol.15; R. Staunton & Council (Moose Fort, MF) to HBC, 17 August 1739, in *Letters from Hudson Bay, 1703–40*, ed. K.G. Davies and A.M. Johnson (London: Hudson's Bay Record Society, 1965) (hereafter cited as *Letters*), 301; R. Norton (Prince of Wales Fort, PWF) to HBC, 16 August 1733, *Letters*, 186; W. Bevan & Council (MF) to HBC, 26 August 1736, *Letters*, 217–18; R. Staunton (AF) to HBC, 21 August 1723, HBCA, A. 11/2, fol. 48; J. Isbister (AF) to HBC, 18 August 1743, HBCA, A. 11/2, fol. 116d; *CHJ Second Series*, xxxvn.

12. Davies, *Royal African Company*, 254; Furber, *John Company at Work*, 19; Davies, "The Living and the Dead," 85–86.
13. For a brief overview of EIC recruitment areas (including those not much explored by scholars), see H.V. Bowen, *Business of Empire*, 271–75. For an organizational chart of the EIC's British administration in 1785, see H.V. Bowen, 186.
14. P.E.H. Hair, Adam Jones, and Robin Law, eds., *Barbot on Guinea* (London: Hakluyt Society, 1992), 405n14.
15. Louise E. Sweet, "Political Tactics of the Peaceful Traders (1616–1853)," in *Proceedings of the Second Congress, Canadian Ethnology Society*, vol. 2, ed. Jim Freedman and Jerome H. Barkow (Ottawa, ON: National Museum of Man, Mercury Series, 1975), 546, 552n6. Also see Davies, "The Living and the Dead," 86.
16. Malachy Postlethwayt, *The Universal Dictionary of Trade and Commerce* (1751), quoted in H.V. Bowen, *Business of Empire*, 9. For a brief overview of the internal EIC debate over maintaining a military presence in the seventeenth century, see P.J. Marshall, "The English in Asia to 1700," in *The Oxford History of the British Empire*, vol. 1, ed. Nicholas Canny (Oxford: Oxford University Press, 1998), 280–81.
17. Quoted in Sushil Chaudhury, "The Imperatives of the Empire," *Studies in History* 8, no. 1, n.s. (1992): 3.
18. David Henige, "Companies Are Always Ungrateful," *African Economic History* 9 (1980): 31, also 30. Seventeenth-century Levant Company traders often set sail with similar expectations of a short stay (perhaps five or seven years) in the East before returning home with a tidy sum (Games, *Web of Empire*, 90).
19. Henige, "Companies Are Always Ungrateful," 32, also 36–37, 42n30. Phipps often complained that honesty met with no reward in Africa (Henige, 32, 39, 43n34). Similar complaints from India can be seen in a 1618 letter from three factors in Bantam to the EIC's court of committees: "At home men are famous for doing nothing; here they are infamous for their honest endeavours" (Chaudhuri, *English East India Company*, 77).
20. See Chaudhuri, *English East India Company*, 77; Furber, *John Company at Work*, 13–14, 27, 338–39; Games, *Web of Empire*, 94.
21. Philip Lawson, *The East India Company* (London: Longman, 1993), 73, 88. H.V. Bowen, *Business of Empire*, sounds two notes of caution: "comparatively few Company servants were either lucky enough, or lived long enough, to be able to retire to Britain with a

substantial fortune" (275); and "the period of easy fortune-making...lasted between 1757 and the mid-1770s" (289).

22. See, for instance, Thomson, *History of Orkney*, 219–20.
23. Seed, *Ceremonies of Possession*, 18.
24. Keith Wrightson, "The Politics of the Parish in Early Modern England," in *The Experience of Authority in Early Modern England*, ed. Paul Griffiths, Adam Fox, and Steve Hindle (New York: St. Martin's Press, 1996), 32.
25. See Tadmor, *Family and Friends*, 41, 63; Laslett, *The World We Have Lost*, 76; Leonore Davidoff, "The Family in Britain," in *The Cambridge Social History of Britain, 1750–1950*, vol. 2, ed. F.M.L. Thompson (Cambridge: Cambridge University Press, 1990), 71; Vickery, *Behind Closed Doors*, 184–85. Also see John E. Foster, "The Indian-Trader in the Hudson Bay Fur Trade Tradition," in *Proceedings of the Second Congress, Canadian Ethnology Society*, vol. 2, ed. Jim Freedman and Jerome H. Barkow (Ottawa, ON: National Museum of Man, Mercury Series, 1975), 574–75.
26. James Horn, "Tobacco Colonies," in *The Oxford History of the British Empire*, vol. 1, ed. Nicholas Canny (Oxford: Oxford University Press, 1998), 189.
27. See Horn, "Tobacco Colonies," 187–88; Boyd Stanley Schlenther, "Religious Faith and Commercial Empire," in *The Oxford History of the British Empire*, vol. 2, ed. P.J. Marshall and Alaine Low (Oxford: Oxford University Press, 1998), 128–31.
28. David Eastwood, *Governing Rural England* (Oxford: Clarendon Press, 1994), 24. Also see Anthony Fletcher and John Stevenson, introduction to *Order and Disorder in Early Modern England*, ed. Fletcher and Stevenson (Cambridge: Cambridge University Press, 1985), 9–10; K.D.M. Snell, "Gravestones, Belonging and Local Attachment in England, 1700–2000," *Past & Present* 179 (May 2003): 100–1, 131–32. Also see John E. Foster, "The Indian-Trader," 577–78. For a discussion of social patterns and popular culture transplanted from Britain to the American colonies through processes of retention, storage, recovery, and borrowing, see Alfred F. Young, "English Plebeian Culture and Eighteenth-Century American Radicalism," in *The Origins of Anglo-American Radicalism*, ed. Margaret Jacob and James Jacob (London: George Allen & Unwin, 1984), 185–212.
29. See Jennifer S.H. Brown, *Strangers in Blood* (Vancouver: University of British Columbia Press, 1980), 20; John E. Foster, "The Indian-Trader," 576–78.
30. Games, *Web of Empire*, 160, 165.
31. Horn, "Tobacco Colonies," 190.
32. H.V. Bowen, *Business of Empire*, 131–32, makes a similar observation about most of the EIC's directors, men of "practical learning" rather than "philosophical or theoretical ideas": "responses to the problems of trade and empire were usually governed by considerations of pragmatism, precedent, and expediency, and there is little evidence to suggest that any more than a few directors ever possessed a far-sighted vision of the development of the Company's affairs."
33. Wrightson, *Earthly Necessities*, 296.
34. Richard Wall, introduction to *Family Forms in Historic Europe*, ed. Richard Wall, Jean Robin, and Peter Laslett (Cambridge: Cambridge University Press, 1983), 6–7; Tadmor, *Family and Friends*, 25; Laslett, "Mean Household Size," 127; Naomi Tadmor, "The Concept

of the Household-Family in Eighteenth-Century England," *Past & Present* 151 (May 1996): 112.

35. Barry Reay, "Kinship and the Neighbourhood in Nineteenth-Century Rural England," *Journal of Family History* 21, no. 1 (January 1996): 99.
36. Tadmor, "Concept," 112, 119–20; Davidoff, "The Family in Britain," 71; Mary Abbott, *Life Cycles in England, 1560–1720* (London: Routledge, 1996), 115–17; K.D.M. Snell, *Annals of the Labouring Poor* (Cambridge: Cambridge University Press, 1985), 321; Vickery, *Behind Closed Doors*, 203; Ann Kussmaul, "The Pattern of Work as the Eighteenth Century Began," in *The Economic History of Britain since 1700*, 2nd ed., ed. Roderick Floud and Donald McCloskey (Cambridge: Cambridge University Press, 1994), 2; Bridget Hill, *Servants* (Oxford: Clarendon Press, 1996), 11–13. Woodward, *Men at Work*, casts some doubt on whether journeymen were included in early modern households (65). For a discussion of household and family from the point of view of feminist historians, see Berg, "Women's Work," 64–98.
37. Tadmor, "Concept," 117–18; Tadmor, *Family and Friends*, 22–24.
38. See Naomi Tadmor, "Early Modern English Kinship in the Long Run," *Continuity and Change* 25, no. 1 (2010): 23–25.
39. Germaine Warkentin, ed., *Pierre-Esprit Radisson: The Collected Writings*, vol. 2 (Toronto: Champlain Society and McGill-Queen's University Press, 2014), 123. For a broader context, see Peter Cook, "Onontio Gives Birth," *Canadian Historical Review* 96, no. 2 (June 2015): 165–92.
40. Tadmor, "Kinship in the Long Run," 26, rejects "the problematic dichotomy between 'interest' and 'emotion.'" Also see Tadmor, *Family and Friends*, 28–29, 175–78, 191–94, 259, and "concept of the household-family," 124. Also Ilana Krausman Ben-Amos, "Gifts and Favors," *Journal of Modern History* 72, no. 2 (June 2000): 295–338; Hainsworth, *Stewards*, 256–61.
41. H. Marten (AF) to W. Richards ("North Main," somewhere up the Albany River), 1 June 1766, HBCA, B. 3/b/3, fol. 4.
42. Tadmor, *Family and Friends*, 27–29; Tadmor, "Concept," 123–26. Also see Ann Kussmaul, *Servants in Husbandry in Early Modern England* (Cambridge: Cambridge University Press, 1981), 31; Robert Paine, "A Theory of Patronage and Brokerage," in *Patrons and Brokers in the East Arctic*, Newfoundland Social and Economic Papers, no. 2, ed. Robert Paine (St. John's: Institute of Social and Economic Research, Memorial University of Newfoundland, 1971), 12.
43. Hainsworth, *Stewards*, 251.
44. See Tadmor, *Family and Friends*, 35; Davidoff, "The Family in Britain," 128; Vickery, *Behind Closed Doors*, 186–87, 201–6; Michael J. Braddick, "Administrative Performance," in *Negotiating Power in Early Modern Society*, ed. Michael J. Braddick and John Walter (Cambridge: Cambridge University Press, 2001), 171–73.
45. Albany Fort Council, trial of John Cartwright, 19 August 1696, HBCA, B. 3/z/2, fol. 2.
46. Albany Fort Council, trial of William Filpott, n.d. [1696], HBCA, B. 3/a/2, fol. 2d. Compare Horn, "Tobacco Colonies," 187: "In a society deeply imbued with patriarchal values, county justices sought to assume the role of fathers of their communities,

dispensing justice, regulating local business, and ensuring the continuance of 'the Amity, Confidence and Quiet that is between men.'"

47. HBC to R. Norton (PWF), private, 25 May 1727, HBCA, A. 6/5, fol. 9d. H. Kelsey (YF) to R. Staunton (PWF), 28 March 1719, HBCA, B. 239/b/1, fol. 13.
48. Michael A. Lacombe, "A Continuall and Dayly Table for Gentlemen of Fashion," *American Historical Review* 115, no. 3 (June 2010), 670, 686.
49. I have taken the middle ground between a higher estimate (Abbott, *Life Cycles*, 111) and a lower one (Davidoff, "The Family in Britain," 87).
50. R. Norton (PWF) to HBC, 23 August 1737, *Letters*, 237–38. Woodward, *Men at Work*, 59–60.
51. Malcolmson, *Life and Labour*, 65; Ben-Amos, *Adolescence and Youth*, 69; Frances J. Shaw, *The Northern and Western Islands of Scotland* (Edinburgh: John Donald, 1980), 191; Tadmor, *Family and Friends*, 35; Kussmaul, *Servants*, 3, 19; Ian D. Whyte, "Migration in Early-Modern Scotland and England," in *Migrants, Emigrants and Immigrants*, ed. Colin G. Pooley and Ian D. Whyte (London: Routledge, 1991), 92. Note that the common experiences of domestic service were not necessarily sufficient to gloss over cultural differences between Orcadian, Scots, and English HBC servants. See Horn and Morgan, "Settlers and Slaves," in Mancke and Shammas, 20.
52. Fletcher and Stevenson, introduction to *Order and Disorder*, 31–33; also see Ben-Amos, *Adolescence and Youth*, 85; Kussmaul, "Pattern of Work," 2; Griffiths, *Youth and Authority*, 299–300; Malcolmson, *Life and Labour*, 66; Pelling, "Apprenticeship," 33. For a note of caution, see Griffiths, 330; Hill, *Servants*, 14–15, 106.
53. Samuel Richardson, *The Apprentice's Vade Mecum: or, Young Man's Pocket-Companion*, ed. A.D. McKillop (Los Angeles: William Andrews Clark Memorial Library, UCLA, 1975; originally published London, 1734), 51; emphasis in the original.
54. Kussmaul, *Servants*, 5–6, 8–9; R. Campbell, *The London Tradesman* (New York: Augustus M. Kelly, 1969; first published 1747, London), 313; Davidoff, "The Family in Britain," 88.
55. Kussmaul, *Servants*, 78–80, 83–84; Malcolmson, *Life and Labour*, 65–67; Tadmor, *Family and Friends*, 35, 38n, 61–62. For a note of caution, see Ben-Amos, *Adolescence and Youth*, 70–71; Laslett, *The World We Have Lost*, 4.
56. J.T. Cliffe, *The World of the Country House in Seventeenth-Century England* (New Haven, CT: Yale University Press, 1999), 91–92. Hainsworth, *Stewards*, 29.
57. Tadmor, *Family and Friends*, 63; Griffiths, *Youth and Authority*, 324; Kussmaul, *Servants*, 31; Laslett, *The World We Have Lost*, 4. Also see Samuel Richardson, *The Apprentice's Vade Mecum*, v.
58. Woodward, *Men at Work*, 12, 25, 51–52; Malcolmson, *Life and Labour*, 23; Davidoff, "The Family in Britain," 78; Laslett, *The World We Have Lost*, 51.
59. Laslett, "Mean Household Size," 126; Kussmaul, *Servants*, 11. English households (averaging two or three servants) were slightly smaller than contemporary Orkney households (which averaged three or four servants); Shaw, *Northern and Western Islands*, 191.
60. Brown, *Strangers in Blood*, 21, 59; John E. Foster, "The Indian-Trader," 579; Cliffe, *World of the Country House*, 116–17. The quotation is from HBC to T. McCliesh Jr & Council (AF), 30 May 1718, HBCA, A. 6/4, fol. 22. Estate stewards remain relatively unstudied outside

of the work of D.R. Hainsworth. Even less scholarly attention has been paid to waged foremen in the workplace; their control of production and of personnel functions, and their equivocal positions between employers and employees, also bears many similarities to the roles played by HBC factors. See Joyce, "Work," 158.

61. Sharon Kettering, *Patrons, Brokers, and Clients in Seventeenth-Century France* (New York: Oxford University Press, 1986), 3.
62. Paine, "Theory of Patronage," 8, 15. Kettering, *Patrons*, 3–4.
63. Paul Griffiths, Adam Fox, and Steve Hindle, introduction to *The Experience of Authority in Early Modern England* (New York: St. Martin's Press, 1996), 3; Joyce, "Work," 158.
64. Hainsworth, *Stewards*, 109.
65. Games, *Web of Empire*, 89.
66. For the EIC, see Makepeace, *East India Company's London Workers*, 197.
67. Paine, "Theory of Patronage," 8, 19–21; Kettering, *Patrons*, 4. This concept is also implicit in much of Hainsworth's work on estate stewards.
68. Hainsworth, *Stewards*, 13.
69. J. Duffield (MF) to J. Isbister (AF), 6 September 1742, HBCA, B. 3/b/1, fol. 4. J. Isbister (AF) to J. Duffield (MF), 13 September 1742, HBCA, B. 3/b/1, fol. 4d.
70. H. Marten (AF) to W. Richards (Henley), 23 June 1766, HBCA, B. 3/b/3, fols. 7–7d. W. Richards ("Henley Flanker") to H. Marten (AF), 1 July 1766, HBCA, B. 3/b/3, fol. 7d.
71. Hainsworth, *Stewards*, 48–49.
72. Daniel Defoe, *The Great Law of Subordination Consider'd* (London, 1724), 97, quoted in E.P. Thompson, "Patricians and Plebs," 43.
73. E.P. Thompson, 43.
74. For Radisson positioning himself as a patron to his nephew and the other Frenchmen at Port Nelson in 1684, see Warkentin, vol. 2, 114–17; but his nephew later expressed deep dissatisfaction with Radisson's performance in that role (vol. 1, 84–86).
75. J. Adams (AF) to HBC, 28 August 1730, HBCA, A. 11/2, fol. 69d; T. McCliesh Jr (YF) to HBC, 7 August 1731, *Letters*, 159; HBC to J. Adams & Council (AF), 20 May 1731, HBCA, A. 6/5, fol. 47d; HBC to R. White (AF), n.d. [11 May 1732], HBCA, A. 6/5, fol. 57d; J. Adams (AF) to HBC, 14 August 1732, HBCA, A. 11/2, fol. 73d; J. Adams & Council (AF) to HBC, 31 July 1733, HBCA, A. 11/2, fol. 77d; HBC to J. Adams & Council (AF), 3 May 1734, HBCA, A. 6/5, fol. 85; J. Adams & Council (AF) to HBC, 12 August 1734, HBCA, A. 11/2, fol. 80d; HBC to R. Norton & Council (PWF), 2 May 1735, HBCA, A. 6/5, fol. 97d; R. Norton & Council (PWF) to HBC, 17 August 1736, *Letters*, 216; R. Norton & Council (PWF) to HBC, 9 August 1740, *Letters*, 320.
76. W. Bevan & Council (MF) to HBC, 23 August 1732, *Letters*, 173; HBCA, A. 16/2, fol. 40; HBC to S. Maidman (MF), 2 May 1735, HBCA, A. 6/5, fol. 99, in response to Maidman's request in a letter the year before (no longer extant).
77. This lack of direct knowledge only seems to have become a serious issue within the company after it began acquiring its territorial empire. See H.V. Bowen, *Business of Empire*, 128–31.
78. Sir John Lowther of Whitehaven to William Christian, 27 December 1681, quoted in Hainsworth, *Stewards*, 108. Also see steward John Peck's advice to Sir John Trevor on the appointment of an understeward, 1652: "It behoves you to make choice of one you

may confide in as not only to receive the rents and return them but also to give you light and intelligence of all things that may redound to your best advantage." Quoted in Hainsworth, 122–23.

79. "Report to the Governor and Committee by John Nixon, 1682," Royal Society, the Boyle Papers (Misc.), XL, printed as appendix A in *Minutes, First Part* (hereafter cited as Nixon), 275. In particular, Nixon was certain that Captain Walker, John Abraham (Walker's first mate), and Thomas Garland (pilot of the *Diligence* and master of the *Hayes* sloop) were going to blame him for the loss of the *Diligence*'s rudder in 1681, a charge he flatly denied (Nixon, 263–64). Hainsworth, *Stewards*, 51–52, observed that it was not uncommon for tenants to appeal to their landlord over the steward's head, alleging "arbitrary and tyrannical behavior." Tenants might travel some distance, "from outlying estates to the landlord's seat, usually preceded by a flurry of warnings from the understeward about the sinister purpose of the visit."

80. Nixon, 274.

81. HBC to J. Nixon (Bottom of the Bay), 15 May 1682, *Copy-Book of Letters Outward &c, Begins 29th May, 1680; Ends 5 July, 1687*, ed. E.E. Rich and A.M. Johnson (Toronto: Champlain Society for the Hudson's Bay Record Society, 1948) (hereafter cited as *L.O. 1680–1687*), 38–39. Also see HBC to H. Sergeant (AF), 22 May 1685, *L.O. 1680–1687*, 144. Compare Hainsworth, *Stewards*, 52: "Interestingly although stewards were often accused by their masters of being too indulgent toward the tenants, stewards were often nervous that they would earn their masters' displeasure by appearing to treat tenants too severely.... Certainly tenants were quick to approach the lord directly if dissatisfied with their treatment from the steward and such appeals to Ceasar were often successful."

82. See Vilhelm Aubert, *The Hidden Society* (Totowa, NJ: Bedminster Press, 1965), 261.

83. W. Richards ("Henley Island") to H. Marten (AF), 15 June 1766, HBCA, B. 3/b/3, fol. 5d.

84. Albany Fort post journal, 24 January 1771, HBCA, B. 3/a/63, fol. 18d.

85. See David Cressy, "Kinship and Kin Interaction in Early Modern England," *Past & Present* 113 (November 1986), 51; Tadmor, *Family and Friends*, 128, 178.

86. G. Spence (AF) to J. Isham (YF), 10 May 1748, HBCA, B. 239/b/5, fol. 8. J. Isham (YF) to G. Spence (AF), 4 July 1748, HBCA, B. 239/b/5, fols. 8d, 9.

87. Campbell, *London Tradesman*, 313; Pelling, "Apprenticeship," 41–42. Also see Tadmor, *Family and Friends*, 157–58; Ben-Amos, *Adolescence and Youth*, 174.

88. E.E. Rich and A.M. Johnson, eds., *James Isham's Observations on Hudsons Bay, 1743, and Notes and Observations on a Book Entitled "A Voyage to Hudsons Bay in the Dobbs Galley," 1749* (London: Hudson's Bay Record Society, 1949), 325; also Brown, *Strangers*, 33.

89. H. Marten (YF) to Thomas Hutchins (AF), 4 February 1779, HBCA, B. 239/b/39, fol. 9d, quoted in *CHJ Second Series*, xx.

90. HBC to H. Pollexfen Sr (MF), private, 23 May 1758, HBCA, A. 5/1, fol. 24d. John Stephenson Jr served under his father, John Sr, on the *Eastmain* sloop between 1757 and 1763: see HBCA, A. 16/4, fol. 22.

91. See Brown, *Strangers*, 32–33; Kussmaul, *Servants*, 55; Vickery, *Behind Closed Doors*, 185–87.

92. See Scott P. Stephen, "'Assistant to York': The Ambiguous Role of Flamborough House, 1749–1759," *Manitoba History* 62 (Winter 2009), 9–21.

93. See Abbott, *Life Cycles*, 113–14.

94. Bishop had served as McCliesh's second at Albany since 1715. He made the declaration in a letter of 30 August 1719, which has not survived. The Committee pointed out the "very great uncertainty" in which it was placed, as the Committee anticipated McCliesh's return to England in 1720 (he actually stayed until 1721), and called Bishop home, "having provided themselves wth a person, who is willing to remain in our Service under whomesoever wee will Appoint, over our Affairs in ye Factory." HBC to N. Bishop (AF), private, 1 June 1720, HBCA, A. 6/4, fol. 45.

95. See, for example, J. Isbister (PWF) to J. Newton (YF), 12 July 1749, HBCA, A. 11/114, fol. 136; J. Isbister (PWF) to J. Isham (YF), 17 January 1751, HBCA, B. 239/b/6, fol. 18; J. Potts (Richmond Fort, RF) to J. Isham (YF), 6 September 1753, HBCA, B. 239/b/12, fol. 1; J. Isham (YF) to J. Potts (RF), 28 June 1754, HBCA, B. 239/b/12, fol. 1d; J. Isham (YF) to F. Jacobs (PWF), 20 January 1756, HBCA, B. 239/b/13, fol. 2.

96. H. Marten (Severn River, SR) to A. Graham (YF), 8 July 1761, HBCA, B. 239/b/22, fol. 8d; Glyndwr Williams, ed., *Andrew Graham's Observations on Hudson's Bay, 1767–91* (London: Hudson's Bay Record Society, 1969), 283.

97. Frits Pannekoek, "'Corruption' at Moose," *The Beaver* 309, no. 4 (Spring 1979): 9.

98. Brown, *Strangers*, 33.

99. Such "social networks" are a major part of Erikson's work on the EIC.

100. HBC to S. Sinclair (AF), 17 June 1693, *L.O. 1688–1696*, 211.

101. A. Beale (AF) to HBC, 23 July 1706, HBCA, A. 11/2, fols. 16–16d.

102. Richardson, *The Apprentice's Vade Mecum*, 42.

103. Tadmor, *Family and Friends*, 167; Davidoff, "The Family in Britain," 72–73, 78; Keith Thomas, *The Ends of Life: Roads to Fulfillment in Early Modern England* (Oxford: Oxford University Press, 2009), 190–97.

104. Felicity Heal, "Food Gifts, the Household and the Politics of Exchange in Early Modern England," *Past & Present* 199 (May 2008): 53. See also Ben-Amos, "Gifts and Favors," 295–338, esp. 298–300; Craig Muldrew, *The Economy of Obligation: The Culture of Credit and Social Relations in Early Modern England* (Basingstoke, UK: Palgrave Macmillan, 1998).

105. This, of course, is how Richard White famously characterized the middle ground between French and Indigenous people in the early modern Great Lakes region (as a process of creative and mutual misunderstanding). It is not the purpose of this book to explore whether such a middle ground was constructed in the HBC's trading relationships, although I certainly hope that it can contribute to such a discussion. Victor Lytwyn, *Muskekowuck Athinuwick* (Winnipeg: University of Manitoba Press, 2002) would be a very useful starting point, but so too would be Bruce M. White's work on the Ojibwa, many aspects of which could be transposed (with some modifications) to the Cree: "'Give Us a Little Milk': The Social and Cultural Meanings of Gift Giving in the Lake Superior Fur Trade," *Minnesota History* 48 (Summer 1982): 60–71; and "A Skilled Game of Exchange: Ojibway Fur Trade Protocol," *Minnesota History* 50, no. 6 (Summer 1987): 229–40.

106. Tadmor, *Family and Friends*, 213, 214–15. Also see Paine, "Theory of Patronage," 12.

107. See Tadmor, *Family and Friends*, 216–36, 279; Richardson, *The Apprentice's Vade Mecum*, 42, 44; Wrightson, *Earthly Necessities*, 82.

108. J. Isham (YF) to J. Potts (MF), 4 July 1748, HBCA, B. 239/b/5, fol. 10; J. Isbister (AF) to J. Isham (YF), 14 May 1747, HBCA, B. 239/b/4, fol. 11; J. Isbister (PWF) to J. Isham (YF), 17 January 1751, HBCA, B. 239/b/6, fols. 20, 21–21d; J. Isham (YF) to J. Isbister (PWF), 24 February 1751, HBCA, B. 239/b/6, fols. 21d–22. Also see Moses Norton (PWF) defending himself against Jacobs's implied charge of enticing YF Indigenous people northward: "Such Unneighbourly Practices Believe me Sir I Shall never make use of" (3 August 1763, HBCA, B. 42/b/9, fol. 6).
109. Michael J. Braddick and John Walter, "Introduction: Grids of Power," in *Negotiating Power in Early Modern Society*, ed. Braddick and Walter (Cambridge: Cambridge University Press, 2001), 5; John Walter, "Public Transcripts, Popular Agency and the Politics of Subsistence in Early Modern England," in *Negotiating Power in Early Modern Society*, ed. Braddick and Walter, 146–47; Edith Burley, *Servants of the Honourable Company* (Don Mills ON: Oxford University Press, 1997), 247–48.
110. Braddick and Walter, "Introduction," 5.
111. Wrightson, *Earthly Necessities*, 325.
112. Braddick and Walter, "Introduction," 5; Laslett, *The World We Have Lost*, 213–20; Whipp, "Labour Markets," 776. Compare Berry's critique of the paradigm of politeness in Britain: "Could not a...repressive civil code of outwardly conformist behaviour in eighteenth-century England nourish an underbelly of impolite resistance?....Where are the hidden transcripts of impolite thought, speech and action in eighteenth-century England?" Helen Berry, "Rethinking Politeness in Eighteenth-Century England," *Transactions of the Royal Historical Society*, sixth series, vol. 11 (2001): 68.
113. This impression is too often accepted at face value; see, for instance, Burley, *Servants of the Honourable Company*, 2. Also Burley suggests that the HBC's post-1770 recruitment policy "never succeeded in yielding a perfectly satisfactory labour force...because it was based on a misunderstanding of the nature of pre-industrial societies" (10). The explanation appears to give servants credit for far more social and political awareness than did the Committee (as "members of the social elite").
114. Braddick and Walter, "Introduction," 5–6; Whipp, "Labour Markets," 775–76; Woodward, *Men at Work*, 207; Richard Price, "The Labour Process," 62, 64; Carolyn Podruchny, *Making the Voyageur World* (Toronto: University of Toronto Press, 2006), 14, 134–64; compare Burley, *Servants of the Honourable Company*, 15–16.
115. Richard J. Preston, "Reflections on Territoriality," *Anthropologica*, new series, 28, no. 1–2 (1986): 16.
116. Joyce, "Work," 162–63; Withington and Shepard, introduction, 6; Wrightson, "Social Order," 194–95, 199.
117. See Braddick and Walter, "Introduction," 6; Wrightson, "Social Order," 193–94; Walter, "Public Transcripts," 124. Also see Withington and Shepard, introduction to *Communities*, 6; Griffiths, Fox, and Hindle, introduction to *The Experience of Authority*, 2; Tim Meldrum, *Domestic Service and Gender, 1660–1750* (Harlow, UK: Pearson, 2000), 4.
118. Laslett, *The World We Have Lost*, 51; *The Batchelor's Directory* (London, 1694), quoted in Vickery, *Behind Closed Doors*, 8.

119. Wrightson, "Social Order," 198–99; Fletcher and Stevenson, introduction, 2; Muldrew, "Interpreting the Market," 163. Although it lies beyond the scope of this study, it would be worthwhile to consider the role of the Homeguard Cree as neighbours in the context of, for instance, Reay, "Kinship," 87–104, or Jeremy Boulton, *Neighbourhood and Society: A London Suburb in the Seventeenth Century* (Cambridge, 1987).

2 THE HUDSON'S BAY COMPANY AS ENTERPRISE AND EMPLOYER

1. Nicholas Canny, "The Origins of Empire: An Introduction," in *The Oxford History of the British Empire*, vol. 1, ed. Nicholas Canny (Oxford: Oxford University Press, 1998), 27, 28; Michael Dove, "Plying the Northernmost Atlantic Trading Route to the New World," in *English Atlantics Revisited*, ed. Nancy L. Rhoden (Montreal: McGill-Queen's University Press, 2007), 186; Norma J. Hall, "Ocean Crossings," *Manitoba History* 71 (Winter 2013): 16–20.
2. This essentially responsive posture was also found in the EIC, where despatches sent to India "were littered with approval, criticism, or outright condemnation of actions that had already been taken in Asia." Only from 1767 onwards did EIC directors take a more proactive approach "in the form of general principles of conduct established with a view to guiding the future actions of senior officers in India." H.V. Bowen, *Business of Empire*, 196, also 183, 194–95.
3. The Newfoundland fishery underwent a similar transition from migratory to resident fishing, but the more dispersed corporate structure of that industry meant that the transition proceeded very differently than it did in Hudson Bay. See Cadigan, "Merchant Capital," 23–24.
4. Games, *Web of Empire*, 14, makes the same point in a more global context.
5. See E.L.J. Coornaert, "European Economic Institutions and the New World," in *The Cambridge Economic History of Europe*, vol. 4, ed. E.E. Rich and C.H. Wilson (Cambridge: Cambridge University Press, 1967), 240; J.H. Parry, introduction to *The Westward Enterprise*, ed. K.R. Andrews, N.P. Canny, and P.E.H. Hair (Liverpool, UK: Liverpool University Press, 1978), 5.
6. Rich, *History*, vol. 1, 62; Daniel Francis and Toby Morantz, *Partners in Furs* (Montreal and Kingston: McGill-Queen's University Press, 1983), 23. For the colonial significance of building houses, see Seed, *Ceremonies of Possession*, 17–19. S.R.H. Jones and Simon P. Ville, "Efficient Transactors or Rent-Seeking Monopolists?," *Journal of Economic History* 56, no. 4 (December 1996): 910, suggested that trading from fortified posts was inefficient and unnecessary and that the HBC's forts were poorly located for trade; for a response, see Carlos and Nicholas, "Theory and History," 917–18.
7. See Rich, *History*, vol. 1, 36–42, 52–53.
8. See Rich, *History*, vol. 1, 53–58; Mancke, *Company of Businessmen*, 15, 23–31. The text of the charter may be found at http://www.gutenberg.org/ebooks/6580.
9. Rich, *History*, vol. 1, 67, claims that "in March and April [1671?] garden seeds were sown and reaped at Charles Fort." For the cultural and imperial significance of gardens, see Seed, *Ceremonies of Possession*, 26–27, 29–30, 37.

10. Rich, *History*, vol. 1, 67; Francis and Morantz, *Partners in Furs*, 24; John Oldmixon, *The History of Hudson's-Bay* (1708), in *Documents Relating to the Early History of Hudson Bay*, ed. J.B. Tyrrell (Toronto: Champlain Society, 1931), 373, 383, 394.
11. Francis and Morantz, *Partners in Furs*, 25; Lytwyn, *Muskekowuck Athinuwick*, 126–27, 239n36. Also see Rich, *History*, vol. 1, 77; Oldmixon, *History of Hudson's-Bay*, 390–91. For some speculation on the early architecture of Moose, see Walter A. Kenyon, *The History of James Bay, 1610–1686* (Toronto: Royal Ontario Museum, 1986), 83–85.
12. Oldmixon, *History of Hudson's-Bay*, 396; Rich, *History*, vol. 1, 78–79; Morgan Lodge (Deal, Kent) to Sir Joseph Williamson, Principal Secretary of State (London), 24 September 1675, quoted in *Minutes*, 74n.
13. *Minutes, First Part*, 13, 14, 19, 22; HBC to J. Nixon (MF), 29 May 1680, *L.O. 1680–1687*, 3.
14. *Minutes, First Part*, 36, 60, 67, 69, 82–83, 107, 117, 125–26, 184, 185; E.E. Rich, ed. *Minutes of the Hudson's Bay Company, 1679–1684: Second Part, 1682–1684* (Toronto: Champlain Society for the Hudson's Bay Record Society, 1946) (hereafter cited as *Minutes, Second Part*), 52, 54, 110–11, 169–70; Alice M. Johnson, "Bayly, Charles," in *Dictionary of Canadian Biography*, ed. David M. Hayne and Francess G. Halpenny, vols. 1–5 (Toronto: University of Toronto Press, 1966–83) (hereafter cited as *DCB*), http://www.biographi.ca/en/bio/bayly_charles_1E.html; Rich, *History*, vol. 1, 76–77.
15. For detailed (and generally more encouraging) analyses of early HBC accounting, see Hugh Grant, "Bookkeeping in the Eighteenth Century," *Archivaria* 43 (Spring 1997): 143–57; and Gary Spraakman, "The Impact of Institutions on Management Accounting Changes at the Hudson's Bay Company, 1670 to 2005," *Journal of Accounting & Organizational Change* 2, no. 2 (2006): 101–22.
16. See HBC to J. Nixon (MF), 21–29 May 1680, *L.O. 1680–1687*, 5. Also see maps in E.E. Rich and A.M. Johnson, eds., *Moose Fort Journals, 1783–85* (London: Hudson's Bay Record Society, 1954), endpiece; and in Kenyon, *History of James Bay*, 12. For the early architectural history of Albany, based largely on extensive archaeological investigation, see Kenyon, 79–84.
17. For an archaeological and historical discussion of the Charlton Island depot, see Kenyon, 60–75.
18. For details on the original shareholders, see Barry M. Gough, "The 'Adventurers of England Trading into Hudson's Bay,'" *Albion* 2, no. 1 (1970): 35–47.
19. See map in Rich and Johnson, *Moose Fort Journals*, endpiece. Francis and Morantz, *Partners in Furs*, 35, 79. For details of the search for minerals, see for instance "Instructions for Cap[tai]n Antho Beale, Now goeing Governor in Hudsons Bay...," 29 May 1711, HBCA, A. 6/3, fol. 109; "Directions for Captn Beale for to Search after Mineralls," 1711, HBCA, A. 6/3, fol. 110d.
20. See Mark L. Thompson, "The Predicament of Ubi," 87; Seed, *Ceremonies of Possession*, 38, 44, 56–63.
21. Rich, *History*, vol. 1, 74–75, 77–79, 119–20.
22. For Canadien traders on the Rupert River, see Cornelius J. Jaenen, ed., *The French Regime in the Upper Country of Canada during the Seventeenth Century* (Toronto: Champlain Society, 1996), 78–79, 192–94. For the Lake Nipigon post, see Victor Lytwyn, *The Fur*

Trade of the Little North (Winnipeg, MB: Rupert's Land Research Centre, 1986), 4. Also see Arthur J. Ray, D. Wayne Moodie, and Conrad E. Heidenreich, "Rupert's Land," in *The Historical Atlas of Canada*, vol. 1 (Toronto: University of Toronto Press, 1987), plate 57.

23. For the question of Englishmen's competence in the Cree dialect in the late seventeenth and early eighteenth centuries see David H. Pentland, "Henry Kelsey's Christmas Message, 1696," in *Linguistic Studies Presented to John L. Finlay*, ed. H.C. Wolfart, Memoir 8, Algonquian and Iroquoian Linguistics (Winnipeg: University of Manitoba, 1991), 134–36.
24. HBC to H. Sergeant (Charlton Island, CI), 27 April 1683, *L.O. 1680–1687*, 75; also Joseph Robson, *An Account of Six Years Residence in Hudson's Bay* (Johnson Reprint, 1965; first published 1752 in London), appendix, 16–17. H. Sergeant (CI) to HBC, 13 September 1683, is no longer extant, though it was extracted in the proceedings of the 1749 parliamentary inquiry and in Robson (appendix, 16) and quoted in *L.O. 1680–1687*, 75n.
25. HBC to H. Sergeant (CI), 22 May 1685, *L.O. 1680–1687*, 141; also Robson, *An Account*, appendix, 17. H. Sergeant (CI) to HBC, 24 August 1685, is no longer extant, though it was extracted in the proceedings of the 1749 parliamentary inquiry and in Robson (appendix, 17), and quoted in *L.O. 1680–1687*, 141n.
26. Michael Dove, "Voyages to Rupert's Land" (unpublished paper presented to the Centre for Rupert's Land Studies Colloquium, Oxford, 2002), 2.
27. Rich, *History*, vol. 1, 113. In 1679 Charles Bayly told Louis Jolliet (who travelled overland from New France to Charles Fort) that he had sixty men in Hudson Bay (Rich, 119–20), but this was probably an exaggeration meant to mislead a potential enemy.
28. Nixon, 250.
29. Rich, *History*, vol. 1, 183.
30. HBC to H. Sergeant (MF), 16 May 1684, *L.O. 1680–1687*, 120; *Minutes, Second Part*, 256. K.G. Davies, "Nixon, John," in *DCB*, http://www.biographi.ca/en/bio/nixon_john_1E.html.
31. For Sergeant, see HBC to J. Knight (AF), 27 April 1683, *L.O. 1680–1687*, 82–83; G.E. Thorman, "Sergeant, Henry," in *DCB*, http://www.biographi.ca/en/bio/sergeant_henry_1E.html ; also see *L.O. 1680–1687*, 388–91. For Verner, see *Minutes, Second Part*, 224, 230.
32. Games, *Web of Empire*, 103–4.
33. This episode was reminiscent of other intra-European encounters in contested colonial spaces; see, for instance, Mark L. Thompson, "The Predicament of Ubi," 86–90.
34. See Jaenen, *The French Regime*, 133–41, 197–207. For Radisson's account of his 1682–83 voyage to Port Nelson for the Compagnie du Nord and of his 1684 voyage for the HBC, see Warkentin, *Pierre-Esprit Radisson*, vol. 2, 1–161. That volume also includes a briefer but somewhat different account by des Groseilliers (206–11). There is no comprehensive study of French activities on Hudson Bay, but for a brief discussion and excerpts from archival sources see Jaenen, 192–274. In Radisson's account he promised to protect the interests of all eight Frenchmen at Port Nelson in 1684 (Warkentin, vol. 2, 105, 117, 129, 155), but he only mentions engaging Chouart and his "interpreter" (presumably one who spoke English, since Chouart was allegedly fluent in Cree) to stay in the country (155). He later mentions leaving Chouart with seven men for the 1683–84 season (89), and he repeats that number in a 1697 account (226).

35. Jaenen, *The French Regime*, 221–22; Rich, *History*, vol. 1, 128, 199–200. Much of the expedition was probably financed by the Compagnie du Nord, the successor to the Compagnie de la Baie d'Hudson (sometimes even called by the same name), and backed by the same major investors.
36. For accounts of the attacks, see Jaenen, *The French Regime*, 231; W.A. Kenyon and J.R. Turnbull, *The Battle for James Bay, 1686* (Toronto: Macmillan, 1971), 68–69, 75–76, 81–82; Rich, *History*, vol. 1, 212–18.
37. Jaenen, *The French Regime*, 222; Rich, *History*, vol. 1, 220–22.
38. See Jaenen, 78; Dove, "Plying," 178–79, 199; *Minutes*, 211; *Minutes, First Part*, xviii, xix, xlii.
39. This war also extended to West Africa, where the RAC suffered at the hands of French marines and privateers, as well as from the Dutch West India Company (despite England and the Netherlands being allied against France). Hair and Law, "The English in West Africa," 258.
40. See, for instance, Davies, *Royal African Company*, 252–53.
41. See Hair and Law, "The English in West Africa," 256–57.
42. "Europeans active in the Atlantic world were very capable of offering rhetorical challenges in the language of law and jurisdiction. In such contested colonial spaces...authorized agents strongly identified themselves according to their national subjecthood—that is, according to their joint statuses as subjects and members of a people. Although these agents projected foremost their status as authorized representatives of their sovereigns, they also employed an ethnic mode of identification as members of European nations." Mark L. Thompson, "Predicament of Ubi," 87.
43. Bruce P. Lenman, "Colonial Wars and Imperial Instability, 1688–1793," in *The Oxford History of the British Empire*, vol. 2, ed. P.J. Marshall and Alaine Low (Oxford: Oxford University Press, 1998), 153.
44. HBC to G. Geyer & Council (YF), 22 May 1690, *L.O. 1688–1696*, 94. For an account of the events of the winter of 1688–89 at Albany, see the affidavit of gunsmith Solomon Nichols, 10 February 1690, *L.O. 1688–1696*, 82; also Rich, *History*, vol. 1, 238–48.
45. Jaenen, *The French Regime*, 250, 272–74; Rich, *History*, vol. 1, 238–48, 268–88, 302–5.
46. Rich, *History*, vol. 1, 302–3.
47. Rich, 302–5, 329–32; J.B. Tyrrell, ed., *Documents Relating to the Early History of Hudson Bay* (Toronto: Champlain Society, 1931), 120–21, 257.
48. For Parsons's and Adams's royal commissions, see *L.O. 1688–1696*, 183–84. For Matthew's commission from the HBC, see *L.O. 1688–1696*, 215.
49. Steele, "The Anointed," 105.
50. *L.O. 1688–1696*, 183n, 184n, 215n.
51. HBC to G. Geyer & Council (YF), 17 June 1693, *L.O. 1688–1696*, 189. For Parsons's commission as deputy governor, see *L.O. 1688–1696*, 214.
52. HBC to J. Knight (London), 17 June 1692, *L.O. 1688–1696*, 146. Although early modern labour relations have received considerable scholarly attention over the last fifty years, wages have not, "particularly the relationship of the wage to time." L.D. Schwarz, "Custom, Wages and Workload in England during Industrialization," *Past & Present* 197 (November 2007): 144. E.P. Thompson's classic article on time and work discipline

continues to exert a strong influence, but see more recent work such as Paul Glennie and Nigel Thrift, "Reworking E.P. Thompson's 'Time, Work-Discipline and Industrial Capitalism,'" *Time and Society* 5, no. 3 (October 1996): 275–99; and Voth, *Time and Work*.

53. Rich, *History*, vol. 1, 336–39.
54. Rich, 349–52.
55. For Geyer, see C. Bayly (Charles Fort, CF) to HBC, September 1678, in Robson, *An Account*, appendix, 15; HBC to G. Geyer (YF), 15 May 1686, *L.O. 1680–1687*, 174; Alice M. Johnson, "Geyer, George," in *DCB*, http://www.biographi.ca/en/bio/geyer_george_1E.html. For Knight, see *Minutes, First Part*, 30n, 180, 215; Ernest S. Dodge, "Knight, James," in *DCB*, http://www.biographi.ca/en/bio/knight_james_2E.html.
56. Rich, *History*, vol. 1, 358, 372, 379, 383, 386.
57. Rich, 376. The French had established Fort Phélipeaux in response to Cree rumours that the English were planning to set up a post there (Rich, 409).
58. J. Fullartine (AF) to HBC, 2 August 1703, HBCA, A. 11/2, fol. 6.
59. For Kelsey's frustration, see Henry Kelsey, "Memorandum of My Abode in Hudsons Bay from 1683 to 1722," in Arthur G. Doughty and Chester Martin, eds., *The Kelsey Papers* (Ottawa, ON: Public Archives of Canada and Public Record Office of Northern Ireland, 1929), 112.
60. J. Fullartine (AF) to HBC, 2 August 1703, HBCA, A. 11/2, fol. 7d; A. Beale (AF) to HBC, 23 July 1706, HBCA, A. 11/2, fol. 15; R. Staunton & Council (MF) to HBC, 17 August 1739, *Letters*, 301; A. Beale (AF) to HBC, 2 August 1714, HBCA, A. 11/2, fols. 23d–24.
61. HBC to G. Geyer & Council (YF), 21 May 1691, *L.O. 1688–1696*, 115, 116, 119, 120–21, 125.
62. For details, see HBC to G. Geyer (YF), 2 June 1688, *L.O. 1688–1696*, 9–10, 18; HBC to Captain James Young (Gravesend), 1 June 1688, *L.O. 1688–1696*, 26; Doughty and Martin, *Kelsey Papers*, 111; James F. Kenney, ed., *The Founding of Churchill, Being the Journal of Captain James Knight* (Toronto: J.M. Dent & Sons, 1932), 20–22.
63. Kenney, 119–20.
64. J. Fullartine (AF) to HBC, 2 August 1703, HBCA, A. 11/2, fol. 4d.
65. HBC to G. Geyer & Council (YF), 6 June 1689, *L.O. 1688–1696*, 79. A French attack on the company's ships that year delayed their journey to the Bay until 1690. HBC to G. Geyer & Council (YF), 6 June 1689, *L.O. 1688–1696*, 79; HBC to G. Geyer & Council (YF), 22 May 1690, *L.O. 1688–1696*, 93.
66. For reference to Dolbey's death and to his widow, Margaret, see HBCA, A. 1/143, fol. 3. For Holstead, Vicary, and Weedon, see *L.O. 1688–1696*, 79n; Rich, *History*, vol. 1, 79n, 192; HBCA, A. 1/14, fol. 15; HBC to G. Geyer & Council (YF), 17 June 1693, *L.O. 1688–1696*, 192.
67. HBC to G. Geyer & Council (YF), 22 May 1690, Robson, *An Account*, appendix, 19; G. Geyer (YF) to HBC, 8 September 1690, Robson, appendix, 19. The "Assinae-poets" are usually identified as Assiniboine, but see Barbara Belyea, "Indians, Asinepoets and Archithinues," in *A Year Inland*, ed. Belyea (Waterloo, ON: Wilfrid Laurier University Press, 2000), 343–68.
68. HBC to G. Geyer & Council (YF), 21 May 1691, *L.O. 1688–1696*, 115; Robson, *An Account*, appendix, 20. Also see G. Geyer & Council (YF) to HBC, 12 September 1691, in Robson,

appendix, 20–21. For Kelsey's wages during this period in his service, see *L.O. 1688–1696*, 382.

69. "Instructions to Capt Henry Kelsey, Govern[o]r of ye Bay & Streights of Hudson, 1718," HBCA, A. 6/4, fol. 27. These instructions were repeated in Henry Kelsey, "Coppy of Instructions to Mr Richd Staunton, Command[e]r in Cheif at Churchill River Hudsons Bay," 27 January 1719, HBCA, B. 239/b/1, fol. 8. Also see the Committee's anxiety upon hearing that a French trader and hiş slave had visited Moose and Albany in 1732–33: HBC to J. Adams & Council (AF), 10 May 1733, HBCA, A. 6/5, fol. 70; HBC to T. McCliesh Jr & Council (YF), 10 May 1733, HBCA, A. 6/5, fol. 73d; HBC to R. Norton & Council (PWF), 10 May 1733, HBCA, A. 6/5, fol. 76d; HBC to W. Bevan & Council (MF), 10 May 1733, HBCA, A. 6/5, fol. 80. The oaths in question are in YF Council Book, HBCA, B. 239/b/1, fols. 5–6; the oath to the company is transcribed in Scott P. Stephen, "Covenant Servants," *Manitoba History* 60 (Spring 2009): 15.
70. HBC to H. Kelsey (YF), private, 30 May 1718, HBCA, A. 6/4, fol. 25; HBC to R. Staunton (PWF), private, 30 May 1718, HBCA, A. 6/4, fol. 25d.
71. York Fort journal, HBCA, B.239/a/2, fol. 27d. Stuart's scanty reports of the journey depict Thanadelthur as the dominant character, with him in a supporting role. See Glyndwr Williams, "Stuart, William," in *DCB*, http://www.biographi.ca/en/bio/stuart_william_2E.html; Sylvia Van Kirk, "Thanadelthur," *The Beaver* (Spring 1974): 40–45; Patricia A. McCormack, "The Many Faces of Thanadelthur," in *Reading Beyond Words*, 2nd ed., ed. Jennifer S.H. Brown and Elizabeth Vibert (Peterborough, ON: Broadview Press, 2003), 329–64. Lytwyn, *Muskekowuck Athinuwick* (71–72), assigned the leading role to the leader of the Lowland Cree of the lower Hayes River (known in HBC documents simply as "the Captain of the River"), whom Knight had chosen to head the expedition.
72. For the trading post, see *Letters*, 64n; Kenney, *Founding of Churchill*, 71. For Norton, see *Letters*, li–liv; Alice M. Johnson, "Norton, Richard," in *DCB*, http://www.biographi.ca/en/bio/norton_richard_3E.html. Exactly where and how far Norton travelled is unknown. Captain William Coats (Norton's brother-in-law) later recorded that, "as he was very young and unqualified for any great matter, I did not find anything remained on his memory, but the danger and terrour he underwent; but to the day of his death he had an affectionate kindness for that people [the Dene]." John Barrow, ed., *The Geography of Hudson's Bay* (London: Hakluyt Society, 1852), 32.
73. HBC to R. Staunton (PWF), 4 June 1719, in Robson, *An Account*, appendix, 26.
74. Trade figures for 1697–1740 can be found in *Letters*, 349–50. Thomas McCliesh Jr believed that Churchill's trade would never justify its expense "by reason most of the fur trade is only a robbing of this place [York]," doubted the presence of copper north of the Churchill River, and cast aspersions on the men prosecuting the white whale fishery near the river's mouth. T. McCliesh Jr (YF) to HBC, 23 August 1723, *Letters*, 94. Notwithstanding some disappointing returns, Prince of Wales Fort became an independent factory in 1731. HBC to T. McCliesh & Council (YF), 20 May 1731, HBCA, A. 6/5, fol. 50.
75. R. Norton (PWF) to HBC, 16 August 1733, *Letters*, 186.

76. W. Bevan & Council (MF) to HBC, 20 August 1734, *Letters*, 197–98. The Committee increased Moose's complement to twenty-eight but then promptly reduced it to twenty-four. HBC to W. Bevan & Council (MF), 2 May 1735, HBCA, A. 6/5, fol. 99d; HBC to W. Bevan & Council (MF), 6 May 1736, HBCA, A. 6/5, fol. 112.

77. J. Isbister (AF) to HBC, 18 August 1743, HBCA, A. 11/2, fol. 116d. Albany's complement had been as high as thirty-six in 1735, when the Committee reduced it to thirty-three: "Orders and Instructions to Captn Thomas Macklish or the Chief and Councill at Albany Fort," 6 May 1736, HBCA, A. 6/5, fol. 105d.

78. The stone fort at Churchill has generated some debate among historians, but see Dove, "Plying," 190–92.

79. HBC to R. Norton & Council (PWF), 10 May 1733, HBCA, A. 6/5, fols. 76–76d. Dove, "Plying," questions the Committee's claims to "very great Charge & Expense" and argues that Robson's estimated cost of no more than £8,000 was probably nearer the mark than the £30,000–40,000 figure that was provided for the parliamentary inquiry: "Evidently, the company was not required to submit its ledger books to the inquiry, for they did not support the company's claims of cost overruns. Rather, the figures tended to support Robson's estimate since there was no noticeable jump in spending on Prince of Wales Fort compared with the other posts in the bay and since there were very few entries relating to anything apart from what could be deemed normal operating expenses" (191).

80. R. Norton (PWF) to HBC, 16 August 1733, *Letters*, 186. Compare the difficulties experienced by factors trying to please the Committee regarding construction (or reconstruction) and renovation projects, to estate stewards trying to please absentee landlords who were rebuilding their manor houses; see Hainsworth, *Stewards*, 236–50.

81. R. Norton (PWF) to HBC, 17 August 1736, *Letters*, 213–14.

82. Minutes of a Council at Prince of Wales Fort, 6 August 1738, *Letters*, 253n, 254n.

83. Rich, *History*, vol. 1, 503–5.

84. See map in Rich and Johnson, *Moose Fort Journals*, endpiece.

85. J. Adams (AF) to HBC, 28 August 1730, HBCA, A. 11/2, fol. 68d; J. Adams (AF) to HBC, 14 August 1732, HBCA, A. 11/2, fol. 73d; Rich, *History*, vol. 1, 505–6.

86. "Orders and Instructions to Captn Thomas Macklish or the Chief and Councill at Albany Fort," 6 May 1736, HBCA, A. 6/5, fols. 106–106d. Also see *Letters*, 215n. Moose was causing the Committee some concern before that: when Thomas McCliesh returned to Hudson Bay as governor in 1735, he was to reside at Albany but was also to have direct authority over Moose as well. HBC to W. Bevan & Council (MF), 2 May 1735, HBCA, A. 6/5, fol. 99d. Richard Staunton was also given command over both Albany and Moose in 1737 but resided at the latter factory so that he could be on hand to "reform" it.

87. W. Bevan & Council (MF) to HBC, 26 August 1736, *Letters*, 218.

88. HBC to W. Bevan (MF), private, 6 May 1736, HBCA, A. 6/5, fol. 113d. "Orders & Instructions to Mr Richd Staunton Chief and the Council at Moose River Fort," 20 May 1737, HBCA, A. 6/5, fol. 120d.

89. "Orders & Instructions to Mr Richd Staunton Chief and the Council at Moose River Fort," 20 May 1737, HBCA, A. 6/5, fols. 120d–121d.

90. T. McCliesh Jr (YF) to HBC, 17 August 1732, *Letters*, 168–69; HBC to T. McCliesh Jr & Council (YF), 10 May 1733, HBCA, A. 6/5, fol. 72.

91. J. Isbister (AF) to J. Duffield (MF), 9 May 1743, HBCA, B. 3/b/1, fol. 20d. Also see Albany Fort journal, 6 May–1 June 1743, HBCA, B. 3/a/34, fols. 36d–42.

92. "A Book of Instructions with the Standard of Trade for Henly House in the Year of our Lord 1751 William Lamb Master," HBCA, A. 11/3, fol. 12; also see John A. Alwin, "The Uncelebrated Boats of the Albany," *The Beaver* 305, no. 4 (Spring 1975): 51.

93. J. Isbister & Council (AF) to HBC, 23 August 1744, HBCA, A. 11/2, fol. 121. He settled for a three-year contract at £30 (rather than the £40 or £50 usually paid to sloop masters). J. Isbister & Council (AF) to HBC, 2 August 1745, HBCA, A. 11/2, fol. 124d. Also see G.E. Thorman, "Isbister, William," in *DCB*, http://www.biographi.ca/en/bio/isbister_william_3E.html.

94. HBC to J. Isbister & Council (AF), 27 May 1755, HBCA, A. 6/9, fol. 4d.

95. Albany Fort journal, 6 March 1755, HBCA, B. 3/a/47, fol. 22. The most complete discussion of the 1754 attack and its consequences is in Charles A. Bishop, "The Henley House Massacres," *The Beaver* 307, no. 2 (Autumn 1976): 36–41.

96. Albany Fort journal, 8 March 1755, HBCA, B. 3/a/47, fols. 25–25d; Howard Robert Baker II, "Law Transplanted, Justice Invented" (master's thesis, University of Manitoba, 1996), 62.

97. "The Examination and Confession of Wappasiss Alias Woudby and his two sons Shanap and Young Snuff ye Blanket when taken by Mr Joseph Isbister Mr Geo Rushworth John Fairfould [Fairfowl] and in the presence of Twenty One Men belonging to Albany Fort June ye 7th Anno 1755..." HBCA, A. 11/2, fols. 165–66. Albany Fort Council, 12 June 1755, HBCA, A. 11/2, fols. 167–167d. For a discussion of the trial from a legal point of view, see Nigol, "Discipline and Discretion," 176–78.

98. H. Pollexfen (MF) to J. Isbister (AF), 18 June 1755, HBCA, A. 11/2, fol. 171. Also see J. Isbister (AF) to J. Isham (YF), 20 March 1756, HBCA, B. 239/b/14, fols. 3d–4; J. Isbister (AF) to J. Isham (YF), 6 June 1756, HBCA, B. 239/b/14, fols. 5d–6; J. Isham (YF) to J. Isbister (AF), 25 July 1756, HBCA, B. 239/b/14, fol. 8.

99. HBC to J. Isbister & Council (AF), 12 May 1756, HBCA, A. 6/9, fol. 29d; HBC to J. Isbister (AF), 12 May 1756, HBCA, A. 5/1, fol. 13d.

100. Jörg Fisch, "Law as a Means and as an End," in *European Expansion and Law*, ed. W.J. Mommson and J.A. De Moor (Oxford, 1992), 21, quoted in Greene, "Empire and Identity," 221.

101. Albany post journal, 3, 7, 12, and 21 June 1755, HBCA, B. 3/a/47. Also see Baker, "Law Transplanted," 64–65; Nigol, "Discipline and Discretion," 176–78; Nigol, "Discipline, Discretion, and Control," 113–54.

102. Despite their charter, the company never had much luck prosecuting interlopers in Britain—a result largely of the post-1688 parliamentary opposition to royal monopolies such as the HBC's. Nevertheless, the HBC's anxiety about interlopers was never matched by much actual threat: we can count on one hand the number of interloping expeditions that successfully made it to Hudson Bay and back during the first hundred years or so. In contrast, the Africa trade was so porous as to undermine the viability of the chartered companies' alleged monopolies. Richardson, "Atlantic Slave Trade," observed: "The scale

of interloping is naturally difficult to quantify and has been the subject of some debate. However, the most careful investigation of the issue has suggested that, at the peak of the Royal African Company's involvement in the slave trade in 1674–86, perhaps one in four of the slaves reaching English America arrived illegally. Moreover, from the mid-1680s the Royal African Company, like its predecessor, the Royal Adventurers, began licensing others to enter the trade" (445), presaging the English government's 1698 decision to open the African trade to all British and colonial merchants upon payment to the RAC of a 10 per cent duty on exports to Africa.

103. Stephen, "Assistant to York," 9–21. In 1755 the Committee—declaring itself "determined to Encourage everything that hath the least shadow of Encreasing the Companys Trade to Advantage and protecting the Rights and priviledges of the English Nation"—also gave Isham permission to send "a sufficient Number of your people...that you shall judge fittest for that purpose" to build a log tent at the "Lower Fork" of the Nelson River, but nothing seems to have come of it. HBC to J. Isham & Council (YF), 27 May 1755, HBCA, A. 6/9, fol. 10d.
104. Richard Beech, Richard Parry, and Humphrey Parry (RF) to HBC, 28 August 1749, HBCA, A. 11/57, fol. 4; J. Potts & Council (RF) to HBC, 15 August 1751, HBCA, A. 11/57, fols. 10, 12. There may have been more than one active mine in the Little Whale River area; see J. Potts & Council (RF) to HBC, 3 September 1750, HBCA, A. 11/57, fol. 7d. HBC to J. Potts & Council (RF), 27 May 1755, HBCA, A. 6/9, fol. 2, referred to summertime trading at Whale River House and at "Longlands Harbour."
105. The most complete discussion of Richmond Fort is in Francis and Morantz, *Partners in Furs*, 65–78.
106. F. Jacobs (YF) to HBC, 20 August 1768, HBCA, A.11/115, fols. 116–116d. See also Glyndwr Williams, *Graham's Observations*, lxiv–lxv, 268n.
107. Glyndwr Williams, lxv.
108. HBC to F. Jacobs (YF), [date?], HBCA, A.6/11, fol. 58d. Also see Rich, *History*, vol. 2, 22; Glyndwr Williams, *Graham's Observations*, lxv–lxvi. In any event, Jacobs had no man fit to command such an undertaking in 1770.
109. A post on Lake Winnipeg or Red River, Graham argued, would drive off interlopers but would drain away the trade from the Bayside factories and would be difficult to supply; a post on the Saskatchewan River might bring in the trade of the Assiniboine and Earchithinues, but problems of transport would make it impractical. Glyndwr Williams, *Graham's Observations*, 260–61, 266. Graham's discussions of inland settlement (both for and against) were often reminiscent of those of his mentor, Isham.
110. Andrew Graham, *Observations on Hudson's Bay*, 1768–1769, HBCA, E. 2/5, fols. 16–16d; also see Glyndwr Williams, *Graham's Observations*, 260.
111. Glyndwr Williams, 264.
112. HBCA, E. 2/5, fol. 16d; Glyndwr Williams, *Graham's Observations*, 269, 270.
113. See HBC to F. Jacobs (YF), private, 12 May 1773, HBCA, A. 6/11, fols. 173d–174.
114. See Rich and Johnson, *Moose Fort Journals*, 334–37; also Francis and Morantz, *Partners in Furs*, 79–81, 101–2. For a brief history of Rupert House, see Rich and Johnson, 344–46.
115. HBC to F. Jacobs (YF), private, 28 May 1773, HBCA, A. 5/1, fol. 149.

116. Michael B. Payne, "Daily Life on Western Hudson Bay, 1714 to 1870" (PHD diss., Carleton University, 1989), 46; *CHJ First Series*, lxxx.

117. For the changing size of the factory's complement, see Payne, "Daily Life," 48. For the black-whale fishery, see HBCA, A. 1/42, fols. 167–167d.

118. For a discussion of the French attacks, see Glyndwr Williams, ed., *Hudson's Bay Miscellany, 1670–1870* (Winnipeg, MB: Hudson's Bay Record Society, 1975), 77–94.

119. See Rich and Johnson, *Moose Fort Journals*, xiv–xvii.

120. Hudson House journal, 22 October 1781, *CHJ Second Series*, 262.

121. William Tomison "received the Disagreeable News of that Devouring Disorder the small pox rageing amongst the Natives, & is carrying all off before It, wherever it Comes & God knowes what will be the End thereof." Cumberland House journal, 17 December 1781, *CHJ Second Series*, 225.

122. Cumberland House journal, 22 January and 1 February 1782, *CHJ Second Series*, 232, 234. Also see Hudson House journal, 9 and 27 November 1781, *CHJ Second Series*, 265, 267.

123. *CHJ Second Series*, lxi; also W. Tomison (CH) to W. Walker (Hudson House), 19 February 1782, *CHJ Second Series*, 237–39. Hudson House journal, 29 November 1781, *CHJ Second Series*, 268.

124. "Minutes of Council held upon the affairs of the Honorable Hudsons Bay Company occasioned by the Unfortunate Capture and Destruction of Prince of Wales & York Forts... at Albany Fort," March 1783, HBCA, A. 11/4, fols. 178–85, quoted in Rich and Johnson, *Moose Fort Journals*, xv–xvii.

125. The post-Utrecht period also differs from the preceding half-century in the availability of records. Although no new kinds of records were created (except perhaps the officers' and servants' ledgers), the increased number of posts resulted in an increased volume of paperwork, and the survival rate for documents of all kinds is much higher. Most of the post journals and all of the officers' and servants' ledgers that have survived date from after 1715.

126. Robson, *An Account*, 6. Also see Dove, "Plying," 175–77.

3 "NO CERTAIN METHOD FOR ANY THING"

1. See Marcus Rediker, *Between the Devil and the Deep Blue Sea* (Cambridge: Cambridge University Press, 1987), 82. *Minutes*, 34.
2. HBC to G. Geyer & Council (YF), 3 June 1687, *L.O. 1680–1687*, 235.
3. HBC to J. Nixon (MF), 29 May 1680, *L.O. 1680–1687*, 8.
4. Nixon, 249. Alternatively, Nixon could have meant gunsmith and edge-tool maker Thomas Wilkinson, who also returned from the Bay in 1681 (see *Minutes, First Part*, 151, 152; HBCA, A. 15/2, fol. 7d).
5. Knight had been a shareholder since 1692 and sat on the Committee from 1700 through 1714. John Fullartine also served on the Committee after retiring from the command of Albany in 1711. Williams, *Miscellany*, 10n.
6. He was also given £30 for paying wage advances to new recruits and to men staying in the country (*Minutes*, 107, 110). Maud M. Hutcheson, "Lydall, William," in *DCB*, http://www.biographi.ca/en/bio/lydall_william_1E.html. Chaudhuri, 77.

7. *Minutes*, 34, 81, 100; *Minutes, First Part*, 338; *Minutes, Second Part*, 213–14; Rich, *History*, vol. 1, 310. For ship's crews, see *Minutes*, 39.

8. Games, *Web of Empire*, 94. Games also noted the EIC's distrust of prospective factors who "had lived outside of England for such extended periods that their fidelity to England might be called into question....[A] lengthy sojourn abroad...made Company members worry about complex personal ties that embedded traders in foreign and rival nations" (95).

9. Nixon, 249.

10. *Minutes*, 24, 42, 88; *Minutes, First Part*, 42, 62.

11. For a more complete discussion of Bayly's life before and during his service in Hudson Bay, see Alice M. Johnson, "Bayly," in *DCB*, vol. 1, 81–84. Also see *Minutes*, li–lvii; Rich, *History*, vol. 1, 65; Mancke, *Company of Businessmen*, 16.

12. Johnson, "Bayly," 82. Although the Society of Friends discouraged its members from engaging in high-risk business ventures, several Quaker families were involved in long-distance trading; see Jacob M. Price, "The Great Quaker Business Families of Eighteenth-Century London," in *The World of William Penn*, ed. R.S. Dunn and M.M. Dunn (Philadelphia: University of Pennsylvania Press, 1986), 363–99.

13. Nixon, 277–78. Also see Rich, *History*, vol. 1, 76–77, 80–81; *Minutes*, 81.

14. Lacombe, "Gentlemen of Fashion," 673.

15. Games, *Web of Empire*, notes that when the EIC selected its first ambassador to the Mughal emperor in 1614, it sought "an Embassadour of extraordinarye Countenance and respect" and chose Sir Thomas Roe, as being a man "of a pregnant understandinge, well spooken, learned, industrious, and of a comelie personage" (154). Roe had no previous mercantile experience but was well connected, had been one of the Royal Council for Virginia, had explored in Brazil, and was later the Levant Company's ambassador in Istanbul.

16. If this was indeed the case, it would contrast with the experience and knowledge that English landlords generally looked for in prospective stewards; see Hainsworth, *Stewards*, 23–24, 27, 29.

17. Mancke, *Company of Businessmen*, 16; John E. Foster, "The Indian-Trader," 576.

18. Nixon, 244–45, 262, 270. Nor was this necessarily confined to the company's early years. In 1755 Joseph Isbister apologized for allowing the supply ship to leave Albany for Moose before it had unloaded all the cargo, "but must remark that when your Captains are In these parts [they] will hardly admit of any Controll but do as they themselves think fit." J. Isbister (AF) to HBC, private, 14 September 1755, HBCA, A. 11/2, fol. 175.

19. Lacombe, "Gentlemen of Fashion," 672.

20. Games, *Web of Empire*, 151, 157.

21. *Minutes*, 108–9; *Minutes, Second Part*, 144. HBC to J. Knight & Council (YF), 31 May 1717, HBCA, A. 6/4, fol. 12d.

22. For Phipps, see HBCA, A. 15/2, fol. 13d; Rich, *History*, vol. 1, 95; *Minutes, First Part*, 165, 174; *L.O. 1680–1687*, 385; Maud M. Hutcheson, "Phipps, Thomas," in *DCB*, http://www.biographi.ca/en/bio/phipps_thomas_1E.html. For Walker, see *Minutes, Second Part*, 83, 83n.

23. *Minutes*, 30, 42, 74, also 100; *Minutes, First Part*, 48; *Minutes, Second Part*, 243.
24. *Minutes, Second Part*, 223.
25. HBCA, A. 1/8, fol. 34d.
26. HBC to J. Nixon (MF), 29 May 1680, *L.O. 1680–1687*, 10.
27. *Minutes, Second Part*, 59. Recall Lord Burghley's advice to his son Robert a century earlier: "Be sure to keep some great man your friend, but trouble him not for trifles. Compliment him often with many, yet small, gifts, and of little charge." Heal, "Food Gifts," 66–67.
28. HBC to J. Nixon (MF), 24 July 1682, *L.O. 1680–1687*, 58–59; HBC to H. Sergeant (MF), 27 April 1683, *L.O. 1680–1687*, 78; HBC to H. Sergeant, 22 May 1685 (AF), *L.O. 1680–1687*, 144; HBC to T. Phipps (YF), 20 May 1686, *L.O. 1680–1687*, 191–94. Compare Phipps Sr to isolated examples of EIC directors engaging in illicit private trade: H.V. Bowen, *Business of Empire*, 123–24.
29. Warkentin, *Pierre-Esprit Radisson*, vol. 2, 151.
30. HBC to J. Knight (AF), 27 April 1683, *L.O. 1680–1687*, 82, 83. No evidence has been found that he actually held HBC stock; *L.O. 1680–1687*, 388.
31. HBC to H. Sergeant (AF), 20 May 1686, *L.O. 1680–1687*, 184–87.
32. See *Minutes, Second Part*, 63, 68, 114, 134, 135, 255. Similarly, brassier Daniel Kingston, who frequently supplied the company with kettles in the 1680s, was attorney for Bayside governors George Geyer (in 1688) and James Knight (in 1683 and 1694). HBC to G. Geyer (YF), 2 June 1688, *L.O. 1688–1696*, 21; *Minutes, Second Part*, 3, 98, 168, 176, 180, 208, 228; HBC to J. Knight (AF), 30 May 1694, *L.O. 1688–1696*, 241.
33. *Minutes, First Part*, 184; HBC to G. Geyer & Council (Port Nelson), 21 May 1691, *L.O. 1688–1696*, 123–24.
34. *Minutes, Second Part*, 242.
35. For James's engagement, see *Minutes, First Part*, 211–12; for Henry, see *Minutes, First Part*, 184, and *Second Part*, 2.
36. For the Savages, see HBCA, A. 14/2, fol. 86d; HBCA, A. 14/3, fols. 82d–83, 106d–107, 108d–109; HBCA, A. 15/1, fols. 12d, 13d, 15d, 27–27d; *Minutes, First Part*, 26–27. For the payment to Patrick Savage for recruiting men, see HBCA, A. 15/1, fol. 13d. For the Fullartines, see HBCA, B. 3/d/5, fols. 7d–8; HBCA, B. 3/d/7, fols. 6d–7; HBCA, B. 3/a/2, fol. 2.
37. *Minutes, Second Part*, 223n, 228. Joshua Allen was bookkeeper at Albany from 1682 to 1685; for family connection, see HBCA, A. 15/3, fol. 152. Joshua was actually a pewterer from London (*Minutes, First Part*, 219) and may also have been related to London blacksmith Christopher Allen, who was engaged for four years in 1684 (*Minutes, Second Part*, 245).
38. See Tim Leunig, Chris Munns, and Patrick Wallis, "Networks in the Premodern Economy," *Journal of Economic History* 71, no. 2 (June 2011): 413–43.
39. Woodward, *Men at Work*, 116; Joan Lane, *Apprenticeship in England, 1600–1914* (Boulder, CO: Westview Press, 1996), 10; Ben-Amos, *Adolescence and Youth*, 158–60. For alehouses, see Clark, "Migrants in the City," 280–81.
40. By about 1698 the Office for Servants in Fleet Street was publishing the weekly *Servants' Guide*, listing vacant situations (Clark, "Migrants in the City," 285). For statute sessions and their declining role in the early eighteenth century, see Kussmaul, *Servants in Husbandry*, 59–61.

41. See, for example, *Minutes*, 27, 33.

42. For the reimbursement, see *Minutes, Second Part*, 93, 106. For Verner standing security, see *Minutes, Second Part*, 102, 104. The one-pound advance paid to James St. Clare (Sinclare) was deducted from Verner's account when Sinclare deserted before sailing for Hudson Bay: *Minutes, Second Part*, 109. This was just one small example of how necessary it was to maintain and manage the flow of cash and credit, "to lubricate the flows of production, distribution, and exchange across the time spans and distances involved in transcontinental commerce" (O'Brien, "Inseparable Connections," 61).

43. For 1684, see *Minutes, Second Part*, 203. For 1691, see HBCA, A.15/3, fol. 184; HBCA, A. 1/13, fol. 10d.

44. For Bringhurst, see HBCA, A. 15/3, fol. 185. For Thoyts, see HBCA, A. 1/27, fol. 17d; HBCA, A. 14/5, fol. 200; HBC to J. Fullartine & Council (AF), 29 May 1710, HBCA, A. 6/3, fol. 100; Williams, *Miscellany*, 15n. For potentially comparable cases in England, see two seventeenth-century examples of Lincoln Cathedral paying to get tradesmen out of prison to work on the church; Woodward, *Men at Work*, 146.

45. HBCA, A. 1/15, fol. 9d.

46. HBCA, A. 1/15, fols. 11d, 12d, 23d; also Rich, *History*, vol. 1, 146, 157.

47. *Minutes, First Part*, 199.

48. Games, *Web of Empire*, 98.

49. HBC to Morgan Lodge (Gravesend), 16 May 1684, *L.O. 1680–1687*, 110. For Lodge as the company's inspection agent, see *L.O. 1680–1687*, 66, 98, 102, 110, 153, 203, 303.

50. "Sailing Orders & Instructions to Capt Richard Ward," 29 May 1711, HBCA, A. 6/3, fol. 111d.

51. Rediker, *Deep Blue Sea*, 24.

52. Jeremy Boulton, "Wage Labour in Seventeenth-Century London," *Economic History Review* 49, no. 2 (1996): 269. Also see Schwarz, *London*, 34.

53. Boulton, "Wage Labour," 287; Elizabeth W. Gilboy, *Wages in Eighteenth Century England* (Cambridge, MA: Harvard University Press, 1934), 222–24; Woodward, *Men at Work*, 177; Nixon, 256, 278, 280.

54. Nixon, 251.

55. Gilboy, *Wages*, 5, 21. This image is being challenged by recent studies of time and labour in early modern England: see, for instance, Voth, *Time and Work*; also Wrightson, *Earthly Necessities*, 321–22.

56. Other parishes directly on the riverside or directly involved with the port of London included St. Katherine Tower, St. George's-in-the-East, St. John Horsleydown, Ratcliffe, Bermondsey, Shadwell, and Poplar and Blackwall (Schwarz, *London*, 9n). The quintessential maritime London parish was Stepney: according to Cheryl Fury, "Elizabethan Seamen," *International Journal of Maritime History* 10 (1998), "in Stepney almost all parish officials were shipmasters or prominent shipwrights," and the vestry book "reads like a 'who's who' of London's maritime elite" between 1579 and 1662 (33). Michael Grimington, prominent in the HBC's maritime service in the generation after 1680, was from Stepney, as were some lesser lights in the land service.

57. See, for instance, Horn, "Tobacco Colonies," 177.

58. Ben-Amos, *Adolescence and Youth*, 97.

59. Domestic servants in London were chiefly supplied from the surrounding rural areas because London servants had acquired such ill repute; they were allegedly "wanton in habit and unscrupulous in practice. Moreover, urban living was supposed to have given them a sophistication characterized by a highly insubordinate spirit and an exceptionally self-interested attitude." Hecht, *Domestic Servant Class*, 9, 11.
60. Peter Burke, "Popular Culture in Seventeenth-Century London," in *Popular Culture in Seventeenth-Century England*, ed. Barry Reay (London: Croom Helm, 1985), 33; Mark S.R. Jenner and Paul Griffiths, introduction to *Londinopolis* (Manchester, UK: Manchester University Press, 2000), 2; Roy Porter, *England in the Eighteenth Century* (London: Folio Society, 1998), 40; Maxine Berg, *The Age of Manufactures* (London: Fontana, 1985), 94.
61. Burke, "Popular Culture," 38, 53. John Rule, *Labouring Classes*, cautioned against assuming "that even the first generation of an urban industrial proletariat was completely uprooted from anything which carried traditional community norms and values" (156–57). Also see Jenner and Griffiths, *Londinopolis*, 2–3.
62. John Wareing, "Changes in the Geographical Distribution of the Recruitment of Apprentices to the London Companies, 1486–1750," *Journal of Historical Geography* 6, no. 3 (July 1980): 242–46; Jeremy Boulton, "Neighbourhood Migration in Early Modern London," in *Migration and Society in Early Modern England*, ed. Peter Clark and David Souden (Totowa, NJ: Barnes & Noble, 1987), 113; Burke, "Popular Culture," 37; Bailyn, introduction, 2.
63. Nixon, 244, 245, 249, 256.
64. Hainsworth, *Stewards*, 51–59.
65. Nixon, 272. It is not clear from the surviving documents of this period whether anyone actually did that.
66. Nixon, 251.
67. Nixon, 277–78.
68. Warkentin, *Pierre-Esprit Radisson*, vol. 2, 151.
69. Nixon, 280. As Nixon suggested, early modern Scotland was highly oriented toward out-migration. T.C. Smout, N.C. Landsman, and T.M. Devine, "Scottish Emigration in the Seventeenth and Eighteenth Centuries," in *Europeans on the Move*, ed. Nicholas Canny (Oxford: Clarendon Press, 1994), 76, 111–12. However, considerably less research has been done on internal and outward population movements in Scotland than in England; Whyte, "Migration," 87.
70. "Among so mobile a population [as the Scots], it is difficult not only to trace Scots, but even to define who they were." Smout, Landsman, and Devine, "Scottish Emigration," 99.
71. For Verner, see Alice M. Johnson, "Verner, Hugh," in *DCB*, http://www.biographi.ca/en/bio/verner_hugh_1E.html. For Anderson and Baine, who were assigned to the *Craven* (Capt. William Bond), see *Minutes, First Part*, 203. Baine died in service, and in December 1683 his wages were paid to his administrator, Samuel Nordon; *Minutes, Second Part*, 166, 173.
72. Brown, *Strangers in Blood*, 26; *Minutes, Second Part*, 86, 88, 90–91, 109.

73. John Crooks was from Prestonpans, and James Swan and David Cleney may have been from there as well (the entry in the minute book is vague); John Pearson was from "Feith" [Leith?]. *Minutes, Second Part*, 203, 234.

74. Clark, "Migrants in the City," 273–74.

75. HBC to J. Bridgar (MF), 20 May 1686, *L.O. 1680–1687*, 176–77.

76. HBC to J. Marsh & Council (AF), 6 June 1689, *L.O. 1688–1696*, 53–54. The Royal African Company faced a similar but more serious problem around this time; see Davies, *Royal African Company*, 253.

77. HBCA, A. 1/18, fol. 15d. His services as a gunner were not required that year, and he did not return to Hudson Bay until 1698, serving at Albany and on the *Hudson's Bay* until 1706.

78. See HBCA, A. 1/15, fols. 9–10d.

79. HBCA, A. 1/15, fols. 17d, 21, 22. Also see Rich, *History*, vol. 1, 336, 370.

80. Rich, *History*, vol. 1, 381. Crimps were agents who traded in recruits for the armed forces or merchant vessels; see Rediker, *Deep Blue Sea*, 81.

81. The first regular recruiting agent employed by the HBC in Stromness was merchant David Geddes, in 1791; Alexander Fenton, *The Northern Isles* (Edinburgh: John Donald, 1978), 596. For a discussion of HBC recruiting agents, see Burley, *Servants*, 80–88.

82. HBC to G. Geyer & Council (YF), 6 June 1689, *L.O. 1688–1696*, 79.

83. HBC to T. McCliesh Jr & Council (AF), 1719 and 1 June 1720, HBCA, A. 6/4, fols. 34, 42; St. Mary's Church (Woodford, Essex) vestry minutes, Essex Record Office, D/P, 167/8/1, 87, quoted in *Letters*, 33n. For Henson (or Hinson), see *Letters*, 76n. For Nicholson's residence and participation in the parish, see HBCA Biographical Sheet, "Nicholson, John," http://www.gov.mb.ca/chc/archives/HBCA/biographical/n/nicholson_john.pdf.

84. HBCA, B. 3/d/11, fol. 14d; "A Coppy of a Counsel Hold at Albany Fort Sepbr ye 1st 1701," HBCA, A. 11/2, fol. 1. Isbister was the first of at least fourteen Isbisters who served the company between 1700 and 1770, most of them sailors or mariners. Also see John Nicks, "Orkneymen in the HBC, 1780–1821," in *Old Trails and New Directions*, ed. Carol M. Judd and Arthur J. Ray (Toronto: University of Toronto Press, 1980), 123–24; Fenton, *Northern Isles*, 596. John Nicks's work remains the most detailed study of Orkneymen in the HBC. Of 121 servants from the parish of Orphir on the main island (Mainland) of Orkney (1780–1821), Nicks was able to link 95 with their baptismal entries, a success rate impossible for any earlier period.

85. Rich, *History*, vol. 1, 377; A. Beale (AF) to HBC, 1 August 1712, *Letters*, 22; HBCA, B. 3/d/21, fols. 55d–58; A. Beale (AF) to HBC, 2 August 1714, HBCA, A. 11/2, fols. 23d–24.

86. For the Russian suggestion, see Rich, *History*, vol. 1, 181. For Lichtenberger, see Francis and Morantz, *Partners in Furs*, 35; also A. Beale (AF) to HBC, 1 August 1712, HBCA, A. 11/2, fol. 19.

87. Rich, *History*, vol. 1, 542; Rediker, *Deep Blue Sea*, 31; Lane, *Apprenticeship*, 83, 88–89; Kussmaul, *Servants*, 166–67; Pelling, "Apprenticeship," 35–36.

88. HBC to G. Geyer & Council (YF), 21 May 1691, *L.O. 1688–1696*, 123.

89. HBC to G. Geyer & Council (YF), 17 June 1692, *L.O. 1688–1696*, 141.

90. Rediker, *Deep Blue Sea*, 32.

91. Baker, "Law Transplanted," compares wartime HBC discipline to military discipline and distinguishes between trials conducted by James Knight during wartime, in which he proceeded "along court-martial procedural lines," and a trial conducted by Knight after the peace of Utrecht, in which he clearly tried to portray his proceedings "as in accord with common law principles" (46–48, 60). However, Baker stressed that the social order of HBC posts, "despite its military cloak" during the 1686–1714 period, "remained fundamentally a social order modelled after the English household" (59).

92. HBC to J. Marsh & Council (AF), 6 June 1689, *L.O. 1688–1696*, 54. For factors complaining about exorbitant wages, see "A Coppy of a Counsel Hold at Albany Fort Sepbr ye 1st 1701," HBCA, A. 11/2, fols. 1–1d; J. Fullartine (AF) to HBC, 2 August 1703, HBCA, A. 11/2, fols. 3–3d; "A Councell Call'd [at Albany] this 11th of Sepr 1705," HBCA, A. 11/2, fol. 9; "A Councell Called the 20th of July 1706," HBCA, A. 11/2, fol. 12; A. Beale (AF) to HBC, 23 July 1706, HBCA, A. 11/2, fol. 15.

93. HBC to J. Knight & Council (AF), 17 June 1693, *L.O. 1688–1696*, 203–4; Thomson, *History of Orkney*, 186.

94. HBC to G. Geyer & Council (YF), 22 May 1690, *L.O. 1688–1696*, 97. For the *Northwest Fox*, see *L.O. 1688–1696*, 16n. In general, men contemplating an Atlantic crossing may have been concerned more about privateers than about warships: French privateers were plundering places in Orkney and Shetland in the 1690s. Thomson, *History of Orkney*, 186.

95. See, for example, the complaint: "First that the warr in Europe makes every thing deare both for trading goods & provisions Next the Warr occasions us to come with greater ships & three times the number of men." HBC to J. Knight & Council (AF), 17 June 1693, *L.O. 1688–1696*, 205.

96. HBC to J. Knight & Council (AF), 30 May 1694, *L.O. 1688–1696*, 230; the same letter later referred to these young men as "stout lusty hands" (232). Knight apparently approved of the 1694 recruits; see HBC to J. Knight & Council (AF), 30 May 1696, *L.O. 1688–1696*, 273.

97. J. Fullartine (AF) to HBC, 2 August 1703, HBCA, A. 11/2, fols. 3–3d; "A Councell Call'd this 11th of Sepr 1705," HBCA, A. 11/2, fol. 9; A. Beale (AF) to HBC, 10 September 1712, HBCA, A. 11/2, fol. 21.

98. In May 1681 the Committee sought a Royal Navy convoy for the company's supply ships; England was not at war, but pirates from the Mediterranean were a palpable threat. *Minutes, First Part*, 80n, 120, 120n.

99. HBC to G. Geyer & Council (YF), 2 June 1688, *L.O. 1688–1696*, 16.

100. HBC to G. Geyer & Council (YF), 22 May 1690, *L.O. 1688–1696*, 100. For Port Nelson's complement, see *L.O. 1688–1696*, xvii.

101. HBC to G. Geyer & Council (YF), 22 May 1690, *L.O. 1688–1696*, 102–3.

102. HBC to G. Geyer & Council (YF), 22 May 1690, *L.O. 1688–1696*, 100, 103.

103. HBC to G. Geyer & Council (YF), 21 May 1691, *L.O. 1688–1696*, 119–20, 125.

104. HBC to G. Geyer & Council (YF), 17 June 1692, *L.O. 1688–1696*, 141–42.

105. HBC to G. Geyer & Council (YF), 17 June 1693, *L.O. 1688–1696*, 191.

106. "A Coppy of a Counsel Hold at Albany Fort Sepbr ye 1st 1701," HBCA, A. 11/2, fol. 1. Edward Williams had served at Albany at least since 1698, went home in 1700, came back in 1701, and remained until 1712. He was identified as a gardener to distinguish him from Edward

Williams the grocer, who served at Albany around the same time. For Perkins's dismissal by mutual consent, see J. Fullartine (AF) to HBC, 2 August 1703, HBCA, A. 11/2, fol. 6.

107. "A Councell Call'd this 11th of Sepbr 1705" (AF), HBCA, A. 11/2, fol. 9.

108. J. Fullartine (AF) to HBC, 2 August 1703, HBCA, A. 11/2, fols. 3–3d. These men were sent out in 1702 but had to winter at Gilpin's Island (Eastmain) and did not arrive at Albany until 1703; see *Letters*, 335. The most likely of these eleven men to have been the exceptions that Fullartine had in mind were mariner Ambrose Yates (who had previously been with the company in 1694–1700, went on to serve in 1702–6, and was part of the Eastmain crew in 1717), smith Thomas Routen (who served in 1702–8 and again in 1711–19), and/or mariner George Lisk (who served until 1720).

109. In 1701 Fullartine persuaded seven old hands (including three former apprentices and three future factors) to stay on, and engaged four men and a boy from the *Pery*; in 1703 he retained one old hand and engaged no one from the ship; in 1705 he retained fourteen old hands (including Tobias Dolbey and Gottlob Augustus Lichtenberger, who had been green hands in 1701) and engaged four men from the *Hudson's Bay* (including Thomas Archard, who had served the company on land in 1678–85, 1691–92, 1699–1700).

110. J. Fullartine (AF) to HBC, 2 August 1703, HBCA, A. 11/2, fol. 5d; "A Councell Call'd this 11th of Sepr 1705," HBCA, A/ 11/2, fol. 9. Fullartine also engaged James Toppey, Thomas Archard, and John Throughgood from the *Hudson's Bay* that year. Spencer spent the winter of 1705–6 at Eastmain; HBCA, B. 3/d/15, fol. 7.

111. Rich, *History*, vol. 1, 389–90; A. Beale (AF) to HBC, 10 September 1712, HBCA, A. 11/2, fol. 21; T. McCliesh Jr (AF) to HBC, 31 August 1719, HBCA, A. 11/2, fol. 39d.

4 "MEN TO DO THE BUSINESS"

1. Albany Fort watches, 7 January 1696, HBCA, B. 3/z/2, fol. 301.

2. HBC to R. Norton & Council (PWF), 25 May 1727, postscript dated 27 May, HBCA, A. 6/5, fol. 9.

3. HBC to W. Richards (AF), 23 May 1764, HBCA, A. 5/1, fol. 56d. In the same year surgeon John Potts was allowed to continue at forty-eight pounds, but he had served longer than Richards and was formerly master of Richmond Fort; HBC to J. Potts (PWF), 23 May 1764, HBCA, A. 5/1, fol. 59d.

4. Bird described Stewart as "infirm, and in years [i.e., old], being of very little use to us." He implied that Whooley was underpaid and underemployed; T. Bird & Council (AF) to HBC, n.d. [1738], HBCA, A. 11/2, fols. 92d–93. Stewart had entered service in 1732 on a five-year contract at £8-10-12-12-14 and stayed an extra year at £14 before going home in 1738; HBCA, A. 16/2, fol. 63; HBCA, A. 16/3, fol. 2; J. Adams & Council (AF) to HBC, 17 August 1737, HBCA, A. 11/2, fol. 89. Whooley had just arrived in Hudson Bay in 1737 on a five-year contract at £4-4-6-6-10; HBCA, A. 16/2, fol. 100; HBCA, A. 16/3, fol. 17.

5. R. Norton (PWF) to HBC, 1731, *Letters*, 163; R. Norton (PWF) to HBC, 1732, *Letters*, 178; HBCA, A. 16/9, fols. 21, 29.

6. HBC to J. Isham (YF), 12 May 1756, HBCA, A. 5/1, fol. 15.

7. T. McCliesh Jr (AF) to HBC, 20 August 1717, HBCA, A. 11/2, fol. 37. The Committee was unable to find a cooper for Albany in 1717, the one whom it engaged for Churchill in 1718

deserted before sailing, and none could be found in 1719. HBC to T. McCliesh Jr (AF), 31 May 1717, HBCA, A. 6/4, fol. 14d; HBC to J. Knight & Council (PWF), 30 May 1718, HBCA, A. 6/4, fol. 21d. Also see HBC to H. Kelsey & Council (YF), 30 May 1718 and 4 June 1719, HBCA, A. 6/4, fols. 24d, 29d.

8. Schwarz, *London*, 95.

9. HBC to T. McCliesh Jr & Council (YF), 20 May 1724, HBCA, A. 6/4, fol. 85d; *Letters*, 99n, 151n; HBCA, A. 1/120, fol. 62. A real bricklayer, James Averill, was sent out to York in 1725; see T. McCliesh Jr (YF) to HBC, 26 August 1725, *Letters*, 109. Hughes's engagement as a bricklayer was not as silly as it might seem. Woodward, *Men at Work*, observed that labourers could sometimes learn some specialist skills through long association with a particular type of craftsman; he cited a 1749 complaint brought against Newcastle bricklayer William Yarrow by his fellow guild members "for saying he had wrought at London with labourers as good workmen as any of the bricklayers in the company" (93).

10. Prince of Wales Fort council minutes, 6 August 1738, *Letters*, 253n; R. Norton (PWF) to HBC, 17 August 1738, *Letters*, 258. Norton called Lovel "a very handy man that way [i.e., coopering] as well as an able sailor." Lovel only stayed for one year, however, because in 1739 Norton again entertained a mariner who could also act as cooper (James Irvin of Stromness); R. Norton & Council (PWF) to HBC, 16 August 1739, *Letters*, 293.

11. Brown, *Strangers in Blood*, 27; Thomson, *History of Orkney*, 187, 216–19; Fenton, *Northern Isles*, 2–9; Shaw, *Northern and Western Islands*, 165–66, 169–71.

12. "Sailing Orders or Instructions to Capt Richd Ward," 15 May 1716 and 31 May 1717, HBCA, A. 6/4, fols. 6, 17; "Sailing Orders or Instructions to Capt Geo Berley," 30 May 1718, HBCA, A. 6/4, fol. 26d; "Sailing Orders and Instructions to Capt Richard Ward, 1719," HBCA, A. 6/4, fol. 36d; "Sailing Orders & Instructions To Capt Jas Belcher Commander of ye Mary Friggt," 1 June 1720, HBCA, A. 6/4, fol. 46.

13. For 1714, see HBCA, B. 3/d/21, fols. 55d–58; A. Beale (AF) to HBC, 2 August 1714, HBCA, A. 11/2, fols. 23d–24. For 1723, see Nicks, "Orkneymen," 123–24, although it is unclear which man he meant. For the list of men, see R. Staunton (AF) to HBC, 21 August 1723, HBCA, A. 11/2, fol. 48.

14. J. Myatt (AF) to HBC, 10 August 1726, HBCA, A. 11/2, fol. 57; also Nicks, "Orkneymen," 102, 123–24. Grimes may have been the "Mr Grimsay" to whom the Committee wrote in January 1708, instructing him to recruit twelve or fourteen servants, lusty young men between twenty and thirty years of age, of whom two were to be tailors; Rich, *History*, vol. 1, 499.

15. J. Myatt (AF) to HBC, 12 August 1727, HBCA, A. 11/2, fol. 59d.

16. HBC to J. Myatt & Council (AF), 25 May 1727, postscript dated 27 May, HBCA, A. 6/5, fol. 3; "Orders and Instructions to Capt Thos Macklish, appointed Governor...," 25 May 1727, postscript dated 27 May, HBCA, A. 6/5, fol. 6; "Sailing Orders and Instructions To Capt George Spurrell," 25 May 1727, postscript dated 26 May, HBCA, A. 6/5, fol. 11d. Also see "Sailing Orders and Instructions to Capt Christo Middleton," 25 May 1727, postscript dated 26 May, HBCA, A. 6/5, fol. 13d; T. McCliesh Jr (YF) to HBC, 16 August 1727, *Letters*, 129. Loutit was a labourer at Albany in 1710–11 and 1715–18; HBCA, B. 3/d/19, fol. 14d; HBCA, B. 3/d/24, fol. 17; HBCA, B. 3/d/25, fol. 86; HBCA, B. 3/d/26, fol. 14d.

17. Dove, "Plying," 186.

18. J. Adams (AF) to HBC, 14 August 1732, HBCA, A. 11/2, fol. 72d. Adams did not name the five men, but four of them can be identified: labourers Hugh Slater, Henry Flett, William Spence, and Robert Corrigall (see HBCA, A. 16/2, fols. 63–69). G. Spence & Council (AF) to HBC, 22 August 1748, HBCA, A. 11/2, fol. 137d. The six labourers brought out in 1748 were Thomas Sclater, James Short, George Isbister, James Leask, and William Miller (all of whom came out on five-year contracts at six pounds per annum); and labourer and tailor Edward Gerick (Garrioch?), who had signed a five-year contract at £4-4-6-6-10 but hanged himself on 24 June 1752. See HBCA, A. 16/3, fols. 68–70. The one non-Orcadian labourer brought to Albany that year, Thomas Austin, was receiving ten pounds per annum for five years (HBCA, A. 16/3, fol. 65), but his higher wages may have been in recognition of some degree of skill as a bricklayer; see G. Spence & Council (AF) to HBC, 4 August 1752, HBCA, A. 11/2, fol. 151.

19. R. Norton (PWF) to HBC, 1731, *Letters*, 162; R. Norton (PWF) to HBC, 16 August 1733, *Letters*, 185; T. White (YF) to HBC, 6 August 1735, *Letters*, 199. Coats only engaged three men (all labourers at £4-4-6-6-10), and White was obliged to re-engage labourer William Dalton for another year at fourteen pounds (his last year's wages), "he being a very good working hand."

20. Tailor Edmund Hay was engaged in the Orkneys in 1727 for four years at £6-8-9-10, considerably less than other company tailors had received in the 1720s: John Long had entered the service at twelve pounds in 1722, and James Brown was engaged as mariner and tailor at twelve pounds in 1725. For Hay, see T. McCliesh Jr (YF) to HBC, 16 August 1727, *Letters*, 128. For Long and Brown, see HBCA, A. 16/1, fol. 21; HBCA, A. 16/2, fol. 22.

21. Brown, *Strangers in Blood*, 27; *Minutes, First Part*, 80n, 120n.

22. J. Myatt (AF) to HBC, 12 August 1727, HBCA, A. 11/2, fol. 61; Rich, *History*, vol. 1, 499. For Sinclair et al., see HBCA, A. 16/2, fols. 31–37. Their shortcomings as mariners must have surprised Myatt because Orkneymen had a reputation as good seamen; see Thomson, *History of Orkney*, 218.

23. Shaw, *Northern and Western Islands*, 133.

24. Instead the Prince of Wales Fort council agreed with its current cooper, James Worrall, for one year at his current salary (twenty-two pounds). R. Norton (PWF) to HBC, 6 August 1728 [1727], *Letters*, 120. HBC to J. Myatt & Council (AF), 25 May 1727, postscript dated 27 May, HBCA, A. 6/5, fol. 3; "Sailing Orders and Instructions To Capt George Spurrell," 25 May 1727, postscript dated 26 May, HBCA, A. 6/5, fol. 11d; "Sailing Orders and Instructions to Capt Christo Middleton," 25 May 1727, postscript dated 26 May, HBCA, A. 6/5, fol. 13d.

25. Gilboy, *Wages*, 40.

26. For mixed occupations, see Shaw, *Northern and Western Islands*, 185, 189–90. For behaviour, see Burley, *Servants*, 11; Thomson, *History of Orkney*, 5–6.

27. For Groundwater, see HBCA, A. 16/2, fol. 54. For Hay, see HBCA, A. 16/3, fols. 54, 59; A. 16/4, fol. 5.

28. Thomson, *History of Orkney*, places HBC service firmly in this context (206), although he observed a cultural element as well: "it was a way of life which combined farming,

travel, comradeship, and adventure in much the same proportions as had once sent their forebears on their Viking voyages" (216). Also see Burley, *Servants*, 71–72.

29. James A. Troup, "Orphir 1821," in *Papers of the 1994 Rupert's Land Colloquium*, ed. Ian MacLaren, Michael Payne, and Heather Rollason (Winnipeg, MB: Centre for Rupert's Land Studies, 1997), 53–54; Thomson, *History of Orkney*, 214, 219–21; Fenton, *Northern Isles*, 596; Shaw, *Northern and Western Islands*, 189.
30. Troup, "Orphir 1821," 58.
31. Thomson, *History of Orkney*, 186–89. For a discussion of agriculture and land tenure in early modern Orkney see Thomson, 190–200, 205–6; Shaw, *Northern and Western Islands*, 21–40, 70–74.
32. Nicks, "Orkneymen," 105–8.
33. Nicks, 107–8.
34. Patrick Bailey, *Orkney* (Newton Abbot, UK: David & Charles, 1971), 196–97; Thomson, *History of Orkney*, 185–87, 219; Shaw, *Northern and Western Islands*, 137, 171; Robert A. Dodgson, *Land and Society in Early Scotland* (Oxford: Clarendon Press, 1981), 304. Thomson compared the relationship of the two towns to the relationship of the eastern and western ports of Scotland, "where older centres looked eastwards to the North Sea, whereas the new and developing ports lay on the west coast and engaged in Atlantic trade" (219).
35. Bailey, *Orkney*, 22. Shaw, *Northern and Western Islands*, 171.
36. "Sailing Orders & Instructions to Captn Michll Grimington," 26 May 1708, HBCA, A. 6/3, fol. 91d.
37. HBCA, A. 16/2, fol. 87.
38. Nicks, "Orkneymen," 113.
39. An "explosion" of educational provision occurred in the early nineteenth century, including schools endowed by former HBC servants Magnus Twatt and James Tait in Orphir, and William Tomison in South Ronaldsay. Thomson, *History of Orkney*, 238–39; Shaw, *Northern and Western Islands*, 144–46.
40. Nicks, "Orkneymen," 113–15.
41. Identifying men's wives from account books is only possible if (a) a man sent home a bill for money to be paid to his wife or to a third party for her subsistence, and (b) the entry of the bill in the account book clearly identifies the woman as his wife. For John Ward, see Moose Factory account books, HBCA, B. 135/d/26, fol. 83; B. 135/d/27, fol. 83; B. 135/d/32, fol. 82; B. 135/d/33, fol. 86; B. 135/d/34, fol. 80d; B. 135/d/35, fol. 84d; B. 135/d/37, fol. 90. For George Sinclair, see HBCA, B. 135/d/33, fol. 86; B. 135/d/35, fol. 84d; B. 135/d/36, fol. 85d; B. 135/d/37, fol. 90. For Thomas Halcro, see HBCA, B. 135/d/36, fol. 85d. In 1763, 1764, and 1766 Thomas Halcro's wife was listed as Marjory Gadus (HBCA, B. 135/d/32, fol. 82; B. 135/d/33, fol. 86d; B. 135/d/35, fol. 84d), but in 1767 Isabel Irwin was listed as his wife, and in 1768 William Cooley (armourer at Moose) ordered two pounds of his salary to be paid to Captain John Horner for the subsistence of Margery Gadus, wife of Thomas Halcro (HBCA, B. 135/d/37, fol. 90).
42. In contrast to the land service, Dove, "Plying," has observed strong family connections in the upper ranks of the HBC's maritime service: "Promotions to captain were made from within and based on connections of kinship, as sons were apprenticed to their fathers.

Commands were not purchased, as they were in the East India service, but in most cases were won by families, a common trend in overseas shipping in their period" (187). The most notable examples were the Fowlers (John, Jonathon, and Jonathon Jr), who made a total of forty-one voyages (1744–74), and the Spurrells (George and his son, Joseph), who between them made forty-eight voyages (1722–63).

43. HBC to M. Norton (PWF), 13 May 1767, HBCA, A. 5/1, fol. 81.
44. J. Myatt (AF) to HBC, 12 August 1727, HBCA, A. 11/2, fols. 59–59d.
45. J. Myatt (AF) to HBC, 12 August 1727, HBCA, A. 11/2, fols. 59–59d; also HBC to J. Myatt & Council (AF), 25 May 1727, HBCA, A. 6/5, fol. 2d.
46. The other new labourers arriving at Albany in 1726 were Matthew Sargent, Randall Butler, and Richard Holmes. HBCA, A. 16/2, fols. 25–28.
47. New head mason Thomas Keyly died shortly after coming ashore in 1731; R. Norton (PWF) to HBC, 1731, *Letters*, 161–62. Tutty requested a raise to twenty pounds per annum "for his encouragement to act in such a station"; R. Norton (PWF) to HBC, 1732, *Letters*, 175–76. Rich, *History*, vol. 1, claimed that ornamental work "was the only craft known to many English masons by the eighteenth century" (533; also see Schwarz, *London*, 34), but he underestimated the diverse experiences of early modern English tradesmen; see Woodward, *Men at Work*, chaps. 1 and 2.
48. HBC to R. Norton & Council (PWF), 10 May 1733, HBCA, A. 6/5, fol. 76. The Committee later regretted this; one of those four masons was Joseph Robson, who became an inveterate critic of the HBC.
49. Rich, *History*, vol. 2, 97–98.
50. HBC to J. Knight & Council (YF), 15 May 1716, HBCA, A. 6/4, fol. 3d.
51. J. Myatt (AF) to HBC, 2 August 1729, HBCA, A. 11/2, fol. 64d; HBC to J. Myatt & Council (AF), 15 May 1730, HBCA, A. 6/5, fol. 36. Rattenbury had served at York in 1714–22 and was a member of Henry Kelsey's council there in 1719 and 1721; HBCA, B. 239/d/7, fol. 6; B. 239/d/12, fol. 5d; B. 239/b/1, fol. 17; H. Kelsey, "Orders and Instructions to be Observed by Capt Anthony Beale in my Absence Untill further Orders from the Compy or Mee," 26 July 1721, HBCA, B. 239/b/2, 7.
52. Lytwyn, *Muskekowuck Athinuwick*, 61.
53. Renée Fossett, *In Order to Live Untroubled: Inuit of the Central Arctic, 1550 to 1940* (Winnipeg: University of Manitoba Press, 2001), 93–94, 108–9. Also see H. Kelsey & Council (YF) to T. McCliesh Jr (AF), 18 January 1720, HBCA, B. 239/b/1, fol. 25d: "I...changed Two of ye Compies Slaves for Two of those Countrey Ladds [i.e., Inuit] and they are very agreeable and Learn English a pace by wch I hope to know wt ye Countrey will afford." The boys were returned to their "friends" that summer, and the company's slaves were brought back to York; H. Kelsey & Council (YF) to T. McCliesh (AF), 25 July 1720, HBCA, B. 239/b/1, fol. 31d.
54. HBCA, B. 3/d/2, fol. 12d, quoted in Lytwyn, *Muskekowuck Athinuwick*, 64. In comparison, in 1736 Joseph Adams at Albany traded one pound of tobacco, one gallon of brandy, and one and one-half yards of blue cloth for an Inuit boy (possibly Jack Eskemay) brought back by a party of Albany River Lowland Cree; Lytwyn, *Muskekowuck Athinuwick*, 65–66.
55. See Jack Eskemay's account in HBCA, A. 16/3, fol. 32.

56. A list of servants at Moose in 1769–70 described Trolio as a labourer (HBCA, B. 135/d/39, fol. 9), but earlier such lists only described him as an "Esquimaux Man" (HBCA, B. 135/d/37, fol. 9; B. 135/d/38, fol. 9). Some idea of his age may be gleaned from references to him as an "Eusquemay Boy" until 1760 (HBCA, B. 135/d/27, fol. 8; B. 135/d/29, fol. 8d). His account was combined with that of English apprentice William Wood until 1759 (HBCA, B. 135/d/27, fol. 8; B. 135/d/28, fol. 8d), and the name Trolio was not used until 1762 (HBCA, B. 135/d/31, fol. 9). Also Lytwyn, *Muskekowuck Athinuwick*, 66. For Trolio in charge of Wapiscogamy House, see Rich and Johnson, *Moose Fort Journals*, 333. For a discussion of both Jack and Trolio, see François Trudel, "Trolio et Jack," *Canadian Journal of Native Studies* 7, no. 1 (1987): 79–93.
57. See Richmond Fort Account Books, 1752–59, HBCA, B. 135/d/3-9. Henry Pollexfen Sr referred to the "Duke of Richmond" as a "boy" in 1754; H. Pollexfen Sr (RF) to HBC, 4 September 1754, HBCA, A. 11/57, fol. 22. "Duke of Richmond" died of a fever at York in June 1761; A. Graham (YF) to F. Jacobs (PWF), 11 July 1761, HBCA, B. 239/b/21, fol. 11d.
58. HBC to T. McCliesh Jr (AF), 31 May 1717, HBCA, A. 6/4, fol. 14d.
59. HBC to W. Richards (Neath), 28 February 1765, HBCA, A.5/1, fol. 62; HBC to Richards (no address), 21 March 1765, HBCA, A. 5/1, fols. 63–63d; HBC to R. Temple [(Berwick)], 5 March 1765, HBCA, A. 5/1, fols. 62d–63; HBC to Thomas Law (at Chauncy Townsends Esqr), 16 April 1765, HBCA, A. 5/1, fols. 63d–64.
60. HBC to W. Richards (Neath), 28 February 1765, HBCA, A. 5/1, fol. 62.
61. For Pollexfen acting on behalf of Peter Knight, see HBC to H. Pollexfen Jr, 28 February 1767, HBCA, A. 5/1, fol. 76d. For Pollexfen acting as agent for the father of Andrew Gerrett, see HBC to H. Pollexfen Jr (Kirkwall), 17 November 1774, HBCA, A. 5/1, fol. 162; HBC to H. Pollexfen Jr (Kirkwall), 28 Janurary 1775, A. 5/1, fol. 163; and HBC to H. Pollexfen Jr (Kirkwall), 4 March 1775, A. 5/1, fols. 163d–164. In 1775 the Committee agreed to hire a cooper recommended by Pollexfen; HBC to H. Pollexfen Jr (Kirkwall), 4 March 1775, HBCA, A. 5/1, fols. 163d–164.
62. See HBCA, A. 32/3, fols. 10–49.
63. For Churchill and Helleker, see HBCA, A. 16/1, fols. 24, 25. For comparable English examples, see Woodward, *Men at Work*, 146; Kussmaul, *Servants*, 31–32. On the reverse side of some of the earliest surviving HBC contracts the new man signed for his advance money; see, for example, John Cromartie's 1780 contract, HBCA, A. 32/1, fol. 10d.
64. HBC to R. Temple (Berwick), 5 March 1765, HBCA, A. 5/1, fols. 62d–63.
65. HBC to W. Richards (Neath), 28 February 1765, HBCA, A. 5/1, fol. 62.
66. HBC to W. Richards (Neath), 21 March 1765, HBCA, A. 5/1, fol. 63.
67. For Coats's role, see R. Norton (PWF) to HBC, 16 August 1733, *Letters*, 185; and T. White (YF) to HBC, 6 August 1735, *Letters*, 199. For McCliesh's role, see HBCA, A. 16/2, fol. 87.
68. HBC to John Stephenson Sr (Stockton, Durham), 20 February 1755, HBCA, A. 5/1, fol. 5d. For the Stephensons' accounts, see HBCA, A. 16/4, fol. 22.
69. HBC to John Garbut (no address), 17 January 1765, HBCA, A. 5/1, fol. 61d; HBC to William Lockey (no address), 7 March 1767, HBCA, A. 5/1, fol. 76d; HBC to Consett Wilson (Stokesley near North Allerton, Yorkshire), 28 January 1769, HBCA, A. 5/1, fol. 93. Wilson had applied to be master of the *Severn* sloop and was offered a position as her mate.

70. Moose Fort journal, 14 September 1741 and 5 January 1742, HBCA, B. 135/a/11, fols. 3d, 27d, quoted in Gerhard Ens, "The Political Economy of the 'Private Trade' on the Hudson Bay," in "*Le Castor Fait Tout*," ed. Bruce G. Trigger, Toby Morantz, and Louise Dechene (Montreal: Lake St. Louis Historical Society, 1987), 402; also see Pannekoek, "'Corruption' at Moose," 9. Joseph Isbister complained of "ye bright Stocton Captn [Coats] who Can in one day oversett a reformation of 2 Years." J. Isbister (AF) to J. Duffield (MF), 13 September 1742, HBCA, B. 3/b/1, fol. 5.
71. HBCA, A. 32/3, fols. 12, 16, 18, 32.
72. See, for instance, "Instructions to Mr Jos Myatt," 25 May 1726, HBCA, A. 6/4, fol. 109.
73. Games, *Web of Empire*, 107.
74. J. Isham & Council (YF) to HBC, 2 September 1755, HBCA, A. 11/114, fol. 185.
75. H. Marten (AF) to HBC, 2 September 1770, HBCA, A. 11/3, fol. 145. For examples of the RAC hiring free Africans and men of mixed African-European ancestry, see Davies, "The Living and the Dead," 85–86.
76. Brown, *Strangers*, 156. For Isham's value as a canoeman, see Cumberland House journal, 30 May 1776, *CHJ First Series*, 52.
77. H. Marten (YF) to R. Temple (AF), 26 October 1759, HBCA, B. 198/b/1, fol. 3; see also York Fort journal, 28 June 1759, HBCA, B. 239/a/46, fol. 37; H. Marten (YF) to F. Jacobs (PWF), 3 July 1759, HBCA, B. 239/b/18, fol. 3; J. Isham (YF) to HBC, 24 August 1759, HBCA, A. 11/114, fol. 23d; Rich, *History*, vol. 2, 1–2.
78. Jean Baptiste D'Laryea (AF) to HBC, private, 21 August 1761, HBCA, A. 11/3, fol. 47; R. Temple & Council (AF) to HBC, 8 September 1760, HBCA, A. 11/3, fol. 43d. Temple (fol. 43d) described D'Laryea as "an Allowed Chief" among the First Nations, but it is unclear to which nation he was referring; if D'Laryea was master at Basquiea as he claimed, he would presumably have been most familiar with the Woodland Cree groups of the upper Nelson and lower Saskatchewan rivers (and perhaps with some of the lower Nelson and Hayes river groups as well), yet the company sent him to Albany, and D'Laryea himself requested to be sent to Moose; J.B. D'Laryea (AF) to HBC, 21 August 1761, HBCA, A. 11/3, fol. 49.
79. D'Laryea also received a total of £50 0s. 2d. for his private trappings (£48 8s. 9d. of that was from his inland journey); HBCA, A. 16/4, fol. 32. Temple commented in 1762, "As to Mr Larlee I am sorry for and shou'd been gladd cou'd I have wrote twice as much in his favour"; R. Temple (AF) to HBC, 31 August 1762, HBCA, A. 11/3, fol. 55. For his part, D'Laryea wrote of Temple in 1761: "Mr Temple is too good humour'd for many people of this place for myself I love him very much he is an amicable Man and deserves all the praise imaginable and has everything much at heart;" J.B. D'Laryea (AF) to HBC, 22 August 1761, HBCA, A. 11/3, fol. 51d. For reports by Upland Cree of D'Laryea's cruelty toward them, and its impact on Albany's trade, see H. Marten (AF) to HBC, private, 24 August 1763, HBCA, A. 11/3, fol. 57; R. Temple (AF) to HBC, private, August 1763, HBCA, A. 11/3, fols. 63–63d; R. Temple & Council (AF) to HBC, 26 August 1763, HBCA, A. 11/3, fol. 59.
80. George E. Thorman, "Maugenest, Germain," in *DCB*, http://www.biographi.ca/en/bio/maugenest_germain_4E.html ; Alice M. Johnson, "Mons. Maugenest suggests…" *Beaver*, outfit 287 (Summer 1956): 49–53.

81. Cumberland House journal, 7–8 February 1777, *CHJ First Series*, 118–21.
82. *CHJ First Series*, lxxviii. Matthew Cocking, "Thoughts on making a Settlement Inland," 1773, HBCA, B. 239/a/69, fol. 52d. Richard Glover unfairly described Louis Primeau as "a lost piece of human flotsam" who had been "stranded" in the west after the fall of New France (*CHJ First Series*, lxxviii). For Primeau's biography, see Sylvia Van Kirk, "Primeau, Louis," in *DCB*, http://www.biographi.ca/en/bio/primeau_louis_4E.html.
83. HBC to F. Jacobs (YF), private, 12 May 1773, HBCA, A. 5/1, fol. 148d. Also see HBC to F. Jacobs & Council (YF), 11 May 1774, HBCA, A. 6/12, fol. 10.
84. Cumberland House journal, 23 May 1777, *CHJ First Series*, 149n.
85. See Jennifer S.H. Brown, "Batt, Isaac," in *DCB*, http://www.biographi.ca/en/bio/batt_isaac_4E.html.
86. Quoted in Rich, *History*, vol. 2, 30. Also see E.B. Kitchen (MF) to HBC, August 1775, quoted in Rich and Johnson, *Moose Fort Journals*, 344–45.
87. Cumberland House journal, 2 July 1776, *CHJ First Series*, 68, also lxxix–lxxx. For the difficulty of proving (or disproving) such accusations, see Podruchny, *Making the Voyageur World*, 159–60.
88. Rich, *History*, vol. 2, 30–31.
89. Rich, *History*, vol. 1, 573.
90. *Letters*, xlv.
91. *CHJ First Series*, lxvii–lxviii, lxxii–lxxiii; *CHJ Second Series*, xiv.
92. York Fort journal, 4 August 1780, HBCA, B. 239/a/78, quoted in *CHJ Second Series*, xxxi; Hudson House journal, 24 April 1781, *CHJ Second Series*, 189.
93. H. Marten & Council (YF) to HBC, 13 September 1780, HBCA, A. 11/116, fol. 75d, quoted in *CHJ Second Series*, xxxiii. Richard Glover observed that the "raw Orkneymen" sent inland were led by experienced inland travellers who "were personally able to carry out any duty their subordinates might have to perform" (*CHJ First Series*, xxvii–xxviii). This contrasts markedly with Burley's observation that in the nineteenth century HBC servants performed tasks no officer would ever do (*Servants*, 12–13, 15).
94. H. Marten (YF) to HBC, 13 September 1780, HBCA, A. 11/116, fol. 75d, quoted in *CHJ First Series*, lxxiii. Also see *CHJ Second Series*, xiv.
95. W. Tomison (CH) to H. Marten (YF), 29 May 1780, *CHJ Second Series*, 50–51; also see W. Tomison (CH) to H. Marten (YF), 7 June 1780, *CHJ Second Series*, 54.
96. *CHJ First Series*, lxxiv–lxxv.
97. HBC to John Favell (MF), 25 May 1762, HBCA, A. 5/1, fols. 46d–47.
98. HBC to M. Norton (PWF), 23 May 1764, HBCA, A. 5/1, fol. 59. Also see William Coats et al. (RF) to HBC, 28 August 1749, HBCA, A. 11/57, fol. 3.
99. Richard I. Ruggles, "Hospital Boys of the Bay," *The Beaver* 308, no. 2 (Autumn 1977): 10.
100. Ruggles, 7, 10.
101. Nixon, 249. To compare the EIC during this period, see John Bowen, "The East India Company's Education of Its Own Servants," *Journal of the Royal Asiatic Society of Great Britain and Ireland* 3, no. 4 (October 1955): 105.

5 "DILIGENT MEN" AND "IDLE FELLOWES"

1. HBC to G. Geyer & Council (YF), 2 June 1688, *L.O. 1688–1696*, 14. Also see HBC to G. Geyer & Council (YF), 17 June 1693, *L.O. 1688–1696*, 189: "As for any men you have there that are Slothfull Drones or from home [i.e., whom] you can expect noe service Pray send them home for England & others that are vigorous nimble and willing & will doe what they are bid may continue there." In the same letter (p. 191) the Committee censured Geyer for sending home apprentice George Holstead early without reason and instructed him not to allow able-bodied men "to depart the Countery till their times be expired but those that are sickly and weak you may send home." Despite the Committee's apparent good opinion of Holstead and his indenture not being expired, he does not appear to have returned to Hudson Bay; see *L.O. 1688–1696*, 79n2.
2. See, for instance, HBC to J. Isbister & Council (AF), 27 May 1755, HBCA, A. 6/9, fol. 3d. The RAC does not appear to have inquired too deeply into the skills of the tradesmen they recruited either; see Davies, "The Living and the Dead," 86–87.
3. HBC to G. Geyer & Council (YF), 21 May 1691, *L.O. 1688–1696*, 120.
4. HBC to J. Adams & Council (AF), 20 May 1737, HBCA, A. 6/5, fol. 118. Also see HBC to T. White & Council (YF), 20 May 1737, HBCA, A. 6/5, fol. 122d; HBC to R. Norton & Council (PWF), 20 May 1737, HBCA, A. 6/5, fol. 125.
5. R. Temple & Council (AF) to HBC, 26 August 1763, HBCA, A. 11/3, fols. 59d, 61; R. Temple (AF) to HBC, private, August 1763, HBCA, A. 11/3, fol. 63; Thomas, *Ends of Life*, 103; Tadmor, *Family and Friends*, 64. Campbell, *London Tradesman*, called idleness on the job "a Crime against Moral Honesty" (313).
6. HBC to T. Walsh (YF), 21 May 1691, *L.O. 1688–1696*, 130. The Committee was asking Walsh to help it persuade George Geyer to stay on as governor of Port Nelson.
7. A. Beale (AF) to HBC, 1 August 1712, HBCA, A. 11/2, fol. 19.
8. HBC to J. Fullartine & Council (AF), 30 May 1705, HBCA, A. 6/3, fol. 71; "A Coppy of a Counsel Hold at Albany Fort Sepbr ye 1st 1701," HBCA, A. 11/2, fol. 1; "A Councell Call'd [at Albany] this 11th of Sepbr 1705," HBCA, A. 11/2, fol. 9; "A Councell Called [at Albany] the 20th of July 1706," HBCA, A. 11/2, fol. 12.
9. HBC to G. Geyer & Council (YF), 2 June 1688, *L.O. 1688–1696*, 9–10, 11, 16; HBC to T. Walsh (SR), 2 June 1688, *L.O. 1688–1696*, 22; HBC to J. Marsh (location unspecified), 18 June 1688, *L.O. 1688–1696*, 40.
10. HBC to G. Geyer & Council (YF), 17 June 1692, *L.O. 1688–1696*, 135; HBC to J. Knight (London?), 17 June 1692, *L.O. 1688–1696*, 144–45.
11. William Fleetwood, *The Relative Duties of Parents and Children, Husbands and Wives, Masters and Servants* (New York: Garland, 1985; first published London: C. Harper, 1705), 366–67, 375–76, 384.
12. HBC to H. Kelsey (AF), 29 May 1710, HBCA, A. 6/3, fol. 100d.
13. HBC to G. Geyer & Council (YF), 17 June 1693, *L.O. 1688–1696*, 189. In the same year the Committee instructed the Albany council to "sett a marke upon all that are slothfull quarelous & cause divisions amongst you, & to Returne home their names." HBC to J. Knight & Council (AF), 17 June 1693, *L.O. 1688–1696*, 201.
14. HBC to S. Missenden (YF), 20 May 1686, *L.O. 1680–1687*, 202.

15. J. Fullartine (AF) to HBC, 2 August 1703, HBCA, A. 11/2, fol. 6. Norcutt kept the Albany accounts in 1703–5 (HBCA, B. 3/d/14, fol. 52). He may have also kept the Eastmain accounts in 1705–6 (see HBCA, B. 3/d/15, fol. 7d), but those have not survived; as the house was only seasonal, the accounts probably consisted of rough daybooks, which were probably not preserved after the information was transferred to the Albany accounts.
16. HBC to G. Geyer (YF), private, 21 May 1691, *L.O. 1688–1696*, 127.
17. HBC to S. Sinclair (AF), 17 June 1693, *L.O. 1688–1696*, 211.
18. J. Fullartine (AF) to HBC, 2 August 1703, HBCA, A. 11/2, fol. 6; HBC to J. Fullartine & Council (AF), 6 June 1698, HBCA, A. 6/3, fol. 39.
19. Kussmaul, *Servants*, 40. Also see Podruchny, *Making the Voyageur World*, 149.
20. J. Fullartine (AF) to HBC, 2 August 1703, HBCA, A. 11/2, fols. 3d, 4. That year Fullartine also mixed payment in kind with money wages to persuade gunner Christopher Spencer to winter in Hudson Bay (forty-eight pounds plus two pounds "in Brandy or some other thing here in ye Country"; ibid.). In 1706 the Albany council granted Thomas Dutton and Edward Williams each thirty pounds plus the value of three pounds in goods from the warehouse; "A Councell Called [at Albany] the 20th of July 1706," HBCA, A. 11/2, fol. 12. Note that even when there was sufficient volume of goods in the factory's warehouse, prices were often a sore point; see, for example, HBC to J. Fullartine & Council (AF), 30 May 1705, HBCA, A. 6/3, fol. 69d.
21. Heal, "Food Gifts," 44; also see Lacombe, "Gentlemen of Fashion," 671. The multiple meanings ascribed to food in the distinctive cultural and class contexts of Hudson Bay deserve a study in their own right; consider, for instance, the prevalence of deer and other ungulates in the traders' diet and the significance of venison in early modern England, versus its more mundane identity in Indigenous cultures. Also worth considering are the social and cultural implications of leaving most of the hunting to Indigenous men in the age of the Black Act (1723). As Heal, "Food Gifts," notes, "The deer parks of the nobility and greater gentry provided one of the most defining aspects of their status...[T]he ability to hunt remained a necessary adjunct to elite power" (58).

    Meanings of food draw our attention to other ways in which English and Indigenous social expectations complemented each other. At least some (if not most) of the "charity" and "debt" offered to Indigenous traders can probably be understood in these terms too; for instance, Ben-Amos, "Gifts and Favors," observes that "the special place of the household was expressed in its hospitality to outsiders....Hospitality in the large houses of the peerage and gentry entailed a distinctive type of reciprocal exchange in which issues of power and prestige, deference and subordination loomed large....Locked in a perpetual duty to return, the poor conferred loyalty and deference in exchange for patronage, favors, and the generosity offered on festive occasions by the elite" (314–15). The Cree would have ascribed their own cultural meanings to these exchanges, but such imagery would have encouraged factors to behave in a particular manner, behaviour that in turn fitted nicely into northern Algonquian notions of hospitality and "pity." For credit and favours, see Ben-Amos, "Gifts and Favors," 328–29.

22. J. Fullartine (AF) to HBC, 2 August 1703, HBCA, A. 11/2, fols. 3d, 4; Albany Fort Council, trial of John Cartwright, 19 August 1696, HBCA, B. 3/z/2, fol. 2; Albert Fort Council, trial of William Filpott, n.d. [1696], HBCA, B. 3/a/2, fol. 2d; H. Kelsey (YF) to R. Staunton (PWF), 28 March 1719, HBCA, B. 239/b/1, fol. 13.

23. A. Beale (AF) to HBC, 23 July 1706, HBCA, A. 11/2, fol. 14d, 15. Beale left the service in 1708 (although he re-engaged in 1711), and his decision may have been prompted by the fact that no supply ship was sent to the Bay in 1707. Ships sailed to Albany in only five of the ten years from 1700 to 1709; *Letters*, 335–36. The post-Utrecht period saw greater regularity and sophistication in the company's shipping: the last ship to winter in the Bay was in 1715, and the last ship lost in the Bay was in 1736. Dove, "Plying," 176–77, 180; Dove, "Voyages to Rupert's Land," 7.

24. Beale also requested "a man fitting for to affisciate Divine Service," but it is unclear whether he considered the absence of such a man to be as great a discouragement as the lack of a surgeon. A. Beale (AF) to HBC, 1 August 1712, HBCA, A. 11/2, fol. 19. The deaths of Bell, Spence, Read, and Johnson were recorded in the Albany account book; "A Mamorandum / Albany Fort, 1711/12," HBCA, B. 3/d/20, fol. 85. The previous year, Albany had buried tailor and accountant James Norcutt and landsmen James Fidler, Oliver Stricklar, and John Sharpe; for the account of the auctions of their effects, see HBCA, B. 3/d/19, fols. 5–5d.

25. J. Fullartine (AF) to HBC, 2 August 1703, HBCA, A. 11/2, fols. 5d, 6. Thomas McCliesh Jr wanted to go home in 1720 because he was "very Desireous of haveing the Happiness to see my wife & children"; T. McCliesh Jr (AF) to HBC, 31 August 1719, HBCA, A. 11/2, fol. 40d. He may also have wanted to come home to defend himself against accusations: in the same letter he denied engaging in private trade (fol. 40) and privately selling goods and provisions to his men (fol. 39d).

26. J. Fullartine (AF) to HBC, 2 August 1703, HBCA, A. 11/2, fol. 5d. Lynier went home in 1703 but re-engaged in 1710 and served at Albany until 1717, when he became "sore afflicted with Lameness" in February, and, "haveing no hopes of his Recovery here," the Albany council granted his request to go home "for the Recovery of his health"; T. McCliesh Jr (AF) to HBC, 20 August 1717, HBCA, A. 11/2, fol. 37. Andrew Johnson was a smith who served at Port Nelson from 1691 to 1694 (when he was captured by the French) and at Albany from 1696 to 1706; he re-engaged again in 1710 (sailing to Albany with Lynier on the *Hudson's Bay* [II]) and died at Albany (where he was apparently serving as gunner) in July 1712. HBCA, A. 15/4, fol. 107; A. 1/26, fol. 8d; A. 15/5, fol. 110; A. 1/29, fol. 7; A. 15/5, fol. 139; A. 1/33, fol. 113d; A. Beale (AF) to HBC, 1 August 1712, HBCA, A. 11/2, fol. 19; *Letters*, 10n, 355.

27. The Committee mentioned twenty-six men by name as having signed one-year contracts in 1712. HBC to A. Beale (AF), 10 June 1713, HBCA, A. 6/3, fols. 120d–121; HBC to A. Beale & Council (AF), 25 May 1714, HBCA, A. 6/3, fol. 128d; A. Beale (AF) to HBC, 2 August 1714, HBCA, A. 11/2, fols. 23d–24.

28. Kussmaul, *Servants*, 73; Ben-Amos, *Adolescence and Youth*, 70–71, 83.

29. R. Staunton (AF) to HBC, 21 August 1723, HBCA, A. 11/2, fol. 48; J. Isham (YF) to HBC, 4 August 1756, HBCA, A. 11/114, fols. 197–197d; A. Beale (PWF) to HBC, 26 July 1729, *Letters*, 140.

30. T. McCliesh Jr (AF) to HBC, 16 July 1716, HBCA, A. 11/2, fol. 27.

31. HBC to J. Knight & Council (YF), 31 May 1717, HBCA, A. 6/4, fol. 12.

32. HBC to J. Adams & Council (AF), 10 May 1733, HBCA, A. 6/5, fol. 68.

33. HBC to James Nicholson (MF), private, 14 May 1771, HBCA, A. 5/1, fol. 128d.

34. J. Knight (YF) to R. Staunton (AF), 28 June 1715, HBCA, A. 6/4, fol. 10; J. Isham (YF) to R. Pilgrim (PWF), 3 January 1747, HBCA, B. 239/b/4, fol. 4d. For a discussion of neighbourly behaviour and expectations in an early modern English parish, see Wrightson, "Politics of the Parish," 18–22. Also see Steve Hindle, "The Keeping of the Public Peace," in *The Experience of Authority in Early Modern England*, ed. Paul Griffiths, Adam Fox, and Steve Hindle (New York: St. Martin's Press, 1996), 213.

35. A. Beale (AF) to HBC, 2 August 1714, HBCA, A. 11/2, fol. 24. In 1723 Thomas McCliesh Jr remarked, "I know Mr Myatt to be honest and careful, and knows the method of trade with those Indians [of Albany River] perfectly, and a man of spirit in face of his enemy"; T. McCliesh Jr (YF) to HBC, 23 August 1723, *Letters*, 96.

36. J. Myatt (AF) to HBC, 22 August 1722, HBCA, A. 11/2, fol. 42. The following year Myatt's successor, Richard Staunton, reported that the surgeon Charles Napper "according to Mr Myats character of him is a very sober & Carefull man, as by me observed since my arival"; R. Staunton (AF) to HBC, 21 August 1723, HBCA, A. 11/2, fol. 46d. Also see R. Staunton (AF) to HBC, 24 August 1725, HBCA, A. 11/2, fol. 53d.

37. T. McCliesh Jr (AF) to HBC, 31 August 1719, HBCA, A. 11/2, fol. 39d.

38. J. Myatt (AF) to HBC, 22 August 1722, HBCA, A. 11/2, fol. 43.

39. R. Staunton (AF) to HBC, 21 August 1723, HBCA, A. 11/2, fols. 46d, 47, 47d. Staunton (fol. 27) felt that Kirke was good only for repairing old guns, not making new ones, and he sent home fifty guns (which Kirke had fitted) to be refitted. This surprised the Committee, to whom Kirke had been recommended as "an Excellent Armourer" and "ye finest Workman." Kirke wanted to go home in 1725 (after only three years' service) and was allowed to do so, "beinge very lazy." HBC to J. Myatt & Council (AF), 24 May 1722, HBCA, A. 6/4, fol. 61d; HBC to R. Staunton & Council (AF), 20 May 1724, HBCA, A. 6/4, fols. 86–86d; R. Staunton (AF) to HBC, 23 August 1724, HBCA, A. 11/2, fol. 51d.

40. R. Staunton (AF) to HBC, 23 August 1724, HBCA, A. 11/2, fol. 50d. For Myatt's praise of Henson's management of the Eastmain trade, see R. Staunton (AF) to HBC, 21 August 1723, HBCA, A. 11/2, fol. 46d. However, Henson died at Albany in 1726; see J. Myatt (AF) to HBC, 10 August 1726, HBCA, A. 11/2, fol. 56. For a suggestion that heavy drinking was a factor, see J. Myatt (AF) to HBC, 12 August 1727, HBCA, A. 11/2, fol. 59.

41. "Instructions to Mr Jos Myatt," 25 May 1726, HBCA, A. 6/4, fol. 110.

42. R. Norton (PWF) to HBC, 23 August 1737, *Letters*, 241, 242. Only Mackcullock was retained in 1738; *Letters*, 241n.

43. R. Staunton & Council (MF) to HBC, 17 August 1739, *Letters*, 306. In 1738 Staunton called Drover "an indifferent [i.e., moderately] honest man and a very good hand" but noted that eight homeward-bound marten skins were his: three of them Drover claimed that

sloop master William Bevan had given him, and five he had trapped himself over the last two winters. R. Staunton & G. Howy (MF) to HBC, August 1738, *Letters*, 269.

44. G. Spence & Council (AF) to HBC, 4 August 1752, HBCA, A. 11/2, fol. 151; J. Isbister & Council (AF) to HBC, 19 September 1754, HBCA, A. 11/2, fol. 161; R. Temple & Council (AF) to HBC, 1 September 1759, HBCA, A. 11/3, fols. 35, 35d; T. White (MF) to J. Isbister (AF), 18 June 1755, HBCA, A. 11/2, fol. 169d.
45. J. Isham & Council (YF) to HBC, 27 July 1740, *Letters*, 312–13.
46. T. McCliesh Jr (YF) to HBC, 23 August 1723, *Letters*, 93.
47. J. Knight (YF) to HBC, 17 September 1716, *Letters*, 69. Knight also pointed out that Vaughan was a ship carpenter as well as a capable mariner. Vaughan actually entered the company's service as a carpenter, being engaged in 1713 for four years at £36-40-40-40, but before sailing he was named mate of the *Prosperous* hoy. During his five years in Hudson Bay (1713–18) Vaughan commanded the *Eastmain* and the *Success*, led woodcutting expeditions at Churchill River, and in 1719 commanded the new sloop *Discovery* on Knight's fatal Arctic voyage; *Letters*, 63n; Kenney, *Founding of Churchill*, 122, 126–27, 133–34.
48. J. Knight (PWF) to T. McCliesh Jr (AF), 11 August 1717, in Kenney, *Founding of Churchill*, 158. Knight was thanking McCliesh for a gift of wine and brandy.
49. T. McCliesh Jr (YF) to HBC, 8 August 1728, *Letters*, 135. Ravilian may have had a drinking problem, but he was not incompetent. McCliesh sent him to Prince of Wales Fort, where Anthony Beale called him "very serviceable not only in fitting up old guns for factory use but also several new guns that has lain for a long time not fit for trade, for want of an armourer here to rectify them, which he has repaired"; A. Beale (PWF) to HBC, 26 July 1729, *Letters*, 139.
50. R. Temple & Council (AF) to HBC, August 1757, HBCA, A. 11/3, fol. 25.
51. R. Temple & Council (AF) to HBC, 25 September 1758, HBCA, A. 11/3, fol. 31; R. Temple & Council (AF) to HBC, 8 September 1760, HBCA, A. 11/3, fol. 43d.
52. G. Spence & Council (AF) to HBC, 4 August 1752, HBCA, A. 11/2, fol. 151. Mackoler died on the passage back to England; HBCA, A. 16/3, fol. 82.
53. H. Marten (AF) to HBC, 27 August 1768, HBCA, A. 11/3, fol. 115d. Humphrey Marten considered "immoderate Drinking" to be as "Pernicious...to your honours Interest" as private trade; H. Marten & Council (AF) to HBC, 15 August 1765, HBCA, A. 11/3, fol. 81.
54. While the Lowland Cree dialect is intelligible to other Cree speakers throughout the western woodlands and northern plains, the Eastmain Cree dialect is noticeably different. Linguist Truman Michelson classified it as a Montagnais-Nascapi dialect and not Cree at all. See Lytwyn, *Muskekowuck Athinuwick*, 12, 57. For differences among Eastmain speakers, see Lytwyn, 57; Francis and Morantz, *Partners in Furs*, 13, 67.
55. HBC to H. Kelsey (AF), 29 May 1710, HBCA, A. 6/3, fol. 100d. The same letter (fol. 101) mentions sending Kelsey "your dixionary [of Cree] Printed that you may the Better Instruct the young Ladds with you, in ye Indian Language."
56. T. Bird (London) to W. Bevan (AF), private, 24 May 1727, HBCA, A. 6/5, fol. 4.
57. J. Myatt (AF) to HBC, 5 August 1728, HBCA, A. 11/2, fol. 63.
58. J. Adams (AF) to HBC, 28 August 1730, HBCA, A. 11/2, fol. 68d.
59. T. Bird & Council (AF) to HBC, n.d. [1738], HBCA, A. 11/2, fol. 93.

60. H. Marten (YF) to HBC, 25 August 1777, HBCA, A. 11/116, fol. 22, quoted in *CHJ First Series*, 181n.
61. H. Marten (YF) to W. Tomison (CH), 1 August 1776, *CHJ First Series*, 87.
62. *CHJ First Series*, lxviii–lxix; H. Marten (YF) to HBC, n.d. [1776], HBCA, A. 11/116, fol. 13d, quoted in *CHJ First Series*, 14n. In 1778 the York council offered him a new contract at high wages (£30) "in Consideration of his known abilities, Fidelity and Courage"; H. Marten & Council (YF) to W. Tomison (CH), 4 August 1778, *CHJ First Series*, 262.
63. T. McCliesh Jr (YF) to HBC, 23 August 1723, *Letters*, 94–95; T. McCliesh Jr (YF) to HBC, 16 August 1724, *Letters*, 97. Wateridge was engaged as a mariner, but always had his eye open for an opportunity: he volunteered for the party that re-established Churchill in 1717 (negotiating a higher wage for himself) and volunteered to help man the new *Whalebone* sloop in 1721 (after its crew refused to winter in the Bay). The Committee took note of McCliesh's 1723 recommendation and left the question of Wateridge's promotion (and qualifications) to his discretion, "if you are satisfied of his ability to discharge ye same"; HBC to T. McCliesh Jr & Council (YF), 20 May 1724, HBCA, A. 6/4, fol. 83d.
64. R. Staunton (AF) to HBC, 21 August 1723, HBCA, A. 11/2, fols. 46d, 48d. Albany's accountant, former apprentice Samuel Hopkins, left Albany "without Leave" on 2 October 1722; HBCA, A. 16/1, p. 5. In response to the Committee's query Staunton described Napper as "very capeable to discharge both offices [i.e., surgeon and accountant], attendinge them with care and dillegence"; R. Staunton (AF) to HBC, 23 August 1724, HBCA, A. 11/2, fol. 50. In HBC to R. Staunton & Council (AF), 19 May 1725, HBCA, A. 6/4, fol. 99d, the Committee promised to "consider him for his trouble in keeping the Books at the expiration of his Contract," but by then Napper had lost Staunton's support and the Committee's good opinion.
65. R. Waggoner & Council (AF) to HBC, 15 August 1739, HBCA, A. 11/2, fol. 99.
66. T. McCliesh Jr (YF) to HBC, 17 August 1732, *Letters*, 169; J. Isham & Council (YF) to HBC, 6 August 1752, HBCA, A. 11/114, fol. 154.
67. J. Isbister & Council (AF) to HBC, 10 September 1756, HBCA, A. 11/3, fol. 9. Harvey got the raise he wanted (from £12 to £14), but only for one year; HBCA, A. 16/3, fol. 97; A. 16/4, fol. 9.
68. J. Isbister & Council (AF) to HBC, 23 August 1744, HBCA, A. 11/2, fol. 121d. The council's letter called Irvin "an able Man, and hath been of infinite Service in carrying on the Building of the Flankers this Year" but "not agreeing with his Master." It is unclear whether "his Master" was Thomas Mitchell of the *Eastmain* or John Longland of the *Phoenix*.
69. J. Myatt (AF) to HBC, 5 August 1728, HBCA, A. 11/2, fol. 63. Joseph Adams also described Waggoner as "being very usefull in many Cases"; J. Adams & Council (AF) to HBC, 31 July 1733, HBCA, A. 11/2, fol. 76d.
70. HBC to J. Adams (AF), private, 24 May 1722, HBCA, A. 6/4, fol. 65. Adams was later chief factor at Albany, from 1730 to 1737. For reference to Adams at Eastmain, see J. Myatt (AF) to HBC, 22 August 1722, HBCA, A. 11/2, fol. 42. Apprentice Richard Norton was also encouraged to "[i]mprove in yr writing, whereby you may be Capable of prefermt"; HBC to R. Norton (PWF), private, 24 May 1722, HBCA, A. 6/4, fol. 65; also H. Kelsey (YF) to

R. Staunton (PWF), 28 March 1719, HBCA, B. 239/b/1, fol. 14. For an argument that literacy was not essential to commercial success in early modern England, see Woodward, *Men at Work*, 81–82.

71. R. Norton (PWF) to HBC, n.d. [1725], *Letters*, 113.
72. T. McCliesh Jr (YF) to HBC, 7 August 1731, *Letters*, 158.
73. HBC to W. Bevan & Council (MF), 10 May 1733, HBCA, A. 6/5, fols. 79d–80.
74. "A Book of Instructions with the Standard of Trade for Henly House in the Year of our Lord 1751 William Lamb Master," HBCA, A. 11/3, fol. 14. It is not clear who wrote these instructions; they were originally signed by George Spence (who was in command at Albany in 1751), but his signature was crossed out in copy and replaced by Joseph Isbister's; a marginal note says that this document was a copy made by Lamb in his own handwriting. Bishop, "The Henley House Massacres," believed that Albany surgeon George Rushworth compiled these instructions (39).
75. *Letters*, 210n; also see HBC to W. Bevan & Council (MF), 3 May 1734, HBCA, A. 6/5, fol. 89d; T. McCliesh Jr, W. Bevan, & Council (MF) to HBC, 24 August 1735, *Letters*, 209–10; Nigol, "Discipline, Discretion and Control," 83–87. Richard Norton was married to McCliesh's daughter; Brown, *Strangers in Blood*, 33. James Norton was sent home in 1735.
76. G. Spence & Council (AF) to HBC, 4 August 1752, HBCA, A. 11/2, fols. 150–150d.
77. T. McCliesh Jr (YF) to HBC, 17 August 1733, *Letters*, 189.
78. J. Myatt (AF) to HBC, 2 August 1729, HBCA, A. 11/2, fol. 64d; J. Adams (AF) to HBC, 28 August 1730, HBCA, A. 11/2, fol. 69.
79. Albany Fort journal, 20 April 1743, HBCA, B. 3/a/34, fol. 34.
80. T. McCliesh Jr (YF) to HBC, 17 August 1732, *Letters*, 169.
81. R. Norton (PWF) to HBC, 23 August 1737, *Letters*, 240.
82. J. Isbister & Council (AF) to HBC, 10 September 1756, HBCA, A. 11/3, fol. 9; A. 16/3, fol. 105; A. 16/4, fol. 13; R. Temple & Council (AF) to HBC, 1 September 1759, HBCA, A. 11/3, fol. 35d; R. Temple & Council (AF) to HBC, 8 September 1760, HBCA, A. 11/3, fol. 43.
83. "Instructions to Capt James Knight now Goeing Governor of the Bay and Streights of Hudsons...," 25 May 1714, HBCA, A. 6/3, fol. 124d. Kenney, *Founding of Churchill*, 112. "Though all names and eaters, they are not all workers": J. Knight (YF) to HBC, 19 September 1714, *Letters*, 37.
84. R. Staunton (AF) to HBC, 23 August 1724, HBCA, A. 11/2, fol. 51d; HBC to R. Staunton & Council (AF), 19 May 1725, HBCA, A. 6/4, fol. 99; R. Staunton (AF) to HBC, 24 August 1725, HBCA, A. 11/2, fol. 53; HBC to R. Staunton & Council (AF), 25 May 1726, HBCA, A. 6/4, fol. 108. R. Staunton (AF) to HBC, 21 August 1723, HBCA, A. 11/2, fol. 48d, referred to Cox as a "Barber," but the officers' and servants' ledger listed Cox as a labourer (HBCA, A. 16/1, p. 9).
85. J. Myatt (AF) to HBC, 10 August 1726, HBCA, A. 11/2, fol. 57; J. Myatt (AF) to HBC, 2 August 1729, HBCA, A. 11/2, fol. 66. Myatt also defended William Bevan (sloop master and trader at Eastmain House) against charges of "Unhansome" behaviour, which Myatt expected Fox to make when he got back to London.
86. HBC to W. Bevan & Council (MF), 3 May 1734, HBCA, A. 6/5, fol. 89d.
87. R. Staunton (AF) to HBC, 21 August 1723, HBCA, A. 11/2, fol. 46.
88. J. Fullartine (AF) to HBC, 2 August 1703, HBCA, A. 11/2, fol. 6; also B. 3/d/13, enclosure.

89. Chambers and Blackburn had "run out more than their wages by changing and trafficking amongst themselves unknown to me" and, along with fellow labourer James Broadbent, have "been guilty of trading with the natives, likewise stealing furs out of the warehouse." T. McCliesh Jr (YF) to HBC, 8 August 1728, *Letters*, 133, 134.
90. R. Norton & Council (PWF) to HBC, 17 August 1736, *Letters*, 215.
91. J. Myatt (AF) to HBC, 10 August 1726, HBCA, A. 11/2, fol. 57. The other two men were cooper Thomas Horn and mariner James Miller. Only the year before, Staunton had reaffirmed his belief that Napper was a "Sober & Carefull Man"; R. Staunton (AF) to HBC, 24 August 1725, HBCA, A. 11/2, fol. 53d. Napper was, in fact, being recalled anyway, as the Committee was disappointed in his desire to sign a new contract for only one year, and in his failure to indicate what wages he wanted; HBC to Charles Napper (AF), private, 25 May 1726, HBCA, A. 6/4, fol. 110d.
92. J. Myatt (AF) to HBC, 2 August 1729, HBCA, A. 11/2, fol. 66. Fox completed his apprenticeship in 1727 and signed a contract that year at fourteen pounds per annum, but it is unclear whether the contract was for three or five years; HBCA, A. 16/2, p. 9.
93. MacKay offered to pay ten pounds for his passage, twice what servants were usually charged for their passages to and from the Bay in such cases; T. McCliesh Jr (YF) to HBC, 16 August 1727, *Letters*, 128.
94. The Committee had asked for a weekly account of York's expenditure of provisions. Knight replied: "I beg the favour of you to recall me rather than to let me lie under any suspicion to make you uneasy, for the little insignificant things you have put upon me is enough to employ me to take me off all other business. And if I do not do it then I lie liable to be charged hereafter for a breach of your orders." J. Knight (YF) to HBC, 17 September 1716, *Letters*, 60.
95. J. Myatt (AF) to HBC, 2 August 1729, HBCA, A. 11/2, fol. 65.
96. J. Myatt (AF) to HBC, 2 August 1729, HBCA, A. 11/2, fol. 64d. The charges against Long are unknown; he appears to have come home in 1721 by his own choice after the Committee refused his request for a raise. HBC to T. McCliesh Jr & Council (AF), 1 June 1720, HBCA, A. 6/4, fol. 42; HBC to T. McCliesh Jr & Council (AF), 26 May 1721, HBCA, A. 6/4, fol. 52d.
97. J. Isbister & Council (AF) to HBC, 9 August 1742, HBCA, A. 11/2, fols. 110–110d.
98. J. Isbister & Council (AF) to HBC, 18 August 1743, HBCA, A. 11/2, fols. 114–114d. The following year Isbister accused Alexander Light (sloop master and trader at Eastmain House, who had gone home in 1743) of purposely making errors in the packing of the Eastmain returns "in order to prejudice us." J. Isbister & Council (AF) to HBC, 23 August 1744, HBCA, A. 11/2, fol. 120.
99. Hainsworth, *Stewards*, 29–30.
100. Dove, "Voyages," 12, observes a similar trend within the company's maritime service. See his figure 1, "Persistence of Captains, 1668–1740," p. 13, which shows the average voyages per captain rising from 1.6 (1668–86) to 10 (1731–40). Also see Dove, "Plying," 186–87.
101. J. Knight (YF) to HBC, 17 September 1716, *Letters*, 66. In the same letter Knight specifically requested former Albany cooper Richard Staunton (who had just gone home) to take the third place in the York chain of command (which was to include Churchill): "I do not know any other servant that you have at home but him that is fit to come in any such

post." The year before, the Committee had sent Knight "7 old Servants" to replace any who were "not fit for our Service"; HBC to J. Knight (YF), 3 June 1715, HBCA, A. 6/3, fol. 133d.

102. J. Isbister & Council (AF) to HBC, 9 August 1742, HBCA, A. 11/2, fol. 111d; J. Isbister & Council (AF) to HBC, 18 August 1743, HBCA, A. 11/2, fol. 116. Drover had served at twenty-eight pounds per annum since 1735, and Isbister increased his wages to thirty pounds; HBCA, A. 16/2, fol. 79; A. 16/3, fol. 27. Peter Isbister Sr, who also engaged in 1735, had been receiving old hand's wages (twelve pounds) since 1740, but they were raised to fourteen pounds for the 1742–43 season; HBCA, A. 16/2, fol. 84; A. 16/3, fol. 22. The largest increase went to Greenwood, who engaged in 1735 at three pounds and whose wages had only risen to six pounds by 1742, but he was given fourteen pounds in 1742–43; HBCA, A. 16/2, fol. 80; A. 16/3, fol. 8. All three men went home in 1743.

103. R. Norton (PWF) to HBC, 23 August 1737, *Letters*, 237; also R. Norton & Council (PWF) to HBC, 17 August 1736, *Letters*, 215; R. Norton & Council (PWF) to HBC, 16 August 1739, *Letters*, 298; J. Isham (YF) to HBC, August 1738, *Letters*, 262.

104. J. Fullartine (AF) to HBC, 2 August 1703, HBCA, A. 11/2, fol. 6. In 1706 Beale (then in command at Albany) praised his deputy, Nathaniel Bishop, in similar terms: "I like [him] very well for I really beleave he is very Honest and Carefull and dose his business very well"; A. Beale (AF) to HBC, 23 July 1706, HBCA, A. 11/2, fol. 16d. Bishop (who served the company almost continuously from 1686 until his death) had the charge of the Eastmain trade in 1715–16 and 1718–20, and Thomas McCliesh Jr unsuccessfully recommended Bishop to succeed him at Albany; T. McCliesh Jr (AF) to HBC, 31 August 1719, HBCA, A. 11/2, fol. 40d. The Committee appointed Bishop to succeed Richard Staunton at Churchill in 1721, but wind and weather prevented Staunton from leaving that year; *Letters*, 66n. Bishop did not take charge until 1722, but by then his health had deteriorated—he suffered from gout and in 1716 had been confined to his room for four months with "a Lameness"—and died on 30 June 1723, "after a long and lingering fit of sickness"; T. McCliesh Jr (AF) to HBC, 20 August 1717, HBCA, A. 11/2, fol. 36d; R. Norton & T. Bird (PWF) to HBC, 3 August 1723, *Letters*, 84.

105. He promised to combine positive reinforcement with "Sever Punishment besides all other Damiges for those that shall be found Fallty"; A. Beale (AF) to HBC, 2 August 1714, HBCA, A. 11/2, fol. 23d.

106. H. Marten (AF) to HBC, private, 17 August 1764, HBCA, A. 11/3, fol. 69. Humble was not given the charge of Henley, apparently because of his inability to speak Cree. See H. Marten (AF) to HBC, private, September 1767, HBCA, A. 11/3, fol. 112. In 1768 Humble signed a three-year contract, thanked the Committee for continuing him in its service, and promised "to make himself acquainted with the Indian Language so as to be of more service to Your Honours in future"; H. Marten & Council (AF) to HBC, 30 August 1768, HBCA, A. 11/3, fol. 119d.

107. Kitchen's assistance was particularly appreciated because Marten was suffering from very poor health, including "a Cancer of the Uvula" that nearly killed him. H. Marten & Council (AF) to HBC, 12 September 1767, HBCA, A. 11/3, fols. 105, 106; H. Marten (AF) to HBC, private, September 1767, HBCA, A. 11/3, fols. 110d–111; H. Marten (AF) to HBC,

private, 27 August 1768, HBCA, A. 11/3, fol. 115. Marten would have replaced Richards at Henley with Kitchen had Kitchen's constitution been strong enough for the journey; H. Marten (AF) to HBC, private, September 1767, HBCA, A. 11/3, fol. 112.

108. HBC to G. Geyer & Council (YF), 2 June 1688, *L.O. 1688–1696*, 8.

109. HBC to G. Geyer & Council (YF), 21 May 1691, *L.O. 1688–1696*, 120.

110. HBC to H. Kelsey & Council (YF), 4 June 1719, HBCA, A. 6/4, fol. 29d; HBC to N. Bishop (AF), private, 4 June 1719, HBCA, A. 6/4, fol. 31d. Similarly, former apprentice and chief factor Anthony Beale re-engaged for four years in 1720; he was appointed to the council at York but was assigned no particular post. The governor there, Henry Kelsey—whose patience had worn very thin during the war years, when Beale and Fullartine took turns occupying the sole position of command—was told to employ Beale however he might be useful and to "entertain him very Civilly"; HBC to H. Kelsey & Council (YF), 1 June 1720, HBCA, A. 6/4, fol. 43d. Also see HBC to J. Myatt & Council (AF), 21 May 1729, HBCA, A. 6/5, fol. 25: "With respect to Alex Thoyts, whom we entertained on account of his having been many years in our service, we never intended he should displace Mr Adams, or any other person, from the station we had fixed them in, but that you should imploy him in such a manner as you thought proper, and about such business he is best able to perform." Carpenter and shipwright Thoyts, who had served at Port Nelson in 1689–93 and at Albany in 1705–ca. 1712 and 1720–27, was apparently under the impression he had been sent out in 1728 as Myatt's "assistant"; J. Myatt (AF) to HBC, 5 August 1728, HBCA, A. 11/2, fol. 62d.

111. HBC to G. Geyer & Council (YF), 21 May 1691, *L.O. 1688–1696*, 117; HBC to T. Walsh (SR), 22 May 1690, *L.O. 1688–1696*, 105. Ann M. Carlos, "Agent Opportunism and the Role of Company Culture," *Business and Economic History* 20 (1991), 146, contrasts this letter with one written to James Nightingale by the Royal African Company's court of assistants (board of directors) around the same time. Nightingale had requested a promotion, which prompted the court to investigate the security (i.e., bond) he had offered for his current position; it did not feel that Nightingale would be able to put up the greater security needed for a higher position and informed him that it could not "preffer any Man to the greatest trust without a suitable Security and if you gett Friends here to strengthen you[r] Security...we shall be ready to bid you welcome." Carlos observed that "not only do the choice of tools used by these two companies differ...but the language used in the letters to express the company's relationship with its managers differs as well." Carlos did not date the letter from which she quoted, but Nightingale was active on the Gold Coast in the early 1680s and was made the factor at James Fort in Accra in the spring of 1681. Robin Law, ed., *The English in West Africa, 1681–1683* (Oxford: Oxford University Press for the British Academy, 1997), 23, 27, 33–34, 158–60, 168, 170–71.

112. HBC to T. Walsh (YF), 21 May 1691, *L.O. 1688–1696*, 130.

113. T. McCliesh Jr (YF) to HBC, 16 August 1730, *Letters*, 151; T. McCliesh Jr (YF) to HBC, 7 August 1731, *Letters*, 158; T. McCliesh Jr (YF) to HBC, 17 August 1732, *Letters*, 170.

114. Adams returned to England for the recovery of his health after the expiration of his apprenticeship in 1723; although he later became chief at Albany (1730–37), he initially re-engaged in 1724 as a labourer at fourteen pounds; see HBCA, A. 16/2, fol. 2. For other

examples, see HBCA, A. 16/2, fol. 27 (Bricker), fol. 44 (Low); A. 16/3, fol. 8 (Greenwood), fol. 10 (Macklin), fol. 33 (Anderson); A. 16/4, fol. 18 (Downs). Bricker also served at sixteen pounds in 1734–36. Low drowned at Albany on 12 June 1736, and Downs died at Albany in 1765.

115. See, for example, HBC to J. Knight & Council (AF), 17 June 1693, *L.O. 1688–1696*, 203–204. That year they sent Albany grain and garden seeds, a book on cultivation, and Stephen Pitts, recommended for his "great Knowledge In all manner of Tillage & agriculture he haveing bin used to itt from his Childhood"; HBC to S. Sinclair (AF), 17 June 1693, *L.O. 1688–1696*, 211–12.

116. HBC to J. Knight & Council (AF), 30 May 1694, *L.O. 1688–1696*, 232.

117. HBC to T. Walsh & Council (YF), 20 May 1694, *L.O. 1688–1696*, 237–38. Of these nineteen, four did not go home as ordered (for reasons unknown) and were taken prisoner when the French captured Port Nelson later that year (*L.O. 1688–1696*, 237n). Of the fifteen who did go home, two later returned to Hudson Bay: Daniel Hardy was at Port Nelson during its brief reoccupation by the English in 1696–97 (HBCA, B. 239/d/6, fols. 60d, 67), and Robert Moore was at Albany in 1700–1 (HBCA, B. 3/d/12, fol. 7d). Verner offered his services to the company in 1697, but no position was available for him; Johnson, "Verner," 657.

118. J. Isbister & Council (AF) to HBC, 23 August 1744, HBCA, A. 11/2, fol. 121d; A 16/3, fols. 39, 42. By 1748, Dikes's wages were up to fourteen pounds (HBCA, A. 16/3, fol. 42), and Dikes was eager to go home. Labourer William Murray, "a Handy Man and able to do the Business of a Cooper," took his place; G. Spence & Council (AF) to HBC, 22 August 1748, HBCA, A. 11/2, fols. 137–137d. Murray's wages were advanced from ten to fourteen pounds (and in 1751 to sixteen pounds), but the Albany officers' and servants' ledger continued to list him as a labourer until 1752; HBCA, A. 16/3, fols. 46, 84.

119. HBC to T. McCliesh Jr & Council (YF), 20 May 1724, HBCA, A. 6/4, fol. 85. Earlier in the letter (fol. 84d) the Committee had instructed the York council not to renew men's contracts for less than two years. Also see HBC to R. Staunton & Council (AF), 20 May 1724, HBCA, A. 6/4, fol. 86d; HBC to R. Norton & Council (PWF), 20 May 1724, HBCA, A. 6/4, fol. 88d.

120. HBC to J. Bridgar (MF), 20 May 1686, *L.O. 1680–1687*, 177.

121. Woodward, *Men at Work*, 12, 161; Cliffe, *World of the Country House*, 105. For discretionary pensions and gratuities in the EIC, see H.V. Bowen, *Business of Empire*, 140–41.

122. *Minutes, First Part*, 26–27.

123. *L.O. 1680–1687*, 378.

124. HBCA, A. 1/8, fol. 11d. In March 1685 the Committee directed Brownson to advise Charles Bridgar on the size of sails to be made for the *Colleton*; HBCA, A. 1/8, fol. 20. Also in March 1685, Brownson re-engaged for three years at thirty-six pounds (HBCA, A. 1/8, fol. 22), but he was captured by the French in July 1686 (HBCA, A. 15/3, fol. 101).

125. HBCA, A. 15/3, fol. 158.

126. HBCA, A. 6/3, fol. 113.

127. HBC to J. Isbister & Council (AF), 12 May 1756, HBCA, A. 6/9, fol. 30.

128. HBCA, A. 16/3, fols. 68, 78, 85, 91, 93. Ash's gratuity was ordered by the Committee in 1755 (HBCA, A. 16/3, fol. 78), but his account was still open in 1762, when the only item listed was the gratuity "intended for a Lawful Heir"; HBCA, A. 16/4, fol. 2. Lamb's administratrix may have been his mother; see HBCA, A. 16/3, fols. 47, 60, 85.
129. Mace went home in 1725 and died in England sometime between October and December that year. *Letters*, 70n; HBC to T. McCliesh Jr & Council (AF), 26 May 1721, HBCA, A. 6/4, fol. 53; A. 16/1, fol. 19; A. 16/2, fol. 11; R. Staunton (AF) to HBC, 23 August 1724, HBCA, A. 11/2, fol. 51d; R. Staunton (AF) to HBC, 24 August 1725, HBCA, A. 11/2, fol. 52d, 53.
130. J. Isham (YF) to HBC, August 1738, *Letters*, 262.
131. G.E. Thorman, "Hopkins, Samuel," in *DCB*, http://www.biographi.ca/en/bio/hopkins_samuel_2E.html; *Letters*, 99n.
132. T. McCliesh Jr (YF) to HBC, 16 August 1730, *Letters*, 150.
133. See, for instance, Ben-Amos, "Gifts and Favors," 310–14.
134. J. Isbister & Council (AF) to HBC, 18 August 1743, HBCA, A. 11/2, fol. 116.
135. "Instructions for Cap[tai]n Antho Beale, Now goeing Governor in Hudsons Bay...," 29 May 1711, HBCA, A. 6/3, fol. 108. Almost identical language was used in "Instructions to Capt James Knight now Goeing Governor of the Bay and Streights of Hudsons...," 25 May 1714, HBCA, A. 6/3, fol. 124d.
136. "Instructions to Mr Jos Myatt," 25 May 1726, HBCA, A. 6/4, fol. 109.

6 THE INLAND EXPERIENCE

1. By the late seventeenth century "the peoples in the post-Columbian countries that faced the Atlantic thought of that ocean as a space in which to *make or imagine physical connections*." Chaplin, "The Atlantic Ocean," 36, also 39–42; emphasis in the original.
2. "Orders to Joseph Smith and Joseph Wagoner," 20 August 1756, HBCA, A. 11/115, fol. 2d. It is unclear who the Sturgeon people were, but Isham's orders to Smith and Waggoner stated (fol. 2) that their "Head Captain...(Washiabutt by Name)...formerly brought 75 Cannoes, but of Late Years has dwindled away to Nothing and even this Year but 13 Cannoes." Also see J.B. D'Laryea (AF) to HBC, private, 22 August 1761, HBCA, A. 11/3, fol. 51.
3. F. Jacobs (PWF) to J. Isham (YF), 30 August 1755, HBCA, B. 239/b/13, fol. 1. For details of the troubles at Whale River see J. Potts (RF) to T. White (MF) and J. Isbister (AF), 15 March 1754, HBCA, A. 11/2, fols. 152–156d; also Francis and Morantz, *Partners in Furs*, 74–75; Fossett, *In Order to Live Untroubled*, 61–62.
4. J. Isbister & Council (AF) to HBC, 13 September 1755, HBCA, A. 11/2, fol. 179. Also see J. Isbister & Council (AF) to HBC, 10 September 1756, HBCA, A. 11/3, fol. 7d.
5. G. Rushworth (AF) to HBC, private, 8 September 1755, HBCA, A. 11/2, fols. 173–174d.
6. HBC to J. Isbister & Council (AF), 12 May 1756, HBCA, A. 6/9, fol. 29d.
7. "It was not owing to an Ill Opinion we had of your Conduct that we sent over another Accountant to relieve you, but from an Apprehension that Officiating as Second, Surgeon and Accountant might be too much for you to go through especially as we saw plainly you were not very Conversant in the latter." HBC to G. Rushworth (AF), private, 12 May 1756, HBCA, A. 5/1, fol. 14.

8. G. Rushworth (AF) to HBC, private, 8 September 1756, HBCA, A. 11/3, fol. 3.
9. J. Isbister & Council (AF) to HBC, 10 September 1756, HBCA, A. 11/3, fol. 7d.
10. R. Temple (AF) to HBC, 7 September 1756, HBCA, A. 11/3, fols. 1–1d.
11. R. Temple & Council (AF) to HBC, 30 May, 6 June, 15 August, 18 August 1757, HBCA, A. 11/3, fol. 17.
12. R. Temple & Council (AF) to HBC, 30 May, 6 June, 15 August, 18 August 1757, HBCA, A. 11/3, fols. 17d–19d; HBC to J. Isbister & Council (AF), 12 May 1756, HBCA, A. 6/9, fol. 29d.
13. R. Temple & Council (AF) to HBC, 30 May, 6 June, 15 August, 18 August 1757, HBCA, A. 11/3, fol. 20. The Albany council was not unhappy to see Joplin depart: "he has this Ship time lay'd one night out of the Factory we think him an improper Person to be Continued"; R. Temple & Council (AF) to HBC, August 1757, HBCA, A. 11/3, fol. 25.
14. R. Temple & Council (AF) to HBC, 30 May, 6 June, 15 August, 18 August 1757, HBCA, A. 11/3, fol. 21.
15. HBC to J. Isbister & Council (AF), 12 May 1756, HBCA, A. 6/9, fol. 29d. For the bounty, see Albany Fort journal, 6 March 1755, HBCA, B. 3/a/47, fol. 22; John S. Long, "In Search of Mr. Bundin," in *Papers of the Twenty-Sixth Algonquian Conference*, ed. David H. Pentland (Winnipeg: University of Manitoba, 1995), 209; Bishop, "The Henley House Massacres," 37.
16. HBC to R. Temple (AF), 23 May 1758, HBCA, A. 5/1, fol. 23d. The Committee had English common law on their side. "A legal guide of 1799 gave the uncontroversial view on the matter: refusing to do the master's business was wrong"; Schwarz, "Custom, Wages and Workload," 158n51. However, the HBC's reluctance to prosecute its own servants has already been noted.
17. R. Temple & Council (AF) to HBC, August 1757, HBCA, A. 11/3, fol. 25.
18. Albany Fort journal, 24 May 1759, HBCA, B. 3/a/51, fol. 51; Long, "In Search of Mr. Bundin," 205. For Clark at Whale River House, see J. Potts (RF) to T. White (MF) and J. Isbister (AF), 15 March 1754, HBCA, A. 11/2, fols. 152–156d. Ward was listed in the Albany officers' and servants' ledger as a sailor between 1756 and 1759 (HBCA, A. 16/3, fol. 111; A. 16/4, fol. 17), but Temple described him in 1758 as "a Boat Builder by Trade and a very handy Young fellow"; R. Temple & Council (AF) to HBC, 25 September 1758, HBCA, A. 11/3, fol. 30d. He returned home in the summer of 1759, when Temple called him "A young Man that has behaved well, and been very usefull to Us"; R. Temple & Council (AF) to HBC, 1 September 1759, HBCA, A. 11/3, fol. 35.
19. Albany Fort journal, 23 September 1759, HBCA, B. 3/a/52, fol. 2d; Long, "In Search of Mr. Bundin," 207. An unsigned letter to HBC, 17 September 1759, HBCA, A. 11/3, fol. 41, detailed the attack on that house, including the death of George Clark, the wounding and courage of John Spence, the brave defending by James Inkster and John Cromartie, and the brave leading by Inkster of the escape. Although Cromartie survived the attack on Henley, he was later "render'd unfit for your Honours Service" by a ruptured hernia and had to go home in 1765; H. Marten & Council (AF) to HBC, 15 August 1765, HBCA, A. 11/3, fol. 80d.
20. Bishop, "The Henley House Massacres," 41; Lytwyn, *Fur Trade*, 8. In a letter to HBC, private, 22 August 1761, HBCA, A. 11/3, fol. 51, J.B. D'Laryea (AF) blamed the French for this

attack on Henley, particularly three men named Boije, Alen Lequout, and Cadotete. Long, "In Search of Mr. Bundin," 203–25, discusses the 1759 attack in detail, incorporating some Cree oral history.

21. Albany Fort journal, 8 October 1759, HBCA, B. 3/a/52, fol. 4; Long, "In Search of Mr. Bundin," 207.
22. Albany Fort journal, 24 August 1764, HBCA, B. 3/a/57, fols. 2d–3.
23. "The Honble Hudsons Bay Companys Servants having refused to go to build a House at Henly the following are their answares on that head" (AF), n.d. [summer 1764], HBCA, A. 11/3, fols. 65–66. For Farrant, see H. Marten & Council (AF) to HBC, 15 August 1765, HBCA, A. 11/3, fol. 80d.
24. Albany Council (AF) to HBC, 15 August 1764, HBCA, A. 11/3, fol. 67.
25. H. Marten (AF) to HBC, 17 August 1764, HBCA, A. 11/3, fols. 68–68d.
26. H. Marten & Council (AF) to HBC, 12 September 1767, HBCA, A. 11/3, fol. 106d; A. 16/4, fol. 46. "Tracking" boats is done when rapids or low water make it difficult or impossible for a fully laden boat to make progress; some or all of the crew get out (and perhaps unload some or all of the cargo to lighten the load further) and walk along the shoreline, dragging the boat with tow ropes.
27. See, for instance, H. Marten (AF) to HBC, private, September 1767, HBCA, A. 11/3, fol. 111d; H. Marten (AF) to HBC, private, 25 August 1769, HBCA, A. 11/3, fols. 126–127; T. Hopkins & Council (AF) to HBC, 28 August 1769, HBCA, A. 11/3, fol. 130; H. Marten (AF) to HBC, private, 2 September 1770, HBCA, A. 11/3, fol. 142d.
28. Williams, *Miscellany*, 87n.
29. R. Temple & Council (AF) to HBC, 30 May, 6 June, 15 August, 18 August 1757, HBCA, A. 11/3, fols. 17–17d.
30. "The Honble Hudsons Bay Companys Servants having refused to go to build a House at Henly the following are their answares on that head" (AF), n.d. [summer 1764], HBCA, A. 11/3, fol. 65.
31. "The Honble Hudsons Bay Companys Servants having refused to go to build a House at Henly the following are their answares on that head" (AF), n.d. [summer 1764], HBCA, A. 11/3, fols. 65–66; R. Temple & Council (AF) to HBC, 18 August 1764, HBCA, A. 11/3, fol. 73d. Although Downs was assigned to a sloop, the council described him as a good sawyer; R. Temple & Council (AF) to HBC, 30 May, 6 June, 15 August, 18 August 1757, HBCA, A. 11/3, fol. 21. Downs had been apprenticed to the company in 1750–57 and served as a labourer from 1757 until his death on 29 August 1764; HBCA, A. 16/3, fols. 75, 112; A. 16/4, fol. 18.
32. H. Marten & Council (AF) to HBC, 15 August 1765, HBCA, A. 11/3, fol. 81d. Atkins—described by Marten as "a bad man"—went home in 1765; H. Marten & Council (AF) to HBC, 15 August 1765, HBCA, A. 11/3, fol. 80d.
33. H. Marten (AF) to W. Richards (Henley), 19 June 1766, HBCA, B. 3/b/3, fol. 5d.
34. Prince of Wales Fort journal, 29 June 1759, HBCA, B. 42/a/52, fol. 37d.
35. Rich and Johnson, *Isham's Observations*, 67–69, 207, 209; Rich, *History*, vol. 1, 525; Thomas Wien, "Selling Beaver Skins in North America and Europe, 1720–1760," *Journal of the Canadian Historical Association* 1, no. 1 (1990): 293–317.

36. See, for example, HBC to J. Isham (YF), 15 May 1760, HBCA, A. 6/9, fols. 128d–129; J. Isham (YF) to HBC, 5 September 1760, HBCA, A. 11/115, fol. 50d.

37. James Isham's "Remarks" on Anthony Henday's inland journal, 1754–1755, HBCA, B. 239/a/40, fol. 38. Isham observed that Henday had been well received inland and that "he does Really believe if English were to go in Land for 2 or 3 years," they could bring many inland groups down to trade; HBCA, B. 239/a/40, fols. 40–40d. Glyndwr Williams, "The Puzzle of Anthony Henday's Journal, 1754–5," *The Beaver* (Winter 1978), 56, has suggested that Henday deliberately suppressed and distorted some aspects of his journal, particularly regarding the willingness of the Earchithinues to come down to Hudson Bay. For the possible identity of the Earchithinues, see Belyea, "Indians," 343–50.

38. HBCA, B. 239/a/40, fol. 41. For Grover, see York Fort journal, 28 June and 2 July 1755, HBCA, B. 239/a/39, fols. 32d–33.

39. F. Jacobs (YF) to M. Norton (PWF), 25 July 1768, HBCA, B. 239/b/29, fol.9d. Andrew Graham believed that the First Nations considered servants as slaves, and gentlemen as "very knowing and great men." "Therefore," he explained, "when they have our men inland, [the First Nations] never mind what they say." Glyndwr Williams, *Graham's Observations*, 262–63.

40. Rich, *History*, vol. 2, 19. Andrew Graham at Severn echoed these concerns the following year; Glyndwr Williams, *Graham's Observations*, 262. Jacobs's and Graham's criticisms were unfair, however, as the Canadiens had not penetrated beyond Rainy Lake before 1767; they had been trying since 1765 but had been blocked by antagonism from local First Nations (probably Ojibwa). Canadien pedlars first reached Lake Winnipeg in the summer or autumn of 1767, after the HBC winterers and Muskego Cree traders had departed the lakeshore for York Fort. Lytwyn, *Fur Trade*, 9.

41. Glyndwr Williams, *Graham's Observations*, 262.

42. Cumberland House journal, 24 January 1777, *CHJ First Series*, 109–10.

43. HBCA, A. 16/31, fols. 77d–78.

44. H. Marten (YF) to HBC, 25 August 1777, HBCA, A. 11/116, fol. 22, quoted in *CHJ First Series*, 142n, 181n.

45. Matthew Cocking's journal, 23 August 1772, HBCA, B. 239/a/69, fol. 11d.

46. Matthew Cocking, "Thoughts on making a Settlement Inland," 1773, HBCA, B. 239/a/69, fol. 53.

47. HBC to F. Jacobs (YF), 28 May 1771, HBCA, A. 5/1, fol. 129.

48. Scholars have generally accepted the traders' reports that Indigenous consumer demand was fairly static during this period and that increasing the purchasing power of fur merely decreased the effort put into commercial trapping. For a recent challenge to this consensus, see Ann M. Carlos and Frank D. Lewis, *Commerce by a Frozen Sea* (Philadelphia: University of Pennsylvania Press, 2010), 130–49.

49. Rich, *History*, vol. 2, 23.

50. William Pink's journal, 7 August 1767, HBCA, B. 239/a/58, fol. 6d. Pink served as a labourer from 1765 through 1770 but spent four of those years (1766–70) on inland wintering journeys.

51. Rich, *History*, vol. 2, 16.

52. Rich, 33.
53. A. Graham (YF) to HBC, 26 August 1772, quoted in Glyndwr Williams, *Graham's Observations*, 290–91. See also Rich, *History*, vol. 2, 27–29; Glyndwr Williams, lxii; *CHJ First Series*, xxi–xxii.
54. Montreal-based trading companies sometimes co-operated in their efforts to control desertion by compiling "blacklists" of deserters; Podruchny, *Making the Voyageur World*, 143.
55. A. Graham (YF) to HBC, 26 August 1772, quoted in Glyndwr Williams, *Graham's Observations*, 288.
56. *CHJ First Series*, xxiii–xxiv. Cole subsequently remained in Canadien employ on the upper Saskatchewan River until he was killed on 22 April 1779 in an argument between some Canadiens and some Cree over a horse; E.E. Rich, "Cole, John," in *DCB*, http://www.biographi.ca/en/bio/cole_john_4E.html.
57. *CHJ First Series*, xxiii.
58. See Rich, *History*, vol. 2, 61–63.
59. For a brief history of Wapiscogamy or Brunswick House (1776–1806), see Rich and Johnson, *Moose Fort Journals*, 331–33.
60. Francis and Morantz, *Partners in Furs*, 102–3.
61. Cumberland House journal, 20 September 1779, *CHJ Second Series*, 15; W. Tomison (Hudson House) to W. Walker (CH), 12 December 1779, *CHJ Second Series*, 27.
62. *CHJ First Series*, xxxiii; Robert Davey et al. (Hudson House) to W. Tomison (CH), 23 May 1781, HBCA, A. 11/116, fol. 83, quoted in *CHJ Second Series*, 183n.
63. *CHJ Second Series*, 183n; H. Marten & Council (YF) to HBC, 1 September 1781, HBCA, A. 11/116, fol. 92, quoted in *CHJ Second Series*, 217n.
64. *CHJ Second Series*, xlix–l; also see Samuel Hearne's journal, 1775, in *Journals of Samuel Hearne and Philip Turnor*, ed. J.B. Tyrrell (Toronto: Champlain Society, 1934), 191.
65. Cumberland House journal, 30 May 1776, *CHJ First Series*, 51–53.
66. Cumberland House journal, 12 May 1777, *CHJ First Series*, 145–46, also 97n; Cumberland House journal, 2 May 1782, *CHJ Second Series*, 249.
67. H. Marten (YF) to HBC, 20 August 1776, HBCA, A. 11/116, fol. 5, quoted in *CHJ Second Series*, xxvi fn; also see *CHJ First Series*, xxxvii. A year earlier Hearne had made a similar complaint about the men of Cumberland; he did not single out Orkneymen as especially culpable, but most of his men were from there; *CHJ Second Series*, xlix–l.
68. York Fort journal, 13 July 1776, HBCA, B. 239/a/73, quoted in *CHJ Second Series*, xxvi.
69. HBC to F. Jacobs (YF), private, 15 May 1776, HBCA, A. 6/12, fol. 54; HBC to H. Marten (YF), private, 14 May 1777, HBCA, A. 6/12, fols. 79–79d.
70. H. Marten (YF) to HBC, 25 August 1777, HBCA, A. 11/116, fol. 22, quoted in *CHJ First Series*, 142n, 181n.
71. H. Marten (YF) to W. Tomison (CH), 11 September 1777, *CHJ First Series*, 226.
72. See the 1777 contract of James Sutherland, aged about twenty-six, of St. Martin in the Fields, who engaged as a tailor for five years at twelve pounds per annum and was posted to Albany; HBCA, A. 32/3, fol. 14. Also see the 1780 contract of John Cromartie of South

Ronaldsay, who engaged as a labourer for five years at six pounds per annum; HBCA, A. 32/1, fol. 10.

73. "Copy of Instructions given by Mr. Humphrey Marten to Mr Matthew Cocking on his going to Cumberland House," n.d. [September 1776], *CHJ First Series*, 347.
74. *CHJ First Series*, xxxvii. For the men's demands (as anxiously recorded by Marten in the York Fort journal), see *CHJ Second Series*, xxvii.
75. H. Marten (YF) to HBC, 4 September 1780, HBCA, A. 11/116, fol. 67, quoted in *CHJ Second Series*, xxxii.
76. *CHJ Second Series*, l.
77. H. Marten (YF) to HBC, 4 September 1780, HBCA, A. 11/116, fol. 67, quoted in *CHJ Second Series*, xxxii. Also see W. Walker (CH) to HBC, 25 July 1777, HBCA, A. 11/116, fol. 19, quoted in *CHJ First Series*, 175n.
78. Albany Fort journal, 9 June 1743, HBCA, B. 3/a/34, fol. 44.
79. Albany Fort journal, 14 June 1743, HBCA, B. 3/a/34, fol. 45d.
80. Tomison was complaining that Marten had not sent any incoming mail up from York the previous autumn; W. Tomison (CH) to H. Marten (YF), 5 June 1781, *CHJ Second Series*, 154.

7 MASTER-SERVANT RELATIONSHIPS

1. HBC to T. McCliesh Jr & Council (YF), 19 May 1725, HBCA, A. 6/4, fol. 95; HBC to J. Myatt (AF), private, 20 May 1724, HBCA, A. 6/4, fol. 87d.
2. Schwarz, "Custom, Wages and Workload," 143, 156.
3. HBC to M. Norton (PWF), private, 14 May 1771, HBCA, A. 5/1, fols. 132d–133. Also see Payne, "Daily Life," 66, 68.
4. Lawson, *East India Company*, 72.
5. Lawson, 72, suggested that a boy could enter the service at age sixteen as a writer and achieve the high rank of senior merchant by age twenty-seven.
6. In the rural estates of many of the gentry there were a few long-serving retainers, but the turnover was steady among the bulk of the domestic and agricultural servants; Cliffe, *World of the Country House*, 91–92. Likewise, naval shipwrights preferred a mix of young and old, good and less good, labourers in their work teams;: John Rule, "The Property of Skill in the Period of Manufacture," in *The Historical Meanings of Work*, ed. Patrick Joyce (Cambridge: Cambridge University Press, 1987), 110.
7. HBC to H. Kelsey (YF), 31 May 1697, HBCA, A. 6/3, fol. 32; R. Staunton (AF) to HBC, 21 August 1723, HBCA, A. 11/2, fol. 47d.
8. For joint management in English companies trading in Africa, see R. Porter, "English Chief Factors on the Gold Coast, 1632–1753," *African Historical Studies* 1, no. 2 (1968): 199–209.
9. York Fort journal, 2 March and 2 April 1762, HBCA, B. 239/a/49, fols. 28d, 34–35.
10. Ann M. Carlos and Stephen Nicholas, "Agency Problems in Early Chartered Companies," *Journal of Economic History* 50, no. 4 (December 1990): 858.
11. Tadmor, *Family and Friends*, 57.
12. This contrasts somewhat with the EIC, whose directors, only from the late 1760s onward, "endeavoured to promote the reform of the Company's civil service in the hope that a

body of men could be created in India whose outlook and attitude were more similar to their own." They attempted "to improve the behaviour, manners, and morals of Company servants, and...very detailed codes of conduct focused attention on junior staff in the hope that extravagance and luxury would be replaced by frugal and sober lifestyles." H.V. Bowen, *Business of Empire*, 212–13.

13. J. Knight (YF) to HBC, 19 September 1714, *Letters*, 37; T. McCliesh Jr (YF) to HBC, 23 August 1723, *Letters*, 96; J. Isham (YF) to HBC, 29 August 1739, *Letters*, 310; J.B. D'Laryea (AF) to HBC, private, 21 August 1761, HBCA, A. 11/3, fol. 47.
14. J. Knight (YF) to Sir Bibye Lake (London), private, 19 September 1714, *Letters*, 37. Richardson, *The Apprentice's Vade Mecum*, recommended an apprentice who "falls into some *casual Lapse*" to "disburthen his Mind of it, and confess it frankly, and resolve to avoid those Occasions for the future that shall lead him into the like Snares....For he that knows his Duty, and will not do it, shews nothing less than an abandon'd Mind" (37–38).
15. HBC to R. Norton (PWF), private, 25 May 1727, HBCA, A. 6/5, fol. 9d.
16. See HBC to T. McCliesh Jr (YF), private, 24 May 1728, HBCA, A. 6/5, fol. 18d; Richardson, *The Apprentice's Vade Mecum*, 49.
17. R. Staunton & G. Howy (MF) to HBC, August 1738, *Letters*, 269; R. Staunton & Council (MF) to HBC, 17 August 1739, *Letters*, 301, 305–6.
18. T. McCliesh Jr (YF) to HBC, 16 August 1724, *Letters*, 97. The Committee's disapproval can be found in HBC to T. McCliesh Jr & Council (YF), 20 May 1724, HBCA, A. 6/4, fol. 83.
19. Hainsworth, *Stewards*, 261. Pollard was partial to an ostentatious turn of phrase: two years earlier, he had written to the Countess of Bath, "I humbly beseech your honour to believe that I value more the least esteem or respect from your honour than the greatest praise or love this country can afford me" (Hainsworth, 49).
20. T. McCliesh Jr (YF) to HBC, 23 August 1723, *Letters*, 94; T. McCliesh Jr (YF) to HBC, 8 August 1728, *Letters*, 137.
21. Isham mentioned, among many other things, that the men were dissatisfied with the quality of sugar ("they thinking it very hard to pay twelvepence a pound for it"), that the coal sent out was so full of stones and dirt that it was dangerous to use in the forge, and that the fort's surgical instruments were dangerously out of repair. J. Isham (YF) to HBC, 20 July 1739, *Letters*, 281–84.
22. Albany Fort journal, 6–7 May 1743, HBCA, B. 3/a/34, fols. 37–38.
23. W. Bevan & Council (MF) to HBC, 15 August 1733, *Letters*, 182.
24. James W. Carey, *Communication as Culture*, rev. ed. (New York: Routledge, 2009), 15, also 12–18. Also see Kenneth J. Banks, *Chasing Empire across the Sea* (Montreal: McGill-Queen's University Press, 2006), 11.
25. See Games, *Web of Empire*, 157.
26. See, for example, Instructions to Captain John Ford, 6 June 1689, *L.O. 1688–1696*, 66; HBC to "the Seamen at Gravesend," 15 June 1689, *L.O. 1688–1696*, 77; HBC to G. Geyer (YF), private, 21 May 1691, *L.O. 1688–1696*, 127; HBC to J. Isham (London), 21 May 1750, HBCA, A. 6/7, fol. 163d; HBC to J. Potts (RF), 22 May 1754, HBCA, A. 5/1, fol. 2; HBC to H. Pollexfen Jr (RF), 27 May 1755, HBCA, A. 5/1, fol. 8; HBC to S. Skrimshire (Flamborough House, FH), HBCA, A. 5/1, fol. 10; HBC to William Grover (PWF), 23 May 1758, HBCA, A. 5/1, fol. 25.

27. H.V. Bowen, *Business of Empire*, 208.

28. HBC to J. Nixon (CI), 15 May 1682, *L.O. 1680–1687*, 39; H. Kelsey (YF) to R. Staunton (PWF), 27 January 1719, HBCA, B. 239/b/1, fol. 10; "Coppy Of the Orders to be observed by Richd Downs & Jno Collinwood," 27 January 1719, HBCA, B. 239/b/1, fol. 11; H. Kelsey (YF) to R. Staunton (PWF), 28 March 1719, HBCA, B. 239/b/1, fol. 15; J.B. D'Laryea (AF) to HBC, 22 August 1761, HBCA, A. 11/3, fol. 51d; H. Marten (SR) to J. Isham (YF), 1 January 1761, HBCA, B. 239/b/22, fol. 3d; H. Marten (AF) to HBC, 24 August 1763, HBCA, A. 11/3, fol. 57; H. Marten (YF) to T. Kitchin (AF), 4 February 1779, HBCA, B. 239/b/39, fol. 9d; *CHJ Second Series*, xx; HBC to R. Norton (PWF), private, 1 June 1720, HBCA, A. 6/4, fol. 45d.

29. See Tadmor, *Family and Friends*, 59–60; Laslett, *The World We Have Lost*, 5; Hecht, *Domestic Servant Class*, 74; E.P. Thompson, "The Patricians and the Plebs," in *Customs in Common*, 64.

30. HBC to J. Nixon (CI), 29 May 1682, *L.O. 1680–1687*, 53–54.

31. HBC to J. Bridgar (MF), 20 May 1686, *L.O. 1680–1687*, 178; HBC to P.E. Radisson (YF), 20 May 1686, *L.O. 1680–1687*, 199–200.

32. J. Isbister & Council (AF) to HBC, 10 September 1756, HBCA, A. 11/3, fol. 7.

33. T. McCliesh Jr (YF) to HBC, 23 August 1723, *Letters*, 92; T. McCliesh Jr (YF) to HBC, 17 August 1732, *Letters*, 169.

34. R. Norton (PWF) to HBC, 14 August 1726, *Letters*, 117; A. Beale (PWF) to HBC, 26 July 1729, *Letters*, 139.

35. Malcolmson, *Life and Labour*, 107; also see Griffiths, *Youth and Authority*, 392; E.P. Thompson, "The Patricians and the Plebs," in *Customs in Common*, 33.However, also see Hecht, *Domestic Servant Class*, 206; Abbott, *Life Cycles*, 113. Laslett, *The World We Have Lost*, referred to "that unquestioning subordination which marked relationships" but added that servants and other subordinates had motives "to dissemble, to conceal resentment, to exaggerate or to feign affection and respect" (213–14).

36. *L.O. 1680–1687*, 313–16, 317.

37. *L.O. 1680–1687*, 321–24. This is also how John Oldmixon portrayed the siege of Albany, although his source is unclear; see Oldmixon, *History of Hudson's-Bay*, 403.

38. Edward Coles et al. (London?) to HBC, n.d. [1688], *L.O. 1680–1687*, 331–32; emphasis added. See also "John Mechen, Edward Coles, Hugh Mitchell, and Wm. Folder, make Oath…," 4 February 1687, *L.O. 1680–1687*, 332–33.

39. Oldmixon, *History of Hudson's-Bay*, 403; Edward Coles et al. (London?) to HBC, n.d. [1688], *L.O. 1680–1687*, 331. Twelve men opted to spend the winter with Lowland Cree families, and four of them appear to have died before spring. Ten men (apparently including Coles et al.) stayed near the post and eked out a very meagre existence for themselves. In the spring they were all taken as prisoners to Canada and then to France, from whence they made their way back to England as best they could. See Edward Coles et al. (London?) to HBC (London), 17 January 1688, *L.O. 1680–1687*, 324–27. Surgeon Edward Evans (whom Sergeant also accused of mutiny) had died in Hudson Bay during the hard winter of 1686–87; his effects were auctioned before the mast for £6 8s.10d. in April 1687; HBCA, A. 15/3, fol. 99. Phillip Scovell and Frederick Johnson may also have died that winter or subsequently (in Canada or in France), as they did not respond to Sergeant's charges

and do not appear in later company records; John Garret and Elias Turner, mentioned by Oldmixon but not by HBC account books, may have suffered a similar fate.

40. *L.O. 1680–1687*, 390–91.

41. See Henige, "Companies Are Always Ungrateful," 27, 29, 33–35, 37, 39–40, 43n34; Chaudhuri, *English East India Company*, 18, 74; Davies, *Royal African Company*, 255–56.

42. J. Knight (PWF) to W. Stuart (YF), 23 August 1717, in Kenney, *Founding of Churchill*, 172. Also see J. Knight (YF) to R. Staunton (AF), 28 June 1715, HBCA, A. 6/4, fol. 9d: "You right that you design home if the Comp doth not Answer your Demand according to Sallery, I wish you well with all my heart, but it does not lye in my power now, to serve you any thing in that matter, & our Ship was gone before I Recd your Letter to write any thing home, but I pray God direct you for ye best whow [whom?] I always shall wish well."

43. J. Knight (PWF) to H. Kelsey (YF), 23 August 1717, in Kenney, *Founding of Churchill*, 175.

44. J. Knight (YF) to HBC, 17 September 1716, *Letters*, 61; T. McCliesh Jr (AF) to HBC, 31 August 1719, HBCA, A. 11/2, fol. 39d; J. Myatt (AF) to HBC, 22 August 1722, HBCA, A. 11/2, fols. 42, 43; R. Staunton (AF) to HBC, 21 August 1723, HBCA, A. 11/2, fol. 46. Staunton later connected the company's "interest" with a factor's "credit" in discussing his own management; R. Staunton & Council (MF) to HBC, 17 August 1739, *Letters*, 305.

45. Faramerz Dabhoiwala, "The Construction of Honour, Reputation, and Status in Late Seventeenth- and Early Eighteenth-Century England," *Transactions of the Royal Historical Society*, sixth series, vol. 6 (1996): 201. Also see Dabhoiwala, 201n1, 202n2; Thomas, *The Ends of Life*, 163–66, 171–79.

46. Hainsworth, *Stewards*, 51.

47. J. Isbister & Council (AF) to HBC, 6 September 1741, HBCA, A. 11/2, fol. 108; A. Graham (YF) to F. Jacobs (PWF), 15 April 1761, HBCA, B. 239/b/21, fol. 7; F. Jacobs (PWF) to A. Graham (YF), 25 April 1761, HBCA, B. 239/b/21, fol. 8d.

48. H. Marten (AF) to George Humble ("Castaway Island," Albany River), 20 June 1766, HBCA, B. 3/b/3, fols. 6d–7.

49. H. Marten & Council (AF) to HBC, 12 September 1767, HBCA, A. 11/3, fol. 107d. Such rhetorical flourishes were part of Marten's prose style, often expressed through the voice of his council. For instance, also see H. Marten & Council (AF) to HBC, 30 August 1768, HBCA, A. 11/3, fol. 118d.

50. T. White (YF) to HBC, 27 August 1736, *Letters*, 221. The "unfortunate crisis" to which he referred was probably the loss of the *Hudson's Bay* frigate and all her cargo in the ice of Hudson Strait on her way to York; *Letters*, 220.

51. J. Isbister (AF) to HBC, private, 14 September 1755, HBCA, A. 11/2, fol. 176. In the official letter to London that year Isbister and his council declared, "We are determined to defend your Factory rights and property to the utmost of our power and make your Orders Sobriety and Virtue the rule of our Conduct"; J. Isbister & Council (AF) to HBC, 13 September 1755, HBCA, A. 11/2, fol. 185.

52. H. Marten (AF) to HBC, private, 27 August 1768, HBCA, A. 11/3, fol. 115; T. Hopkins (AF) to HBC, private, 30 August 1768, HBCA, A. 11/3, fol. 124.

53. Fleetwood, *Relative Duties*, 362–63, 376; also Richardson, *The Apprentice's Vade Mecum*, vi, 21, 24; Tadmor, *Friends and Family*, 60–62; Wrightson, *Earthly Necessities*, chap. 13.

54. H. Kelsey & Council (YF) to R. Staunton (PWF), 12 April 1720, HBCA, B. 239/b/1, fol. 27.
55. Wrightson, *Earthly Necessities*, 301.
56. HBC to T. White & Council (YF), 6 May 1736, HBCA, A. 6/5, fol. 107; HBC to T. White (YF), private, 6 May 1736, HBCA, A. 6/5, fol. 113.
57. HBC to G. Geyer & Council (YF), 22 May 1690, *L.O. 1688–1696*, 99–100; W. Bevan & Council (MF) to HBC, 20 August 1734, *Letters*, 196, 198. Also see R. Staunton & G. Howy (MF) to HBC, August 1738, *Letters*, 265.
58. HBC to W. Bevan & Council (MF), 3 May 1734, HBCA, A. 6/5, fol. 89.
59. H. Marten & Council (AF) to HBC, 23 August 1766, HBCA, A. 11/3, fol. 92d; H. Marten & Council (AF) to HBC, 30 August 1768, HBCA, A. 11/3, fol. 118d; H. Marten (AF) to HBC, 3 September 1771, HBCA, A. 11/3, fol. 169.
60. H. Marten (AF) to HBC, 17 August 1764, HBCA, A. 11/3, fols. 68–68d; H. Marten (AF) to HBC, September 1767, HBCA, A. 11/3, fol. 111d; H. Marten & Council (AF) to HBC, 30 August 1768, HBCA, A. 11/3, fol. 121. Marten's reference to "the loss of Your Servants" probably referred to the drowning deaths of John Stone and Daniel Bryan on 15 September 1766.
61. HBC to J. Knight & Council (AF), 17 June 1693, *L.O. 1688–1696*, 201; HBC to J. Fullartine & Council (AF), 26 May 1708, HBCA, A. 6/3, fol. 91.
62. Games, *Web of Empire*, 87.
63. T. McCliesh Jr (AF) to HBC, 31 August 1719, HBCA, A. 11/2, fol. 39d; T. White (MF) to J. Isbister (AF), 18 June 1755, HBCA, A. 11/2, fol. 170; G. Rushworth (AF) to HBC, 8 September 1755, HBCA, A. 11/2, fol. 173d; J. Isbister & Council (AF) to HBC, 13 September 1755, HBCA, A. 11/2, fol. 178. Divine service was supposed to be a regular part of life at all HBC posts from the earliest years onward. Many post journals mention it, but few (if any) are as detailed as James Isham's 1750–51 York Fort journal (HBCA, B. 239/a/34), in which he lists the readings and sermons each Sunday.
64. Richardson, *The Apprentice's Vade Mecum*, 24.
65. Richardson, 50.
66. Fleetwood, *Relative Duties*, 340–41, 387. These comments were part of two sermons on St. Paul's first letter to the Colossians: "Servants, obey, in all things, your Masters according to the Flesh; not with Eye-service, as Men-pleasers, but in singleness of heart fearing God: And whatsoever you do, do it heartily as unto the Lord, and not unto Men: Knowing that of the Lord ye shall receive the reward of the Inheritance; for ye serve the Lord Christ" (1 Colossians 3:22–24; see Fleetwood, 339, 365). Fleetwood interpreted St. Paul's words as instructions to "*obey your Masters in all things, according to your Contract and Agreement, behave your selves as diligently and faithfully, as you have promised them to do*" (347, also 349–50, 356–59; emphasis in the original).
67. For example, York armourer Christopher Bannister asked Governor McCliesh to write to the Committee on his behalf in 1727; HBC to T. McCliesh Jr & Council (YF), 24 May 1728, HBCA, A. 6/5, fol. 18. HBC to J. Myatt & Council (AF), 21 May 1729, HBCA, A. 6/5, fol. 26, refers to Rowland Waggoner "having wrote to us, to know what is due to him from the

Company," but as he was illiterate, we may suppose that a friend or co-worker wrote the letter for him.

68. HBC to H. Kelsey (AF), 29 May 1712, HBCA, A. 6/3, fol. 118d; HBC to T. McCliesh Jr (AF), 29 May 1712, HBCA, A. 6/3, fol. 119. Also see HBC to James Liner (AF), 3 June 1715, HBCA, A. 6/3, fol. 137d; T. McCliesh Jr (YF) to HBC, 16 August 1727, *Letters*, 128; A. Beale (PWF) to HBC, 1730, *Letters*, 156; T. White (YF) to HBC, 6 August 1735, *Letters*, 200. Logan's contract expired the following year; Thomas White called him "a very honest, sober, diligent person, and one very deserving your honours' favour"; T. White (YF) to HBC, 6 August 1735, *Letters*, 200. Logan was favoured with a two-year contract at sixteen pounds; T. White (YF) to HBC, 27 August 1736, *Letters*, 221. Labourer William Mackcullock wrote to the Committee from Prince of Wales Fort in 1737, but the Committee does not appear to have replied, so the council took it upon itself to re-engage him for two years at his last year's wages (ten pounds, which was what he had asked for); PWF Council minutes, 6 August 1738, *Letters*, 253n.
69. G. Spence & Council (AF) to HBC, 4 August 1752, HBCA, A. 11/2, fols. 150–51; T. McCliesh Jr (YF) to HBC, 17 August 1732, *Letters*, 169.
70. T. McCliesh Jr (YF) to HBC, 16 August 1724, *Letters*, 97; J. Adams (AF) to HBC, 14 August 1732, HBCA, A. 11/2, fol. 72d. White's letter is not extant, but the Committee's reply is; HBC to R. White (AF), n.d. [11 May 1732], HBCA, A. 6/5, fol. 57d. The company was willing to re-engage White, but negotiations in London during the winter of 1733–34 broke down; the two parties finally came to terms in 1735, and he went out as second at PWF; HBC to J. Adams & Council (AF), 3 May 1734, HBCA, A. 6/5, fol. 85; HBC to R. Norton & Council (PWF), 2 May 1735, HBCA, A. 6/5, fol. 97d. White's wages were not small. He entered the service at twelve pounds in 1726 and was up to twenty-five pounds in 1731–32 and thirty pounds in 1732–33. He also sent home private trappings in most years, ranging in value from £3 1s. 7d. in 1729 to £9 7s. 3d. in 1730; HBCA, A. 16/2, fol. 24. Churchill accountant Thomas Bird, who had served the company for considerably longer than White had (and who replaced White at Albany), was receiving thirty pounds in 1731–32; HBCA, A. 16/9, fol. 17.
71. HBC to T. McCliesh Jr & Council (AF), 30 May 1718, HBCA, A. 6/4, fols. 22–22d.
72. G. Rushworth (AF) to HBC, 8 September 1755, HBCA, A. 11/2, fol. 173d; H. Marten (AF) to HBC, private, 22 August 1766, HBCA, A. 11/3, fol. 103d; H. Marten (AF) to HBC, private, September 1767, HBCA, A. 11/3, fol. 111.
73. The Committee had to remind the sloop masters in western Hudson Bay that they still had to obey the factors' commands; HBC to T. McCliesh Jr & Council (York), 20 May 1724, HBCA, A. 6/4, fol. 84; HBC to R. Norton & Council (PWF), 20 May 1724, HBCA, A. 6/4, fol. 88d.
74. S. Skrimshire (YF) to HBC, private, 8 August 1751, HBCA, A. 11/114, fols. 144–45.
75. H. Marten (AF) to HBC, private, 15 September 1765, HBCA, A. 11/3, fol. 90. He sent the same gift in 1767; H. Marten (AF) to HBC, private, September 1767, HBCA, A. 11/3, fol. 112.
76. Heal, "Food Gifts," 53–56, 67.
77. J. Knight (YF) to Sir Bibye Lake (London), private, 19 September 1714, *Letters*, 37–38; J. Knight (YF) to Captain John Merry (London), private, 19 September 1714, *Letters*, 38–39; J.

Knight (YF) to HBC, 17 September 1716, *Letters*, 61. The northern country to which Knight referred was the lower Churchill River valley and the coastline north of the river's mouth.

78. We see a similar situation in the EIC during its pre-Plassey days, when stock turnover was limited and the high degree of continuity within the court of directors was barely disrupted by a 1734 bylaw requiring directors to stand down for one year after serving four consecutive years. See H.V. Bowen, *Business of Empire*, 57–68, 126–27.
79. See HBC to J. Nixon (MF), 29 May 1680, *L.O. 1680–1687*, 10; HBC to P.E. Radisson (YF), 20 May 1686, *L.O. 1680–1687*, 199–200.
80. H.V. Bowen, *Business of Empire*, 120–21.
81. HBC to G. Geyer & Council (YF), 2 June 1688, *L.O. 1688–1696*, 8, 13; HBC to P.E. Radisson (YF) 20 May 1686, *L.O. 1680–1687*, 199.
82. T. McCliesh Jr (AF) to HBC, 12 September 1716, HBCA, A. 11/2, fol. 34d; J. Myatt (AF) to HBC, 12 August 1727, HBCA, A. 11/2, fol. 60d; Moose Fort journal, 8 September 1741, HBCA, B. 135/a/11, fol. 3. Some censure of Staunton's management may also be read into the Albany council's (or Captain Christopher Middleton's) choice of Joseph Isbister to command that factory after Rowland Waggoner's death in 1740, "[c]ontrary to Mr Stauntons will," although the process is very unclear; see *Letters*, 323n. For similar cases of excuses and counter-accusations in the Royal African Company, see Davies, *Royal African Company*, 255–56. Kathleen Venema, "As We Are Both Deceived," RHETOR 1 (2004), suggests some useful sociolinguistic approaches to this issue.
83. He did not name the "Transgressors" but referred the Committee to Captain George Berley of the *Albany* for further information, "haveing Calld my Informers before him; and the rest of the Councell"; T. McCliesh Jr (AF) to HBC, 12 September 1716, HBCA, A. 11/2, fol. 34d.
84. J. Myatt (AF) to HBC, 12 August 1727, HBCA, A. 11/2, fol. 60d. John Newton defended himself against similar charges during his brief command of York: "I have, and hope shall Continue to make it the Rule of my Conduct to do as I should think it Reasonable to be dealt by, to every One under Mee, if I should have happen'd to think different from any and thereby occasion'd any Complaints to be made against Mee, I am Quite easy about it, As I am very Certain Your Honours will never Censure Mee unheard." J. Newton (YF) to HBC, 12 August 1749, HBCA, A. 11/114, fol. 135d. Richardson, *The Apprentice's Vade Mecum*, advised apprentices "in your Business, to be serious, grave, even-temper'd, and respectful to every Body; and this you may be, and yet be chearful and pleasant: For there is a proper Medium between *Moroseness* and *Melancholy* on one Hand, and *Flippancy* and *Pertness* on the other" (29).
85. R. Staunton (AF) to HBC, 21 August 1723, HBCA, A. 11/2, fol. 46.
86. Prince of Wales Fort journal, 3 June 1732, HBCA, B. 42/a/12, fol. 30.
87. Prince of Wales Fort journal, 27 September 1740, HBCA, B. 42/a/21, fol. 18.
88. Nixon, 257.
89. HBC to H. Kelsey & Council (YF), 26 May 1721, HBCA, A. 6/4, fol. 50. "Our Masters will not aprove of his [George Saunders's] takeing up their brandy at Six & Selling it at twelve Shills, pr Galln, neither would I have you allow him so to do for I will not allow any Such

extortiong here"; H. Kelsey (YF) to R. Staunton (PWF), 28 March 1719, HBCA, B. 239/b/1, fol. 14d. For the importance of drams in the Montreal-based trade, see Podruchny, *Making the Voyageur World*, 149–51.

90. HBC to Christopher Gofton (MF), private, 17 May 1770, HBCA, A. 5/1, fol. 112; HBC to F. Jacobs (YF), private, 12 May 1773, HBCA, A. 5/1, fol. 148d.

91. Rule, *Experience of Labour*, 201; Sarah Jordan, "From Grotesque Bodies to Useful Hands," *Eighteenth-Century Life* 25 (Autumn 2001): 63–65.

92. J. Knight (YF) to R. Staunton (AF), 28 June 1715, HBCA, A. 6/4, fol. 8d. Grimington avoided further censure, however, and continued to serve the company until at least 1719; *Letters*, 45n. Also see HBC to J. Myatt & Council (AF), 24 May 1728, HBCA, A. 6/5, fol. 16d: "with respect to those servants who are guilty of drinking to excess and neglect their duty or are disobedient to command we hope you will not fail to send us their characters when they return home that they may not be again entertained in our Service."

93. J. Adams (AF) to HBC, 14 August 1732, HBCA, A. 11/2, fol. 72d; J. Adams & Council (AF) to HBC, 31 July 1733, HBCA, A. 11/2, fol. 77d.

94. "Orders and Instructions to Captn Thomas Macklish or the Chief and Councill at Albany Fort," 6 May 1736, HBCA, A. 6/5, fol. 105. Rumours of Gunn's behaviour had reached Albany via Cree traders at least two years earlier; see J. Adams & Council (AF) to HBC, 12 August 1734, HBCA, A. 11/2, fol. 80d.

95. *Letters*, xlvi; also see J. Adams (AF) to HBC, 14 August 1732, HBCA, A. 11/2, fol. 73d. R. Staunton & G. Howy (MF) to HBC, August 1738, *Letters*, 265.

96. J. Isham (YF) to HBC, August 1738, *Letters*, 260–62; PWF Council to HBC, 1 August 1738, *Letters*, 243; T. Bird & Council (AF) to HBC, [1738], *Letters*, 273. In 1740 the Albany council informed the Committee, "As we are of Opinion that Mr Birds Death might be hastened by an immoderate use of Liquors, we shall take particular care to prevent all your Servants from being guilty of that vice, the Thought of the Calamities of our Neighbouring Factory at the Late dreadful fire being continually before our Eyes"; J. Isbister & Council (AF) to HBC, 24 August 1740, HBCA, A. 11/2, fol. 102d.

97. R. Staunton (MF) to HBC, August 1738, *Letters*, 270; also R. Staunton & G. Howy (MF) to HBC, August 1738, *Letters*, 267. Staunton claimed that Thomas Render (Moose's first chief) "as I have been informed was an honest man which was one as they termed it would neither eat oats himself nor suffer any other within his knowledge, which I take to be the same as if they had said if he would not be a rogue himself nor suffer any other within his knowledge to be so, for they soon worked him out of his place and got another [John Jewer] which they brought into the crimes with themselves and then they made a tool of him" (*Letters*, 271).

98. R. Staunton (MF) to HBC, August 1738, *Letters*, 270.

99. R. Staunton (MF) to HBC, August 1738, *Letters*, 266.

100. J. Isham (YF) to HBC, 29 August 1739, *Letters*, 308; J. Myatt (AF) to HBC, 10 August 1726, HBCA, A. 11/2, fol. 57; HBC to John Favell (MF), private, 14 May 1766, HBCA, A. 5/1, fol. 72d; R. Staunton & Council (MF) to HBC, 20 August 1737, *Letters*, 236. Staunton was astonished the following year when Captain Christopher Middleton allowed Booth, then serving as a carpenter on the *Hudson's Bay* [V], to come ashore at Moose; R. Staunton & G. Howy (MF)

to HBC, August 1738, *Letters*, 269. Mincyn also returned to company service and caused problems for John Potts at Richmond; however, Potts chose not to send him home in 1753, because "his behaviour has been somthing better than formerly"; J. Potts & Council (RF) to HBC, 31 August 1753, HBCA, A. 11/57, fol. 19d. Mincyn remained in the service until his death ("being quite wore out") at York in April 1761; A. Graham (YF) to H. Marten (SR), 12 May 1761, HBCA, B. 239/b/22, fol. 7d.

101. R. Staunton & G. Howy (MF) to HBC, August 1738, *Letters*, 270–71. McCliesh had re-engaged in 1735 as "Governor in Hudson Bay" and sailed to Albany, where he was to have succeeded chief factor Joseph Adams and to have supervised business at Moose, but severe illness ("A Violent pain in his breast with A Difficulty of breathing ever Since his Arrival in Hudsons Straights") forced him to return home; T. McCliesh Jr & Council (AF) to HBC, 19 August 1735, HBCA, A. 11/2, fol. 82. He went out again the following year but returned home due to ill health; T. McCliesh Jr & Council (AF) to HBC, 2 September 1736, A. 11/2, fol. 86. He again re-engaged in 1737, but his contract was cancelled before the ships sailed. McCliesh was at least in his late fifties, having first entered the company's service in 1698; Alice M. Johnson, "McCliesh, Thomas," in *DCB*, http://www.biographi.ca/en/bio/mccliesh_thomas_3E.html.

102. R. Staunton & G. Howy (MF) to HBC, August 1738, *Letters*, 270.

103. R. Pilgrim (PWF) to J. Isham (YF), 17 February 1748, HBCA, B. 239/b/5, fol. 5d.

104. Albany Fort journal, 1 February 1756, HBCA, B. 3/a/48, fol. 16.

105. Albany Fort journal, 1 September 1756, HBCA, B. 3/a/48, fols. 38d–39.

106. J. Isbister & Council (AF) to HBC, 13 September 1755, HBCA, A. 11/2, fol. 182; HBC to J. Isbister & Council (AF), 12 May 1756, HBCA, A. 6/9, fol. 30; J. Isbister & Council (AF) to HBC, 10 September 1756, HBCA, A. 11/3, fol. 8d; A. 16/3, fol. 94. For Stephens's (and Jopling's) misbehaviour, see Albany Fort journal, 1–2 February, 13 March, 5 and 10–11 April, 29 August, 6 September 1756, HBCA, B. 3/a/48, fols. 16, 20–20d, 22d–23d, 38–39d. The severity of Stephens's crime in scaling the walls at night lay not in breaching the physical and social barrier between the Englishmen and the Indigenous "Other" but in breaching the physical and social boundaries and thresholds of the household. See Vickery, *Behind Closed Doors*, 28–34.

107. Albany Fort journal, 3 October 1722, HBCA, B. 3/a/11, fol. 7; 1 and 17 May 1723, HBCA, B. 3/a/11, fols. 22d, 24–24d. Hopkins had been sent to Albany "on Purpose to keep our Accompts...because there are but few but what are Wilde that offer their Service to us for that Employment"; HBC to J. Knight (YF), 3 June 1715, HBCA, A. 6/3, fol. 133. Yet McCliesh was told to take "great Care" of apprentices John Henson, Joseph Adams, and Samuel Hopkins, "that they be well used & taught to Read"; HBC to T. McCliesh Jr (AF), 3 June 1715, HBCA, A. 6/3, fol. 135.

108. HBC to T. McCliesh Jr & Council (YF), 20 May 1724, HBCA, A. 6/4, fol. 85d; T. McCliesh Jr (YF) to HBC, 26 August 1725, *Letters*, 109; HBC to S. Hopkins (YF), private, 25 May 1726, HBCA, A. 6/4, fol. 115d; T. McCliesh Jr (YF) to HBC, 7 August 1731, *Letters*, 158. Also see Thorman, "Hopkins," 291.

109. The Committee mentioned to Staunton that French traders were reportedly moving into the upper Albany River valley; "Instructions for Mr Richd Staunton, now going over Governor at Albany Fort," 17 May 1723, HBCA, A. 6/4, fol. 75.
110. HBC to J. Myatt (AF), private, 17 May 1723, HBCA, A. 6/4, fol. 74d.
111. For Staunton's praise of Myatt's management, see R. Staunton (AF) to HBC, 21 August 1723, HBCA, A. 11/2, fol. 46. The Committee responded favourably in HBC to R. Staunton & Council (AF), 20 May 1724, HBCA, A. 6/4, fol. 86, and in HBC to J. Myatt (AF), private, 20 May 1724, HBCA, A. 6/4, fol. 87d.
112. T. McCliesh Jr (YF) to HBC, 16 August 1724, *Letters*, 99; W. Bevan & Council (MF) to HBC, 20 August 1734, *Letters*, 197; R. Waggoner & Council (AF) to HBC, 15 August 1739, HBCA, A. 11/2, fol. 97d. Macklin served at Albany as a labourer and a tailor until 1742, and his wages were increased from ten to fourteen pounds in 1740 (HBCA, A. 16/2, fol. 83; A. 16/3, fol. 10). Fosset appears to have gone home in 1738 (HBCA, A. 16/3, fol. 13).
113. Moose Fort journal, 5 December 1741, B. 135/a/11, quoted in Nigol, "Discipline, Discretion, and Control," 174. Also see the case of Prince of Wales Fort armourer John Watson's misdemeanours and possible mental illness in 1748: Nigol, "Discipline, Discretion and Control," 78–79. For a suggestion that "over much lenity" had led to "as great a share of Contempt" at Albany and Moose, see T. White (YF) to J. Isbister (AF), 29 June 1742, HBCA, B. 3/b/1, fol. 2.
114. HBC to H. Kelsey (YF), private, [4 June] 1719, HBCA, A. 6/4, fol. 32. Kelsey provides some clues to the nature of these accusations in H. Kelsey & Council (YF) to R. Staunton (PWF), 1 February 1720, HBCA, B. 239/b/1, fol. 26. At least some of the accusations came from James Knight, who blamed Kelsey for allegedly deceiving him about the availability of provisions at Churchill River; Kenney, *Founding of Churchill*, 137.
115. HBC to H. Kelsey (YF), private, 26 May 1721, HBCA, A. 6/4, fol. 51.
116. HBC to H. Jones (YF), private, 31 May 1763, HBCA, A. 5/1, fol. 53.
117. HBC to A. Graham (YF), private, 27 May 1766, HBCA, A. 5/1, fol. 73d.
118. Griffiths, *Youth and Authority*, 342–44.
119. J. Isbister & Council (AF) to HBC, 6 September 1741, HBCA, A. 11/2, fol. 106d; R. Staunton & G. Howy (MF) to HBC, August 1738, *Letters*, 265, 271.
120. J. Myatt (AF) to HBC, 5 August 1728, HBCA, A. 11/2, fol. 62d; J. Adams (AF) to HBC, 14 August 1732, HBCA, A. 11/2, fol. 73d; R. Staunton & Council (MF) to HBC, 17 August 1739, *Letters*, 306; J. Potts & Council (RF) to HBC, 3 September 1750, HBCA, A. 11/57, fol. 9; also J. Potts & Council (RF) to HBC, 10 August 1752, HBCA, A. 11/57, fol. 15d.
121. H. Kelsey (YF) to John Scroggs (PWF), 31 January 1722, HBCA, B. 239/b/3, p. 10. Factors were not to let their guards down in peacetime, however. When Thomas McCliesh Jr was given the command of Albany in 1715, he was ordered to train his men in small arms and to keep a strict watch "that you be not Surprized, remembring how often We have Suffered by the Carelessness or Cowardice of our Commander in times of Peace"; HBC to T. McCliesh Jr (AF), 3 June 1715, HBCA, A. 6/3, fol. 134d.

8 TENSIONS WITHIN THE HOUSEHOLD MODEL

1. W. Bevan & Council (MF) to HBC, 26 August 1736, *Letters*, 217–18; J. Isbister & Council (AF) to HBC, 24 August 1740, HBCA, A. 11/2, fol. 102.
2. Tadmor, "Kinship in the Long Run," 27.
3. HBC to J. Knight (YF), 3 June 1715, HBCA, A. 6/3, fol. 132. Also see HBC to J. Adams & Council (AF), 11 May 1732, HBCA, A. 6/5, fol. 56. In 1721 the Committee complained that Richard Staunton's previous letter had failed to mention his desire to come home and that they had learned of his intention "by a Letter you wrote your Wife"; Mrs. Staunton may have passed on her husband's wishes, but the word choices imply that the Committee had read the letter before she ever received it. HBC to R. Staunton (PWF), private, 26 May 1721, HBCA, A. 6/4, fol. 52.
4. *Minutes*, 38, 72, 75, 77, 83.
5. *Minutes*, 82, 88, 97, 103.
6. Mancke, *Company of Businessmen*, 26–27. For a similar situation and response, see HBC to J. Fullartine (AF), private, 6 June 1698, HBCA, A. 6/3, fol. 39d.
7. *Minutes, First Part*, 64, 72, 77, 123; HBC to J. Fullartine & Council (AF), 29 May 1710, HBCA, A. 6/3, fol. 100; Carlos and Nicholas, "Giants of an Earlier Capitalism," 135.
8. *Minutes, Second Part*, 20; also 21, 28, 111, 129, 132, 134, 143, 245, 249. London Minute Books, HBCA, A. 1/8, fols. 25d, 27. Their reluctance may have also stemmed from the apparent inconstancy of Governor John Abraham, who (according to Radisson) had rescinded his permission for Chouart and the others to stay in the country, instead ordering them to be seized and brought on board the ship; Warkentin, *Pierre-Esprit Radisson*, vol. 2, 154–59. Radisson claimed that they had already taken the oath of fidelity before they left Port Nelson, but this may have been part of his overall strategy to safeguard their interests by emphasizing their (and his) loyalty to the company; in the same paragraph he explains how they could have captured and burned the HBC ships and retaken their trading post with ease, "But to do that, they would have had to mistrust everything I had said to them and to be as ill disposed to the service of the company as the governor was" (Warkentin, 159). Abraham had made it clear that he did not trust Radisson or the other Frenchmen, while Radisson knew that his own credibility rested in part upon his ability to carry through the promises that he had made to Chouart and the others.
9. Rich, *History*, vol. 1, 182. "The pelts were then to be sold by the company at its open sales, so that there would be no rivalry in price or quality for the London furriers' custom, and the servants were given 'so much money as the Company shall think fitt'" (Rich, *History*, vol. 1, 184).
10. For instance, see Hainsworth, *Stewards*, 31–37, for the range of licit and illicit perquisites enjoyed by estate stewards.
11. Rich, *History*, vol. 1, 184; Richardson, *The Apprentice's Vade Mecum*, 6–7; emphasis in the original. Also see Schwarz, "Custom, Wages and Workload," 158–59.
12. Games, *Web of Empire*, 89, 129–30.
13. Peter Pope, "The Practice of Portage in the Early Modern North Atlantic," *Journal of the Canadian Historical Association* 6, no. 1 (1995), notes some legal texts of 1661, 1679, and 1705 that suggest portage was no longer common on English ships (28). Rediker, *Deep*

Blue Sea, suggests that mariners were still carrying private cargo but were now paying freight on it (130–32). Pope questions Rediker's reading of his evidence and argues: "Eighteenth-century American wage agreements, or portledge bills, often specified under the heading 'privilege' the amount of venture to be carried freight-free, i.e., as portage....Acceptance of privilege, for men as well as for master, recurs in various other sources, suggesting that portage [the freight-free carriage of private goods by mariners], and not merely venture [private goods carried, freight paid or not], continued to be common enough in the colonial New England trades to the West Indies, Isle Royale, and Newofundland" (28–29). Note that this is part of the scholarly debate whether early modern mariners were "merchants in the forecastle" (Allan A. Arnold) or members of a maritime proletariat (Rediker). Note that Pope is not entirely convinced by either Arnold or Rediker.

14. Pope, "Practice of Portage," 37.
15. Davies, *Royal African Company*, 110–11, 252, 258, 297; also Carlos, "Agent Opportunism," 145. Carlos and Nicholas, "Giants of an Earlier Capitalism," gave the base salary in 1680 as £600 per annum (134–35).
16. Chaudhuri, *English East India Company*, 74, 83, 84, 87–88; Gary M. Anderson, Robert E. McCormick, and Robert D. Tollison, "The Economic Organization of the English East India Company," in *Trade in the Pre-Modern Era, 1400–1700*, ed. Douglas A. Irwin (Cheltenham, UK: Elgar, 1996), vol. 1, 471, 473, 474; Furber, *John Company at Work*, 4–5, 13–14, 21.
17. H.V. Bowen, *Business of Empire*, 270.
18. Erikson, *Between Monopoly and Free Trade*, 5, 14.
19. Erikson, 1–3. For important earlier discussions of private trade, see P.J. Marshall, *East Indian Fortunes: The British in Bengal in the Eighteenth Century* (Oxford: Clarendon Press, 1976), esp. 159–79; Ian Bruce Watson, *Foundations for Empire: English Private Trade in India, 1659–1760* (New Delhi, India: Vikas, 1980), chap. 3.
20. H.V. Bowen, *Business of Empire*, 185–87.
21. Erikson, *Between Monopoly and Free Trade*, admits this but explicitly avoids addressing that issue, focusing instead on the role of private trade in the EIC's commercial success (14). For a forceful discussion of the political machinations of private trade interests within the EIC, see Chaudhury, "Imperatives of the Empire," 1–12.
22. H.V. Bowen, *Business of Empire*, 207. In response, see Erikson, *Between Monopoly and Free Trade*, 14–15.
23. Erikson, 20.
24. Holden Furber, *Rival Empires of Trade in the Orient, 1600–1800* (1976), 227, quoted in H.V. Bowen, *Business of Empire*, 22. Bowen noted that "Furber thought that the word 'façade' was perhaps 'too strong,' but he confessed [he] could not think of a better one" (H.V. Bowen, 22n65). For *carapace*, see Sanjay Subrahmanyam, "Introduction: The Indian Ocean World and Ashin Das Gupta," in *The World of the Indian Ocean Merchant, 1500–1800: Collected Essays of Ashin Das Gupta*, ed. Uma Das Gupta (Delhi, India, 2001), 17.
25. H.V. Bowen, *Business of Empire*, 12, also 21.
26. H.V. Bowen, 21.

27. Rich, *History*, vol. 1, 374; T. McCliesh Jr (AF) to HBC, 16 July 1716, HBCA, A. 11/2, fols. 26d–27. In 1722 the Committee chastised Henry Kelsey for not sending men's private furs home with the returns from York and Churchill; HBC to H. Kelsey & Council (YF), 24 May 1722, HBCA, A. 6/4, fol. 59d.
28. HBC to H. Kelsey & Council (YF), 4 June 1719, HBCA, A. 6/4, fol. 29d; Carlos and Nicholas, "Agency Problems," 866; also HBC to H. Kelsey & Council (YF), 26 May 1721, HBCA, A. 6/4, fols. 49d–50; HBC to H. Kelsey (YF), private, 26 May 1721, HBCA, A. 6/4, fol. 51; G. Spence & Council (AF) to HBC, 1 August 1751, HBCA, A. 11/2, fol. 148d.
29. For example, see HBC to J. Knight (YF), 3 June 1715, HBCA, A. 6/3, fol. 133; J. Knight (YF) to HBC, 17 September 1716, *Letters*, 58, 58n; HBC to J. Myatt & Council (AF), 25 May 1727, HBCA, A. 6/5, fol. 1d; R. Norton (PWF) to HBC, 6 August 1728 [1727], *Letters*, 120, 120n; Francis and Morantz, *Partners in Furs*, 91–92; Rich, *History*, vol. 1, 486.
30. For a list of furs sent home by the men, see Albany Fort journal, 27 February 1716, HBCA, B. 3/a/9, fol. 7d.
31. T. Bird (London) to Matthew Sargent (AF), private, 21 May 1729, HBCA, A. 6/5, fol. 26d; HBC to J. Myatt & Council (AF), 15 May 1730, HBCA, A. 6/5, fols. 36d–37. Moose accountant Samuel Maidman appears to have made a similar request but met with a less sympathetic response; T. Bird (London) to S. Maidman (MF), 11 May 1732, HBCA, A. 6/5, fol. 64d.
32. See Williams, *Graham's Observations*, 282.
33. HBC to J. Adams & Council (AF), 20 May 1737, HBCA, A. 6/5, fol. 119. Fourteen marten skins found in a chest belonging to one of the men, labourer Thomas Lowe, had been sent home with the official cargo. Lowe's account was posthumously credited with £1 15s. 7d. for the marten skins and 11s. 4d. for "Sundry Peices [*sic*] of Beaver sent home after his decease"; HBCA, A. 16/2, fol. 44.
34. HBC Bye-Laws, HBCA, A. 37/41, fol. 81d.
35. For example, see contract of John Cromartie, signed 20 June 1780, HBCA, A. 32/1, fol. 10.
36. T. McCliesh Jr (YF) to HBC, 16 August 1727, *Letters*, 128; T. McCliesh Jr (YF) to HBC, 8 August 1728, *Letters*, 133; T. McCliesh Jr (YF) to HBC, 1 August 1729, *Letters*, 144.
37. Ann M. Carlos and Jamie Brown Kruse, "The Decline of the Royal African Company," *Economic History Review* 49, no. 2 (1996): 298–99; also Carlos, "Agent Opportunism," 150.
38. See "Orders and Instructions to Mr Richd Norton or the Chief and Council at Prince of Wales Fort," 6 May 1736, HBCA, A. 6/5, fols. 110–110d; also see *Letters*, 215n. These concerns were not new; see, for instance, H. Kelsey (YF) to R. Staunton (PWF), 28 March 1719, HBCA, B. 239/b/1, fol. 12d.
39. R. Staunton & G. Howy (MF) to HBC, August 1738, *Letters*, 267, 271.
40. HBC to R. Staunton & G. Howy (MF), 18 May 1738, HBCA, A. 6/6, fol. 19d; also see *Letters*, 265n. HBC to H. Marten (AF), 8 May 1770, HBCA, A. 5/1, fol. 105d.
41. J. Isham (YF) to HBC, August 1738, *Letters*, 263; R. Norton & Council (PWF) to HBC, 16 August 1739, *Letters*, 296.
42. Williams, *Graham's Observations*, 282–84; Robson, *An Account*, 40; A.R. Michell, "The European Fisheries in Early Modern History," in *The Cambridge Economic History of*

Europe, vol. 5, ed. E.E. Rich and C.H. Wilson (Cambridge: Cambridge University Press, 1977), 183.

43. HBC to H. Marten (AF), 8 May 1770, HBCA, A. 5/1, fols. 105d–107; HBC to F. Jacobs (YF), 10 May 1770, HBCA, A. 5/1, fols. 113d, 116–116d; HBC to I. Needham (no address), 14 December 1769, HBCA, A. 10/1, fol. 12; *CHJ First Series*, xxxvii.
44. Williams, *Graham's Observations*, 282–83.
45. H. Marten (AF) to HBC, 2 September 1770, HBCA, A. 11/3, fols. 142d–143. It is not clear whether the four persons to whom he refers are members of his Indigenous family or the gentlemen's mess.
46. H. Marten (AF) to HBC, 2 September 1770, HBCA, A. 11/3, fol. 145.
47. H. Marten & Council (AF) to HBC, 3 September 1770, HBCA, A. 11/3, fol. 149d.
48. Hair, Jones, and Law, *Barbot on Guinea*, 351; emphasis in the original. The Earl Marischal used exactly the same phrase ("make hay while the sun shines") in a letter to William Fullerton Elphinstone about the East India trade, 20 November 1768, quoted in H.V. Bowen, *Business of Empire*, 270.
49. Anderson, McCormick, and Tollison, "Economic Organization," 474. Also see Carlos and Nicholas, "Giants of an Earlier Capitalism," 135–36.
50. Hair, Jones, and Law, *Barbot on Guinea*, 393. Also see Carlos, "Agent Opportunism," 150.
51. HBC to H. Marten (AF), 8 May 1770, HBCA, A. 5/1, fol. 107.
52. Hainsworth, *Stewards*, 251, 253.
53. HBC to H. Marten (AF), private, 20 May 1772, HBCA, A. 5/1, fol. 137. Also see HBC to T. Moore (AF), private, 20 May 1772, HBCA, A. 5/1, fol. 138d. H.V. Bowen, *Business of Empire*, observed that the EIC's directors sanctioned significant salary increases "in the hope that this would help to create a more professional and well-ordered civil service whose members were not preoccupied with the pursuit of private profit, and as a result the average official earnings in the Bengal civil service rose from less [than] £150 a year before 1757 to £2,261 a year in 1783" (213–14). Also see H.V. Bowen, 209.
54. Laslett, *The World We Have Lost*, 99; Wall, introduction, 13; Woodward, *Men at Work*, 59–60.
55. Richardson was concerned that the young man would acquire a family before he was able to support it by lawful means, and lose the chance to marry for money later in life. "As a natural Consequence of his Indiscretion, he would, very probably, be forced to drudge on in the lowest Part of his Business, a *Servant* to Servants; and, what is still worse, his innocent Children would be involved in all the Misfortunes of their imprudent Parents." Richardson, *The Apprentice's Vade Mecum*, 3–5; emphasis in the original.
56. *Minutes, First Part*, 199. Considering that the Committee here was referring to tradesmen, it may have meant *bachelor* in the older sense of a junior member of a trade guild. For the apparent preference for bachelors, also see, for instance, *Minutes, First Part*, xxxiv; Heather Rollason Driscoll, "A Most Important Chain of Connection," in *From Rupert's Land to Canada: Essays in Honour of John E. Foster*, ed. T. Binnema, G.J. Ens, and R.C. Macleod (Edmonton: University of Alberta Press, 2001), 87–88.
57. Clark, "Migrants in the City," 271. For the EIC's policy of banning its servants from bringing wives to India, as well as some ingenious attempts to circumvent that policy, see Games, *Web of Empire*, 104.

58. Brown, *Strangers in Blood*, 11. The quotation comes from the Committee's reply to Mary Dalton's 1680 petition (*Minutes, First Part*, 55), but the same wording (with slight variations) can be found in other petitions of that period; see, for example, the petitions of Rebecca Kildale, Mrs. Brownstone, Mrs. Verner, and Mrs. Garland in 1682, *Minutes, First Part*, 170, 212, 217, 218. For a broader context in which to set such letters, see Nancy Christie, "A 'Painful Dependence,'" in *Mapping the Margins*, ed. Nancy Christie and Michael Gauvreau (Montreal: Montreal-Queen's University Press, 2004), 69–102.
59. T. McCliesh Jr (YF) to HBC, 8 August 1728, *Letters*, 135; HBC to T. McCliesh Jr & Council (YF), 24 May 1728, HBCA, A. 6/5, fol. 18.
60. T. McCliesh Jr (YF) to HBC, 23 August 1723, *Letters*, 93. Fettus served at Churchill (1725–30) and at Albany and Moose (1731–37). He may have gone home in 1730, which might explain why his wages dropped from fourteen pounds in 1728–30 back down to his original ten pounds per annum in 1731–33 (he was back up to fourteen pounds in 1735–37). He made payments to his wife in 1727 (£3), 1731 (£2 5s. 0d.), 1733 (£3), and 1737 (£6). HBCA, A. 16/2, fol. 51; A. 16/9, fol. 13.
61. T. McCliesh Jr (YF) to HBC, 16 August 1730, *Letters*, 150.
62. T. McCliesh Jr (AF) to HBC, 31 August 1719, HBCA, A. 11/2, fol. 40d; T. McCliesh Jr (YF) to HBC, 16 August 1724, *Letters*, 100; T. McCliesh Jr (YF) to HBC, 17 August 1733, *Letters*, 188. McCliesh's family probably consisted mainly of servants and relatives other than offspring: between his entry into the service in 1698 and counting his family in 1724, he had only spent the winters of 1707–8, 1714–15, and 1721–22 in England.
63. T. Hopkins (AF) to HBC, private, 30 August 1768, HBCA, A. 11/3, fol. 124.
64. Abbott, *Life Cycles*, 131. Also see Snell, *Annals*, 360–64.
65. T. Bird (London) to George Lisk (AF), 25 May 1726, HBCA, A. 6/4, fol. 111d. Also see HBC to A. Beale & Council (PWF), 23 May 1728, HBCA, A. 6/5, fol. 19d: "Acquaint James Fettus and John Moor we have paid their wives each £3, they having petitioned us for the same, being in great want." Also HBC to R. Norton & Council (PWF), 20 May 1737, HBCA, A. 6/5, fol. 125: "[A]cquaint Thomas Lukyn surgeon that Conformable to his request Wee have paid...seven pounds to his wife She being in great Want, and expect he will write Us word what sum he wou'd have Us pay her this Year on his acco[un]tt Wee being fully satisfied she is his lawfull Wife and has not wherewithal to Subsist."
66. T. Bird (London) to Nicholas Coxworthy (PWF), private, 25 May 1726, HBCA, A. 6/4, fol. 118.
67. Elizabeth Jane Errington, "Webs of Affection and Obligation," *Journal of the Canadian Historical Association* 19, no. 1 (2008): 3. Most of the existing literature focuses on the nineteenth century, but see Elizabeth Jane Errington, *Emigrant Worlds and Transatlantic Communities* (Montreal: McGill-Queen's University Press, 2007). Cressy, "Kinship," suggests that transatlantic migration may have heightened the sense of membership in some extended families; also see Cressy, *Coming Over: Migration and Communication between England and New England in the Seventeenth Century* (Cambridge: Cambridge University Press, 1987), 263–91.
68. *Minutes, First Part*, 151; also see Brown, *Strangers in Blood*, 11–12.
69. HBCA, A. 15/3, fols. 39, 99, 102.

70. See Aubert, *Hidden Society*, 268–69.

71. *Minutes, First Part*, 53, 56, 71. In 1682 Thomas Walsh's return was requested by Thomas and Alice Walsh, possibly his parents (*Minutes, First Part*, 170–71), and Jacob Robinson's mother successfully petitioned for a raise in her son's salary (*Minutes, First Part*, 210).

72. HBC to J. Knight & Council (AF), 30 May 1696, *L.O. 1688–1696*, 274, 274n; HBCA, A. 15/5, fol. 12.

73. Brown, *Strangers in Blood*, 12–13, 52, 76; Sylvia Van Kirk, *Many Tender Ties* (Winnipeg, MB: Watson & Dwyer, 1980), 14–15.

74. Joseph Robson referred to Henry Kelsey's Indigenous companion as his "wife" (Robson, *An Account*, 72), but his account was recorded at least eleven years after Kelsey had left Hudson Bay; though the account is certainly plausible, there is only circumstantial evidence to corroborate it; Pentland, "Henry Kelsey's Christmas Message," 128–31. Also see Brown, *Strangers in Blood*, 52–53; Van Kirk, *Many Tender Ties*, 64. See Games, *Web of Empire*, 104–7, 324n86, for a brief discussion of the multiple terms (and their multiple meanings) used by English traders in Japan to describe their Japanese female companions in the early seventeenth century.

75. Captain George Spurrell called these payments "a very ancient custom" and "a thing in all shipping in Christendom allowed," usually amounting to "a month's pay from a foremast man"; George Spurrell & Council (PWF) to HBC, 1 August 1738, *Letters*, 247. J. Isham (YF) to HBC, August 1738, *Letters*, 261. Also see T. Bird & Council (AF) to HBC, n.d. [1738], HBCA, A. 11/2, fols. 93–93d.

76. Rebecca Probert and Liam D'arcy Brown, "The Impact of the Clandestine Marriages Act," *Continuity and Change* 23, no. 2 (2008): 311, 326; Gill Newton, "Clandestine Marriage in Early Modern London," *Continuity and Change* 29, no. 2 (2014): 152–53.

77. Articles agreed upon for the surrender of Albany, 16 July 1686, *L.O. 1680–1687*, 319; see also *L.O. 1680–1687*, 388–89.

78. *Minutes, Second Part*, 224, 230; Brown, *Strangers in Blood*, 10. For comparable examples in the RAC, see Davies, "The Living and the Dead," 87–88.

79. HBC to H. Sergeant (AF), 20 May 1686, *L.O. 1680–1687*, 186; HBC to G. Geyer & Council (YF), 3 June 1687, *L.O. 1680–1687*, 235; Brown, *Strangers in Blood*, 10–11.

80. See, for example, Games, *Web of Empire*, 105, 133–34. More generally, see Ann Laura Stoler, *Carnal Knowledge and Imperial Power: Race and the Intimate in Colonial Rule* (Berkeley: University of California Press, 2002).

81. Tadmor, "Kinship in the Long Run," 26–27.

82. See Henry Sergeant's description of the French attacks, 4 November 1687, *L.O. 1680–1687*, 313.

83. *Letters*, 33n, 233n; Brown, *Strangers in Blood*, 53; Van Kirk, *Many Tender Ties*, 29.

84. In return for this service Duffield was to receive all of Waggoner's "other goods and effects," which Gerhard Ens suggested were related to private trade. Captain William Coats appears to have had a dispute with Duffield over Waggoner's will and claimed that he (Coats) had been cheated of some property. See Moose Fort journal, 1742–43, HBCA, B. 135/a/12, fol. 11; Ens, 395n. Waggoner's will is in the National Archives (formerly the Public Record Office), Kew, England, PROB 11/706/240.

85. Brown, *Strangers in Blood*, 53–54; Van Kirk, *Many Tender Ties*, 48–49.
86. Brown, 54–56; Van Kirk, 64.
87. Van Kirk, 37–38.
88. Rich and Johnson, *Isham's Observations*, 322; Brown, *Strangers in Blood*, 55.
89. *Letters*, 292n.
90. H. Marten (AF) to HBC, private, 2 September 1770, HBCA, A. 11/3, fol. 145.
91. HBC to Capt. J. Richards (Gravesend), 28 May 1771, HBCA, A. 5/1, fol. 126. Andrew Graham employed a similar tactic in his ultimately successful attempts to bring his half-Cree son and daughter to Britain in the 1770s; see Williams, *Graham's Observations*, 344–50.
92. Williams, 248; John E. Foster, "The Indian-Trader," 579.
93. G. Rushworth (AF) to HBC, private, 8 September 1755, HBCA, A. 11/2, fol. 174; also see Van Kirk, *Many Tender Ties*, 260n58; Pannekoek, "'Corruption' at Moose," 5. However, Van Kirk, *Many Tender Ties*, believed that Isham's example was more commonly followed than Graham's comments suggested (41); also see Pannekoek, 6, 9.
94. Vickery, *Behind Closed Doors*, 29.
95. Greene, "Empire and Identity," 210.
96. See John E. Foster, "The Indian-Trader," 579; Ens, "Political Economy," 397.
97. Moose Fort journal, 12 February 1742, HBCA, B. 135/a/11, fols. 35d–36, quoted in Ens, "Political Economy," 400. Also see Pannekoek, "'Corruption' at Moose," 5. Games, *Web of Empire*, observed that "[i]n the seventeenth century, English people believed that a person could be transformed by external factors and, indeed, by his very garb; wearing foreign clothes might fundamentally change a man. Travel could alter an individual, shaking his sense of self at its very core.... [This posed a] problem for the large trading companies that relied on loyal employees far from their control, thousands of miles away. How could men be loyal when the very experience of leaving home, necessary for their business, undermined their attachment to home?" (97).
98. Ens, "Political Economy," 385; Carol Judd, "Housing the Homeguard at Moose Factory," *Canadian Journal of Native Studies* 3, no. 1 (1983): 25–26. In contrast to Frost's long service on land (he had entered the service in 1719), Duffield had served as steward on various HBC ships since 1731, and the command of Moose was his first posting on land. Pannekoek, "'Corruption' at Moose," emphasized Frost's power and entrepreneurship, describing him as "knowledgeable in all the Indian ways and connected to a number of Indian women who ran his traplines" (6).
99. Ens, "Political Economy," 397.
100. This inhibited the development of a Metis identity among these communities during this period. See Ens, "Political Economy," 410.
101. Albany Fort journal, 24 January 1771, HBCA, B. 3/a/63, fol. 18d.
102. John E. Foster, "The Indian-Trader," 579; Ens, "Political Economy," 397.
103. Quoted in Van Kirk, *Many Tender Ties*, 17. Also see Lytwyn, *Muskekowuck Athinuwick*, 15–17.
104. HBCA, B. 3/a/63, fol. 14, quoted in Van Kirk, *Many Tender Ties*, 17.
105. Van Kirk, 28–29.
106. See, for instance, Wrightson, *Earthly Necessities*, 290–306.
107. T. McCliesh Jr (YF) to HBC, 16 August 1724, *Letters*, 98.

108. Van Kirk, *Many Tender Ties*, 43; HBCA, B. 135/a/11, fols. 46–47, 64–66.

109. Rich and Johnson, *Isham's Observations*, 95.

110. Van Kirk, *Many Tender Ties*, 42; HBCA, B. 239/a/50, fols. 5–5d.

111. Albany Fort journal, 7 January 1754, HBCA, B. 3/a/46, fol. 17; Van Kirk, *Many Tender Ties*, 42. Statton's wages in 1753–54 were twenty-five pounds. He went home in 1754 at the expiration of his contract; HBCA, A. 16/3, fol. 71; J. Isbister & Council (AF) to HBC, 19 September 1754, HBCA, A. 11/2, fol. 160d.

112. Albany Fort journal, 10 September 1753, HBCA, B. 3/a/46, fols. 4d–5. Also see Albany Fort journal, 7 January 1754, HBCA, B. 3/a/46, fol. 17.

113. J. Isham & Council (YF) to HBC, 2 September 1755, HBCA, A. 11/114, fol. 188; J. Isham (YF) to HBC, 13 August 1756, HBCA, A. 11/114, fol. 192.

114. H. Marten (AF) to HBC, private, 3 September 1771, HBCA, A. 11/3, fol. 169.

115. H. Marten (YF) to HBC, 28 August 1781, HBCA, A. 11/116, fol. 87; quoted in *CHJ Second Series*, footnote, xxi.

116. R. Temple (AF) to HBC, private, 31 August 1762, HBCA, A. 11/3, fol. 55.

117. HBC to H. Marten (AF), private, 20 May 1772, HBCA, A. 5/1, fol. 137.

118. R. Norton & T. Bird (PWF) to HBC, 3 August 1723, *Letters*, 86; R. Norton (PWF) to HBC, n.d. [1725], *Letters*, 112; HBC to R. Norton & Council (PWF), 25 May 1726, HBCA, A. 6/4, fol. 116; R. Norton (PWF) to HBC, 14 August 1726, *Letters*, 117–18; HBCA, A. 16/9, fol. 3. Hawes had been engaged at twenty-six pounds; HBCA, A. 16/9, fol. 15.

119. A. Beale (PWF) to HBC, 26 July 1729, *Letters*, 140. Thomas McCliesh Jr would have welcomed Frost's transfer, "for a man that understands bricklayer's business is much wanted at this place," but he doubted that Frost would be willing to come to York; T. McCliesh Jr (YF) to HBC, 1 August 1729, *Letters*, 143, 144. Also see HBC to T. McCliesh Jr (YF), private, 21 May 1729, HBCA, A. 6/5, fol. 28.

120. W. Bevan & Council (MF) to HBC, 15 August 1733, *Letters*, 182; T. McCliesh Jr & Council (MF) to HBC, 24 August 1735, *Letters*, 209; HBCA, A. 16/2, fol. 41.

121. Duffield complained that Frost had "corrupted all the Englishmen" since 1730, and made him the focus of his struggle against private trade; Ens, "Political Economy," 400.

122. Ens, 400n.

123. T. McCliesh Jr (YF) to HBC, 1 August 1729, *Letters*, 143, 144.

124. Moose Fort journal, 12 February 1742, HBCA, B. 135/a/11, fols. 35d–36, quoted in Ens, "Political Economy," 400.

CONCLUSION

1. Sidney Pollard, *The Genesis of Modern Management* (London: Edward Arnold, 1965), 121, 160; Makepeace, *East India Company's London Workers*, 198.

2. Pollard, *Genesis of Modern Management*, made this point about labour in the early industrial factories (161).

3. It is only with hindsight that we can point to Utrecht as ushering in decades of peace in Hudson Bay. At the time, the future did not seem so certain, and the continuing sense of vulnerability can be seen in the instructions given by the Committee to its supply-ship captains regarding how much ransom it was willing to pay in case the ships and crews

were captured by an enemy. See HBC to Captain Richard Ward (Gravesend), 5 June 1717, HBCA, A. 6/4, fol. 19d.

4. HBC to G. Geyer & Council (YF), 2 June 1688, *L.O. 1688–1696*, 8. For comparable preferences within the EIC, see Makepeace, *East India Company's London Workers*, 198–99.
5. Matthew Cocking, "Thoughts on Making a Settlement Inland," 1773, HBCA, B.239/a/69, fol. 53.
6. Between 1782 and 1821 the HBC built more than two hundred trading posts, although most lasted no more than five years; see Burley, *Servants of the Honourable Company*, 5.

APPENDIX

1. Hainsworth, *Stewards*, 17.
2. David W. Galenson, *White Servitude in Colonial America* (Cambridge: Cambridge University Press, 1981), 39, 45–47, 51–54.
3. Woodward, *Men at Work*, 64–65; Schwarz, *London*, 48–49. For problematic interpretation of historic occupation labels, see Peter H. Lindert, "English Occupations, 1670–1811," *Journal of Economic History* 40, no. 4 (December 1980): 693.
4. Gilboy, *Wages*, 224; Woodward, *Men at Work*, 40; Malcolmson, *Life and Labour*, 40; Joyce, "Work," 143. Although the terms *tradesman*, *craftsman*, and *artisan* are used interchangeably in this study, it should be noted that none of these terms is unproblematic; see Rule, "The Property of Skill," 102; also Joyce, "Work," 143.
5. Lane, *Apprenticeship*, 12, 131–32.
6. Campbell, *The London Tradesman*, 47, described a surgeon as "only employed in the Cure of Wounds, Bruises, Contusions, Ulcers, and Eruptions in the outward Parts, in Trepanning, Cutting, or Scarifying, and Amputations...He applies only topical Medicines...but is rarely concerned in any inward Applications; nor is supposed conversant with Pharmacy of any sort." For surgeons in the Royal Navy, see Campbell, 53.
7. Lane, *Apprenticeship*, 149.
8. Campbell, *The London Tradesman*, 240, 242.
9. Campbell, 241.
10. Lane, *Apprenticeship*, 141; Campbell, *The London Tradesman*, 159–61.
11. Campbell, 158–59; Lane, 141, 144–45.
12. B.W.E. Alford and T.C. Barker, *A History of the Carpenters Company* (London: George Allen & Unwin, 1968), 116; Campbell, *The London Tradesman*, 244, 299.
13. Campbell, 192–93.
14. Campbell, 192–93; Lane, *Apprenticeship*, 120–21. Homeguard Cree were groups of Muskego (Swampy) or Lowland Cree who had altered their seasonal patterns and more or less attached themselves to HBC posts as hunters or other service providers for at least part of the year.
15. According to Hatfield, "Mariners," "at least in the early seventeenth century, the term mariner did not carry status connotations and referred to any one involved in the sailing of ships. Masters and ship captains were often of high status and served in various political offices" (351n23).

16. Kussmaul, *Servants*, 6, 135, also 136–42, table A1.1, "The Usage of 'Servant' and 'Labourer,' 1360–1850." Woodward, *Men at Work*, 93, also 1, 94, 96; Galenson, *White Servitude*, 60–61.
17. Raymond Williams, *Keywords*, 145–48. Also see White and Vann, "The Invention of English Individualism," 357–59.
18. Raymond Williams, *Keywords*, 274–75.
19. Games, *Web of Empire*, 84.
20. Games, 149–50.
21. Thomas McCliesh Jr commanded York while he was governor in 1722–26 and 1727–34, and he would have resided at Albany in 1735 and in 1736 had illness not forced him to return home both times.
22. Raymond Williams, *Keywords*, 156–57; also see Pollard, *Genesis of Modern Management*, 104.
23. In particular, see Carlos and Nicholas, "Theory and History," 916–24; and Carlos and Nicholas, "Giants of an Earlier Capitalism," 118–39.
24. Hainsworth, *Stewards*, 42.
25. Raymond Williams, *Keywords*, 44–45.

Bibliography

PRIMARY SOURCES

Hudson's Bay Company Archives (HBCA) at the Archives of Manitoba

A. 1/8–42: London Minute Books, 1684–1766

A. 1/120: London Minute Books (Foul Copies), 1721–1726

A. 1/143: London Minute Books, Sub-Committee for Trade, 1717–1731

A. 5/1: London Correspondence Outward—General Series, 1753–1776

A. 6/3–11: London Correspondence Outward—HBC Official, 1696–1773

A. 10/1: London Correspondence Inward—General, 1712–1816

A. 11/2–3: London Correspondence Inward from Albany, 1701–1774

A. 11/57: London Correspondence Inward from Richmond, Severn, & Eastmain, 1749–1791

A. 11/114–116: London Correspondence Inward from York, 1716–1787

A. 14/1–5: Grand Ledger, 1667–1697

A. 15/1–5: Grand Journal, 1676–1713

A. 16/1–4: Officers' and Servants' Ledger—Albany, 1719–1780

A. 16/9–11: Officers' and Servants' Ledger—Churchill (PWF), 1725–1793

A. 16/31: Officers' and Servants' Ledger—York, 1738–1760

A. 32/1–3: Servants' Contracts, 1776–1791

A. 36/1a: Officers' and Servants' Wills, 1763–1863

A. 37/41: Bye-Laws, 1739–1952

A. 66/2: Papers re: Pension & Benefit Schemes, 1711–1863

B. 3/a/2–63: Post Journals—Albany, 1706–1771

B. 42/a/52: Post Journals—Churchill (PWF), 1758/59

B. 135/a/1–12: Post Journals—Moose, 1730–1743

B. 239/a/1–50: Post Journals—York, 1714–1763

B. 239/a/40: Inland Journal—Anthony Henday, 1754/55

B. 239/a/43: Inland Journal—Joseph Smith, 1756/57

B. 239/a/58, 61: Inland Journals—William Pink, 1767/68, 1768/69

B. 239/a/69: Inland Journal—Matthew Cocking, 1772/73

B. 3/b/1–19: Correspondence Books—Albany, 1742–1782

B. 198/b/1: Correspondence Books—Severn, 1759/60

B. 239/b/1–29: Correspondence Books—York, 1718–1768

B. 3/d/1–28: Account Books—Albany, 1692–1720

B. 42/d/1–5: Account Books—Churchill (Prince of Wales Fort), 1717–1725

B. 135/d/1–39: Account Books—Moose, 1730–1770

B. 182/d/1–9: Account Books—Fort Richmond, 1751–1759

B. 198/d/1–12: Account Books—Severn, 1759–1770

B. 239/d/1–15: Account Books—York, 1688–1725

E. 2/1–2: James Isham, *Observations on Hudson's Bay*, 1742–43

E. 2/4–13: Andrew Graham, *Observations on Hudson's Bay*, 1767–92

G. 1–2: Manuscript Maps, ca. 1719–ca. 1929

P.: Documentary Art Collection

Biographical Sheets. https://www.gov.mb.ca/chc/archives/HBCA/biographical/index.html.

Barrow, John, ed. *The Geography of Hudson's Bay: Being the Remarks of Captain W. Coats*. London: Hakluyt Society, 1852.

Campbell, R. *The London Tradesman*. New York: Augustus M. Kelley, 1969. First published 1747 (London).

Davies, K.G. and A.M. Johnson, eds. *Letters from Hudson Bay, 1703–40*. With an introduction by Richard Glover. London: Hudson's Bay Record Society, 1965.

Doughty, Arthur G., and Chester Martin, eds. *The Kelsey Papers*. Ottawa, ON: Public Archives of Canada and Public Record Office of Northern Ireland, 1929.

Fleetwood, William. *The Relative Duties of Parents and Children, Husbands and Wives, Masters and Servants*. New York: Garland, 1985. First published 1705 by C. Harper (London).

Hair, P.E.H., Adam Jones, and Robin Law, eds. *Barbot on Guinea: The Writings of Jean Barbot on West Africa, 1678–1712*. London: Hakluyt Society, 1992.

Jaenen, Cornelius J., ed. *The French Regime in the Upper Country of Canada during the Seventeenth Century*. Toronto: Champlain Society, 1996.

Kenney, James F., ed. *The Founding of Churchill, Being the Journal of Captain James Knight, Governor-in-Chief in Hudson Bay, from the 14th of July to the 13th of September, 1717*. Toronto: J.M. Dent & Sons, 1932.

Kenyon, W.A., and J.R. Turnbull. *The Battle for James Bay, 1686*. Toronto: Macmillan, 1971.

Law, Robin, ed. *The English in West Africa, 1681–1683: The Local Correspondence of the Royal African Company of England, 1681–1699; Part 1*. Oxford: Oxford University Press for the British Academy, 1997.

Nixon, John. "Report to the Governor and Committee by John Nixon, 1682." Appendix A in *Minutes of the Hudson's Bay Company, 1679–1684: First Part, 1679–1682*, edited by E.E. Rich, 239–304. Royal Society, Boyle Papers (Misc.), XL. Toronto: Champlain Society for the Hudson's Bay Record Society, 1945.

Oldmixon, John. *The History of Hudson's-Bay* (1708). In *Documents Relating to the Early History of Hudson Bay*, edited by J.B. Tyrrell, 371–410. Toronto: Champlain Society, 1931.

Rich, E.E., ed. *Minutes of the Hudson's Bay Company, 1671–1674*. With an introduction by Sir John Clapham. Toronto: Champlain Society for the Hudson's Bay Record Society, 1942.

———. *Minutes of the Hudson's Bay Company, 1679–1684: First Part, 1679–1682*. With an introduction by G.N. Clark. Toronto: Champlain Society for the Hudson's Bay Record Society, 1945.

———. *Minutes of the Hudson's Bay Company, 1679–1684: Second Part, 1682–1684*. With an introduction by G.N. Clark. Toronto: Champlain Society for the Hudson's Bay Record Society, 1946.

Rich, E.E., and A.M. Johnson, eds. *Copy-Book of Letters Outward &c, Begins 29th May, 1680; Ends 5 July, 1687*. With an introduction by E.G.R. Taylor. Toronto: Champlain Society for the Hudson's Bay Record Society, 1948.

———. *Cumberland House Journals and Inland Journal, 1775–82: First Series, 1775–79*. With an introduction by Richard Glover. London: Hudson's Bay Record Society, 1951.

———. *Cumberland House Journals and Inland Journal, 1775–82: Second Series, 1779–82*. With an introduction by Richard Glover. London: Hudson's Bay Record Society, 1952.

———. *Hudson's Bay Copy Booke of Letters Commissions Instructions Outward, 1688–1696*. With an introduction by K.G. Davies. London: Hudson's Bay Record Society, 1957.

———. *James Isham's Observations on Hudsons Bay, 1743, and Notes and Observations on a Book Entitled "A Voyage to Hudsons Bay in the Dobbs Galley," 1749*. London: Hudson's Bay Record Society, 1949.

———. *Moose Fort Journals, 1783–85*. With an introduction by G.P. de T. Glazebrook. London: Hudson's Bay Record Society, 1954.

Richardson, Samuel. *The Apprentice's Vade Mecum: or, Young Man's Pocket-Companion*. Edited and introduced by A.D. McKillop. Augustan Reprint Society nos. 169–170. Los Angeles: William Andrews Clark Memorial Library, UCLA, 1975. First published 1734 (London).

Robson, Joseph. *An Account of Six Years Residence in Hudson's Bay*. Johnson Reprint, New York, 1965. First published 1752 (London).

Tyrrell, J.B., ed. *Documents Relating to the Early History of Hudson Bay*. Toronto: Champlain Society, 1931.

———. *Journals of Samuel Hearne and Philip Turnor*. Toronto: Champlain Society, 1934.

Warkentin, Germaine, ed. *Pierre-Esprit Radisson: The Collected Writings*. Vol. 2. Toronto: Champlain Society and McGill-Queen's University Press, 2014.

Williams, Glyndwr, ed. *Andrew Graham's Observations on Hudson's Bay, 1767–91*. With an introduction by Richard Glover. London: Hudson's Bay Record Society, 1969.

———. *Hudson's Bay Miscellany, 1670–1870*. Winnipeg, MB: Hudson's Bay Record Society, 1975.

SECONDARY SOURCES

Abbott, Mary. *Life Cycles in England, 1560–1720*. London: Routledge, 1996.

Alford, B.W.E., and T.C. Barker. *A History of the Carpenters Company*. London: George Allen & Unwin, 1968.

Alwin, John A. "The Uncelebrated Boats of the Albany." *The Beaver* 305, no. 4 (Spring 1975): 47–53.

Anderson, Gary M., Robert E. McCormick, and Robert D. Tollison. "The Economic Organization of the English East India Company." In *Trade in the Pre-modern Era, 1400–1700*, edited by Douglas A. Irwin, vol. 1, 466–83. Cheltenham, UK: Elgar, 1996.

Ashton, T.S. *Economic Fluctuations in England, 1700–1800*. Oxford: Clarendon Press, 1959.

Aubert, Vilhelm. *The Hidden Society*. Totowa, NJ: Bedminster Press, 1965.

Bailey, Patrick. *Orkney*. Newton Abbot, UK: David & Charles, 1971.

Bailyn, Bernard. "Introduction: Europeans on the Move, 1500–1800." In *Europeans on the Move: Studies on European Migration, 1500–1800*, edited by Nicholas Canny, 1–5. Oxford: Clarendon Press, 1994.

Baker, Howard Robert II. "Law Transplanted, Justice Invented: Sources of Law for the Hudson's Bay Company in Rupert's Land, 1670–1870." Master's thesis, Interdisciplinary Studies (Law, History, Sociology), University of Manitoba, 1996.

Banks, Kenneth J. *Chasing Empire across the Sea: Communications and the State in the French Atlantic, 1713–1763*. Montreal: McGill-Queen's University Press, 2006.

Belyea, Barbara. "Indians, Asinepoets and Archithinues." In *A Year Inland: The Journal of a Hudson's Bay Company Winterer*, edited by Barbara Belyea, 343–68. Waterloo, ON: Wilfrid Laurier University Press, 2000.

Ben-Amos, Ilana Krausman. *Adolescence and Youth in Early Modern England*. New Haven, CT: Yale University Press, 1994.

———. "Gifts and Favors: Informal Support in Early Modern England." *Journal of Modern History* 72, no. 2 (June 2000): 295–338.

Berg, Maxine. *The Age of Manufactures: Industry, Innovation and Work in Britain, 1700–1820*. London: Fontana, 1985.

———. "Women's Work, Mechanisation and the Early Phases of Industrialisation in England." In *The Historical Meanings of Work*, edited by Patrick Joyce, 64–98. Cambridge: Cambridge University Press, 1987.

Berry, Helen. "Rethinking Politeness in Eighteenth-Century England: Moll King's Coffee House and the Significance of 'Flash Talk.'" *Transactions of the Royal Historical Society*, sixth series, 11 (2001): 65–81.

Bishop, Charles A. "The Henley House Massacres." *The Beaver* 307, no. 2 (Autumn 1976): 36–41.

Bliss, Michael. *Northern Enterprise: Five Centuries of Canadian Business*. Toronto: McClelland & Stewart, 1987.

Boulton, Jeremy. "Neighbourhood Migration in Early Modern London." In *Migration and Society in Early Modern England*, edited by Peter Clark and David Souden, 107–49. Totowa, NJ: Barnes & Noble, 1987.

———. "Wage Labour in Seventeenth-Century London." *Economic History Review* 49, no. 2 (1996): 268–90.

Bowen, H.V. *The Business of Empire: The East India Company and Imperial Britain, 1756–1833*. Cambridge: Cambridge University Press, 2006.

Bowen, John. "The East India Company's Education of Its Own Servants." *Journal of the Royal Asiatic Society of Great Britain and Ireland* 3, no. 4 (October 1955): 105–23.

Braddick, Michael J. "Administrative Performance: The Representation of Political Authority in Early Modern England." In *Negotiating Power in Early Modern Society: Order, Hierarchy and Subordination in Britain and Ireland*, edited by Michael J. Braddick and John Walter, 166–87. Cambridge: Cambridge University Press, 2001.

Braddick, Michael J., and John Walter. "Introduction: Grids of Power; Order, Hierarchy and Subordination in Early Modern Society." In *Negotiating Power in Early Modern Society: Order, Hierarchy and Subordination in Britain and Ireland*, edited by Braddick and Walter, 1–42. Cambridge: Cambridge University Press, 2001.

Brown, Jennifer S.H. "Batt, Isaac." In Hayne and Halpenny, *Dictionary of Canadian Biography*. http://www.biographi.ca/en/bio/batt_isaac_4E.html.

———. *Strangers in Blood: Fur Trade Company Families in Indian Country*. Vancouver: University of British Columbia Press, 1980.

Burke, Peter. "Popular Culture in Seventeenth-Century London." In *Popular Culture in Seventeenth-Century England*, edited by Barry Reay, 31–58. London: Croom Helm, 1985.

Burley, Edith. *Servants of the Honourable Company: Work, Discipline, and Conflict in the Hudson's Bay Company, 1770–1870*. Don Mills, ON: Oxford University Press, 1997.

Burnett, John. *A History of the Cost of Living*. Harmondsworth, UK: Penguin, 1969.

Bushnell, Amy Turner. "Indigenous America and the Limits of the Atlantic World, 1493–1825." In *Atlantic History: A Critical Appraisal*, edited by Jack P. Greene and Philip D. Morgan, 191–221. Oxford: Oxford University Press, 2009.

Cadigan, Sean T. "Merchant Capital, the State, and Labour in a British Colony: Servant-Master Relations and Capital Accumulation in Newfoundland's Northeast-Coast Fishery, 1775–1799." *Journal of the Canadian Historical Association* 2, no. 1 (1991): 17–42.

Calhoun, C.J. "Community: Toward a Variable Conceptualization for Comparative Research." *Social History* 5, no. 1 (January 1980): 105–29.

Canny, Nicholas. "In Search of a Better Home? European Overseas Migration, 1500–1800." In *Europeans on the Move: Studies on European Migration, 1500–1800*, edited by Nicholas Canny, 263–83. Oxford: Clarendon Press, 1994.

———. "The Origins of Empire: An Introduction." In *The Origins of Empire: British Overseas Enterprise to the Close of the Seventeenth Century*, edited by Nicholas Canny, 1–33. Vol. 1 of *The Oxford History of the British Empire*. Oxford: Oxford University Press, 1998.

Carey, James W. *Communication as Culture: Essays on Media and Society*. Rev. ed. New York: Routledge, 2009.

Carlos, Ann M. "Agent Opportunism and the Role of Company Culture: The Hudson's Bay and Royal African Companies Compared." *Business and Economic History* 20 (1991): 142–51.

Carlos, Ann M., and Jamie Brown Kruse. "The Decline of the Royal African Company: Fringe Firms and the Role of the Charter." *Economic History Review* 49, no. 2 (1996): 291–313.

Carlos, Ann M., and Frank D. Lewis. *Commerce by a Frozen Sea: Native Americans and the European Fur Trade*. Philadelphia: University of Pennsylvania Press, 2010.

Carlos, Ann M., and Stephen Nicholas. "Agency Problems in Early Chartered Companies: The Case of the Hudson's Bay Company." *Journal of Economic History* 50, no. 4 (December 1990): 853–75.

———. "'Giants of an Earlier Capitalism': The Chartered Trading Companies as Modern Multinationals." In *Trade in the Pre-modern Era, 1400–1700*, edited by Douglas A. Irwin, vol. 1, 118–39. Cheltenham, UK: Elgar, 1996.

———. "Theory and History: Seventeenth-Century Joint-Stock Chartered Trading Companies." *Journal of Economic History* 56, no. 4 (December 1996): 916–24.

Chakrabarty, Dipesh. "The Muddle of Modernity." *American Historical Review* 116, no. 3 (2011): 663–75.

Chaplin, Joyce E. "The Atlantic Ocean and Its Contemporary Meanings, 1492–1808." In *Atlantic History: A Critical Appraisal*, edited by Jack P. Greene and Philip D. Morgan, 35–51. Oxford: Oxford University Press, 2009.

Chaudhuri, K.N. *The English East India Company: The Study of an Early Joint-Stock Company, 1600–1640*. London: Frank Cass, 1965.

Chaudhury, Sushil. "The Imperatives of the Empire: Private Trade, Sub-imperialism and the British Attack on Chandernagore, March 1757." *Studies in History*, n.s., 8, no. 1 (1992): 1–12.

Christie, Nancy. "A 'Painful Dependence': Female Begging Letters and the Familial Economy of Obligation." In *Mapping the Margins: The Family and Social Discipline in Canada, 1700–1975*, edited by Nancy Christie and Michael Gauvreau, 69–102. Montreal: McGill-Queen's University Press, 2004.

Clark, Peter. "Migrants in the City: The Process of Social Adaptation in English Towns, 1500–1800." In *Migration and Society in Early Modern England*, edited by Peter Clark and David Souden, 267–91. Totowa, NJ: Barnes & Noble, 1987.

———. "Migration in England during the Late Seventeenth and Early Eighteenth Centuries." *Past & Present* 83 (May 1979): 57–90.

Clark, Peter, and David Souden. Introduction to *Migration and Society in Early Modern England*, edited by Peter Clark and David Souden, 11–48. Totowa, NJ: Barnes & Noble, 1987.

Cliffe, J.T. *The World of the Country House in Seventeenth-Century England*. New Haven, CT: Yale University Press, 1999.

Cook, Peter. "Onontio Gives Birth: How the French in Canada Became Fathers to Their Indigenous Allies, 1645–73." *Canadian Historical Review* 96, no. 2 (June 2015): 165–92.

Coornaert, E.L.J. "European Economic Institutions and the New World; The Chartered Companies." In *The Economy of Expanding Europe in the Sixteenth and Seventeenth Centuries*, edited by E.E. Rich and C.H. Wilson, 220–74. Vol. 4 of *The Cambridge Economic History of Europe*. Cambridge: Cambridge University Press, 1967.

Cressy, David. *Coming Over: Migration and Communication between England and New England in the Seventeenth Century*. Cambridge: Cambridge University Press, 1987.

———. "Kinship and Kin Interaction in Early Modern England." *Past & Present* 113 (November 1986): 38–69.

Dabhoiwala, Faramerz. "The Construction of Honour, Reputation and Status in Late Seventeenth- and Early Eighteenth-Century England." *Transactions of the Royal Historical Society*, sixth series, 6 (1996): 201–13.

Davidoff, Leonore. "The Family in Britain." In *People and Their Environment*, edited by F.M.L. Thompson, 71–129. Vol. 2 of *The Cambridge Social History of Britain, 1750–1950*. Cambridge: Cambridge University Press, 1990.

Davies, K.G. "The Living and the Dead: White Mortality in West Africa, 1684–1732." In *Race and Slavery in the Western Hemisphere: Quantitative Studies*, edited by Stanley L. Engerman and Eugene D. Genovese, 83–98. Princeton, NJ: Princeton University Press, 1975.

———. "Nixon, John." In Hayne and Halpenny, *Dictionary of Canadian Biography*. http://www.biographi.ca/en/bio/nixon_john_1E.html.

———. *The Royal African Company*. London: Longmans, Green, 1957.

Dodge, Ernest S. "Knight, James." In Hayne and Halpenny, *Dictionary of Canadian Biography*. http://www.biographi.ca/en/bio/knight_james_2E.html.

Dodgson, Robert A. *Land and Society in Early Scotland*. Oxford: Clarendon Press, 1981.

Dove, Michael. "Plying the Northernmost Atlantic Trading Route to the New World: The Hudson's Bay Company and British Seaborne Empire." In *English Atlantics Revisited: Essays Honouring Professor Ian K. Steele*, edited by Nancy L. Rhoden, 174–205. Montreal: McGill-Queen's University Press, 2007.

———. "Voyages to Rupert's Land: The Hudson's Bay Company's Maritime Component, 1670–1770." Paper presented to the Centre for Rupert's Land Studies Colloquium, Oxford, April 2002.

Dunn, Richard S. "Servants and Slaves: The Recruitment and Employment of Labor." In *Colonial British America: Essays in the New History of the Early Modern Era*, edited by Jack P. Greene and J.R. Pole, 157–94. Baltimore, MD: Johns Hopkins University Press, 1984.

Eastwood, David. *Governing Rural England: Tradition and Transformation in Local Government, 1780–1840*. Oxford: Clarendon Press, 1994.

Ens, Gerhard. "The Political Economy of the 'Private Trade' on the Hudson Bay: The Example of Moose Factory, 1741–1744." In *"Le Castor Fait Tout": Selected Papers of the Fifth North American Fur Trade Conference, 1985*, edited by Bruce G. Trigger, Toby Morantz, and Louise Dechene, 382–410. Montreal: Lake St. Louis Historical Society, 1987.

Erikson, Emily. *Between Monopoly and Free Trade: The English East India Company, 1600–1757*. Princeton, NJ: Princeton University Press, 2014.

Errington, Elizabeth Jane. *Emigrant Worlds and Transatlantic Communities*. Montreal: McGill-Queen's University Press, 2007.

———. "Webs of Affection and Obligation: Glimpse into Families and Nineteenth Century Transatlantic Communities." *Journal of the Canadian Historical Association* 19, no. 1 (2008): 1–26.

Fenton, Alexander. *The Northern Isles: Orkney and Shetland*. Edinburgh: John Donald, 1978.

Fletcher, Anthony, and John Stevenson. Introduction to *Order and Disorder in Early Modern England*, edited by Fletcher and Stevenson, 1–40. Cambridge: Cambridge University Press, 1985.

Fossett, Renée. *In Order to Live Untroubled: Inuit of the Central Arctic, 1550 to 1940*. Winnipeg: University of Manitoba Press, 2001.

Foster, Hamar. "Law and Necessity in Western Rupert's Land and Beyond, 1670–1870." In *Laws and Societies in the Canadian Prairie West, 1670–1940*, edited by Louis A. Knafla and Jonathon Swainger, 57–91. Vancouver: University of British Columbia Press, 2005.

Foster, John E. "The Indian-Trader in the Hudson Bay Fur Trade Tradition." In *Proceedings of the Second Congress, Canadian Ethnology Society*, vol. 2, edited by Jim Freedman and Jerome H. Barkow, 571–85. Mercury Series. Ottawa, ON: National Museum of Man, 1975.

Francis, Daniel, and Toby Morantz. *Partners in Furs: A History of the Fur Trade in Eastern James Bay, 1600–1870*. Montreal and Kingston: McGill-Queen's University Press, 1983.

Furber, Holden. *John Company at Work: A Study of European Expansion in India in the Late Eighteenth Century*. Cambridge, MA: Harvard University Press, 1948.

Fury, Cheryl. "Elizabethan Seamen: Their Lives Ashore." *International Journal of Maritime History* 10 (1998): 1–40.

Galenson, David W. *White Servitude in Colonial America: An Economic Analysis*. Cambridge: Cambridge University Press, 1981.

Games, Alison. *The Web of Empire: English Cosmopolitans in an Age of Expansion, 1560–1660*. Oxford: Oxford University Press, 2008.

Gilboy, Elizabeth W. *Wages in Eighteenth Century England*. Cambridge, MA: Harvard University Press, 1934.

Glennie, Paul, and Nigel Thrift, "Reworking E.P. Thompson's 'Time, Work-Discipline and Industrial Capitalism.'" *Time and Society* 5, no. 3 (October 1996): 275–99.

Goldring, Philip. "Labour Records of the Hudson's Bay Company, 1821–1870." *Archivaria* 11 (Winter 1980/81): 53–86.

Gough, Barry M. "The 'Adventurers of England Trading into Hudson's Bay': A Study of the Founding Members of the Hudson's Bay Company, 1665–1670." *Albion* 2, no. 1 (1970): 35–47.

Grant, Hugh. "Bookkeeping in the Eighteenth Century: The Grand Journal and Grand Ledger of the Hudson's Bay Company." *Archivaria* 43 (Spring 1997): 143–57.

Greene, Jack P. "Empire and Identity from the Glorious Revolution to the American Revolution." In *The Eighteenth Century*, edited by P.J. Marshall and Alaine Low, 208–30. Vol. 2 of *The Oxford History of the British Empire*. Oxford: Oxford University Press, 1998.

Griffiths, Paul. *Youth and Authority: Formative Experiences in England, 1560–1640*. Oxford: Clarendon Press, 1996.

Griffiths, Paul, Adam Fox, and Steve Hindle. Introduction to *The Experience of Authority in Early Modern England*, edited by Griffiths, Fox, and Hindle, 1–9. New York: St. Martin's Press, 1996.

Hainsworth, D.R. *Stewards, Lords, and People: The Estate Steward and His World in Later Stuart England*. Cambridge: Cambridge University Press, 1992.

Hair, P.E.H., and Robin Law. "The English in West Africa to 1700." In *The Origins of Empire: British Overseas Enterprise to the Close of the Seventeenth Century*, edited by Nicholas Canny, 241–63. Vol. 1 of *The Oxford History of the British Empire*. Oxford: Oxford University Press, 1998.

Hall, Norma J. "Ocean Crossings: Hudson's Bay Company Seafaring in a Northern North Atlantic World." *Manitoba History* 71 (Winter 2013): 16–20.

Hatfield, April Lee. "Mariners, Merchants, and Colonists in Seventeenth-Century English America." In *The Creation of the British Atlantic World*, edited by Elizabeth Mancke and Carole Shammas, 139–59. Baltimore, MD: Johns Hopkins University Press, 2005.

Hayne, David M., and Francess G. Halpenny, eds. *Dictionary of Canadian Biography*. Vols. 1–5. Toronto: University of Toronto Press, 1966–83.

Heal, Felicity. "Food Gifts, the Household and the Politics of Exchange in Early Modern England." *Past & Present* 199 (May 2008): 41–70.

Hecht, J. Jean. *The Domestic Servant Class in Eighteenth-Century England*. London: Routledge & Kegan Paul, 1956.

Henige, David. "'Companies Are Always Ungrateful': James Phipps of Cape Coast, a Victim of the African Trade." *African Economic History* 9 (1980): 27–47.

Hill, Bridget. *Servants: English Domestics in the Eighteenth Century*. Oxford: Clarendon Press, 1996.

Hindle, Steve. "The Keeping of the Public Peace." In *The Experience of Authority in Early Modern England*, edited by Paul Griffiths, Adam Fox, and Steve Hindle, 213–48. New York: St. Martin's Press, 1996.

Horn, James. "British Diaspora: Emigration from Britain, 1680–1815." In *The Eighteenth Century*, edited by P.J. Marshall and Alaine Low, 28–52. Vol. 2 of *The Oxford History of the British Empire*. Oxford: Oxford University Press, 1998.

———. "Tobacco Colonies: The Shaping of English Society in the Seventeeth-Century Chesapeake." In *The Origins of Empire: British Overseas Enterprise to the Close of the Seventeenth Century*, edited by Nicholas Canny, 170–92. Vol. 1 of *The Oxford History of the British Empire*. Oxford: Oxford University Press, 1998.

Horn, James, and Philip D. Morgan. "Settlers and Slaves: European and African Migrations to Early Modern British America." In *The Creation of the British Atlantic World*, edited by Elizabeth Mancke and Carole Shammas, 19–44. Baltimore, MD: Johns Hopkins University Press, 2005.

Hutcheson, Maud M. "Lydall, William." In Hayne and Halpenny, *Dictionary of Canadian Biography*. http://www.biographi.ca/en/bio/lydall_william_1E.html.

———. "Phipps, Thomas." In Hayne and Halpenny, *Dictionary of Canadian Biography*. http://www.biographi.ca/en/bio/phipps_thomas_1E.html.

Innis, Harold. *The Fur Trade in Canada*. Rev. ed. Toronto: University of Toronto Press, 1999.

Jenner, Mark S.R., and Paul Griffiths. Introduction to *Londinopolis: Essays in the Cultural and Social History of Early Modern London*, edited by Griffiths and Jenner, 1–23. Manchester, UK: Manchester University Press, 2000.

Johnson, Alice M. "Bayly, Charles." In Hayne and Halpenny, *Dictionary of Canadian Biography*. http://www.biographi.ca/en/bio/bayly_charles_1E.html.

———. "Geyer, George." In Hayne and Halpenny, *Dictionary of Canadian Biography*. http://www.biographi.ca/en/bio/geyer_george_1E.html.

———. "McCliesh, Thomas." In Hayne and Halpenny, *Dictionary of Canadian Biography*. http://www.biographi.ca/en/bio/mccliesh_thomas_3E.html.

———. "Mons. Maugenest Suggests…." *The Beaver*, Outfit 287 (Summer 1956): 49–53.

———. "Norton, Richard." In Hayne and Halpenny, *Dictionary of Canadian Biography*. http://www.biographi.ca/en/bio/norton_richard_3E.html.

———. "Verner, Hugh." In Hayne and Halpenny, *Dictionary of Canadian Biography*. http://www.biographi.ca/en/bio/verner_hugh_1E.html.

Jones, Geoffrey. *Merchants to Multinationals: British Trading Companies in the Nineteenth and Twentieth Centuries*. Oxford: Oxford University Press, 2000.

Jones, S.R.H., and Simon P. Ville. "Efficient Transactors or Rent-Seeking Monopolists? The Rationale for Early Chartered Trading Companies." *Journal of Economic History* 56, no. 4 (December 1996): 898–915.

Jordan, Sarah. "From Grotesque Bodies to Useful Hands: Idleness, Industry, and the Labouring Class." *Eighteenth-Century Life* 25 (Autumn 2001): 62–79.

Joyce, Patrick. "The Historical Meanings of Work: An Introduction." In *The Historical Meanings of Work*, edited by Patrick Joyce, 1–30. Cambridge: Cambridge University Press, 1987.

———. "Labour, Capital and Compromise: A Response to Richard Price." *Social History* 9, no. 1 (January 1984): 67–76.

———. "Languages of Reciprocity and Conflict: A Further Response to Richard Price." *Social History* 9, no. 2 (May 1984): 225–31.

———. "Work." In *People and Their Environment*, edited by F.M.L. Thompson, 131–94. Vol. 2 of *The Cambridge Social History of Britain, 1750–1950*. Cambridge: Cambridge University Press, 1990.

Judd, Carol. "Housing the Homeguard at Moose Factory: 1730–1982." *Canadian Journal of Native Studies* 3, no. 1 (1983): 23–37.

Kenyon, Walter A. *The History of James Bay, 1610–1686: A Study in Historical Archaeology*. Archaeology Monograph 10. Toronto: Royal Ontario Museum, 1986.

Kettering, Sharon. *Patrons, Brokers, and Clients in Seventeenth-Century France*. New York: Oxford University Press, 1986.

Kussmaul, Ann. "The Pattern of Work as the Eighteenth Century Began." In *The Economic History of Britain since 1700*, 2nd ed., edited by Roderick Floud and Donald McCloskey, 1–11. Cambridge: Cambridge University Press, 1994.

———. *Servants in Husbandry in Early Modern England*. Cambridge: Cambridge University Press, 1981.

Lacombe, Michael A. "'A Continuall and Dayly Table for Gentlemen of Fashion': Humanism, Food, and Authority at Jamestown, 1607–1609." *American Historical Review* 115, no. 3 (June 2010): 669–87.

Lane, Joan. *Apprenticeship in England, 1600–1914*. Boulder, CO: Westview Press, 1996.

Laslett, Peter. "Mean Household Size in England since the Sixteenth Century." In *Household and Family in Past Times*, edited by Peter Laslett and Richard Wall, 125–58. Cambridge: Cambridge University Press, 1972.

———. *The World We Have Lost: Further Explored*. 3rd ed. London: Methuen, 1983.

Lawson, Philip. *The East India Company: A History*. London: Longman, 1993.

Lenman, Bruce P. "Colonial Wars and Imperial Instability, 1688–1793." In *The Eighteenth Century*, edited by P.J. Marshall and Alaine Low, 151–68. Vol. 2 of *The Oxford History of the British Empire*. Oxford: Oxford University Press, 1998.

Leunig, Tim, Chris Minns, and Patrick Wallis. "Networks in the Premodern Economy: The Market for London Apprenticeships, 1600–1749." *Journal of Economic History* 71, no. 2 (June 2011): 413–43.

Lindert, Peter H. "English Occupations, 1670–1811." *Journal of Economic History* 40, no. 4 (December 1980): 685–712.

Long, John S. "In Search of Mr. Bundin: Henley House 1759 Revisited." In *Papers of the Twenty-Sixth Algonquian Conference*, edited by David H. Pentland, 203–25. Winnipeg: University of Manitoba, 1995.

Lytwyn, Victor. *The Fur Trade of the Little North: Indians, Pedlars, and Englishmen East of Lake Winnipeg, 1760–1821*. Winnipeg, MB: Rupert's Land Research Centre, 1986.

———. *Muskekowuck Athinuwick: Original People of the Great Swampy Land*. Winnipeg: University of Manitoba Press, 2002.

Makahonuk, Glen. "Wage-Labour in the Northwest Fur Trade Economy, 1760–1849." *Saskatchewan History* 41, no. 1 (Winter 1988): 1–17.

Makepeace, Margaret. *The East India Company's London Workers: Management of the Warehouse Labourers, 1800–1858*. Woodbridge, UK: Boydell Press, 2010.

Malcolmson, Robert W. *Life and Labour in England, 1700–1780*. New York: St. Martin's Press, 1981.

Mancke, Elizabeth. "Another British America: A Canadian Model for the Early Modern British Empire." *Journal of Imperial and Commonwealth History* 25, no. 1 (1997): 1–36.

———. "Chartered Enterprises and the Evolution of the British Atlantic World." In *The Creation of the British Atlantic World*, edited by Elizabeth Mancke and Carole Shammas, 237–62. Baltimore, MD: Johns Hopkins University Press, 2005.

———. *A Company of Businessmen: The Hudson's Bay Company and Long-Distance Trade, 1670–1730*. Winnipeg, MB: Rupert's Land Research Centre, 1988.

Marshall, P.J. *East Indian Fortunes: The British in Bengal in the Eighteenth Century*. Oxford: Clarendon Press, 1976.

———. "The English in Asia to 1700." In *The Origins of Empire: British Overseas Enterprise to the Close of the Seventeenth Century*, edited by Nicholas Canny, 264–85. Vol. 1 of *The Oxford History of the British Empire*. Oxford: Oxford University Press, 1998.

McCormack, Patricia A. "The Many Faces of Thanadelthur: Documents, Stories, and Images." In *Reading Beyond Words: Contexts for Native History*, 2nd ed., edited by Jennifer S.H. Brown and Elizabeth Vibert, 329–64. Peterborough, ON: Broadview Press, 2003.

Meldrum, Tim. *Domestic Service and Gender, 1660–1750: Life and Work in the London Household*. Harlow, UK: Pearson, 2000.

Michell, A.R. "The European Fisheries in Early Modern History." In *The Economic Organization of Early Modern Europe*, edited by E.E. Rich and C.H. Wilson, 133–84. Vol. 5 of *The Cambridge Economic History of Europe*. Cambridge: Cambridge University Press, 1977.

Morgan, Philip D., and Jack P. Greene. "Introduction: The Present State of Atlantic History." In *Atlantic History: A Critical Appraisal*, edited by Greene and Morgan, 3–33. Oxford: Oxford University Press, 2009.

Muldrew, Craig. *The Economy of Obligation: The Culture of Credit and Social Relations in Early Modern England* (Basingstoke, UK: Palgrave Macmillan, 1998).

———. "Interpreting the Market: The Ethics of Credit and Community Relations in Early Modern England." *Social History* 18, no. 2 (May 1993): 163–83.

Newton, Gill. "Clandestine Marriage in Early Modern London: When, Where and Why?" *Continuity and Change* 29, no. 2 (2014): 151–80.

Nicks, John. "Orkneymen in the HBC, 1780–1821." In *Old Trails and New Directions: Selected Papers of the Third North American Fur Trade Conference*, edited by Carol M. Judd and Arthur J. Ray, 102–26. Toronto: University of Toronto Press, 1980.

Nigol, Paul C. "Discipline and Discretion in the Mid-Eighteenth-Century Hudson's Bay Company Private Justice System." In *Laws and Societies in the Canadian Prairie West, 1670–1940*, edited by Louis A. Knafla and Jonathon Swainger, 150–82. Vancouver: University of British Columbia Press, 2005.

———. "Discipline, Discretion and Control: The Private Justice System of the Hudson's Bay Company in Rupert's Land, 1670–1770." PHD diss., History, University of Calgary, 2001.

O'Brien, Patrick K. "Inseparable Connections: Trade, Economy, Fiscal State, and the Expansion of Empire, 1688–1815." In *The Eighteenth Century*, edited by P.J. Marshall and Alaine Low, 53–77. Vol. 2 of *The Oxford History of the British Empire*. Oxford: Oxford University Press, 1998.

Offutt, William M. "The Atlantic Rules: The Legalistic Turn in Colonial British America." In *The Creation of the British Atlantic World*, edited by Elizabeth Mancke and Carole Shammas, 160–81. Baltimore, MD: Johns Hopkins University Press, 2005.

O'Leary, Michael, Wanda Orlikowski, and JoAnne Yates. "Distributed Work over the Centuries: Trust and Control in the Hudson's Bay Company, 1670–1826." In *Distributed Work*, edited by Pamela Hinds and Sara Kiesler, 27–54. Cambridge, MA: MIT Press, 2002.

Paine, Robert. "A Theory of Patronage and Brokerage." In *Patrons and Brokers in the East Arctic*, edited by Paine, 8–21. Newfoundland Social and Economic Papers, no. 2. St. John's: Institute of Social and Economic Research, Memorial University of Newfoundland, 1971.

Pannekoek, Frits. "'Corruption' at Moose." *The Beaver* 309, no. 4 (Spring 1979): 4–11.

Parry, J.H. "Introduction: The English in the New World." In *The Westward Enterprise: English Activities in Ireland, the Atlantic, and America 1480–1650*, edited by K.R. Andrews, N.P. Canny, and P.E.H. Hair, 1–16. Liverpool, UK: Liverpool University Press, 1978.

Payne, Michael B. "Daily Life on Western Hudson Bay, 1714 to 1870: A Social History of York Factory and Churchill." PHD diss., History, Carleton University, 1989.

Pelling, Margaret. "Apprenticeship, Health and Social Cohesion in Early Modern London." *History Workshop* 37 (Spring 1994): 33–56.

Pentland, David H. "Henry Kelsey's Christmas Message, 1696." In *Linguistic Studies Presented to John L. Finlay*, edited by H.C. Wolfart, 127–38. Algonquian and Iroquoian Linguistics, Memoir 8. Winnipeg: University of Manitoba, 1991.

Podruchny, Carolyn. *Making the Voyageur World: Travelers and Traders in the North American Fur Trade*. Toronto: University of Toronto Press, 2006.

Pollard, Sidney. *The Genesis of Modern Management: A Study of the Industrial Revolution in Great Britain*. London: Edward Arnold, 1965.

Pope, Peter. "The Practice of Portage in the Early Modern North Atlantic: Introduction to an Issue in Maritime Historical Anthropology." *Journal of the Canadian Historical Association* 6, no. 1 (1995): 19–41.

Porter, R. "English Chief Factors on the Gold Coast, 1632–1753." *African Historical Studies* 1, no. 2 (1968): 199–209.

Porter, Roy. *England in the Eighteenth Century*. London: Folio Society, 1998.

Preston, Richard J. "Reflections on Territoriality." In "Who Owns the Beaver? Northern Algonquian Land Tenure Reconsidered." Special issue, *Anthropologica*, n.s., 28, no. 1–2 (1986): 11–17.

Price, Jacob M. "The Great Quaker Business Families of Eighteenth-Century London: The Rise and Fall of a Sectarian Patriciate." In *The World of William Penn*, edited by R.S. Dunn and M.M. Dunn, 363–99. Philadelphia: University of Pennsylvania Press, 1986.

Price, Richard. "Conflict and Co-operation: A Reply to Patrick Joyce." *Social History* 9, no. 2 (May 1984): 217–24.

———. "The Labour Process and Labour History." *Social History* 8, no. 1 (January 1983): 57–75.

Probert, Rebecca, and Liam D'arcy Brown. "The Impact of the Clandestine Marriages Act: Three Case-Studies in Conformity." *Continuity and Change* 23, no. 2 (2008): 309–30.

Ray, Arthur J., D. Wayne Moodie, and Conrad E. Heidenreich. "Rupert's Land." In *The Historical Atlas of Canada*, vol. 1, plate 57. Toronto: University of Toronto Press, 1987.

Reay, Barry. "Kinship and the Neighbourhood in Nineteenth-Century Rural England: The Myth of the Autonomous Nuclear Family." *Journal of Family History* 21, no. 1 (January 1996): 87–104.

Rediker, Marcus. *Between the Devil and the Deep Blue Sea: Merchant Seamen, Pirates, and the Anglo-American Maritime World, 1700–1750*. Cambridge: Cambridge University Press, 1987.

Rich, E.E. "Cole, John." In Hayne and Halpenny, *Dictionary of Canadian Biography*. http://www.biographi.ca/en/bio/cole_john_4E.html.

———. *The History of the Hudson's Bay Company, 1670–1870*. 2 vols. London: Hudson's Bay Record Society, 1958, 1959.

Richardson, David. "The British Empire and the Atlantic Slave Trade, 1660–1807." In *The Eighteenth Century*, edited by P.J. Marshall and Alaine Low, 440–64. Vol. 2 of *The Oxford History of the British Empire*. Oxford: Oxford University Press, 1998.

Rollason Driscoll, Heather. "'A Most Important Chain of Connection': Marriage in the Hudson's Bay Company." In *From Rupert's Land to Canada: Essays in Honour of John E. Foster*, edited by T. Binnema, G.J. Ens, and R.C. Macleod, 81–107. Edmonton: University of Alberta Press, 2001.

Ruggles, Richard I. "Hospital Boys of the Bay." *The Beaver* 308, no. 2 (Autumn 1977): 4–11.

Rule, John. *The Experience of Labour in Eighteenth-Century English Industry*. New York: St. Martin's Press, 1981.

———. *The Labouring Classes in Early Industrial England, 1750–1850*. London: Longman, 1986.

———. "The Property of Skill in the Period of Manufacture." In *The Historical Meanings of Work*, edited by Patrick Joyce, 99–118. Cambridge: Cambridge University Press, 1987.

Schlenther, Boyd Stanley. "Religious Faith and Commercial Empire." In *The Eighteenth Century*, edited by P.J. Marshall and Alaine Low, 128–50. Vol. 2 of *The Oxford History of the British Empire*. Oxford: Oxford University Press, 1998.

Schwarz, L.D. "Custom, Wages and Workload in England during Industrialization." *Past & Present* 197 (November 2007): 143–75.

———. *London in the Age of Industrialization: Entrepreneurs, Labour Force and Living Conditions, 1700–1850*. Cambridge: Cambridge University Press, 1992.

Seed, Patricia. *Ceremonies of Possession in Europe's Conquest of the New World, 1492–1640*. Cambridge: Cambridge University Press, 1995.

Shammas, Carole. Introduction to *The Creation of the British Atlantic World*, edited by Elizabeth Mancke and Carole Shammas, 1–16. Baltimore, MD: Johns Hopkins University Press, 2005.

Shaw, Frances J. *The Northern and Western Islands of Scotland: Their Economy and Society in the Seventeenth Century*. Edinburgh: John Donald, 1980.

Smandych, Russell, and Rick Linden. "Administering Justice without the State: A Study of the Private Justice System of the Hudson's Bay Company to 1800." *Canadian Journal of Law and Society* 11 (1996): 21–61.

Smolenski, John. "Introduction: The Ordering of Authority in the Colonial Americas." In *New World Orders: Violence, Sanction, and Authority in the Colonial Americas*, edited by John Smolenski and Thomas J. Humphrey, 1–16. Philadelphia: University of Pennsylvania Press, 2005.

Smout, T.C., N.C. Landsman, and T.M. Devine. "Scottish Emigration in the Seventeenth and Eighteenth Centuries." In *Europeans on the Move: Studies on European Migration, 1500–1800*, edited by Nicholas Canny, 76–112. Oxford: Clarendon Press, 1994.

Snell, K.D.M. *Annals of the Labouring Poor: Social Change and Agrarian England, 1660–1900*. Cambridge: Cambridge University Press, 1985.

———. "Gravestones, Belonging and Local Attachment in England, 1700–2000." *Past & Present* 179 (May 2003): 97–134.

Spraakman, Gary. "The Impact of Institutions on Management Accounting Changes at the Hudson's Bay Company, 1670 to 2005." *Journal of Accounting & Organizational Change* 2, no. 2 (2006): 101–22.

Steele, Ian K. "The Anointed, the Appointed, and the Elected: Governance of the British Empire, 1689–1784." In *The Eighteenth Century*, edited by P.J. Marshall and Alaine Low, 105–27. Vol. 2 of *The Oxford History of the British Empire*. Oxford: Oxford University Press, 1998.

Stephen, Scott P. "'Assistant to York': The Ambiguous Role of Flamborough House, 1749–1759." *Manitoba History* 62 (Winter 2009): 9–21.

———. "'Covenant Servants': Contract, Negotiation, and Accommodation in Hudson Bay, 1670–1782." *Manitoba History* 60 (Spring 2009): 14–27.

Stevenson, John. "The 'Moral Economy' of the English Crowd: Myth and Reality." In *Order and Disorder in Early Modern England*, edited by Anthony Fletcher and John Stevenson, 218–38. Cambridge: Cambridge University Press, 1985.

Sweeny, Robert C.H. "Understanding Work Historically: A Reflection Prompted by Two Recent Studies of the Fur Trade." *Labour / Le Travail* 41 (Spring 1997): 243–52.

Sweet, Louise E. "Political Tactics of the Peaceful Traders (1616–1853): How the British Came to Control the Persian Gulf." In *Proceedings of the Second Congress, Canadian Ethnology Society*, vol. 2, edited by Jim Freedman and Jerome H. Barkow, 534–54. Mercury Series. Ottawa, ON: National Museum of Man, 1975.

Tadmor, Naomi. "The Concept of the Household-Family in Eighteenth-Century England." *Past & Present* 151 (May 1996): 111–40.

———. "Early Modern English Kinship in the Long Run: Reflections on Continuity and Change." *Continuity and Change* 25, no. 1 (2010): 23–25.

———. *Family and Friends in Eighteenth-Century England: Household, Kinship, and Patronage*. Cambridge: Cambridge University Press, 2001.

Thomas, Keith. *The Ends of Life: Roads to Fulfillment in Early Modern England*. Oxford: Oxford University Press, 2009.

Thompson, E.P., ed. *Customs in Common: Studies in Traditional Popular Culture*. New York: New Press, 1993.

———. "Eighteenth-Century English Society: Class Struggle without Class?" *Social History* 3, no. 2 (1978): 133–65.

———. "The Moral Economy of the English Crowd in the Eighteenth Century." *Past & Present* 50 (1971): 76–136.

———. "Patricians and Plebs." In *Customs in Common*, edited by E.P. Thompson, 16–96.

Thompson, Mark L. "'The Predicament of Ubi': Locating Authority and National Identity in the Seventeenth-Century English Atlantic." In *The Creation of the British Atlantic World*, edited by Elizabeth Mancke and Carole Shammas, 71–92. Baltimore, MD: Johns Hopkins University Press, 2005.

Thomson, William P.L. *History of Orkney*. Edinburgh: Mercat Press, 1987.

Thorman, G.E. "Hopkins, Samuel." In Hayne and Halpenny, *Dictionary of Canadian Biography*. http://www.biographi.ca/en/bio/hopkins_samuel_2E.html.

———. "Isbister, William." In Hayne and Halpenny, *Dictionary of Canadian Biography*. http://www.biographi.ca/en/bio/isbister_william_3E.html.

———. "Maugenest (Maugenest, *dit* Saint-Auron, Saint-Horan, Saint-Jorand, or Saint-Terone), Germain." In Hayne and Halpenny, *Dictionary of Canadian Biography*. http://www.biographi.ca/en/bio/maugenest_germain_4E.html.

———. "Sergeant, Henry." In Hayne and Halpenny, *Dictionary of Canadian Biography*. http://www.biographi.ca/en/bio/sergeant_henry_1E.html.

Troup, James A. "Orphir 1821: Attractions of Hudson's Bay Company Service." In *Papers of the 1994 Rupert's Land Colloquium*, edited by Ian MacLaren, Michael Payne, and Heather Rollason, 51–58. Winnipeg, MB: Centre for Rupert's Land Studies, 1997.

Trudel, François. "Trolio et Jack: Deux Inuit au service de la Compagnie de la Baie d'Hudson au XVIIIe siècle." *Canadian Journal of Native Studies* 7, no. 1 (1987): 79–93.

Van Kirk, Sylvia. *Many Tender Ties: Women in Fur Trade Society in Western Canada, 1670–1870*. Winnipeg, MB: Watson & Dwyer, 1980.

———. "Primeau (Primault, Primo), Louis (Lewis) (Nick'a'thu'tin)." In Hayne and Halpenny, *Dictionary of Canadian Biography*. http://www.biographi.ca/en/bio/primeau_louis_4E.html.

———. "Thanadelthur." *The Beaver* (Spring 1974): 40–45.

Venema, Kathleen. "'As We Are Both Deceived': Strategies of Status Repair in 19thC Hudson's Bay Company Correspondence." RHETOR 1 (2004). http://www.rhetcanada.org/wp-content/uploads/2015/05/Rhetor1_Venema.pdf.

Vickery, Amanda. *Behind Closed Doors: At Home in Georgian England*. New Haven, CT: Yale University Press, 2009.

Voth, Hans-Joachim. *Time and Work in England, 1750–1820*. Oxford: Clarendon Press, 2000.

Wall, Richard. Introduction to *Family Forms in Historic Europe*, edited by Richard Wall, Jean Robin, and Peter Laslett, 1–64. Cambridge: Cambridge University Press, 1983.

Walter, John. "Public Transcripts, Popular Agency and the Politics of Subsistence in Early Modern England." In *Negotiating Power in Early Modern Society: Order, Hierarchy and Subordination in Britain and Ireland*, edited by Braddick and Walter, 123–48. Cambridge: Cambridge University Press, 2001.

Wareing, John. "Changes in the Geographical Distribution of the Recruitment of Apprentices to the London Companies, 1486–1750." *Journal of Historical Geography* 6, no. 3 (July 1980): 241–49.

Watson, Ian Bruce. *Foundations for Empire: English Private Trade in India, 1659–1760*. New Delhi, India: Vikas, 1980.

Weir, Robert M. "'Shaftesbury's Darling': British Settlement in the Carolinas at the Close of the Seventeenth Century." In *The Origins of Empire: British Overseas Enterprise to the Close of the Seventeenth Century*, edited by Nicholas Canny, 375–97. Vol. 1 of *The Oxford History of the British Empire*. Oxford: Oxford University Press, 1998.

Whipp, Richard. "Labour Markets and Communities: An Historical View." *Sociological Review* 33, no. 4 (1985): 768–91.

White, Stephen D., and Richard T. Vann. "The Invention of English Individualism: Alan Macfarlane and the Modernization of Pre-modern England." *Social History* 8, no. 3 (October 1983): 345–63.

Whyte, Ian D. "Migration in Early-Modern Scotland and England: A Comparative Perspective." In *Migrants, Emigrants and Immigrants: A Social History of Migration*, edited by Colin G. Pooley and Ian D. Whyte, 87–105. London: Routledge, 1991.

Wien, Thomas. "Selling Beaver Skins in North America and Europe, 1720–1760: The Uses of Fur-Trade Imperialism." *Journal of the Canadian Historical Association* 1, no. 1 (1990): 293–317.

Williams, Glyndwr. "The Puzzle of Anthony Henday's Journal, 1754–5." *The Beaver* (Winter 1978): 41–56.

———. "Stuart, William." In Hayne and Halpenny, *Dictionary of Canadian Biography*. http://www.biographi.ca/en/bio/stuart_william_2E.html.

Williams, Raymond. *Keywords: A Vocabulary of Culture and Society*. New York: Oxford University Press, 1976.

Withington, Phil, and Alexandra Shepard. Introduction to *Communities in Early Modern England: Networks, Place, Rhetoric*, edited by Alexandra Shepard and Phil Withington, 1–15. Manchester, UK: Manchester University Press, 2000.

Woodward, Donald. *Men at Work: Labourers and Building Craftsmen in the Towns of Northern England, 1450–1750*. Cambridge: Cambridge University Press, 1995.

Wrightson, Keith. *Earthly Necessities: Economic Lives in Early Modern Britain*. New Haven, CT: Yale University Press, 2000.

———. "The Politics of the Parish in Early Modern England." In *The Experience of Authority in Early Modern England*, edited by Paul Griffiths, Adam Fox, and Steve Hindle, 10–46. New York: St. Martin's Press, 1996.

———. "The Social Order of Early Modern England: Three Approaches." In *The World We Have Gained: Histories of Population and Social Structures*, edited by Lloyd Bonfield, Richard M. Smith, and Keith Wrightson, 177–202. Oxford: Basil Blackwell, 1986.

Young, Alfred F. "English Plebeian Culture and Eighteenth-Century American Radicalism." In *The Origins of Anglo-American Radicalism*, edited by Margaret Jacob and James Jacob, 185–212. London: George Allen & Unwin, 1984.

Index

Other Titles from University of Alberta Press

Metis Pioneers

Marie Rose Delorme Smith and Isabella Clark Hardisty Lougheed

DORIS JEANNE MACKINNON

Two remarkable Metis women's lives during the prairie west's transition from the fur trade.

Fur Trade Letters of Willie Traill 1864–1893

WILLIAM EDWARD TRAILL

K. DOUGLAS MUNRO, *Editor*

Gritty, deeply touching, fascinating, informative; these letters show the joys and heartbreaking challenges of family life in the fur trade.

From Rupert's Land to Canada

Essays in Honour of John E. Foster

THEODORE BINNEMA, GERHARD J. ENS & ROD MACLEOD, *Editors*

A cross-disciplinary examination of the fur trade, playing with ideas that re-imagine the Canadian West.

More information at uap.ualberta.ca